CHARLES JAMES FOX
(From a Painting by Sir Joshua Reynolds)

THE EARLY HISTORY

OF

CHARLES JAMES FOX

BY

GEORGE OTTO TREVELYAN, M.P.

AUTHOR OF

"THE LIFE AND LETTERS OF LORD MACAULAY"

HARPER & BROTHERS, PUBLISHERS

NEW YORK AND LONDON

1900

CONTENTS.

CHAPTER I.

Stephen Fox.—His Career Abroad and at Home.—His Wealth, and the Use he made of it.—His Domestic History.—Henry Fox.—His Marriage.—His Opposition to the Marriage Act.—His Style of Speaking. —Outbreak of the Seven Years' War.—Fox in the Pay-office, and Pitt Master of the Nation.—Accession of George the Third, and Downfall of Newcastle and Pitt. — Bute's Unpopularity. — Fox undertakes to carry the Peace through Parliament.—The Methods by which he made good his Promise.—He Retires from the House of Commons with the Title of Lord Holland.—His Quarrel with Lord Shelburne and with Rigby. — Hatred with which Lord Holland was regarded by the Country...Page 1

CHAPTER II.

1749–1768.

Lord Holland in his own Family.—Birth of Charles James Fox.—His Childhood.—Wandsworth.—Eton and Paris.—Dr. Barnard.—The Musæ Etonenses.—Picture at Holland House.—Lady Sarah Lennox.—Fox at Oxford.—Tour in Italy.—Fox's Industry and Accomplishments.—His Return to England... 35

CHAPTER III.

London Society at the Time that Fox entered the Great World.—Its Narrow Limits and Agreeable Character. — Prevalent Dissipation and Frivolity.—The Duke of Grafton.—Rigby.—Lord Weymouth.— Lord Sandwich.—Fox in the Inner Circle of Fashion.—Lord March.— Brooks's Club. — Gaming. — Extravagance. — Drinking and Gout. — George the Third's Temperate and Hardy Habits.—State of Religion among the Upper Classes.—Political Life in 1768.—Sinecures.—Pensions and Places, English, Irish, and Colonial.—Other Forms of Corruption.—The Venality of Parliament.—Low Morality of Public Men, and Discontent of the Nation.—Office and Opposition.—Fox's Political Teachers.. 61

CHAPTER IV.

George the Third.—His Education.—His Assiduity in Public Business.—
His Theory of Personal Government. — The King's Friends. — The
King's Interference in the Details of Parliament and of Elections.—His
Dislike of the Whigs.—Formation of the Whig Party.—Lord Rockingham's Administration.—His Dismissal.—Lord Chatham's Government
and the Successive Changes in its Composition.—General Election of
1768.—Fox chosen for Midhurst.—His Political Opinions and Prejudices.—He selects his Party and takes his Seat.—Lord Shelburne.—
Fox as a Young Politician ....Page 102

CHAPTER V.
1768–1769.

Fox's Maiden Speech.—Wilkes.—His Early Life. — The *North Briton*
and the "Essay on Woman."—Persecution of Wilkes.—His Exile.—
Churchill.—Return of Wilkes, and his Election for Middlesex.—Disturbances in London.—Fatal Affray between the Troops and the People.—Determination of the Court to crush Wilkes.—Conflict between
the House of Commons and the Middlesex Electors.—Enthusiasm in
the City on Behalf of Wilkes.—Dingley.—Riot at Brentford.—Weakness of the Civil Arm.—Colonel Luttrell.—His Cause espoused by the
Foxes.—Great Debates in Parliament.—Rhetorical Successes of Charles
Fox.—The King and Wilkes.—Burke on the Middlesex Election.—
Proceedings during the Recess. — Recovery of Lord Chatham. — His
Reconciliation with the Grenvilles and the Whigs........................ 138

CHAPTER VI.
1770.

The Effect produced upon the Political World by the Reappearance of
Lord Chatham.—His Speech upon the Address.—Camden and Granby
separate themselves from their Colleagues.—Savile rebukes the House
of Commons.—Charles Yorke and the Great Seal.—The Duke of Graf-
ton resigns. — David Hume. — Lord North goes to the Treasury. —
George the Third, his Ministers and his Policy.—George Grenville on
Election Petitions and the Civil List.—Chatham denounces the Cor-
ruption of Parliament.—Symptoms of Popular Discontent.—The City's
Remonstrance presented to the King and condemned by Parliament.—
Imminent Danger of a Collision between the Nation and its Rulers.—
The Letter to the King.—Horace Walpole on the Situation.—The Per-
sonal Character of Wilkes, and its Influence upon the History of the

Country.—Wilkes regains his Liberty.—His Subsequent Career, and the Final Solution of the Controversy about the Middlesex Election..Page 193

CHAPTER VII.

The Favorable Conditions for taking Rank as an Orator under which Fox entered Parliament.—His Early Career.—He becomes a Junior Lord of the Admiralty.—His Father's Pride and Pleasure.—Lord Holland's Unpopularity.—The Balances of the Pay-office.—Lord Holland's Indulgence towards his Children.—King's Gate.—Charles Fox and his Studies.—His Passion for Poetry.—Naples.—Paris.—Intimate Relations between the Good Society of France and England.—Shopping in Paris.—Intellectual Commerce between the Two Countries.—Feelings of Fox towards France.—Madame du Deffand.—Fitzpatrick.—Mrs. Crewe.—Private Theatricals.—Effect of his Stage Experience on Fox's Speaking.. 245

CHAPTER VIII.
1770–1771.

The Law of Libel.—Great Speech by Charles Fox, and Burke's Reply.—Final Solution of the Question.—Contest of Parliament with the Reporters.—Scene in the Lords.—Indignation of the Commons.—Artful Conduct of Charles Fox.—Lord George Germaine's Duel.—The Onslows.—Their Warfare with the Press.—The King begins to take an Interest in the Controversy.—A Night of Divisions.—John Wheble.—Interference of Wilkes.—Miller Arrested, and Discharged by the Guildhall Bench.—Proceedings in the House of Commons against the Lord Mayor and Alderman Oliver.—Rebellion of the King's Friends against Lord North.—Fiery Speech of Charles Fox.—Feeling against him in the Country.—March of the City upon Westminster.—Violent Conduct of the Majority in the House.—Wedderburn's Defection from the Opposition.—Popular Excitement outside Parliament.—Fox and North Maltreated.—The Lord Mayor and the Alderman Committed to the Tower.—Their Imprisonment and Release.—Testimonial to Wilkes.—Establishment of the Freedom of Reporting Debates in Parliament... 289

CHAPTER IX.
1771–1772.

Fox at this Period a Consistent Defender of the King's System.—The Case of New Shoreham.—The Grenville Act.—Quarrel between Fox

and Wedderburn.—The Duke of Portland and Sir James Lowther.—
The Nullum Tempus Bill.—Mnemon.—Pertinacity of Sir James Lowther.—Sir William Meredith introduces an Amending Bill, which is
opposed, and at length defeated, by Fox. — Fox and Burke. — Fox
sends a Challenge to an Unknown Adversary.—The Petition of the
Clergy, and its Fate.—Story of Mr. Lindsey.—The Dissenters' Relief
Bill.—Priestley and the Early Unitarians.—Courage and Independence
of Charles Fox...Page 348

CHAPTER X.

1772–1774.

The Moral Danger of the Position in which Fox now stood.—He attacks Lord North on the Church Nullum Tempus Bill, and resigns
the Admiralty.—The Motives of his Conduct.—Marriages of the Dukes
of Cumberland and Gloucester.—Anger of the King.—The Royal Marriage Bill.—The Bill gets through the Lords, is strenuously opposed
in the Commons, and with difficulty passes into Law.—Strong Feeling
of Fox on the Question.—His Earnest Efforts against the Measure.—
His Sentiments with Regard to Women, and his Eager Care of their
Rights and Interests in Parliament.—His Private Life.—The Betting-
book at Brooks's.—Personal Tastes and Habits of Charles Fox.—His
Extravagance and Indebtedness.—Horace Walpole on Fox.—Influence
and Popularity of the Young Man in the House of Commons.—Fox
goes to the Treasury.—Lord Clive.—Fox and Johnson.—John Horne
Tooke.—Fox leaves the Ministry, never to return......................... 390

INDEX.. 453

THE EARLY HISTORY

OF

CHARLES JAMES FOX.

CHAPTER I.

Stephen Fox.—His Career Abroad and at Home.—His Wealth, and the Use he made of it.—His Domestic History.—Henry Fox.—His Marriage.—His Opposition to the Marriage Act.—His Style of Speaking.—Outbreak of the Seven Years' War.—Fox in the Pay-office, and Pitt Master of the Nation.—Accession of George the Third, and Downfall of Newcastle and Pitt.—Bute's Unpopularity.—Fox undertakes to carry the Peace through Parliament. — The Methods by which he made good his Promise.—He retires from the House of Commons with the Title of Lord Holland.—His Quarrel with Lord Shelburne and with Rigby.—Hatred with which Lord Holland was regarded by the Country.

CHARLES JAMES FOX, our first great statesman of the modern school, was closely connected with scenes which lie far back in English history. His grandfather, if not the most well-graced, was at any rate one of the best-paid, actors on the stage of the seventeenth century. Sir Stephen Fox was born in 1627. "The founder of our family," says the third Lord Holland, "seems, notwithstanding some little venial endeavors of his posterity to conceal it, to have been of a very humble stock;" and Sir Stephen's biographer and panegyrist, writing within a year of his death, has very little to tell which can destroy the effect of this frank confession.[1] As a boy,

---

[1] It is difficult to overrate the value of the "Memorials and Correspondence of Charles James Fox," which Lord Holland commenced, and Lord Russell continued, to edit. But for their labor of love, a biography of

Fox is said to have been in the choir of Salisbury Cathedral; and (what proved more to the purpose with reference to his future career) he was well and early grounded in the art of book-keeping. At the age of fifteen his "beauty of person and towardliness of disposition" recommended him to the notice of the Earl of Northumberland, High Admiral of England. Thence he passed into the household of the earl's brother, Lord Percy, and had, no doubt, his share in the good living for which, even at the height of the Civil War, that nobleman's table was famous.[1] Fox, who was a cavalier as soon as he was anything, was employed on the staff in an administrative capacity during the campaign which ended at Worcester; and after the battle was over he took an active part in assisting the escape of Prince Charles to Normandy.

The prince passed the next few years at Paris in great distress. In 1652 the French Court relieved his more pressing necessities by an allowance of six thousand francs a month— a pension very much smaller, and less regularly paid, than that which, as King of England, he afterwards enjoyed from the same quarter. As time went on, it began to be understood at the Louvre that Cromwell would be better pleased if the royal fugitive could be induced to shift his quarters. Charles was made to perceive that he had outstayed his welcome, and gladly entered into an arrangement by which he was enabled to leave Paris out of debt, and to settle elsewhere with a fair prospect of paying his way if his household could only be managed with the requisite economy. At this juncture Clar-

---

the great Whig would be an ungrateful, if not an impossible, task. The "Memoirs of the Life of Sir S. Fox, Kt., from his First Entrance upon the Stage of Action under the Lord Piercy till his Decease," were published in the year 1717. With regard to Sir Stephen's extraction, the writer is content to say, "As it is not material to enter into the genealogy of the family on the side of his father, who was of substance enough to breed up his son in a liberal education, so it is altogether needless to ransack the Heralds' Office for the origin and descent of his mother."

[1] Clarendon tells us of Lord Percy that "though he did not draw the good fellows to him by drinking, yet he ate well; which, in the general scarcity of that time, drew many votaries to him."

endon, as true a friend as prince ever had, did his master the inestimable service of persuading him to put his affairs unreservedly into the hands of Stephen Fox, "a young man bred under the severe discipline of the Lord Peircy, very well qualified with languages, and all other parts of clerkship, honesty, and discretion that were necessary for the discharge of such a trust." Fox thoroughly answered the expectations of his patron. At whichever of the German capitals or Low-Country watering-places the prince preferred to fix his modest court, he never was without the means of living in comfort and respectability, and from that day forth he knew nothing more of the lowest humiliations of exile. Fox was the first to bring his employer the news of Cromwell's death, and to salute him as the real King of Great Britain, "since he that had caused him to be only titularly so was no longer to be numbered among the living." Very little else of a definite nature is told about him in his biography, and probably very little else was known to its author, as may be gathered from the fact that, of the hundred and forty-nine pages which the book contains, no less than sixty-seven are consumed in an account of the state reception which the Dutch authorities gave to Charles in 1660, when he was on his way to England to receive the crown.

As soon as the master had his own again, the servant's fortunes rose rapidly. Fox was appointed first clerk of the Board of Green Cloth, paymaster to two regiments, and, before long, paymaster-general of all his Majesty's forces in England. Later on in his career he became Master of the Horse, and one of the Lords Commissioners of the Treasury. He was knighted. He obtained the reversion of a rich sinecure. The people of Salisbury, "for the love they bore to a gentleman who did them the honor of owing his birth to their neighborhood," chose him as their member, and, when he retired from Parliament, transferred their loyalty to his son.[1] When James acceded to the throne, the royal seduc-

---

[1] Fox showed his gratitude to the church in whose precinct he was educated after a fashion which churchmen of our day would hardly ap-

tions which prevailed over the faint Protestantism of Sunderland were tried upon Fox; but he resisted the offer of a peerage, and stuck manfully to his religion. The priests intrigued to have him removed from the Commission of the Treasury; but the king, who, with all his faults, understood public business as well as any man in the country, insisted on keeping Fox and Godolphin as coadjutors and instructors to the untrained Roman Catholic courtiers who formed the majority of the Board. When the Prince of Orange landed, the Bishop of London, whom a very moderate amount of persecution had converted from a preacher of non-resistance into a recruiting-officer for rebellion, endeavored to tamper with the fidelity of Fox; but the old placeman refused to take part against a monarch "whose and his brother's bread he had so plentifully eaten of." Sir Stephen, however, was not a Hyde or a Montrose. The best that his biographer can find to say for his loyalty is that "he never appeared at his Highness's court to make his compliments there till the king had left the country." William had no great difficulty in persuading him to take his seat once more at his accustomed boards. Thenceforward, whatever changes might occur at the Treasury, Fox's name was always on the new Commission. The veteran was sorely tried when Montague, who numbered only half his years, clambered over his head into the first position in the State; but ere long the storm of faction and jealousy hurled Montague from office, and when the sky was clear again Sir Stephen still was at his post, unappalled and unscathed. A favorite with twelve successive parliaments and with four monarchs, it was not until Anne had mounted the throne that he at length retired into private life.

His places were enormously lucrative, and he was soon rolling in wealth, "honestly got, and unenvied," says Evelyn; "which is next to a miracle." Evelyn himself informs us how Sir Stephen contrived to escape the evil eye which or-

---

preciate. The canon who preached his funeral sermon tells us that "he pewed the body of the cathedral church at Sarum in a very neat manner, suitable to the neatness of that church, of which he was in many ways a great benefactor."

dinarily pursues a self-made man.   At the height of his prosperity he continued "as humble and ready to do a courtesy
as ever he was."   He was honorably mindful of the source
whence his opulence was mainly derived, and, after twenty
years at the Pay-office, he bethought him of a magnificent device for restoring to the army some part of the fortune which
he had got by it.   He it was who inspired Charles with that
idea of founding an asylum for disabled soldiers, the credit of
which is generally ascribed to a less respectable quarter.   Sir
Stephen furnished much more than the first suggestion.   He
fostered the enterprise, through all its stages, with well-judged
but unstinted supplies of money; and if his original intentions were carried out, his contribution to the building and
maintenance of Chelsea Hospital can have fallen little short
of a hundred thousand pounds.

Sir Stephen's domestic annals were at least as remarkable
as his public history.   Somewhere about 1654, he married the
sister of the king's surgeon, by whom he had nine children.
In 1682 he made over the paymastership to his eldest son,
Charles, who, three years afterwards, at a great political crisis,
preferred a clear conscience to the emoluments of his place,
and, by the single act of his life which remains on record,
proved that he was worthy of giving a name to his nephew.[1]
Sir Stephen married his eldest daughter to Lord Cornwallis,
a nobleman who habitually "lost as much as any one would
trust him, but was not quite as ready at paying," and whose
gambling-scrapes sadly ruffled the serenity of one who is de-

---

[1] In 1685 the Opposition protested against granting money to James
the Second until grievances had been redressed.   When the division
was taken, "to the dismay," writes Macaulay, "of the ministers, many
persons whose votes the court had absolutely depended on were seen
moving towards the door.   Among them was Charles Fox, paymaster of
the forces, and son of Sir Stephen Fox, clerk of the Green Cloth.   The
paymaster had been induced by his friends to absent himself during
part of the discussion.   But his anxiety had become insupportable.   He
came down to the Speaker's chamber, heard part of the debate, withdrew, and, after hesitating for an hour or two between conscience and
five thousand pounds a year, took a manly resolution and rushed into
the House just in time to vote."

scribed by Grammont, in terms which read oddly as applied to any of the name of Fox, as among "the richest and most regular men in England." The old gentleman did not fail to profit by his dear-bought experience; and Evelyn gives an amusing sketch of the grave and dexterous courtesy with which he foiled an attempt, on the part of Lady Sunderland, to saddle him with a second high-born and expensive son-in-law. His sons were all childless; and, at the age of seventy-six, after his retirement from the Treasury, "unwilling that so plentiful an estate should go out of the name, and being of a vegete and hale constitution," he took to wife the daughter of a Grantham clergyman, who brought him twins within the twelvemonth. Two more children were born before Sir Stephen's death, which took place at his Chiswick villa in the year 1716. He had attended Charles the First on the scaffold, and he lived to discuss the execution of Lord Derwentwater. One of his daughters by the first marriage is said to have died while a baby. Lady Sarah Napier, the sister of his daughter-in-law, survived until the year 1826; and there is no reason to question the tradition that Charles Fox had two aunts who died a hundred and seventy years from each other.

Lady Fox outlived her husband only three years. Sir Godfrey Kneller, in the picture at Holland House, endows her with small and pretty features, and hair and complexion as dark as her grandson's. A fortnight before her death she called her children together, and made them a quaint little address which shows that she had already discerned the tendencies of the family character. "Don't be a fop, don't be a rake," she said to her eldest son. "Mind on your name—Stephen Fox; that, I hope, will keep you from being wicked. You, Harry, having a less fortune, won't be subject to so many temptations; but withstand those you have when you grow up. Then you'll learn to swear, to rake about, to game, and at last be ruined by those you unhappily think your friends. Love your brother, Stephen; I charge you all love one another. You have enemies enough; make not one another so." In after-years Henry Fox, the most fiercely hated public man of his own, or perhaps of any other, generation, may have called to mind these affectionate forebodings, which can still be read in his own boyish handwriting.

Stephen became, in course of time, Earl of Ilchester, and the founder of a house which has steadily grown in prosperity and general esteem. Henry Fox had a stormy and dissolute youth, and did not turn to serious affairs until he had wasted some of his best years and the greater part of his patrimony. He was thirty when he entered Parliament, and thirty-two before he got office, an age at which his son was the first man in the House of Commons. Any chance of Henry Fox being a Jacobite was effectually extinguished by his early distaste for certain doleful ceremonies with which the 30th of January was honored in the paternal household. His principles, if they could be dignified by such a title, were Whig, and he owed his first place to Walpole, whose favor he repaid by a fidelity which that statesman seldom experienced, and never expected.[1] To the end of his life, Fox made Sir Robert's quarrels his own. He could not forgive Lord Hardwicke for deserting their common chief, as the great chancellor in after-years had ample reason to know. "Mr. Fox," wrote Bubb Dodington, "had something very frank and open about him. If he had any dislike to me, it must be from my hating Sir Robert Walpole; for Fox really loved that man." He would have nothing to do with the administration which had profited by his leader's fall; and it was not until Pelham became prime-minister, on the recommendation, and almost under the auspices, of Walpole, that Fox consented to return to public employment as a Commissioner of the Treasury.

The first exploit by which he attracted the attention of the world was not performed in his capacity of an administrator. Horace Walpole has left us the description of a ball given in the days when his father was still in power; and it must be

---

[1] A colleague of Sir Robert Walpole said to him in the House of Commons, while Winnington was speaking, "That young dog promised that he would always stand by us." "I advise my young men never to use 'always,'" was the quiet reply.

confessed that there are some features in the picture which modern London might copy with advantage. " There were one hundred and ninety-seven persons at Sir Thomas's, and yet nobody felt a crowd. He had taken off all his doors, and so separated the old and the young that neither were inconvenienced with the other. The ball began at eight. Except Lady Ancram, no married woman danced. The beauties were the Duke of Richmond's two daughters, and their mother, still handsomer than they. The duke sat by his wife all night, kissing her hand." It is strange to reflect that this pair of lovely girls, and a third sister whose turn to be the reigning toast was still in the future, were destined to be the mothers of Charles Fox, Sir Charles Napier, and Lord Edward Fitzgerald. Forcibly, indeed, does such a thought bring it home to the mind that the period of which this book will treat was the transition between the old order of things and the new.

A more curious illustration of the sentiments and manners of the past could not easily be found than the story of Henry Fox's marriage. Fox lost his heart to Lady Caroline Lennox, and won hers in return. He made a formal application for her hand, but the duke and duchess would not hear of it ; and Lady Caroline's relatives were already looking around for a more eligible suitor, when, early in the month of May, 1744, the town was convulsed by the intelligence that the lovers had settled the matter by a secret wedding, which, in those days, was a much less arduous operation than at present. The sensation was instant and tremendous. At the opera the news ran along the front boxes " exactly like fire in a train of gunpowder." It was said at the time that more noise could hardly have been made if the Princess Caroline had gone off with her dancing-master. All the blood royal was up in arms to avenge what was esteemed an outrage upon the memory of his sacred Majesty Charles the Second, who, if he had been alive to see it, would have been infinitely diverted by the catastrophe, and would doubtless have taken his great-granddaughter's part. Sir Charles Hanbury Williams, who had lent his house for the marriage, found that his complicity was like to have cost him his red ribbon. The father and mother of the young lady put off their social engagements, and hurried away to hide their vexation at their country-seat. There is something irresistibly comical in the letters of condolence which came pouring in upon them at Goodwood. Lord Ilchester wrote to exculpate himself and his wife from any previous knowledge of his brother's designs. Lord Lincoln had heard, with the greatest uneasiness, that he and his sister had been "falsely and villanously" charged with being concerned in so unhappy and imprudent a business. The Duke of Newcastle buzzed round the court, mumbling and bewailing to every peer he met about "this most unfortunate affair," till he was unlucky enough to fall into the hands of Lord Carteret.[1] "I thought," said Carteret, "that our fleet was beaten, or that Mons had been betrayed to the French. At last it came out that Harry Fox was married, which I knew before. This man, who is secretary of state, cannot be consoled because two people, to neither of whom he is any relation, were married without their parents' consent!" The prime-minister, who both liked and feared Fox, would have been very glad to have left the matter alone, and the more so because Miss Pelham stoutly refused to abandon her friend Lady Caroline, and, in the vigorous language which young women then allowed themselves to use, declared to any one who denied Mr. Fox's claim to be called a gentleman that if Lord Ilchester had been free to present himself, the duke and duchess would both have jumped at the match. She was now, she

---

[1] Lord Carteret, afterwards Earl Granville, is the only person of whom we hear too little in the voluminous memoirs of his time. His flashes of jovial common-sense never fail to infuse some human interest into the dreary political period which coincided with the ascendency of the Pelhams. Unfortunately he loved his ease better than his country, and was only too ready to lounge away his life in the background, "resigned," says Mr. Carlyle, "in a big contemptuous way to have had his really considerable career closed upon him by the smallest of mankind," and known in history chiefly for "occasional spurts of strong rugged speech which come from him, and a good deal of wine taken into him." Two bottles of burgundy were his daily allowance.

said, in other people's power, but before long would be her
own mistress and able to please herself; which meant that
she was on the eve of being married to Lord Lincoln, who, no
doubt, soon found occasion to repent that he had been in such
a hurry to take the wrong side in so interesting a controversy.
In order to keep on terms with the Duke of Richmond, Pelham thought it necessary to speak with grave disapproval of
his audacious subordinate, and, during at least a twelvemonth,
continued to address him as "Dear Sir" instead of "Dear
Harry." But the anger of a minister against a formidable
member of Parliament is not an enduring or implacable emotion, and Fox soon discovered that his political future had
gained a great deal more than it had lost by his having aspired to a duke's daughter. The parents remained obdurate
from 1744 to 1748; but even they melted at last, and, in a
letter which is extant, announced to their erring daughter
that the conflict between reason and nature was over, and that
tenderness had carried the day. The birth of a son, whom
the duke candidly admits to be an "innocent child," contributed not a little to this change of feeling; and, when Fox had
for years been secretary at war, a privy-councillor, and the
readiest speaker in the House of Commons, he was solemnly
forgiven for having married above his station.

Charles Fox's mother, if pictures may be trusted (and in
her day they spoke true), must, at each successive stage of
life, have possessed in a high degree the charms appropriate
to her years. Hogarth makes her the prettiest and most
prominent figure in a delicious group of small actors and
actresses just out of the nursery, who are playing the "Con-
quest of Mexico" by the fireside for the amusement of the
Duke of Cumberland; and her latest portrait, taken when
her hair was gray, is marked by a tranquil, serious expression,
which is singularly winning. Fox and Lady Caroline were,
from first to last, an enviable couple. They lived together
most happily for more than thirty years, and the wife survived
the husband not quite so many days. Neither of them ever
knew content except in the possession, or the immediate expectation, of the other's company; and their correspondence

continued to be that of lovers until their long honeymoon was finally over. "Indeed, my dear angel," wrote Fox, twelve years after marriage, "you have no reason to be peevish with me. Ask yourself whether you know an instance of my want of confidence in you, or of your want of power with me. Upon my word, you do not. I wrote to you yesterday. I rode to town this morning; found six people in my house; went to court, Parliament, dined late, and am at this moment waited for at the Speaker's. What can I more than snatch this time to tell you that I am, for me, well, and that I love you dearly?" Perfect trust and passionate affection breathe through every page of the letters, so close upon each other in date, and so ungrudging in length, in which Henry Fox's easy, kindly, and humorous words

> "Lie disordered in the paper, just
> As hearty nature speaks them."

Fox has left on the history of his times a testimony to his conjugal regard which is highly characteristic of the man. In the reign of George the Second the scandal of the old marriage laws had come to a head. Those facilities for extemporizing a wedding, which are not without inconvenience in the north of our island, had proved far too lax for the warmer and less provident temperament of Englishmen. The vision of a broken-down parson ready, without asking questions, to marry any man to any woman for a crown and a bottle was an ever-present terror to guardians and parents. Numerous were the cases in which boys of rank had become the prey of infamous harpies, and girls with money or beauty had found that the services of a clergyman were employed as a cloak for plunder or seduction. A sham marriage enters into the plot of half the novels of that period; and the fate which in fiction poor Olivia Primrose suffered, and the future Lady Grandison narrowly escaped, became a terrible reality to many of their sex. Nor were the miseries entailed by such practices confined to a single generation. The succession to property was rendered doubtful and insecure; every day in term-time produced hearings in Chancery, or appeals in the Lords, concerning the validity of a marriage which had been solemnized thirty years before in the back-parlor of a public-house, or in some still more degraded haunt of vice; and the children might be ruined by an act of momentary folly committed when the father was a midshipman on leave from Sheerness, or a Westminster boy out for a half-holiday.

In the year 1753, Lord Hardwicke undertook to remedy the evil. He introduced a bill which made effectual provision for putting a stop to the Fleet marriages; but his measure was so constructed as to inflict a new injustice upon a section of the community which had already endured enough from the partiality of our legislature. The chancellor insisted that everybody, including Roman Catholics and Dissenters, must either be married according to the ritual of the establishment, or not be married at all, whatever objections they might entertain to a service some passages of which cause even the most devout pair of Church people to wince when it is read over them. The bill got easily through the Lords; but as soon as it appeared in the House of Commons it aroused an opposition, vigorous, obstinate, and intensely clever, but in which it is difficult to discover a single trace of public spirit. Little or nothing was said about the grievance of the Nonconformists—a grievance which, in our century, it took eight sessions to redress. Other grave defects, productive in coming years of infinite confusion and litigation, were left unnoticed by orators who lavished their flowers of rhetoric and wit upon prophecies that the bill would check population and reduce England to a third-rate power, and that fine ladies would never consent to be asked for three Sundays running in the parish church. Charles Townshend delighted the House, never very critical of a new argument, by a pathetic appeal on behalf of younger sons, whom Lord Hardwicke's bill would debar from running away with heiresses. Were fresh shackles, he asked, to be forged in order that men of abilities might be prevented from rising to a level with their elder brothers?[1] It was on this occasion that Townshend

---

[1] Charles Townshend discovered, in the course of the next year, that

first brought into successful play his rare personal advantages. His elegant and commanding figure, his vehement yet graceful action, his clear voice and cheery laugh, the art (said an acute observer) with which he disguised everything but his vanity, completely carried away with him an audience which thenceforward he always had at his command.

The encounter in which Charles Townshend won his spurs was only a preliminary skirmish. "The speeches," says Walpole, "had hitherto been flourishes in the air. At last the real enemy came forth, Mr. Fox, who neither spared the bill nor the author of it; as, wherever he laid his finger, it was not wont to be light." A law which annulled a marriage made without consent of parents, and which treated the principals in the transaction as common felons, was, not unnaturally, resented by the hero of the most famous runaway match of the generation. Fired with indignation at what he regarded as an affront to the romance of his life—a sentiment which never died out of his family, for neither Charles Fox nor the third Lord Holland could speak of the Marriage Act with patience—he stood forth as the champion of oppressed lovers, and declared that it was cruel to force upon the country a measure which, from the first word to the last, was dictated by aristocratic pride and heartlessness. He had high words with his own leader on every clause, and almost on every sentence; but, while striking at Pelham, he was really belaboring Lord Hardwicke in effigy. "I will speak so loud," he cried, "that I will be heard outside the House;" and heard he was to such effect that the lord chancellor's life became a burden to him as long as the bill remained in the Commons. Day after day the secretary at war made the highest lay dignitary in the kingdom a butt for his unsparing ridicule and invective; until at length a ludicrous simile, applied to his lordship amidst

---

the new act did not stand in the way of a younger son who wanted to make a great marriage, if only he would be content with a dowager. He proved an excellent husband, though he was rather too fond of amusing his company by congratulating his wife on her good-luck with a freedom suited rather to his century than to ours.

roars of laughter, proved too much for the filial and professional feelings of Charles Yorke, who, as the son of his father, had already a great business in Chancery, and who was beginning to make his mark in Parliament as a cultured but somewhat affected speaker. With a sensitiveness of which he was one day to give a tragical proof, the young man started to his feet, descanted in high-flown terms upon Lord Hardwicke's office and character, and denounced the insolence of his assailant as "new in Parliament, new in politics, and new in ambition." The secretary at war, in his reply, rang the changes on these sententious periods with the pitiless skill of a veteran gladiator, and, none the worse for the correction, returned to the charge on the third reading, and kept the ear of the House for a full hour and a half, while he fought his battles over again in a speech of which one fragment fortunately remains to us as a sample of the source whence the prince of all debaters inherited his unrivalled facility. Fox was insisting that the measure was so intolerably rigorous, and at the same time so carelessly framed, that the ministers themselves, whom the chancellor had told off to be its body-guard, for very shame had been forced to amend it until its own father would fail to recognize it; and with that he flourished a copy of the bill, on which the alterations were written in red ink. "How bloody it looks!" said the solicitor-general. "Yes," cried Fox; "but thou canst not say I did it. See what a rent the learned Casca made;" and he pointed to a clause which had been altered by the solicitor-general himself. "Through this the well-beloved Brutus stabbed;" and here he indicated Pelham with an emphatic gesture. To a well-disciplined member of a modern government there is something grotesque in the reflection that the actors in such a scene were all ranged side by side along the same Treasury bench.

Lord Hardwicke was wise enough to remember that an orator whose anger is real cannot safely trust himself to the impulse of the moment. Taking his revenge with discretion, he read in the House of Lords an elaborate philippic, in which he designated his traducer as "a dark and insidious genius, the engine of personality and faction." Then, hav-

ing referred to some sentences of apology which Fox had
had the grace to utter, but which, it must be allowed, bore a
very small proportion to the magnitude of the offence, the
injured chancellor concluded in a style half - way between
good prose and bad verse, "I despise the invective, and I despise the retractation. I despise the scurrility, and I despise
the adulation." The report of this outburst came to Fox
while he was amusing himself at Vauxhall; whereupon he
gathered round him a knot of young members of Parliament
(a class among whom, like his son after him, he was always
a great authority), and assured them, in his most animated
language, that if the session had lasted another fortnight
he would have paid off Lord Hardwicke with interest. In
his wrath he sought an interview with the king, and began
to complain of the chancellor; but his Majesty cut him
short with the remark that Fox had only himself to blame
for the quarrel, and that he had given at least as good as
he had got. The secretary at war declared to the king,
on his honor, that there had been nothing factious or un-
derhand in his behavior. "The moment you give me your
honor," was the reply, "I believe you; but I must tell you,
as I am no liar, that you have been much suspected." Before he quitted the royal presence, Fox, utilizing the opportunity with an effrontery which was all his own, had contrived to extract from his Majesty the promise of a small
sinecure.

His conduct on the Marriage Bill did Fox no harm either
in the cabinet or in the closet. "The king," said the Duke
of Cumberland to him, "will like you the better for what
has passed. He thinks you a man, and he knows that none
of the rest have the spirit of a mouse." He had won the
respect of his official superiors by showing that, in case of
need, he could fight for his own hand. The time was approaching when, if Fox had had a particle of patriotism or
disinterestedness in his composition, he might have left behind him one of the greatest names in English history. In
March, 1754, Pelham died suddenly, and the inheritance of
Sir Robert Walpole was open to any one who had the

strength to seize and to hold it.[1] The Duke of Newcastle
succeeded to his brother's place at the Treasury; but everybody was aware that the substance of authority, then as now,
would rest with the leader of the House of Commons. It
took Newcastle eighteen months to learn this obvious truth.
Avaricious of power, which he hoarded, but knew not how
to employ, he selected Sir Thomas Robinson, a dull diplomatist, ignorant of the very phraseology of debate, to speak for
a government in which Fox was secretary at war and Pitt
paymaster-general. Sir Thomas soon had reason to wish
himself safely back in the embassy at Vienna. Acting heartily in concert, for the first and last time in their lives, his
terrible subordinates divided between them the easy task of
making their chief ridiculous. Pitt would crush Sir Thomas
beneath the weight of his august insolence, and then would
be rebuked by Fox in an exquisitely humorous strain of
ironical loyalty; and their victim dreaded the defence even
more than the attack. Murray, the attorney-general, whose
close reasoning and copious and polished diction qualified
him to hold his own against any single adversary, did not
venture to face such a combination of talent; and when Pitt,
tired of his inglorious sport, began to strike at higher game,
Newcastle was frightened into acknowledging that something
must be sacrificed in order to preserve himself from the fate
of his puppet. In 1755, Fox was invited to join the cabinet,
into which he had not as yet obtained admission, and was
asked whether he would consent to act under Sir Thomas
Robinson. " What is acting under him?" he answered,
laughing. " If we both rise to speak, I will yield to him.
If there is a meeting of the council, it will be his paper and
his pens and his green table." [2] The offer, however, was ac-

---

[1] Pelham died at six in the morning. By eight o'clock Fox had begun his round of calls upon the deceased minister's possible successors,
and before noon he had obtained an interview with the bereaved brother.

[2] Fox wrote to his wife, in the last fortnight of 1754, " I must tell you
a compliment of Lord Granville's imagination, and whether I tell you because it is pretty or because it flatters me, or both, you may judge. I
was not present. 'They must,' says he, 'gain Fox. They must not

cepted, and the redoubtable alliance dissolved; but Fox permanently suffered in reputation by this breach of faith towards his great rival, whose honor the nation had already begun to identify with its own.

The world wondered that so grasping a man should have given himself away for so little; but Fox had judged the situation with a discerning eye. Before the year had ended, he was secretary of state and leader of the House of Commons. And now began a duel of giants, which lasted, with varying fortune, over the space of three sessions and through four changes of government. The antagonists were not ill-matched. Fox, unattractive in person and with defective elocution, surpassed all the orators of his time in the force, the abundance, and the justness of the proofs and illustrations with which he supported and explained his views. His homely yet pointed and vehement method of debate was admirably suited to the taste of hearers who disliked set speeches, and no longer relished the similes, metaphors, and historical parallels which formerly were in vogue, and in whose minds the increasing study of pamphlets and newspapers had begun to create a demand for practical arguments founded upon the solid facts of the case. Fox was the sworn enemy of lawyers who had seats in Parliament. "He loved disputing as much as they do," wrote Horace Walpole; "but he loved sense, which they make a trade of perplexing." It was well said that Fox always spoke to the question, and Pitt to the passion; and in ordinary times an orator who speaks to the question is master of the field. But the time, far from being ordinary, was pregnant with events so momentous that it would be difficult to find words which could describe them, or rhetoric which could exaggerate them. Problems had long been ripe for solution which concerned not only the British kingdom, but all the civilized, and almost the whole of the inhabited, world. Whether France or England was to rule in India; whether the French man-

---

think it keeps him under in the House of Commons. They cannot keep him under. Mix liquors together, and the spirit will be uppermost.'"

2

ners, language, and institutions, or the English, were to prevail over the immense continent of North America; whether Germany was to have a national existence; whether Spain was to monopolize the commerce of the tropics; who was to command the ocean; who was to be dominant in the islands of the Caribbean Sea; what power was to possess the choice stands for business in the great market of the globe: these were only some among the issues which had to be decided during the period when Fox and Pitt were in the prime of their vigor and at the summit of their fame.

On the 18th of May, 1756, the unofficial hostilities between France and England, which had been smouldering or blazing for the space of four years on the shores of the Carnatic, and along the valleys of the St. Lawrence, the Ohio, and the Mississippi, were sanctioned and extended by an open declaration of war—a war destined to be the most profitable and the most glorious that this country ever waged. As is usual, however, with our glorious wars, the earlier operations brought us nothing but disaster and disgrace. Byng's unhappy blunder, and the loss of Minorca, which was to our ancestors what Malta is to us, had given rise to an uneasy feeling that our navy was not to be relied on. For the first time since the Dutch were in the Medway, that humiliating misgiving took firm hold of the public imagination; and, as an inevitable consequence, came the terrors of a possible invasion. The English people were in that state of fury and suspicion which no rulers dare face except such as are rendered fearless by the consciousness of integrity, and the determination to do their duty for duty's sake.[1] The whole herd of aristocratic jobbers and political adventurers were eager to throw upon each other the responsibility of defending the nation over whose plunder, in quiet years, they were never weary of squabbling. Scared by the first mutter of the storm, Newcastle ran whimpering to Granville, and

---

[1] When the invasion was first talked of, the Duke of Cumberland was told that the people wished to see him at the head of the army. " I do not believe," was his fine answer, " that the command will be offered to me, but when no wise man would accept it and no honest man would refuse it."

begged him to accept the Treasury. "I thought," said Granville, "I had cured you of such offers. I will be hanged a little before I take your place, rather than a little after." Fox carried his woes to the same quarter, and, forgetful for a moment that he was talking to the shrewdest observer within a mile of St. James's, set down his pusillanimity to the score of his unambitious temper. "Fox," said Lord Granville, "I don't love to have you say things that will not be believed. If you was of my age, very well. I have put on my nightcap, but you *should* be ambitious. I want to instil a nobler ambition into you; to make you knock the heads of the kings of Europe together, and jumble something out of it that may be of service to the country." But there was no chord in Fox's nature which responded to such exhortations, and, at a crisis when the English secretary of state might have been more powerful than the King of France and as celebrated as Frederic of Prussia, he could think of no bolder course than to resign the seals. The largest bribes that even Newcastle had ever offered were pressed upon Murray, and pressed in vain, if only he would consent to stand during a single session, or at least during a single debate, between an incapable government and an angry nation which had Pitt for its champion. But Murray knew better than his tempter how irresistible were the thunderbolts of the Great Commoner at a time when the political atmosphere was in so perilous a condition of electricity. In the calm of the House of Lords, and amidst the congenial labors of the King's Bench, he waited with patient dignity till the opportunity came when he could repay the Earl of Chatham something of what he had endured at the hands of William Pitt.

The story of the long political crisis which agitated Downing Street during the first twelvemonth of the Seven Years' War is not edifying or pleasant reading. "The hour," wrote Carlyle, "is great; and the honorable gentlemen, I must say, are small;" but they had among them one who was equal to the hour. "Your country," said Frederic to our envoy at Berlin, "has been long in labor, and has suffered much; but at last she has produced a man." Pitt had

unbounded confidence in himself, and, most fortunately for
England, his oratory was peculiarly adapted to the purpose
of communicating that confidence to others. " Pitt spoke to
raise himself," said one who did not altogether love him ; and
certainly his elevated and audacious eloquence inspired all
who heard him with a conviction that he was endowed with
rare courage and decision at a season when rare courage and
decision in high quarters were worth twenty millions a year
to the nation. That close connection between energy of
speech and vigor of action, which is much more common than
the enemies of popular government are willing to suppose,
found in him its most splendid exemplification. Without a
moment of hesitation, without a twinge of diffidence, he set
himself at the head of his countrymen ; and they, placing
their blood and treasure at his disposal, believing all that he
asserted, paying all that he demanded, undertaking everything that he advised, followed him through an unbroken
course of effort and victory with an enterprise and a resolution worthy of his own. The nation which lately had been
in a panic because a score of French battalions were quartered between Brest and Dunkirk, was soon paramount in
every corner of the world into which a British keel could
float or a British cannon could be dragged. " I shall burn all
my Greek and Latin books," said Horace Walpole, who had
in him more of the patriot than it was his humor to admit.
" They are histories of little people. The Romans never
conquered the world till they had conquered three parts of
it, and were three hundred years about it. We subdue the
globe in three campaigns ; and a globe, let me tell you, as
big again as it was in their days." " You would not know
your country again," he writes to Sir Horace Mann at Florence. " You left it a private little island, living upon its
means. You would find it the capital of the world ; St. James's
Street crowded with nabobs and American chiefs, and Mr.
Pitt attended in his Sabine farm by Eastern monarchs, waiting till the gout has gone out of his foot for an audience. I
shall be in town to-morrow, and perhaps able to wrap up and
send you half a dozen French standards in my postscript."

While the renown of the great Englishman was spread over three continents by a series of triumphs vast, rapid, and durable beyond any which are related in the pages of Curtius or Livy, at home his empire was unbounded, and even undisputed. During four whole sessions his opponents never ventured to test the opinion of Parliament by calling for a vote. Politics, said Walpole, seemed to have gone into winter-quarters. Charges of inconsistency, of recklessness, of profusion, were disdainfully cast aside, and ere long ceased to be uttered. A flash of his eye, a wave of his hand, a contemptuous shrug of his shoulders, were an adequate reply to speeches an hour long, bristling with figures and quotations. When he thought fit to break silence, every phrase had the weight of a despot's edict. One fiery sentence carried the Prussian subsidy. Another made the House of Commons forget, in its exultation at hearing how America was to be conquered in Germany, that almost on that day year it had been cheering Pitt while he declaimed against the folly of a Hanoverian war. Parliament was willing to remember only what he chose; and the few orators from whom he had anything to fear found excellent reasons for allowing his statements to pass uncriticised. A minister who wanted nothing for his own share except the honor of serving his country had ample means of providing every mouth with the sop which it loved the best. Fox became paymaster of the forces. Murray, in his own province as high-minded and public-spirited as the secretary of state himself, was already absorbed in his thirty years' labor of adjusting the ancient common-law of England to the multifarious needs of modern society. To the Duke of Newcastle had been allotted the uncontrolled patronage of every office in the kingdom which did not affect the conduct of the war. As long as Pitt might appoint whom he liked to command expeditions, to defend fortresses, and to represent Great Britain in the belligerent courts, the whole army of placemen, from tellers of the Exchequer to tide-waiters, were welcome to carry their hopes and their homage to the old intriguer, who could not endure that any one besides himself should be the dictator of the backstairs and the antechamber. The Great Commoner might work his will upon France and Austria without a whisper of interference, while Newcastle was making partisans, while Mansfield was making law, and while Fox was making money.

He made money to his heart's content. Pitt, when at the Pay-office, had magnanimously refused to follow the example of his predecessors and enrich himself by trading with the national funds which were in his custody ; but Henry Fox was not the man to forego his legal privileges from any quixotic notions of principle or nicety. It was enough for him if he kept on the safe side of a parliamentary impeachment. The years during which he had been secretary at war were long remembered by army agents and contractors as a golden age of peculation ; and he now saw before him a prospect of secure and almost boundless gain. He was in a position to take full advantage of the favorable condition of the money-market. Half the brokers in Lombard Street were discounting bills at a war rate of interest with cash supplied to them out of the public balances, at a time when those balances had been swollen to an unprecedented amount by the loans and taxes that went to feed a contest which embraced the world. Every new regiment that was mustered ; every fresh ship that was in commission ; every additional ally who applied for a subsidy ; every captured province or colony which had to be provided with a staff of salaried administrators, brought grist to the mill of the paymaster. Intent upon heaping up a colossal fortune, which his sons were to dissipate even more quickly than he had amassed it, he tamely consented to abandon everything which makes ambition honorable and self-seeking respectable. He sank from a cabinet minister into an underling, and from the spokesman of a government into the mute occupant of a remote corner of the Treasury bench. Rich and inglorious, he played Crassus to his rival's Cæsar, until an unexpected turn in politics tempted him to quit that comfortable obscurity from which it would have been well for his memory if he had never emerged.[1]

---

[1] The extent of Lord Holland's gains may be estimated by a compari-

The death of George the Second was the signal for a transformation of the government as complete, if not as sudden, as any which could have occurred at Constantinople or St. Petersburg. The strong narrow mind of the young monarch, which soon learned to work in its own direction, as long as it continued to work at all, was first set in motion by the external influence of a favorite. Lord Bute, the groom of the stole, who stood highest in the graces both of the princess royal and her son, regarded Pitt as aspiring mediocrity will always regard born greatness, and had taught his royal pupil to dislike and distrust the noblest subject that King of England ever had. The invincible loyalty of the secretary of state kept him at his post for a year after his authority had begun to decline; but in October, 1761, Bute enjoyed the satisfaction of being congratulated on the fall of the eminent man whom he had the impertinence to envy. Lord Melcombe, the unsavory associations of whose career are more readily recalled by his earlier designation of Bubb Dodington, had been tempted forth by the genial sunshine of the new reign to flutter feebly for a short season around his ancient haunts. " I sincerely wish your lordship joy," he writes in a letter which is among the gems of the Bute correspondence, " of being delivered of a most impracticable colleague, his Majesty of a most imperious servant, and the country of a most dangerous minister. I am told that the people are sullen about it." It

---

son between his financial position when he took the Pay-office and when he quitted it. In the will which he made in middle life he left eight thousand pounds, and eleven hundred a year to his wife. At his death, in 1774, he left Lady Holland two thousand a year, Holland House, and government securities to the amount, it is said, of a hundred and twenty thousand pounds. To Stephen Fox he had already given between four and five thousand a year in land. To Charles he bequeathed the property in Kent, and nine hundred a year; to his son Henry an estate in the North, and five hundred a year; while the young men got among them fifty thousand pounds in money, and a sinecure valued at twenty-three hundred a year. It must be remembered that Lord Holland had already paid for the two eldest at least a couple of hundred thousand pounds of debts.

was Pitt's misfortune that his extraordinary achievements were accomplished at a period when the poetry of our nation was at its lowest ebb. The pen of Churchill, who was his sincere admirer, was never potent except when dipped in gall;[1] and to be sung by the Whiteheads was a more serious calamity than to be libelled by Wilkes. In default of the praise of writers whose praise was worth having, it was something to be made the object of Bubb Dodington's abuse. No direct panegyric could tell more in Pitt's favor than the ill-will with which the most notorious of court sycophants and Treasury leeches honored the minister who had long been the bane of all his tribe.

In the course of the ensuing summer, Newcastle was bullied into resigning the Treasury, and Bute became prime-minister. The first act of his administration was to put an end to hostilities. On the third of November, 1762, the Duke of Bedford and the Duc de Nivernois signed the preliminaries of peace at Fontainebleau. The conditions were not those which England had a right to demand as the outcome of such a war; but if Bute had been allowed his own way in the cabinet, she would have had even less cause to look back with complacency upon her long roll of sacrifices and successes. Our people already detested the prime-minister as a Scotchman who rode rough-shod over Englishmen, and as an upstart who had displaced his betters;[2] and they were now excited to fury by the belief that he had made use of a position which he never could have won in fair political fight to barter away the good

---

[1] It is pitiable to compare with the native vigor of Churchill's attacks upon the Earl of Sandwich and Lord Holland the bathos which degrades his attempt to exalt Chatham:

"Though scandal would our patriot's name impeach,
And rails at virtue which she cannot reach,
What honest man but would with joy submit
To bleed with Cato and retire with Pitt?"

[2] Bute became prime-minister at the end of May. On the twentieth of June Walpole writes, "The new administration begins tempestuously. My father was not more abused after twenty years than Lord Bute is in twenty days."

faith of the nation. They had been proud of their share in the Continental war. It was largely due to them that Frederic had been able to make head against the gigantic coalition which threatened his destruction, and they keenly felt the disgrace of having deserted him before the close of his immortal struggle. It was said that this minion from north of Tweed, not content with supplanting the greatest of English statesmen, had betrayed a foreign ruler whose alliance was an honor to the whole community. The public resentment was sharpened by a report that the prime-minister entertained a grudge against Frederic on the score of an epigram which, in his character of an indiscreet man of letters, that monarch had levelled against the Scotch—a rumor not very credible with regard to the friend and brother-soldier of the Keiths. So odious was the peace that Bute's conduct was generally attributed to the basest of all motives. A notion that his pockets were full of louis-d'ors was current, not only with the populace, but among men of sense and position who ought to have taken the trouble to make themselves better informed; and the vulgar suspicion was carried to such a pitch that an imputation of corruption was extended to the Duke of Bedford, who, if it had come to bribing, might, without sensibly feeling the loss, have bought up out of his private fortune the French plenipotentiary, with Madame Pompadour to boot.

False or true, the charges had to be met, and an approval of the preliminaries extorted from Parliament. Bute had nothing to fear from the House of Lords; but the House of Commons, ill as it represented the nation, was drawn from the classes who create and share public opinion, and was accessible to the spell of Pitt's genius. The time had come for employing every species of influence, honorable, questionable, and discreditable, which the government had in store. Money and intimidation might carry the day, if only the cabinet could secure the services of a skilful speaker. It was essential for success that a case should be made out plausible enough to afford members a pretext for voting against the wishes and convictions of the nation. The emergency demanded a leader of undaunted courage and long parliamentary experience, with a tongue in his head, and without a scruple in his conscience. Such a man was not easily to be found. Sir Francis Dashwood, the Chancellor of the Exchequer, was as poor a creature as ever held high office, with nothing to recommend him except the reputation for cleverness which usually attaches to a libertine; Charles Townshend had upon him the curse of Reuben;[1] and George Grenville was too little of an orator for one part of the work which had to be done, and not enough of a reprobate for the other. The king measured the situation accurately. "We must call in bad men," he said, "to govern bad men," and, in his despair, he turned to Fox. The paymaster, who had got everything that he wanted except a peerage, and who hated the long hours of the House of Commons, was very unwilling to incur trouble and unpopularity in defence of a minister whom he would have seen on his way to Tower Hill with the most perfect indifference. But a statesman in the long run must yield to royal solicitations, if he can give no better ground for resisting than his own laziness and satiety.[2] Fox entered the cabinet, and assured the king that Parliament should approve the peace by as large a majority as his Majesty could possibly desire.

---

[1] In a very curious paper addressed to Lord Bute, dated March, 1763, Fox writes, "I have said nothing of Charles Townshend. He must be left to that worst enemy, himself; care only being taken that no agreeableness, no wit, no zealous and clever behavior, ever betray you into trusting him for half an hour." Sir Francis Dashwood is justly described by Wilkes as one who, "from puzzling all his life at tavern bills, was called by Lord Bute to administer the finances of a kingdom above one hundred millions in debt."

[2] "I cannot be minister," so Fox wrote in the year 1756, "without being the prime-minister. I am not capable of it. Richelieu, were he alive, could not guide the councils of a nation, if he could not, from November to April, have above two hours in four-and-twenty to think of anything but the House of Commons." That Fox was far from eager to undertake the lead in 1762 is incontestably shown by Lord Edmund Fitzmaurice in his "Life of Lord Shelburne"—a work which has done much to clear up the disputed points and to vivify the lay figures of political history. In volume ii., page 180, there is the prettiest story that ever was told.

There was no time to be lost. The new leader was hardly
in his saddle by the beginning of November, and it was necessary that the victory should be secured before the House
adjourned for the Christmas holidays. Fox possessed all the
qualities which could command success in such an undertaking—perverted ability, impudence, cynicism, misdirected courage, an unequalled knowledge of all that was worst in human
nature and least admirable in human affairs. No cupidity was
left untempted, no fear or foible unplayed on, no stone un-
turned beneath which one of the creeping things of politics
might chance to be lying. Every office-holder in Parliament
was given to understand that his place depended upon his
vote; and every office-seeker got a promise that, when the
battle was won, he should have his share in the spoils, and
should step into some post of dignity and emolument from
which an honester man than himself had been expelled. Money flowed like water; and any honorable gentleman who was
too proud to pocket a bank-note had almost unlimited choice
as to the form of bargain under which he preferred to sell
himself. The terms of one, at least, among these negotiations
still remain on paper. Fox appears to have evinced his respect for the memory of Sir Robert Walpole by expending a
quite exceptional amount of delicacy over the business of
buying his old leader's grandson. Approaching Lord Orford
through his uncle Horace, he offered him the rangership of
the London parks, which he estimated at more than two thousand pounds a year. "Such an income," he wrote, "might, if
not prevent, at least procrastinate your nephew's ruin. I find
nobody knows his lordship's thoughts on the present state of
politics. Now, are you willing, and are you the proper person,
to tell Lord Orford that I will do my best to procure this employment for him if I can soon learn that he desires it? If he
does choose it, I doubt not of his and his friend Boone's hearty
assistance; and I believe I shall see you, too, much oftener in
the House of Commons. This is offering you a bribe, but 'tis
such a one as one honest good-natured man may without offence offer to another." It may well be imagined that a search
among the archives of our old country-seats might bring to

light a curious collection of documents, signed "Henry Fox," and dated in November, 1762, when it is recollected that the letter quoted above was addressed to one who, in spite of certain faults of character, was known far and wide as a man of strict honor and a most independent politician.

When Parliament met, it was at once evident that Fox had got value for his money. A motion for delay was defeated by two hundred and thirteen votes to seventy-four, and an address approving the peace was carried by three hundred and nineteen votes to sixty-five. The fight was over, and the butchery began. Every one who belonged to the beaten party was sacrificed without mercy, with all his kindred and dependents; and those public officers who were unlucky enough to have no political connections fared as ill as the civil population of a district which is the seat of war between two contending armies. Clerks, messengers, excisemen, coast-guardsmen, and pensioners were ruined by shoals because they had no vote for a member of Parliament, or because they had supported a member who had opposed the peace. An inquisition was held into the antecedents of every man, woman, or child who subsisted on public money; and it was said that a noted political lady, ambitious of emulating the exploits of Fulvia in the second triumvirate, had volunteered to bring her feminine acuteness to the aid of the committee of proscription. The old servants and poor relations of peers who had refused to abandon Pitt were hunted from their employments, and thrown back on the world without regard to age or sex or merit. But, to do the ministers justice, they had no respect of persons. They struck high and low with unflinching impartiality. No class fared worse than the Whig magnates to whom and to whose fathers George the Third owed his throne. Forgetting, what even the despots of Webster's ghastly dramas remembered, that

> " Princes give rewards with their own hands,
> But death and punishment by the hands of others,"

the king, with his own pen, dashed the Duke of Devonshire's name off the list of privy-councillors—an act of evil omen, "dipped," said Walpole, "in a deeper dye than I like in politics." The lovers of liberty and order perceived with dismay that their monarch was at heart a Stuart. "Strip the Duke of Newcastle of his three lieutenancies," wrote Fox. "Then go on to the general rout, but let this beginning be made immediately." On the same day that the veteran ex-minister was thus rewarded for his services to the House of Hanover, two young noblemen who before long were to occupy conspicuous stations, the Duke of Grafton and the Marquis of Rockingham, were summarily dismissed from the lord-lieutenancies of their respective counties. The Duke of Devonshire, with proper spirit, insisted on sharing the honorable disgrace of his friends, and placed the Lord-lieutenancy of Derbyshire at the disposal of the government. Every post where a Whig had been drawing salary or exercising authority was now filled by a young Tory or an old Jacobite. It was said in the newspapers that Bute had turned out everybody whom the Duke of Newcastle had helped to bring in, except the king.

Whenever his cold-blooded rigor flagged, Fox was hounded on to his prey by his relentless and rapacious colleagues. "Before another question comes," said Lord Shelburne, "let the two hundred and thirteen taste some of the plunder of the seventy-four." Bute, paraphrasing in a clumsy sentence the concise wish of the Roman tyrant, expressed a hope that "everything the king detests will be gathered into one ostensible heap, and formed either to be destroyed by him, or, by getting the better, to lead him in chains." Rigby, the worst of the graceless clique who lived upon the Duke of Bedford's influence and reputation, boasted to his patron of the share which he had in encouraging Fox to make a clean sweep of the public offices. The court was beside itself with glee; and the princess royal, glad at heart for Bute, but affecting to rejoice because her son was at length king in fact as well as in name, led the chorus of jubilation. She had a right to triumph. A woman's favor and a stripling's whim had proved strong enough to balk the wishes of a nation; for the people, and especially the Londoners, to whom Pitt was dearer than ever, did not by any means participate in the satisfaction of their rulers. The gratitude and affection with which the city continued to regard the man who had made it the first capital in the world seemed equally criminal and contemptible in the eyes of those who, for England's sins, were now her masters. Rigby, who had never been loyal to anything but his bread and butter, recommended the Common Council, now that Pitt's cause was irretrievably lost, to throw over their idol, and fall to their proper business of lighting their lamps and flushing their sewers; and the prime-minister could at length sneer with impunity at "the city's darling," an epithet which doubtless seemed infinitely ridiculous to the luckiest of royal minions.

To the chief of this crew retribution was not long in coming. Fox had abandoned the men with whom he had acted for five-and-twenty years, in order to place himself at the head of a faction which hated him as politicians in all times and all countries hate those who differ from them about a question of disputed succession to the throne. The injuries and affronts which he had inflicted upon those who once had been his allies had cut him off from any chance of reconciliation with his former party. The Whigs, whom he had evicted and insulted; the Jacobites, who had always regarded his family as a tribe of renegades; the lawyers, whom he had so often beaten at their own weapons; his very mercenaries, who, now that they had fulfilled their part of the bargain by voting for the peace, were in a hurry to prove to their seducer that they no longer considered themselves in his debt—one and all vied with each other in harassing and humiliating their common enemy. One day there was a motion for inquiry into the accounts of the Pay-office, and the names of four members who were known to be in his confidence were ostentatiously struck off the list of the proposed committee. On another occasion the House of Commons pretended to suspect that its leader had forged the names which were attached to a trumpery petition. When, after reiterated provocations, he showed signs of temper, he was treated to a lecture by one of Pitt's partisans, who desired him, for the credit of his position, to save

appearances. " It is not my habit," he replied, " to mind appearances, but realities." His audience, catching at the opportunity with ill-natured adroitnesss, smothered the last two
words of the sentence in a shout of insolent laughter; and
Fox, as he sat down, declared, in the bitterness of his heart,
that no man in his situation had ever been so used before.
The most unforgiving and ingenious of his victims could
not have invented for him a more appropriate punishment
than the task of guiding the deliberations of an assembly
whose respect he had forfeited and whose regard he had
never possessed.

His only object now was to withdraw from his uneasy pre-
eminence, and to carry into his retreat as much booty as he
could contrive to pack. Loaded with sinecures and reversions
for himself and his children, he was still unsatisfied unless he
could obtain his peerage without losing his paymastership.
It may well be believed that the aspirants whom he left behind him with their fortunes still unmade were not pleased
at seeing a prize of five-and-twenty thousand a year carried
out of the ring; and, before the matter could be settled, Fox
and Shelburne were involved in an ignoble and tortuous altercation which ruined anything that remained of the elder
statesman's good fame, and hampered the younger with a reputation for duplicity from which he was never able to shake
himself free. Fox may be said to have won the last of his
fights; for he became Lord Holland, kept the Pay-office, and
got the credit of having made the best known of political rep-
artees; [1] while Shelburne gained nothing by the business except a nickname. But there were many to whom the quarrel
served as a pretext for turning against a man who henceforward would have nothing to give; and Fox, if he did not
know it before, now learned what the friendship of self-inter-
ested men was worth. Calcraft, his creature and cousin, whom
he had raised to vast opulence from a clerkship of forty pounds

---

[1] Lord Bute had endeavored to do his best for Shelburne by charac-
terizing the affair as " a pious fraud." " I can see the fraud plain enough,"
said Fox; " but where is the piety?"

a year, was Shelburne's most active partisan in the controversy; and when Fox, relying on the tender recollections of a hundred jobs which they had perpetrated in common, appealed to Rigby for sympathy and advice, his confidences were rejected with a brutality which, if they had been younger men, could only have been expiated at the swordpoint.[1]

Up to November, 1762, Fox had passed for a sharp, self-seeking politician, formidable in debate and still more formidable in intrigue, who would recoil from nothing to gain his ends, but who was no worse at bottom than most of the people by whom he was surrounded. No one expected him to prefer the advantage of the State to his own; but, on the other hand, no one accused him of having ill-used any individual who did not stand in the way of his personal profit and advancement. When once his exorbitant appetite was in course of being gratified, he was not the man to grudge others their share. He was accounted as one who made it his rule to live and let live on the public, to stick by those who had stuck by him, and to observe the laws of that honor which proverbially exists among the class to which so many placemen of his day belonged. Nobody thought well of him except his wife, his children, and his servants; but not a few had a kindly feeling towards him, and liked him the better for his disclaiming any pretence to a virtue of which, after all, he was not more devoid than some of his seemlier competitors.

But the five months which Henry Fox spent in Bute's cabinet entirely reversed the opinion entertained of him by his equals, and undid him in the estimation of his countrymen at large. He had not played fair. He had broken the rules of the game. He had deserted his comrades, and had attacked

---

[1] Fox met Rigby's chariot in St. James's Street, and, leaning over the door, began to abuse Shelburne as "a perfidious and infamous liar." "You tell your story of Shelburne," rejoined the other. "*He* has a damned one to tell of you, and I do not trouble myself which is the truth;" and, pushing Fox's elbow from the window, Rigby ordered his coachman to drive away.

them with an animosity which would have been indecent if directed against the most inveterate of foes. He had cruelly wronged a multitude of humble people who had hitherto been exempted from the severities of party warfare. And all this he had apparently done in the wantonness of deliberate but almost aimless malice; without any benefit to himself which could compensate for a tithe of the unpopularity that pursued him into his retirement, and attended him to his grave. There was no crime of which the public believed him incapable, and not very many which he was not expressly charged with having committed. In the political literature of the next eleven years, Lord Holland supplied an unfailing synonym for tyrant, incendiary, and public robber. Whenever the reader lights upon the title which Fox had waded through so much to earn, it is ten to one that within the next half-dozen lines there will be found an allusion to the gallows;[1] and, what is more significant than the direct vituperation with which he was assailed, he is nowhere mentioned in terms of praise or charity or even of indifference. Junius, his only friend among the satirists who wrote between the Peace of Paris and the outbreak of the American war, proved his good-will by abstaining from any reference to the hated name. Mason branded Lord Holland in his smoothest, and

---

[1] A ferocious libel, published originally under Churchill's initials, with much else that affords desultory but not unprofitable reading on an idle afternoon, may be noticed in the "Foundling for Wit"—a collection of extracts, elegant and otherwise, published in annual volumes between the years 1768 and 1773. The ghost of a felon who had lately died at Tyburn for forging Lord Holland's name to a lease appears to the paymaster-general as he lies in his bedroom at Holland House,

> " revolving future schemes
> His country to betray."

The most vigorous lines read like a horrible travesty of the last verse in " Edwin and Angelina."

> " Not all thy art or wealth can e'er
> Avert the stern decree;
> The same base hand that stretched my neck
> Shall do the same for thee."

3

Churchill in his most pointed, verse.[1] The men of fashion whom he had helped into comfortable places, and in whose company he had drunk whole cellarfuls of claret, were at the pains to collect, and republish in a permanent shape, all the savage lampoons which might inform posterity how universally their old boon companion was detested. And Gray summed up the popular abhorrence in stanzas of extraordinary power, which describe the fallen statesman, "old, and abandoned by each venal friend," as consumed by an undying rancor against the people of London on account of their fidelity to Pitt.[2] With an energy such as he nowhere else expends upon contemporary themes, the poet depicts Lord Holland in his gloomy retreat on the bleak shore of the North Foreland, which he had made still more hideous with mimic ruins in order to feed his diseased fancy with an image of the desolation to which he would have condemned the disobedient city, if only he had met with colleagues bold enough to carry out his atrocious designs.

---

[1]   " Lift against virtue Power's oppressive rod;
         Betray thy country, and deny thy God;
         And, in one general comprehensive line
         To group (which volumes scarcely could define),
         Whate'er of sin and dulness can be said,
         Join to a Fox's heart a Dashwood's head."
                         CHURCHILL, *Epistle to Hogarth.*

[2] Gray, with an affectation unworthy of his powers, gives the title of an "Impromptu" to a performance which, by its condensation of meaning and lucidity of expression, recalls the "Elegy in a Country Churchyard." Such lines as these are not produced offhand:

         " Ah! said the sighing peer, had Bute been true,
           Nor Murray's, Rigby's, Bedford's friendship vain;
         Far better scenes than these had blessed our view,
           And realized the beauties which we feign.

       "Purged by the sword, and purified by fire,
           Then had we seen proud London's hated walls.
         Owls would have hooted in Saint Peter's choir,
           And foxes stunk and littered in Saint Paul's."

CHAPTER II.

1749–1768.

Lord Holland in his own Family.—Birth of Charles James Fox.—His Childhood.—Wandsworth.—Eton and Paris.—Dr. Barnard.—The Musæ Etonenses.—Picture at Holland House.—Lady Sarah Lennox.—Fox at Oxford.—Tour in Italy.—Fox's Industry and Accomplishments.—His Return to England.

LORD HOLLAND was neither so wicked nor so unhappy as the world supposed him. He had never courted esteem, and, while his health was still fairly good and his nerves strong, he cared not a farthing for popularity. He looked upon the public as a milch-cow, which might bellow and toss its horns as much as ever it pleased, now that he had filled his pail and had placed the gate between himself and the animal. But, though he had no self-respect to wound, he could be touched through his affection; for this political buccaneer, whose hand had been against every man and in every corner of the national till, was in private a warm-hearted and faithful friend. Lord Holland cannot be called nice in the choice of some among the objects on whom he bestowed his regard; but, once given, it never was withdrawn. He had attached himself to Rigby with a devotion most unusual in an intimacy made at Newmarket, and cemented over the bottle;[1] and his feelings were more deeply and more permanently hurt by the unkindness of one coarse and corrupt adventurer than by the contempt and aversion of every honest man in the country who read the newspapers. To the end of his life he could not

---

[1] " I dined at Holland House," wrote Rigby on one occasion, " where, though I drank claret with the master of it from dinner till two o'clock in the morning, I could not wash away the sorrow he is in at the shocking condition his eldest boy is in—a distemper they call Sanvitoss dance. I believe I spell it damnably."

mention his old associate without a touch of pathos which has
its effect even upon those whose reason inclines them to regard his expressions of tenderness as the lamentations of a
rogue who has been jockeyed by his accomplice. " I loved
him," he says to George Selwyn; "and whether to feel or
not to feel on such an occasion be most worthy of a man, I
won't dispute; but the fact is that I have been, and still am,
whenever I think of it, very unhappy." Six years after the
breach he was still writing in the same strain. " There is one
question which, I hope, will not be asked—

> 'Has life no sourness, drawn so near its end ?'

Indeed it has; yet I guard against it as much as possible, and
am weak enough sometimes to think that if Rigby chiefly, and
some others, had pleased, I should have walked down the vale
of years more easily. But it is weak in me to think so often
as I do of Rigby, and you will be ashamed of me."

Whatever Lord Holland suffered by the coldness and
treachery of the outside world was amply made up to him
within his domestic circle. As will always be the case with
a man of strong intelligence and commanding powers, who
has the gift of forgetting himself in others, there was no limit
to the attachment which he inspired and the happiness which
he spread around him. In all that he said and wrote, his inability to recognize the existence of public duty contrasts singularly with his admirable unconsciousness that he had any
claims whatever upon those whom he loved; and, as a sure
result, he was not more hated abroad than adored at home.
That home presented a beautiful picture of undoubting and
undoubted affection; of perfect similarity in tastes and pursuits; of mutual appreciation, which thorough knowledge of
the world, and the strong sense inherent in the Fox character,
never allowed to degenerate into mutual adulation. There
seldom were children who might so easily have been guided
into the straight and noble path, if the father had possessed a
just conception of the distinction between right and wrong;
but the notion of making anybody of whom he was fond uncomfortable, for the sake of so very doubtful an end as the

attainment of self-control, was altogether foreign to his creed and his disposition. However, if the sterner virtues were wanting among his young people, the graces were there in abundance. Never was the natural man more dangerously attractive than in Lord Holland's family; and most of all in the third son, a boy who was the pride and light of the house, with his sweet temper, his rare talents, and his inexhaustible vivacity.[1]

Charles James Fox was born on the twenty-fourth January, 1749. His father was already tenant of the suburban palace and paradise from which he was to derive his title; but it was a work of no small time and labor to prepare the mansion for its great destinies, and the noise of carpenters and the bustle of upholsterers obliged Lady Caroline to choose a lodging in Conduit Street for the scene of an event which would have added distinction even to Holland House.[2] Holland House, however, was the seat of Charles's boyhood; and his earliest associations were connected with its lofty avenues, its trim gardens, its broad stretches of deep grass, its fantastic gables, its endless vista of boudoirs, libraries, and drawing-rooms, each more home-like and habitable than the last. All who knew him at this stage of his existence recollected him as at once the most forward and the most engaging of small creatures.

---

[1] Lord Holland had four sons—Stephen, Henry (who died so young that well-informed writers have called Charles the second son), Charles, and Henry Edward.

[2] Fox bought Holland House in 1767. Up to that date he paid for the property a rent less than is asked for five out of six among the hundreds of dwellings which now fringe its northern and eastern outskirts, but which have not been permitted to invade the sacred enclosure. "It will be a great pity," wrote Scott, "when this ancient house must come down and give way to rows and crescents. One is chiefly affected by the air of deep seclusion which is spread around the domain." This was the limit of what Sir Walter would say in favor of a building which he was perhaps too good a Tory to admire as it deserved. Walpole, writing in 1747, says, "Mr. Fox gave a great ball last week in Holland House, which he has taken for a long term, and where he is making great improvements. It is a brave old house, and belonged to the gallant Earl of Holland, the lover of Charles the First's queen."

His father worshipped him from the very first. "Dear Caroline," he writes in March, 1752, "send me word by the bearer how my dear Charles does. Send John Walker to-morrow morning with another account, for I propose shooting, and not being in till three or four. I can do nothing in the anxiety of not hearing of him." On another occasion Henry Fox thus replies to a complaint that he was too much absorbed in politics to please so loving a wife and so fond a mother. "I am very sorry to hear of poor dear Thumb's being so bad in his cough. For God's sake, have the greatest attention for him. If he is ill, you will see whether my state affairs make me forget domestic affection or no. But I pray God no trial of that kind may ever happen to me." "I do believe," he says elsewhere, "Ste has his share of favor in a proper way for his age; but I suppose Charles is so continually at home, and Ste so continually abroad, which must give Charles an advantage with those who stay at home. Don't be peevish, pray, with the dear child for that, nor for anything else; neither will you seriously, I know; for he has made you love him as much as all of us."

The father might honestly repudiate a charge of favoritism; for the love which Charles enjoyed was never at the expense of his brothers. "I got to Holland House," wrote Fox, "last night at seven; found all the boys well; but, to say the truth, took most notice of Charles. I never saw him better or more merry. Harry was just gone to bed and fast asleep. I saw him this morning, when he entered into the conversation very much by signs, but does not speak a word." And again, "I rode to Holland House this morning, and found Harry in his nurse's arms in the park, looking very cold but very well. I called him Squeaker. He looked at me and laughed, but, on the whole, appeared to like my horse better than me." But, however ready Henry Fox might be to pet and spoil the others, it was impossible not to be on rather exceptional terms with a little fellow who made himself a companion at an age when most children are only amusing as playthings. "I dined at home to-day *tête-à-tête* with Charles," wrote the statesman to his wife when the boy was hardly three years old, "intending to do business; but he has found me pleasanter employment. I grow immoderately fond of him." "Is he my sensible child still?" he asks, in December, 1754; and in a subsequent letter he answers his own question by describing his five-year-old son as "very well, very pert, very argumentative," overflowing with good-humor, and so mad about the stage that he was reading every play on which he could lay his tiny hands. In 1756, Charles had gone, as usual, to the theatre. "He says," wrote Fox to Lady Caroline, "he loves you as well indeed, but sticks to it that you are not so handsome as I am, and therefore that he had rather be like me; and he was displeased this morning when Miss Bellamy found out, as I always do, his great resemblance to you." And, a few days later, "Charles is perfectly well, and Mrs. Farmer is therefore sorry that 'Alexander the Great' was acted to-night, because she wished him two or three days of confirmed health before he ventured. But he is gone to eat biscuit there for supper, and to come the moment the play is over to take his rhubarb. Charles is now in perfect health and spirits as it is possible for any animal to be. He is all life, spirit, motion, and good-humor. He says I look like a villain though; and is sure everybody in the House of Commons that don't know me must take me for such." Better testimony to his marvellous but not ungraceful precocity than the admiration of an indulgent father is given by Charles Fox himself, who remembered being present in the room when his mother made a desponding remark about his passionate temper. "Never mind," said Henry Fox, always for leaving both well and ill alone. "He is a very sensible little fellow, and will learn to cure himself." "I will not deny," said Charles, when he told the story, "that I was a very sensible little boy—a very clever little boy. What I heard made an impression on me, and was of use to me afterwards." If he mended his faults so readily, it certainly is a pity that he did not overhear more of the parental criticisms; for of correction and reprimand he received little or none. "Let nothing be done to break his spirit," Lord Holland used to say. "The world will do that business fast enough." The impression left by the father's subservience to all the child's whims and fancies is preserved in many well-known anecdotes which, for the most part, are probably mythical. The shortest and best of these stories is to the effect that Charles declared his intention to destroy a watch. "Well," said Lord Holland, "if you must, I suppose you must."

The boy very soon got beyond the teaching of women, as women then were educated. There was truth in the taunt which, long afterwards, the satirists levelled against him : how,

> "born a disputant, a sophist bred,
> His nurse he silenced and his tutor led."

An unlucky blunder which poor Lady Caroline made in a question of Roman history settled at once and forever her claims as an instructress in the estimation of her irrepressible son ; and, when just turned of seven, he was sent to a school at Wandsworth, then much in vogue among the aristocracy. The master was a Monsieur Pampellonne, from whom Charles Fox perhaps acquired his excellent French accent. This change in his circumstances was ordained, like everything else, by his own will and pleasure. Nothing can be more quaint and droll than the respectful delicacy with which the most headstrong and audacious man in England propounded the question of home or school for the consideration of his small lord and master. "I beg to know," Fox wrote, in February, 1756, "what disposition Charles comes up in, and which you would have me encourage, his going immediately to Wandsworth, or staying till he can go to Eton." And, shortly afterwards, "I was going to dine _tête-à-tête_ with Charles, when I was sent for to the House of Commons. It proved a false alarm, and only prevented my dining with him, but not playing at picket with him and Peter. He is infinitely engaging, and clever and pretty. He coughs a little, and is hot. Would it not be best to persuade him to go to Wandsworth for his health?" At last the decision came. "Charles," wrote his father, "determines to go to Wandsworth." Eighteen months afterwards he determined to go to Eton, and to Eton he accordingly went. There he studied hard, under the care and direction of the Rev. Dr. Francis, known among boys as one of the innumerable translators of Horace, and among men as the father of a writer who has contrived to occupy a greater space in the annals of literature than if he had been undisputed author of the "Areopagitica" and the "Thoughts on the Cause of the Present Discontents." In a happy hour for his own future repose, Lord Holland repaid the services of Dr. Francis by procuring for his promising son Philip a clerkship in the office of the secretary of state.[1]

Though saddled with the encumbrance of a private tutor, Charles Fox was highly popular among his schoolfellows. There was that about him which everywhere made him the king of his company, without effort on his own part, or jealousy on the part of others. Young and old alike watched with hope and delight the development of that fascinating yet masterful character. Lord Holland was proud and glad to admit that the son bade fair to be "as much and as universally beloved" as ever the father was hated. When the boy was still in his fourteenth year, the Duke of Devonshire, who was not a man to sow compliments broadcast, concluded a letter, addressed to the paymaster on high matters of State,

---

[1] Dr. Francis had kept a school at Esher, in Surrey. Gibbon, who was with him for a few weeks at the age of fourteen, complains that "he preferred the pleasures of London to the instruction of his pupils." With a view of reconciling his tastes and his duties, Francis became private chaplain to Lady Holland, and was domesticated in her family. He taught Lady Sarah Lennox to declaim, and Charles Fox to read. Dr. Francis pronounced Lord Holland himself the very worst reader he ever heard; a defect which the Doctor attributed to the last cause which any one would have suspected—his having begun to read the Bible too early.

Another member of the staff of Holland House was Sir George Macartney, a handsome dashing young Irishman, who acted as a sort of travelling tutor and companion to Charles. Macartney, who had to a remarkable degree the talent of success, talked and pushed himself into a celebrity among his contemporaries of which their descendants have ceased to take much account. He became no less a personage than Lord Macartney, President of Madras, Governor of the Cape of Good Hope, and Ambassador to China. The influence and position which Lord Holland enjoyed in his lifetime must have been very great when measured by the number and importance of his satellites.

with the words "Commend me to your son Charles for his sagacity." Never was there a more gracious child, more rich in promise, more prone to good, when, in the spring of 1763, the devil entered into the heart of Lord Holland. Harassed by his dispute with Lord Shelburne, and not unwilling to withdraw himself and his new title for a time from the notice of his countrymen, he could think of no better diversion than to take Charles from his books, and convey him to the Continent on a round of idleness and dissipation. At Spa his amusement was to send his son every night to the gaming-table with a pocketful of gold; and (if family tradition may be trusted where it tells against family credit) the parent took not a little pains to contrive that the boy should leave France a finished rake.[1] After four months spent in this fashion, Charles, of his own accord, persuaded his father to send him back to Eton, where he passed another year with more advantage to himself than to the school. His Parisian experiences, aided by his rare social talents and an unbounded command of cash, produced a visible and durable change for the worse in the morals and habits of the place.[2]

---

[1] Lord Russell's "Life and Times of Charles James Fox," vol. i. p. 4.

[2] The parents of some among our golden youth would do well to notice the epithet attached by a born gentleman to the expense and luxury in which Henry Fox brought up his family. "He educated his children," said Lord Shelburne, "without the least regard to morality, and with such extravagant vulgar indulgence that the great change which has taken place among our youth has been dated from the time of his son's going to Eton."

The discipline of the school in Dr. Barnard's day was none of the best. Mr. Whately, in a letter published among the Grenville papers, relates that he was riding through Eton with Lady Mulgrave, accompanied by her child on a pony, when something in their appearance caught the fancy of the boys, who at once proceeded to mob the party. Things were beginning to look serious, when George Grenville's son, who happened luckily to be in the crowd, came to the rescue. "Her ladyship was frightened, dismounted, and fled for refuge into Lord Mulgrave's chaise, leaving me and the little urchin in the midst of the circle. My good friend Tom give me a wink and a whisper, advising me to make my retreat as soon as possible. I followed his advice, and think he got me out of a scrape." This, says the editor of the papers, was an early

Dr. Barnard, the head-master, a man who had too much spirit, humor, and independence ever to become one of George the Third's bishops, did his best to laugh Charles out of his fopperies and improprieties; but he had not the heart to deal sharply with a lad whom he loved all the better for being, like himself, "rather a mutineer than a courtier." The Doctor was great in elocution. His reading of the Church Service has been cited as "absolute perfection;" and his pulpit manner was much admired, perhaps rather in consequence than in spite of its haste and vehemence. The same description exactly applies to the declamation of his pupil; but, long before he sat under Dr. Barnard, Charles Fox could get quite as many words into a minute as the conditions of human respiration would allow. He could always obtain leave to run up to London when an interesting question was on in the House of Commons.[1] The head-master, with good reason, attended carefully to the rhetorical training of boys who had boroughs waiting for them as soon as they came of age; and Fox, with his repertory of favorite passages from the dramatists, and his passion for an argument, was always to the front both in the speech-room and the debating society. A tribute to his school-boy eloquence remains in the shape of a dozen contemporary couplets from the facile pen of Lord Carlisle, of which the best that can be said is that they are no worse than anything which his lordship's celebrated kinsman produced while he was still at Harrow.[2]

---

indication of the sagacity and discretion for which Mr. Thomas Grenville was so eminently distinguished during his long career.

[1] "The Speaker," wrote Henry Fox, in November, 1763, "fell ill, which disappointed Charles of a debate on Friday."

[2]   "How will, my Fox, alone, thy strength of parts
Shake the loud senate, animate the hearts
Of fearful statesmen, while around you stand
Both Peers and Commons listening your command!
While Tully's sense its weight to you affords,
His nervous sweetness shall adorn your words.
What praise to Pitt, to Townshend, e'er was due,
In future times, my Fox, shall wait on you."

These lines are quite up to the standard of the poem on "Childish

Dr. Barnard possessed what is by far the rarest among all the qualities of an instructor, the tolerance that will permit clever boys to be clever in their own way. The insipidity of school and college exercises, which is ordinarily charged to the account of the author, is quite as often due to the fastidiousness of the judges whom it is his aim to please. Those who insist on perfect good taste and demure propriety in the productions of the young may get taste and propriety, but they will get nothing more; as may be seen by any one who compares the value of everything which has been written to win the verdict of professors and masters of colleges, with much that has been given to the world by men, no older than undergraduates, who have boldly obeyed the impulse of their unfettered genius. All the prize verse of Cam and Isis together is not worth half a canto of "Childe Harold," or ten stanzas of the "Hymn on the Nativity." The schoolmasters of North and Fox, though they had not a Milton or a Byron to educate, were too sensible to be annoyed by the crudity or terrified by the audacity of aspiring sixteen; and beneath the rule of Dr. Barnard and his predecessor the Eton muse was distinguished by a pleasant spice of originality, which is nowhere so marked as in the effusions of the two lads who were destined to shake the senate by their dissensions, and to ruin each other by their fatal reconciliation. Among all Fox's imitations of the classical writers, there is nothing dull or commonplace except a Greek idyl in which a party of shepherds discourse about a recent eclipse in a vein something too sceptical and materialistic for Arcadia—a performance which, at the worst, displays an acquaintance with Theocritus creditable to so young a scholar. A piece of a much higher order is a farewell to Eton, in which the boy addresses Dr. Barnard as the English Quintilian, and describes himself as more fondly attached to the Playing-fields than even to the groves and

---

Recollections" in the "Hours of Idleness;" with the additional advantage that Lord Carlisle called Fox by his proper name, while Byron addressed his schoolfellows as Euryalus and Lycus and Alonzo, and, without any excuse on the score of metre, must needs speak of Harrow as Ida.

lawns of Holland House.[1] But still more full of spirit and
promise are the elegies in which Lord North and his future
rival sang their premature loves. "Laura, indeed," wrote
North, "is fair, and Lydia too is fair. Fairer is Aula, but
fairer after another model. Small art thou, Chloris; but not
small is thy glory, as of a violet that nestles lowly in the dew."
As for Clarissa, the young connoisseur tells us, in the very
neatest of pentameters, that, while each separate feature fails
to please, she pleases as a whole. In Latin quite as good,
and with an even more astonishing air of maturity, Charles
Fox celebrates the dove as the courser of Venus, and the discreet and silent messenger of divided lovers.[2] As for himself, his sighs are directed to Susanna, a name so ill adapted
to Ovidian poetry that it can hardly have been fictitious. His
goddess, in all likelihood, was his cousin Lady Susan Strangways, a daughter of Lord Ilchester, between whom and himself there existed a disparity of years quite sufficient to attract
the homage of a schoolboy.

The young Etonian is as alive as ever on the canvas of one
of Sir Joshua's very best pictures. There he may be seen,
smart, but rather untidy, in a blue laced coat, looking amaz-

---

[1] " Ut patriæ (neque enim ingratus natalia rura
　　　Præposui campis, mater Etona, tuis),
　Ut patriæ, carisque sodalibus, ut tibi dicam,
　　　Anglice, supremum, Quintiliane, Vale.

[2] " Nempe, alis invecta tuis, tibi semper amores
　　　Fidit in amplexus Martis itura Venus.
　Garrulitas nostræ quondam temeraria linguæ
　　　Indicio prodit multa tacenda levi;
　At tibi vox nulla est."

There is a sort of fifth-form coxcombry about the lines which must have
tickled such a humorist as Dr. Barnard.

"If I had a boy," said Fox to Samuel Rogers, "I would make him
write verses. It is the only way to know the meaning of words." An
Etonian to the backbone, he maintained to the end of his life that none
but those who had learned the art within the shadow of Henry the
Sixth's Chapel ever acquired " a correct notion of Greek, or even Latin,
metre."

ingly old for fourteen, with his jet-black curls, and his strongly
moulded rounded features of a Jewish cast—if that nation
could be associated with poor Charles Fox in any connection
but one. The boy is represented with a paper in his hand,
from which he is apparently holding forth for the benefit of
his pretty cousin, and his prettier aunt, of whom the former
was soon to marry an actor, and the latter had already refused
a king. Lady Sarah Lennox, as the sweetest of little children,
had been the pet of old George the Second. Her mother died
before she had left the nursery, and she was thenceforward
brought up, rather as a daughter than a sister, by the Duchess of Leinster and Lady Caroline Fox. She was not likely
long to be a burden on her chaperons. "Her great beauty,"
said Henry Fox, "was a peculiarity of countenance that made
her at the same time different from, and prettier than, any
other girl I ever saw." In January, 1761, Horace Walpole
gives an enthusiastic account of some private theatricals performed at Holland House, in which she played Jane Shore,
of all parts to be selected for a young lady who still was, or
ought to have been, in the schoolroom. "Lady Sarah," writes
Walpole, "was more beautiful than you can conceive. No
Magdalene by Correggio was half so lovely and expressive."[1]
So thought the king, who, in the first flush of his royalty,
imagined that his mother and his groom of the stole would
allow him to choose a wife for himself. He sent his proposal, couched in terms somewhat unusual, but quite unmistakable, through Lady Susan Strangways, who, as he well knew,
was in the habit of spending half her days at Holland House.
The next time that Lady Sarah Lennox appeared at court,

---

[1] In the large picture at Holland House Reynolds has concentrated his
strength upon young Charles Fox, and does scanty justice to the ladies;
but there is another Sir Joshua, engraved in the second volume of
"George Selwyn and his Contemporaries," which has immortalized such
a face as may not be seen in a generation. "In white, and with her hair
about her ears," this exquisite portrait exactly answers to Walpole's description of Lady Sarah as Jane Shore. The expression, which is studied
to suit the character, says everything for the consummate art of the
painter, and not a little for the lady's proficiency as an actress.

the king took her aside into a bow-window, and asked whether she had got his message, and what she thought of it. "Tell
me," he pleaded, "for my happiness depends on it." "Nothing, sir," replied the lady, who, to say truth, had just then
some one else in her head. "Nothing comes of nothing,"
said his Majesty; and he turned away in manifest vexation,
having done his duty under difficulties to which a monarch
has a right to anticipate that he will never find himself exposed.

Lady Sarah, while spending her Easter in the country, had
the misfortune to fall with her horse and break her leg. The
king questioned Henry Fox closely and anxiously about her
state, with signs of deep feeling which were meant to be observed. The evidences of his devotion were duly conveyed
to the right quarter by means of a minute report from the
paymaster to his wife, who was nursing her sister down in
Somersetshire.[1] Six weeks of unwelcome leisure enabled Lady
Sarah to reconsider the whole matter; and, before the summer had set in, she was back in London, knowing her own
mind, and looking more beautiful than ever. The town began
to talk. "The birthday," wrote Walpole on the thirteenth of
June, "exceeded the splendor of the 'Arabian Nights.' Do
you remember one of those stories where a prince has eight
statues of diamonds, which he overlooks because he fancies
he wants a ninth; and the ninth proves to be pure flesh and
blood? Somehow or other, Lady Sarah is the ninth statue."
A witty lady of rank, who had reason to be proud of her figure, caught Lady Sarah by the skirt as she was entering the
presence chamber in the order of precedence. "Do," she said,
"let me go in before you this once, for you never will have
another opportunity of seeing my beautiful back." June was
passed in a flutter of hope and agitation; but the princess
royal had no mind to be mother-in-law even to so bewitching
a Cinderella. The letter in which Lady Sarah announces to

---

[1] "If Lady Sarah don't be quiet," wrote Henry Fox to his wife on the
nineteenth of April, 1761, "it will be the longer before she can dance, and
show her pretty self to advantage."

her friend Lady Susan that her hopes were at an end—a letter the spelling and punctuation of which prove that the
writer was worthy to occupy the throne of Anne and Mary
of Orange—is the most charming of all the documents which
bear upon English history.[1] His Majesty treated her with
marked distinction both then and afterwards; but it was a
cruel courtesy to name her as a bridesmaid. Lady Sarah,
however, had her revenge. Walpole, in the narrative of the
royal wedding which he sent to General Conway, tells us that,
" with neither features nor air, she was by far the chief angel ;"
and it was an easy triumph to outshine a bride whose looks
never earned her a compliment until, after the lapse of many
years, her own chamberlain ventured to express his belief
that " the bloom of her ugliness was going off." Time, which
was kind to Queen Charlotte, bore lightly on her rival. In
1781 the Prince of Wales declared that Lady Sarah could not
have been more lovely in the days when his father was at
her feet. She became the mother of the most illustrious family of heroes that ever graced the roll of the British army.
Twice on the evening of a hard-fought battle Lord Wellington snatched a moment to let her know that two Napiers had
been gloriously wounded. Within a few hours after he had

---

[1] The most delightful passage, if it were possible to make a choice, is
that in which Lady Sarah carefully defines the extent and nature of her
disappointment. " I did not cry I assure you which I believe you will, as
I know you were more set upon it than I was, the thing I am most angry
at is looking so like a fool as I shall for having gone so often for nothing, but I don't much care, if he was to change his mind again (which
can't be tho') and not give a *very very* good reason for his conduct I
would not have him." The whole letter, with much else of the highest
value and interest, may be found in Princess Mary Liechtenstein's volumes. When Sir William Napier, the historian of the Peninsular War,
was seventeen, he spelled as badly as his mother at the same age, and
minded his stops, if possible, even less; but his early letters, like hers,
positively sparkle with fire and fun. He certainly inherited her beauty.
An officer who saw him, for the first time, left for dead under a tree at
Casal Noval, where he had been shot down within a few yards of the
French muzzles, thought him the handsomest man he had ever met or
dreamed of.

been helped down the breach of Ciudad Rodrigo, the second of the three, writing with his left hand, told her that he had lost his best arm at the head of the storming party. With sons as good as they were brave and gifted, every one of whom loved her as she deserved, she had little reason to envy her old admirer the moral reputation, the martial exploits, or the filial affection of the Prince of Wales and the Duke of York.

Charles Fox left Eton for Oxford in 1764. He was entered at Hertford College, which, crushed down for a time by its wealthier neighbors in the struggle for academical existence, has in our own day been munificently re-endowed as a train-ing-school of principles and ideas very different from those ordinarily associated with the name of its greatest son. Early in George the Third's reign the college flourished under the care of Dr. Newcome, a good, wise, and learned divine, who afterwards became Primate of Ireland on the nomination of Lord Fitzwilliam. A poor foundation has attractions for none but rich scholars; and Dr. Newcome's pupils were, for the most part, young men of family. The first Lord Malmesbury, who was in the same set as Charles Fox, though not in the same college, informs us that the lads who ranked as gentle-men-commoners enjoyed the privilege of living as they pleased, and were never called upon to attend either lectures or hall or chapel. "The men," says his lordship, "with whom I lived were very pleasant, but very idle, fellows. Our life was an imitation of high life in London. Luckily, drinking was not the fashion; but what we did drink was claret, and we had our regular round of evening card-parties, to the great annoyance of our finances. It has often been a matter of surprise to me how so many of us made our way so well in the world, and so creditably." [1]

---

[1] Lord Malmesbury was the son of Mr. Harris, a member of Parliament and a placeman, with a love for the by-ways of literature. When he took his seat in the House of Commons, John Townshend asked who he was, and, being told that he had written on "Grammar and Harmony," ob-served, "Why does he come here, where he will find neither?"

Among these pleasant fellows Charles Fox passed for the pleasantest; but idle he was not. He read as hard as any young Englishman who does not look to university success for his livelihood or advancement will ever read for reading's sake. He gave himself diligently to mathematics, which he liked "vastly." "I believe they are useful," he writes, "and I am sure they are entertaining, which is alone enough to recommend them to me." Pursuing them with zest at the age when they most rapidly and effectually fulfil their special function of bracing the reasoning faculties for future use, he got more profit from them than if he had been a senior wrangler. "I did not," said Fox, speaking of the University, "expect my life here could be so pleasant as I find it; but I really think, to a man who reads a great deal, there cannot be a more agreeable place." He loved Oxford as dearly as did Shelley, and for the same reasons, and quitted it almost as much against his will.[1] By his own request he was permitted to spend a second year at college, where he resided continuously, both in and out of term-time, whenever his father could be induced to spare his company. He remained at Oxford during the long vacation of 1765, reading as if his bread depended on a fellowship, and was seldom to be seen outside his own rooms, except when standing at the bookseller's counter, deep in Ford or Massinger. He was one of those students who do not need the spur. "Application like yours," wrote Dr. Newcome, "requires some intermission, and you are the only person with whom I have ever had connection to whom I could say this." Many years afterwards, when Charles Fox was secretary of state, he took the precaution of carrying his old tutor's letter in his pocketbook as a tes-

---

[1] Shelley's happy and peaceful industry at Oxford, and his misery when he was driven forth from that quiet haven into a world where he was as much at home as a bird-of-paradise on the side of Bencruachan, are portrayed with almost preternatural vividness in Hogg's strange fragment of biography, perhaps the most interesting book in our language that has never been republished.

timonial ready to be produced whenever he was rallied for laziness by his colleagues in the cabinet.[1]

Three more years of such a life would have fortified his character and moulded his tastes; would have preserved him from untold evil, and quadrupled his influence as a statesman. But everything which the poor fellow tried to do for himself was undone by the fatal caprice of his father. "Charles," wrote Lord Holland, in July, 1765, "is now at Oxford studying very hard, after two months at Paris, which he relished as much as ever. Such a mixture was never seen; but, extraordinary as it is, it seems likely to do very well." His lordship, like many other people, apparently thought that a theory of education cannot be pushed too far. Two months of foreign travel had agreed so well with his son that two years of it might effect wonders. In the spring of 1766, Charles was taken from Oxford; and in the autumn Lord and Lady Holland once more started for the Continent. Travelling in patriarchal fashion, with three sons and a daughter-in-law, they made their way slowly to Naples. There they spent the winter, with much benefit to Lord Holland's now declining health. The old statesman showed better in retirement than in office. Those who lived with him found much pleasure and little trouble in amusing one who was a delightful companion to others and to himself. His love of reading had many years before excited the envy of Sir Robert Walpole, who anticipated with positive dismay the time when a mind for whose activity the business of three kingdoms hardly sufficed would be reduced to seek occupation within the walls of the library

---

[1] A letter from Dr. Newcome to his one industrious pupil indicates that the curriculum at Hertford College was not exceptionally severe. It appears that when Charles Fox was away at Paris or in London, the scientific studies of the other young Whigs remained in abeyance. "As to trigonometry," says the Doctor, "it is a matter of entire indifference to the other geometricians of the college whether they proceed to the other branches of mathematics immediately, or wait a term or two longer. You need not, therefore, interrupt your amusements by severe studies, for it is wholly unnecessary to take a step onward without you, and therefore we shall stop until we have the pleasure of your company."

at Houghton.   Lord Holland, if politics had left him any superfluous energy, might have made a respectable figure as an
author.   His clear but unpretentious letters are those of a
good writer who was not fond of putting pen to paper, and
he could turn a verse with the best of the clever people of
fashion to whom rhyming was then an indispensable accomplishment.   Several of his fugitive pieces bear the date of
this tour; and the most telling lines that he ever wrote, inspired by the unfailing theme of Rigby's ingratitude, were
actually composed, as they profess to have been composed,
during his return journey over the pass of Mont Cenis.[1]

Charles had arranged that Lord Carlisle should join him in
the course of the winter, so that the two friends might make
the tour of Italy together; but when the time came, the young
nobleman would not leave London, where he was fluttering
round the shrine of no less a goddess than Lady Sarah.[2]

---

[1] This little poem, in something over a score of couplets, expresses
Lord Holland's acknowledgment to Italy for having repaired his "shattered nerves," and enabled him to look back with equanimity on the infidelity and selfishness of his former colleagues.

> "Slight was the pain they gave, and short its date.
> I found I could not both despise and hate.
> But, Rigby, what I did for thee endure!
> Thy serpent's tooth admitted of no cure.
> Lost converse, never thought of without tears!
> Lost promised hope of my declining years!
> Oh, what a heavy task 'tis to remove
> Th' accustomed ties of confidence and love!
> Friendship in anguish turned away her face,
> While cunning Interest sneered at her disgrace."

[2] Lord Holland addressed from Naples a poetical remonstrance to his
sister-in-law on her cruelty to Lord Carlisle, in imitation of Horace's appeal to Lydia in behalf of Sybaris.   The opening lines,

> "Sally, Sally, don't deny,"

are very pretty, in spite of a false rhyme and an asseveration that is far
too strong for the occasion.   The second stanza will bear transcription:

> "Manly exercise and sport,
>   Hunting, and the tennis-court,

When April came, Lord and Lady Holland returned to England; while Charles, who at all times in his life could obtain as many companions as he wanted by holding up his finger, remained on the Continent with Lord Fitzwilliam, and Mr. Uvedale Price, an Eton acquaintance of his own age. In the following October the old people crossed the Channel again, but got no farther than the South of France, where they made an unbroken stay of six months. They were followed by Lord Carlisle, who at length tore himself away from London, and set forth upon his "necessary banishment;" broken-hearted, of course, but, as is pretty evident from his subsequent correspondence, by no means inconsolable. Lord Holland, who had been wofully bored at Nice,[1] though he admitted that angels could not enjoy better weather, was sincerely grateful for the trouble which the young men took to amuse "one," he writes, "so universally despised as I am. Lord Carlisle is very good to Charles, and Charles to me, to be so cheerful as they are in this dull place." "Harry," he says elsewhere, speaking of his youngest son, "will lose no learning by being with Charles, instead of being at Eton. I am sure I am a great gainer by the latter's kind and cheerful stay here; and if I were to go on expatiating upon his and Lord

---

> And riding-school no more divert;
> Newmarket does, for there you flirt.
>   But why does he no longer dream
>   Of yellow Tiber and its shore?
>   Of his friend Charles's favorite scheme,
>   On waking, think no more?"

[1] Charles had called on Lord Breadalbane to make inquiries about Nice, and brought Lord Holland back a most uninviting account. "The commandant, le Comte de Nangis, of a good family in Savoy, and his lady are very polite, and were extremely obliging to Lord and Lady Glenorchy. There is an assembly at his house every evening, consisting of from fifteen to twenty-five ladies, and men in proportion, where they play cards very low. There is no other meeting of company in the town, and consequently very little, or rather no, amusement. The lodgings are bad, with bare walls and brick floors, and there is certainly nothing to invite strangers thither but the air. The best house to be let is a new-built one in the square, but quite unfurnished."

Carlisle's merits, I should never have done.   They have, and promise, every agreeable and good quality; and will not despise themselves, or be despised by other people, at least these forty years."   Forty years from that time Charles Fox was in Westminster Abbey, and Lord Carlisle was patiently submitting to the alternate praises and insults of his fiery young cousin: conduct for which Byron, when his arrogance had been corrected by the experience of a real sorrow, made memorable atonement in his noblest poem.[1]

Early in 1768 Lord Carlisle set off upon a journey, the stages of which may be traced in his letters to George Selwyn —letters so good as to arouse a regret that the writer did not devote himself to a province of literature in which he might have been mentioned with Walpole, instead of manufacturing poetry which it was flattery to compare with Roscommon's. Accompanied by Lord Kildare, he crossed the Alps in a style very different from that in which Englishmen of his age cross them now; in a chair carried by six men, shuddering at every step, and tortured by apprehensions for the safety of his dog, which, bolder than himself, ventured now and then to look over the edge of a precipice.   The scenery of a fine pass inspired him with no ideas except those of horror and melancholy; and he never speaks of "beauties" until he is safe and warm in the Opera-house at Turin.[2]   At Genoa he met Charles Fox, who, like a good son, had stayed at Nice till the last moment; and the three friends went by Piacenza, Parma, and Bologna to Florence, and thence to Rome.   The history of their proceedings may be read in the fourth book of the "Dunciad." Lads of eighteen and nineteen, who had been their own masters almost since they could remember; bearing names that were a passport to any circle; with unimpaired health, and a credit at their banker's which they were not yet old enough to have exhausted, made their grand tour after much the

---

[1] "Childe Harold," canto iii., stanzas xxix. and xxx.

[2] Three years previously to this, Wilkes pronounces the Apennines to be "not near so high nor so horrid as the Alps.   On the Alps you see very few tolerable spots."

same fashion at all periods of the eighteenth century; and it is unnecessary to repeat what Pope has told in a manner that surpasses himself. Travelling with eight servants apiece; noticed by queens; treated as equals by ambassadors; losing their hearts in one palace and their money in another, and yet, on the whole, getting into less mischief in high society than when left to their own devices, they

> " sauntered Europe round,
> And gathered every vice on Christian ground;
> Saw every court; heard every king declare
> His royal sense of operas or the fair;
> Tried all *hors-d'œuvres*, all *liqueurs* defined,
> Judicious drank, and greatly daring dined." [1]

Fox threw into his follies a vivacity and an originality which were meant for better things. Looking forward to the day when, as arbiter of dress, he was to lead the taste of the town through all stages from coxcombry to slovenliness, he spared no pains to equip himself for the exercise of his lofty functions. He tried upon Italian dandies the effect of the queer little French hat and the red heels with which he designed to astonish his brother-macaronies of St. James's Street; and, before he and his friend left the Continent, the pair of scape-

---

[1] The memoirs of last century swarm with proofs that young Englishmen of family were only too well received in Continental, and most of all in Italian, drawing-rooms. The nobleman who, rather by contrast to the others of his name than for any exceptionally heinous misdoings of his own, goes by the sobriquet of " the bad Lord Lyttelton," dated his moral ruin from his grand tour, when he fought two duels and found the women " all Armidas." It might have been thought that young George Grenville's report of his experiences at Naples in the year 1774 was over-colored, if it had been addressed to any less respectable correspondent than Lord Temple. A nephew may be trusted to say the best for the society in which he lives when writing to an uncle by whose aid he expects to come into Parliament. At Vienna, Grenville complains that very few ladies of rank would allow him the honor of their acquaintance without insisting on his purchasing it at the loo-table—a condition which would not have stood much in the way of Charles Fox or Lord Carlisle, whose confidences to George Selwyn are such as irresistibly to suggest a wish that they were both back at Eton in the hands of a head-master who knew his duty.

graces drove post all the way from Paris to Lyons in order to select patterns for their embroidered waistcoats.

In one respect Fox did not resemble Pope's hero. Unlike the youth who

"Spoiled his own language and acquired no more,"

he came back from the Continent an excellent linguist, and a better English scholar than ever. He was fairly contented with the knowledge which, as the fruit of his industry at Oxford, he had obtained of Greek and Latin; and his standard was not a low one. He bade Virgil and Euripides lie by till such time as he could read them again with something of the pleasure of novelty; and from the day that he landed at Genoa he flung himself into the delights of Italian literature with all the vehemence of his ardent nature. "For God's sake," he wrote to his friend Fitzpatrick, "learn Italian as fast as you can, to read Ariosto. There is more good poetry in Italian than in all other languages I understand put together. Make haste and read all these things, that you may be fit to talk to Christians." Every moment that could be spared from gaming and flirting he spent in devouring Dante and Ariosto, or in drudging his way through Guicciardini and Davila. He had a student's instinct for getting at the heart of a language. Like other men who look forward to reading with their knees in the fire or with their elbows in the grass, he knew that he must begin with the dictionary and the exercise-book. While a boy, he had as much French as most diplomatists would think sufficient for a lifetime. Lord Holland has preserved a copy of verses written by Charles at Eton which, in three years out of four, would still win him the prize in French composition at any of our public schools.[1] But he was dissatisfied

---

[1] When, in after-days, these verses were brought to the notice of Fox, he spoke of them as worthless. "I did not," he said, "at that time know the rules of French versification." The subject, indeed, of the lines was not likely to please many besides his father; for they consist in a eulogy on the "digne citoyen" Lord Bute at the expense of Chatham, who is denounced as "un fourbe orateur," the idol and tyrant of a land which the poet blushes to call his country.

with his own proficiency. "As to French," he says, "I am far from being so thorough a master of it as I could wish; but I know so much of it that I could perfect myself at any time with very little trouble, especially if I pass three or four months in France." First and last, he passed a great deal more than three or four months in that seductive country, and few besides himself would have spoken slightingly of the trouble which he bestowed on the task of acquiring its language. He adopted the useful custom of writing from France in French to the friends with whom he could take that liberty. Much of what he had to say he put into the shape of verses, over the construction of which he must have expended no small labor; and any error in rhyme or prosody which he suspected himself of having committed in a letter that had been already despatched he took care to point out and amend in the next. His exertions were not thrown away. None ever found fault with his French except Napoleon, the purity of whose own accent was by no means above criticism. When Fox revisited Paris after the Peace of Amiens, the survivors of the eighteenth-century society, who were venturing once more to show themselves in their old haunts, were astonished by the spirit and correctness with which he reproduced the phraseology in which President Henault talked to Madame du Deffand and the Duchesse de la Vallière in the days before the guillotine had been heard of.

There are some who apparently study the histories of distinguished men in order to find illustrations of the theory that fame in after-life does not necessarily depend upon habits of work formed betimes and persistently maintained. Readers of this class will derive even less than their usual consolation and encouragement from the career of Fox. The third Lord Holland, who knew his uncle far better than all other people together who have recorded their impressions of his character, tells us that the most marked and enduring feature in his disposition was his invincible propensity "to labor at excellence." His rule in small things, as in great, was the homely proverb that what is worth doing at all is worth doing well. His verses of society were polished with a care which

their merit not unfrequently repaid. He ranked high among
chess-players, and was constantly and eagerly extending his
researches into the science of the game. When secretary of
state, he did something to improve his hand by taking lessons,
and writing copies like a schoolboy. At the head of his own
table, he helped the turbot and the fowls according to the directions of a treatise on carving which lay beside him on the
cloth. As soon as he had finally determined to settle in the
country, he devoted himself to the art of gardening with a
success to which St. Anne's Hill still bears agreeable testimony. He could hold his own at tennis after he was well on
in years and of a bulk proportioned to his weight in the balance of political power; and when an admiring spectator
asked him how he contrived to return so many of the difficult
balls, " It is," he replied, " because I am a very painstaking
man." Whatever hand or mind or tongue found to do, he
did it with his might; and he had his reward; for the practice of working at the top of his forces became so much a part
of his nature that he was never at a loss when the occasion
demanded a sudden and exceptional effort. A young senator,
who feels that he has it in him, eagerly asks to be told the
secret of eloquence; and veterans can give him no better receipt than the humble advice, whatever he is about, always to
do his utmost.[1] It is said that armies can be disciplined to
such a point that the soldier will find the battle-field a relaxation from the hardships and restraints of the drill-ground;
and the orator who, when taken unawares, retorts upon his

---

[1] The collection of aphorisms which Mr. Ruskin composed for the instruction of a young Italian painter may be studied with benefit by aspirants in oratory. "Stop," says Mr. Ruskin, "the moment you feel a
difficulty, and your drawing will be the best you can do, but you will
not be able to do another so good to-morrow. Put your full strength
out the moment you feel a difficulty, and you will spoil your drawing
to-day, but you will do better than your to-day's best to-morrow." The
processes of true art are much the same in all its branches. A public
speaker may learn more from Herr Klesmer's discourse in "Daniel Deronda" on the training of a public performer than from twenty professed
treatises on rhetoric.

assailant with a shower of sentences so apt that they might each have been coined for the purpose of the moment has purchased his enviable gift by many an hour of unseen and apparently objectless labor, which few among his audience, even with such a prize in prospect, could ever prevail upon themselves to undertake.

In August, 1768, Fox waited upon Voltaire at his villa by the Lake of Geneva. The old man was very gracious, treated his guest to chocolate, and did him the easy favor of pointing out some of his own writings which had a tendency to counteract the influence of religious prejudice. "Voilà," said the patriarch, "des livres dont il faut se munir."[1] Charles had just then very little attention to spare for theological controversy, even in the enticing guise which it assumes in the "Ingénu" and the "Philosophical Dictionary." With his head full of politics, he was proceeding homewards to commence the business of his life. The world in which he found himself on his arrival in England differed so essentially from our own that it would be a gross injustice to the memory of Fox if I were to plunge into the narrative of his actions without previously describing, to the best of my power, the society in which he moved, the moral atmosphere which he breathed, and the temptations by which he was assailed. Never was there a man whose faults were so largely those of his time; while his eminent merits, and enormous services to the country, were so peculiarly his own. When we compare the state of public life as he entered it and as he left it, and when we reflect how preponderating a share he cheerfully bore in the gigantic labors and sacrifices by which a change for the better was gradually and painfully secured,

---

[1] Fox took other opportunities of improving his acquaintance with Voltaire, who acknowledged his next visit in a letter to Lord Holland, the first sentences of which run thus: "Yr son is an English lad, and j an old frenchman. He is healthy, and j sick. Yet j love him with all my heart, not only for his father, but for him self." On this occasion Voltaire gave Charles a dinner in his "little caban," where the young man was soon privileged to come and go at will.

we shall confess that, besides his unquestioned title to an affection which, after the lapse of three quarters of a century, is still rather personal than historical, he has a claim to our unstinted gratitude, and to no scanty measure of esteem.

CHAPTER III.

London Society at the Time that Fox entered the Great World.—Its
Narrow Limits and Agreeable Character. — Prevalent Dissipation
and Frivolity.—The Duke of Grafton.—Rigby.—Lord Weymouth.—
Lord Sandwich.—Fox in the Inner Circle of Fashion.—Lord March.—
Brooks's Club. —·Gaming. — Extravagance. — Drinking and Gout. —
George the Third's Temperate and Hardy Habits.—State of Religion
among the Upper Classes.—Political Life in 1768.—Sinecures.—Pensions and Places, English, Irish, and Colonial.—Other Forms of Corruption.—The Venality of Parliament.—Low Morality of Public Men,
and Discontent of the Nation.—Office and Opposition.—Fox's Political
Teachers.

MORAL considerations apart, no more desirable lot can well
be imagined for a human being than that he should be included in the ranks of a highly civilized aristocracy at the
culminating moment of its vigor. A society so broad and
strongly based that within its own borders it can safely permit absolute liberty of thought and speech ; whose members
are so numerous that they are able to believe, with some
show of reason, that the interests of the State are identical
with their own, and at the same time so privileged that they
are sure to get the best of everything which is to be had, is
a society uniting, as far as those members are concerned,
most of the advantages and all the attractions both of a popular and an oligarchical form of government. It is in such
societies that existence has been enjoyed most keenly, and
that books have been written which communicate a sense of
that enjoyment most vividly to posterity. The records of
other periods may do more to illustrate the working of political forces and to clear up the problems of historical science ; the literature of other periods may be richer in wealth
of thought and nobler in depth of feeling; but a student
who loves to dwell upon times when men lived so intensely
and wrote so joyously that their past seems to us as our

present will never tire of recurring to the Athens of Alcibiades and Aristophanes, the Rome of Mark Antony and Cicero, and the London of Charles Townshend and Horace
Walpole. The special charm of the literature produced in
communities so constituted is that in those communities, and
in those alone, personal allusion, the most effective weapon
in the armory of letters, can be employed with a certainty of
success. A few thousand people who thought that the world
was made for them, and that all outside their own fraternity
were unworthy of notice or criticism, bestowed upon each
other an amount of attention quite inconceivable to us who
count our equals by millions. The actions, the fortunes, and
the peculiarities of every one who belonged to the ruling
class became matters of such importance to his fellows that
satire and gossip were elevated into branches of the highest
literary art. Every hit in an Athenian burlesque was recognized on the instant by every individual in an audience
which comprised the whole body of free-born citizens. The
names and habits of every parasite and informer and legacy-
hunter within the circuit of the Seven Hills were accurately
known to every Roman who had enough spare sesterces to
purchase a manuscript of Juvenal. In the eighteenth century, in our own country, the same causes produced the same
results; and the flavor of the immortal impertinences which
two thousand years before were directed against Pericles and
Euripides may be recognized in the letters which, when
George the Third was young, were handed about among a
knot of men of fashion and family who could never have
enough of discussing the characters and ambitions, the incomes and genealogies, the scrapes and the gallantries, of
everybody who had admission to the circle within which
their lives were passed.

The society pictured in these letters had much the same relation to what is called good society now that the "Boar Hunt"
by Velasquez, in the National Gallery, with its groups of
stately cavaliers, courteous to each other, and unmindful of
all besides, bears to the scene of confused bustle and dubious
enjoyment represented in the "Derby Day" of Mr. Frith. So

far from being a vast and ill-defined region, capable of almost infinite expansion, into which anybody can work his way who has a little money and a great deal of leisure, and who is willing to invest his industry in the undertaking, good society, when Lord Chesterfield was its oracle and George Selwyn its father-confessor, was enclosed within ascertained and narrow boundaries. The extent of those boundaries was so familiar to all who were admitted and all who were excluded that a great lady, when she gave an evening-party, would content herself with sending cards to the women, while she left the men to judge for themselves whether they had a right to come, or not. Within the charmed precincts there prevailed an easy and natural mode of intercourse which in some respects must have been singularly delightful. Secure of his own position, and with no desire to contest the social claims of others, a man was satisfied, and sometimes only too easily satisfied, to show himself exactly as he was. There was no use in trying to impose upon people who had been his schoolfellows at Eton, his brother-officers in the Guards, his colleagues in Parliament, his partners at whist, his cronies at the club, his companions in a hundred revels. Every friend with whom he lived was acquainted with every circumstance in his career and every turn in his affairs—who had jilted him, and who had schemed for him; how many thousands a year had been allowed him by his father, and how many hundreds he allowed his son; how much of his rent-roll was unmortgaged, and how much wood was left uncut in his plantations; what chance he had of getting heard at two in the morning in the House of Commons, and what influence he possessed over the corporation of his neighboring borough. Unable to dazzle those for whose good opinion he cared, it only remained for him to amuse them; and the light and elegant effusions in which the fine gentlemen of White's and Arthur's rivalled, and, as some think, excelled, the wittiest pens of France remain to prove of what Englishmen are capable when they devote the best of their energy to the business of being frivolous.

The frivolity of the last century was not confined to the

youthful, the foolish, or even to the idle. There never will be a generation which cannot supply a parallel to the lads who, in order that they might the better hear the nonsense which they were talking across a tavern table, had Pall Mall laid down with straw at the cost of fifty shillings a head for the party; or to the younger brother who gave half a guinea every morning to the flower-woman who brought him a nose-gay of roses for his button-hole.[1] These follies are of all times; but what was peculiar to the period when Charles Fox took his seat in Parliament and his place in society consisted in the phenomenon (for to our ideas it is nothing else) that men of age and standing, of strong mental powers and refined cultivation, lived openly, shamelessly, and habitually, in the face of all England, as no one who had any care for his reputation would now live during a single fortnight of the year at Monaco. As a sequel to such home-teaching as Lord Holland was qualified to impart, the young fellow, on his entrance into the great world, was called upon to shape his life according to the models that the public opinion of the day held up for his imitation; and the examples which he saw around him would have tempted cooler blood than his, and turned even a more tranquil brain. The ministers who guided the State, whom the king delighted to honor, who had the charge of public decency and order, who named the fathers of the Church, whose duty it was (to use the words of their monarch) "to prevent any alterations in so essential a part of the Constitution as everything that relates to religion,"[2] were conspicuous for impudent vice, for daily dissipation, for pranks which would have been regarded as childish and unbecoming by the cornets of a crack cavalry regiment in the worst days of military license. The Duke of Grafton flaunted at Ascot races with a mistress whom he had picked up in the street, and paraded her at the opera when the royal party were in their box.[3] So public an outrage on the part of the first ser-

---

[1] Walpole to Mann, September 9, 1771; May 6, 1770.
[2] The king to Lord North, April 2, 1772.
[3] Junius has made the Duke of Grafton and Miss Nancy Parsons almost

vant of the crown roused a momentary indignation even in hardened minds. " Libertine men," writes an active politician in April, 1768, " are as much offended as prudish women ; and it is impossible he should think of remaining minister." But George the Third was willing that the Duke of Grafton should bring whom he pleased under the same roof as the queen, so long as he kept such people as Rockingham and Burke and Richmond out of the cabinet. Where the king gave his confidence, it was not for his subjects to play the Puritan, or, at any rate, for those among his subjects who lived upon the good graces of the prime-minister ; and in the following August, when Miss Parsons showed herself at the Ridotto, she was followed about by as large a crowd as ever of smart gentlemen who wanted commissionerships for themselves and deaneries for their younger brothers.[1]

In point of both the lesser and the greater morals there was little to choose between the head of the government and his subordinates. The paymaster of the forces was Rigby, a man of whom it may be literally said that the only merit he possessed, or cared to claim, was that he drank fair. This virtue had stood him in good stead when secretary to the Duke of Bedford in Ireland, to whom he was invaluable for the skill with which he conducted the operation of washing away disaffection in floods of the viceregal claret. He took care to keep the lord-lieutenant informed of the zeal which he expended on this important service. " We liked each other," he writes on one such occasion, " well enough not to part till three in the morning ; long before which time the company was reduced to a *tête-à-tête*, except one other, drunk and asleep in the corner of the room." Rigby, however, in the matter of sobriety, did not observe what Burke calls " the morality of geography." As he drank at Dublin, so he drank in Lon-

---

as famous as Antony and Cleopatra ; but the most discreditable features of the story are known by the casual and somewhat contemptuous comments of a number of men who socially were the prime-minister's equals, and who had no sufficient motive, political or personal, for depicting him to each other as worse than he was.

[1] Mr. Whately to Mr. Grenville, April 22 and August 24, 1768.

don, and as he drank in London, so he drank in the country. A letter of Garrick's almost implies that the paymaster fixed his residence among the swamps of Essex in order that he might have an excuse for using brandy as the rest of the world used small-beer. With no lack of mother-wit, and prepared, according to the character of his company, to please by the coarsest jollity or the most insinuating good-breeding, he was a dangerous guide to the sons and nephews of his own contemporaries. When he first appeared as a man about town, he was detected as having been at the bottom of at least one discreditable frolic;[1] and he did not improve with years. At the Pay-office, in which paradise of jobbery he contrived to settle himself as a permanent occupant, he kept open house for the members of several successive administrations, according to his own notions of what open house should mean. But the cup of his excesses, to employ a metaphor which he would have appreciated, was at length full; and he lived to learn, in impoverishment and disgrace, that a purer generation had drawn somewhat tighter than in the halcyon days of Lord Holland the limits within which public money might be diverted to the maintenance of private debauchery.

When the Duke of Grafton was at the Treasury, the seals were held by Lord Weymouth, the son of Earl Granville's daughter. With more than his grandfather's capacity for liquor, he had inherited a fair portion of his abilities; and anybody who cared to sit up with the secretary of state till

---

[1] Sir Charles Hanbury Williams gave George Selwyn a sad account of a young Hobart, whom the latter was trying to keep out of mischief. "The moment your back was turned he flew out; went to Lady Tankerville's drum-major, having unfortunately dined that day with Rigby, who plied his head with too many bumpers, and also made him a present of some Chinese crackers. Armed in this manner, he entered the assembly, gave a string of four-and-twenty crackers to Lady Lucy Clinton, and bid her put it in the candle, which she very innocently did. When the first went off, she threw the rest on the tea-table, where, one after another, they all went off, with much noise and not a little stink. Lady Lucy was very plentifully abused, and Mr. Hobart had his share. Few women will courtesy to him, and I question if he'll ever lead anybody to their chair again as long as he lives."

the hours were no longer small might obtain a fair notion how Carteret used to talk towards the end of his second bottle. It would have been well for Lord Weymouth if his nights had been consumed exclusively in drinking, for he was an ardent and most unlucky gambler, and by the age of one-and-thirty he had played away his fortune, his credit, and his honor. His house swarmed with bailiffs; and when he sought refuge at the club, he found himself among people whose money he had tried to win without having any of his own to lose, and who had told him their opinion of his conduct in terms which he was not in a position, and (as some suspected) not of a nature, to resent. He was on the point of levanting for France when, as a last resource, his grandfather's friends bethought them that he had not yet tried public life. "He must have bread, my lord," wrote Junius; "or, rather, he must have wine;" and, as it was convenient that his first services to the State should be rendered at a distance from the scene of his earlier exploits, he was appointed Lord-lieutenant of Ireland. The Dublin tradesmen, however, did not relish the prospect of having a bankrupt nobleman quartered upon them for five or six years, in order that at the end of that time he might be able to show his face again at White's. The spirit which, fifty years before, had refused to put up with the bad halfpence of the dominant country again began to show itself; Lord Weymouth's nomination was rescinded; and, to console him for the rebuff, he was made Secretary of State for the Northern Department, and intrusted with half the work that is now done by the Foreign Office, and with the undivided charge of the internal administration of the kingdom. He did not pay his new duties the compliment of making the very slightest alteration in his habits. He still boozed till daylight, and dozed into the afternoon; and his public exertions were confined to occasional speeches, which his admirers extolled as preternaturally sagacious, and which his severest critics admitted to be pithy. "If I paid nobody," wrote Walpole, "and went drunk to bed every morning at six, I might expect to be called out of bed by two in the afternoon to save the nation and govern the House of Lords by two or three sentences as profound and short as the proverbs of Solomon."

Lord Weymouth's successor as secretary of state was the most eminent, and possibly the most disreputable, member of the Bedford connection. The Earl of Sandwich was excellent as the chief of a department. He rose about the time that his predecessor retired to rest, and remained, till what then was a late dinner-hour, closely absorbed in methodical and most effectual labor. "Sandwich's industry to carry a point in view," says Walpole, "was so remarkable that the world mistook it for abilities;" and if genius has been rightly defined as the capability of taking trouble, the world was not far wrong. Like all great administrators, he loved his own way, and rarely failed to get it; but outside the walls of his office his way was seldom or never a good one. He shocked even his own generation by the immorality of his private life, if such a term can be applied to the undisguised and unabashed libertinism that he carried to the very verge of a tomb which did not close on him until he had misspent three quarters of a century. He survived a whole succession of scandals, the least flagrant of which would have been fatal to any one but him. Nothing substantially injured him in the estimation of his countrymen, because no possible revelation could make them think worse of him than they thought already. When he was advanced in age, and at the head of what was just then the most important branch of the public service, he was involved in one of those tragedies of the police-court by means of which the retribution of publicity sometimes overtakes the voluptuary who imagines that his wealth has fenced him securely from the consequences of his sin. But no coroner's inquest, or cross-examination at the Old Bailey, could elicit anything which would add a shade to such a character. The blood had been washed from the steps of the theatre; the gallows had been erected and taken down; the poor creature who had been the object of a murderous rivalry was quiet in her grave;[1] and the noble earl was still at the

---

[1] "The poor assassin was executed yesterday. The same day Charles

Admiralty, giving his unhonored name to the discoveries of
our most celebrated navigator, and fitting out expeditions
which might reduce the Puritans of New England and the
Quakers of Philadelphia, to the necessity of contributing to
the taxes out of which he replenished his cellar and his se-
raglio.   Corrupt, tyrannical, and brazen-faced as a politician,
and destitute, as was seen in his conduct to Wilkes, of that
last relic of virtue, fidelity towards the partners of his secret
and pleasant vices, political satire itself tried in vain to exaggerate the turpitude of Sandwich.

> " Too infamous to have a friend ;
>   Too bad for bad men to commend,
>   Or good to name ; beneath whose weight
>   Earth groans ; who hath been spared by fate
>   Only to show, on mercy's plan,
>   How far and long God bears with man."

Even this masterpiece of truculence was no libel upon one
who had still eight-and-twenty years to pass in living up to
the character which Churchill had given him in his wrath.

"Such," cried Junius, "is the council by which the best of
sovereigns is advised, and the greatest nation upon earth governed."[1]   The humiliation and resentment with which decent
Englishmen saw this train of Bacchanals scouring through the
high places of the State is a key to the unexampled popularity of that writer who, under twenty different signatures
drawn from the pages of Plutarch and Tacitus, lashed the
self-will and self-delusion of the king, and the rapacity and
dissoluteness of his ministers.   The spectacle of "the Duke
of Grafton, like an apprentice, thinking that the world should
be postponed to a horse-race, and the Bedfords not caring
what disgraces we undergo, while each of them has three
thousand pounds a year and three thousand bottles of claret

Fox moved for the removal of Lord Sandwich, but was beaten by a large
majority; for in Parliament the ministers can still gain victories" (Walpole to Mann, April 20, 1779).

[1] The letter containing this sentence is signed "Atticus;" but it was
published among the works of Junius, and is indisputably from his pen.

and champagne," [1] did more than his own somewhat grandiose
eloquence and over-labored sarcasm to endow Junius with a
power in the country second only to that of Chatham, and a
fame hardly less universal than the notoriety of Wilkes. But
in the eyes of George the Third the righteous anger of his
people was only another form of disloyalty. Intent, heart and
soul, on his favorite scheme for establishing a system of personal rule, under which all the threads of administration
should centre in the royal closet, he entertained an instinctive antipathy to high-minded and independent men of all
political parties. He selected his instruments among those
who were willing to be subservient because they had no self-
respect to lose. "His Majesty," wrote Burke, "never was in
better spirits. He has got a ministry weak and dependent;
and, what is better, willing to continue so." [2] Serenely satisfied with his success in weeding out of the government everybody whom the nation trusted and esteemed, he felt it an insult to himself that his subjects should murmur when they
saw honest and patriotic statesmen forbidden to devote their
talents to the service of the public, while the prosperity and
honor of the country were committed to the charge of men
not one of whom any private person in his senses would
choose as a steward or receive as a son-in-law. According to
his Majesty's theory, his favor was a testimonial which the
world was bound to accept. The royal confidence could turn
Sir Francis Dashwood into a sage and Lord George Sackville
into a hero; could make a Cato the censor of the Earl of
Sandwich, and a Scipio of the Duke of Grafton. Among the
innumerable evil results of George the Third's policy, not
the least disastrous was that the supporters of that policy considered themselves bound to maintain that men like Lord
Weymouth and Rigby were no worse than men like the Duke
of Richmond and the Marquis of Rockingham. Personal morality became a party question; the standard of virtue was

---

[1] Walpole to Conway, June 16, 1768. The allusion to the Duke of
Grafton has been softened by the omission of three words.

[2] Burke to the Marquis of Rockingham, August 1, 1767.

lowered to meet the convenience of the court; and whoever was desirous of evincing his attachment to the king was in a hurry to assure mankind that he condoned the vices of the minister.

It must have been an edifying lesson in ethics for the Cambridge undergraduates when the Earl of Sandwich put himself up for the high-stewardship of their university, within six weeks of the time that his initiation into the orgies and blasphemies of Medmenham Abbey had become matter for comment throughout the length and breadth of England.[1] The post had been vacated by the death of Lord Hardwicke; and, scandalized by the prospect of such a successor to an office which his father had dignified, the deceased nobleman's eldest son announced himself as a rival candidate. The more respectable masters of arts declared their preference for a peer whose literary tastes and exemplary conduct fairly entitled him to an academical compliment, and asked each other what single qualification his opponent possessed which could recommend him to the suffrages of a corporate body pledged to the encouragement of religious education. Gray, in a very superior specimen of that class of pasquinades which a hot contest at the university never fails to produce, endeavored to establish a connection between the Earl of Sandwich and Bibli-

---

[1] Medmenham Abbey, formerly a convent of Cistercian monks, was a ruin finely situated on the Thames, near Marlow. A society of dissipated men of fashion who dubbed themselves "The Franciscans," after their founder, Sir Francis Dashwood, repaired and fitted up the buildings and laid out the grounds as a retreat where they might indulge with impunity in their peculiar notions of enjoyment. Little is known with certainty about their proceedings; but that little is more than enough. Selwyn, as an undergraduate, was expelled from Oxford with every mark of ignominy for an act of profane buffoonery which, in an aggravated form, was performed nightly at Medmenham by the Chancellor of the Exchequer for the amusement of a circle of privy-councillors and members of Parliament. The door of the abbey may still be seen surmounted by the motto "Fay ce que voudras." The other inscriptions which disgraced the natural beauty of the groves and gardens survive only in books which fortunately no one, except an historian, is under any obligation to consult.

cal theology, on the ground that a precedent for most of his
vices could be found in the history of one or another of the
patriarchs. But Lord Hardwicke's adherents soon found that
the matter was beyond a joke. Sandwich, who was the most
consummate electioneerer of the day, left his character to
take care of itself, and applied all his activity and experience
to the familiar business of getting votes. He bribed; he
promised; he canvassed every country clergyman who had
kept his name on the books. He wrote fawning letters to
men of his own rank, begging them to exert their influence
over their private chaplains and the incumbents and expect-
ants of the livings which were in their gift. He fetched one
voter out of a mad-house, and another all the way from the
Isle of Man; and such were the ill-feeling and confusion which
he created in university society that his own cousins, who had
gone down from London to do what they could for him among
their college acquaintances, freely expressed their disgust at
finding the Cambridge senate treated like a constituency of
potwallopers. When the poll closed, both sides claimed a
majority of one. The undergraduates, who were for Lord
Hardwicke to a man, burst into the senate-house, elected one
of their own number high steward, and chaired him as the
representative of their favorite; and when, in the course of
the next month, Sandwich dined with the fellows of Trinity,
the students rose from their seats and quitted the hall in a
body as soon as he had taken his place at the high table. But
the self-seeking and sycophancy of their elders and instructors
were proof against any conceivable rebuke. Four years afterwards, at a time when the Duke of Grafton was at once the
greatest dispenser of patronage and the most notorious evil
liver in the kingdom, the chancellorship of Cambridge happened to fall vacant; and the young prime-minister was selected to preside over a university which, if he had been in *statu
pupillari*, the proctors would soon have made too hot to hold
him. Well might Junius congratulate his grace on his amicable relations with "that seat of learning which, in contemplation of the system of your life, the comparative purity of
your manners with those of your high steward, and a thousand

other recommending circumstances, has chosen you to encourage the growing virtue of their youth and to preside over their education." [1]

There is no form of personal example more sure to be observed and copied than that which a political leader presents to the younger portion of his followers ; and it may well be believed that Charles Fox, entering public life at an age when in our generation he would still be a freshman at college, was not likely to get much good by studying the patterns in fashion among the party to which Lord Holland ordained that he should belong. Youth as he was, and absolutely in the

---

[1] The Duke of Grafton was chosen Chancellor of Cambridge in July, 1769. Gray stooped to compose the words of an ode which was performed at the installation. A comparison between this production and his squib on Lord Sandwich goes far to bear out the dictum of his old pupil, Horace Walpole, that Gray's natural turn was for " things of humor." It is melancholy to find the author of " The Bard " invoking all the heroes and benefactors of the university—Milton, Newton,

> " Great Edward with the lilies on his brow
> From haughty Gallia torn,"

" sad Chatillon and princely Clare," and " either Henry,"

> " The murdered saint, and the majestic lord
> That broke the bonds of Rome,"

to welcome a nobleman who would have found himself much more at home with Poins and Pistol and Mrs. Quickly than in the august company which the poet provided for him. The very depth of incongruity was sounded in the passage,

> " Hence avaunt—'tis holy ground—
> Comus and his midnight crew !"

An injunction which, if obeyed, would have prevented most of the prime-minister's colleagues from being present at the installation of their chief. It was long before Gray heard the last of his ode, every line of which appeared to be written with a view to parody. The wits of the Opposition took special delight in illustrating his assertion that the muse

> " No vulgar praise, no venal incense, flings,"

by reminding the world that the Duke of Grafton had appointed him professor of history at Cambridge in the course of the previous twelve-month.

hands of a parent whose fascinating manners aided and disguised an uncommon force of will, and to whom every corner
of the great world was intimately known, he had little choice
in this or in any other vital matter. His bench in Parliament was ready for him, and his niche in society. Few have
had the downward path made smoother before them, or strewn
with brighter flowers and more deadly berries. He was received with open arms by all that was most select and least
censorious in London. Those barriers that divide the outer
court from the inner sanctum—barriers within which Burke
and Sheridan never stepped, and which his own father with
difficulty surmounted—did not exist for him. Like Byron,
Fox had no occasion to seek admission into what is called the
highest circle, but was part of it from the first.[1] Instead of
being tolerated by fine gentlemen, he was one of themselves
—hand and glove with every noble rake who filled his pockets from the Exchequer and emptied them over the hazard-
table; and smiled on by all the dowagers and maids of honor
as to the state of whose jointures and complexions our envoy
at Florence was kept so regularly and minutely informed. It
would be unchivalrous to revive the personal history of too
many among the fair dames to whom, and about whom, Walpole indited his letters, even though a century has elapsed
since they were laid elsewhere than in their husband's family
vault.[2] What were the morals of the bolder sex among Lord
Holland's friends may be gathered from the correspondence
of the Earl of March, in which a man past forty describes to
a man of nearly fifty the life which, without affectation of

---

[1] "I liked the dandies," said Byron. "They were always civil to me,
though in general they disliked literary people. The truth is that,
though I gave up the business early, I had a tinge of dandyism in my
minority, and retained enough of it to conciliate the great ones."

[2] The foot-notes to Walpole's "Correspondence," and the short personal histories in Selwyn's "Memoirs," leave on the mind of the reader
an impression that, among the ladies of their set, the usual destiny was
in France to be guillotined and in England to be divorced. "Augustus
Hervey," writes Walpole, "asked Lord Bolingbroke t'other day who was
his proctor, as he would have asked for his tailor."

concealment, was led by persons high in rank, rich in official employments, well seen at court, and to whom every door in Mayfair was as freely open as to young Lord Hardwicke or old Lord Mansfield. March was in no sense one of those whom the gods loved. As Duke of Queensberry, at nearer ninety than eighty years of age, he was still rolling in wealth, still wallowing in sin, and regarded by his countrymen as one whom it was hardly decent to name, because he did not choose, out of respect for the public opinion of 1808, to discontinue a mode of existence which in 1768 was almost a thing of course among the men to whose care and guidance Lord Holland intrusted the unformed character of his idolized boy.[1]

What a mere boy he was when his father, as if ambitious of making him not less invulnerable to shame than himself, plunged him into the flood of town dissipation as suddenly and as completely as Achilles was dipped in Styx, may be judged by the date at which his name appears in the books of Brooks's. This society, the most famous political club that will ever have existed in England—because, before any noteworthy rival was in the field, our politics had already outgrown St. James's Street—was not political in its origin. In the first list of its members the Duke of Grafton and Lord Weymouth are shown side by side with the Duke of Richmond and the Duke of Portland.[2] Brooks's took its rise from

---

[1] The Duke of Queensberry is the crucial instance among bad men, as Samuel Johnson is the crucial instance among the good, that the dread of the undiscovered future has no necessary connection with the consciousness of an ill-spent life. Amidst a great deal in the received account of his last days which may be charitably set down as fabulous, this much is clear, that he met death with well-bred indifference.

[2] The rules of admission were evidently inspired by the caution of social, and not political, prudence. The ballot took place between eleven at night and one in the morning; a single black ball excluded; and a member of Brooks's who joined any other club except White's was at once struck off the books. The establishment was formed by one Almack, a wine-merchant, who was strictly enjoined to " sell no wines, that the club approves of, out of the house." Almack was soon succeeded by Mr. Brooks. The present house was built on the site of the old one in 1778, and not long afterwards Brooks,

the inclination of men who moved in the same social orbit
to live together more freely and familiarly than was compati-
ble with the publicity of a coffee-house; and how free and
familiar was the life of marquises and cabinet ministers, when
no one was there to watch them, the club rules most agreeably
testify. Dinner was served at half-past four, and the bill was
brought in at seven. Supper began at eleven and ended at
half an hour after midnight. The cost of the dinner was
eight shillings a head, and of the supper six; and any one
who had been present during any part of the meal hours paid
his share of the wine, in accordance with that old law of
British conviviality which so long held good in the commercial room, and which has not yet died out from the bar mess.
No gaming was allowed over the decanters and glasses, "except tossing up for reckonings," under penalty of standing
treat for the whole party; and at cards or hazard no one
might stake on credit, nor borrow from any of the players or
bystanders. But with these regulations began and ended all
the restraint which the club imposed, or affected to impose,
upon the gambling propensities of its members. The rule
about ready money was soon a dead letter; and if ever a
difficulty was made, Mr. Brooks, to his cost, was always at
hand with the few hundred guineas which were required to
spare any of his patrons the annoyance of leaving a well-
placed chair at the faro-bank or a well-matched rubber of
whist.[1] Gentlemen were welcome to go on losing as long as

"Who, nursed in clubs, disdains a vulgar trade,
Exults to trust, and blushes to be paid,"

retired from the management, and, not unnaturally, died poor.

The managers of Brooks's have courteously permitted me to extract
from the books of the club anything that bears upon the career and
habits of its greatest member.

[1] "I won four hundred pounds last night," wrote Fitzpatrick, "which
was immediately appropriated to Mr. Martindale, to whom I still owe
three hundred pounds; and I am in Brooks's books for twice that sum."
Within the same ten pages of Selwyn's "Correspondence" are letters
from two earls, one of whom relates how, in a moment of "cursed folly,"
he raised his account with Brooks from one hundred to five hundred

the most sanguine of their adversaries was willing to trust them; and when, at the age of sixteen, Charles Fox entered the club, which he was to render illustrious, he found himself surrounded with every facility for ruining himself with the least delay and in the best of company.

If the habits of life which prevailed within the walls of Brooks's differed from those of the world outside, they did not differ for the worse. The men who swept up the gold and tilted out the dice on the old round-table in the drawing-room on whose broad and glistening surface the weekly journals now lie of an evening in innocent array, played more comfortably and more good-humoredly than elsewhere, but they did not play for higher stakes. Society in those days was one vast casino. On whatever pretext, and under whatever circumstances, half a dozen people of fashion found themselves together—whether for music or dancing or politics, or for drinking the waters[1] or each other's wine—the box was sure to be rattling, and the cards were being cut and shuffled. The passion for gambling was not weakened or di-

---

pounds; while the other writes, " Having lost a very monstrous sum of money last night, if it is not very inconvenient to you, I should be glad of the money you owe me. If it is, I must pay what I can, and desire Brooks to trust me for the remainder." The scion of another noble house is immortalized in the club books by an entry which appears against his name, scrawled in the headlong indignation of some loser who had been balked of his revenge. " Having won only £12,000 during the last two months, retired in disgust, March 21, 1772; and that he may never return is the ardent wish of members."

[1] Bath had been a headquarters of gambling all through the reign of George the Second. "Were it not," wrote Lord Chesterfield, "for the comfort of returning health, I believe I should hang myself; I am so weary of sauntering about without knowing what to do, or of playing at low play, which I hate, for the sake of avoiding high, which I love." Lord Chesterfield's receipt for prudence did not suit the more fervid temperament of Pulteney, one of whose jeremiads over his own losses concludes with a wish which would have gone home to Charles Fox. " On Friday next we leave this place—an unlucky one for me, for I have lost between five and six hundred pounds at it. Would it was to be paid, like the Jew's of Venice, with flesh instead of money ! I think I could spare some pounds of that without any detriment."

verted by the rival attractions of female society; for the
surest road into the graces of a fine lady was to be known
as one who betted freely and lost handsomely; and too often
it was no bar to a young fellow's advancement if he contrived
to be short-sighted at a critical moment in the game, and was
above having a long memory with regard to his unpaid win-
nings. It was next to impossible for a lad still in his teens
to keep himself from the clutch of these elegant harpies,
when men who were renowned as talkers in half the capitals
of Europe complained that the eagerness of the women to
levy blackmail on their friends and acquaintances was the destruction of all pleasant and rational intercourse in London
drawing-rooms. "The ladies," said Horace Walpole, "game
too deep for me. The last time I was in town Lady Hertford wanted one, and I lost fifty-six guineas before I could
say an Ave-Maria. I do not know a teaspoonful of news.
I could tell you what was trumps, but that was all I heard."
On a summer night at Bedford House, with windows open
on the garden, and French horns and clarionets on the gravel
walks, the guests had no ears for anything beyond the cant
phrases of the card-table. There was limited loo for the
Princess Amelia, and unlimited loo for the Duchess of Grafton; and it was noticed that when a pipe and tabor were introduced, and the furniture was shifted for a minuet, her
royal highness took advantage of the confusion to desert
her own for the duchess's party. During a long and fierce
debate on Wilkes, and a close division — so close that two
votes were purchased with two peerages, and that invalids
were brought down in flannels and blankets, till the floor of
the House was compared to the pavement of Bethesda—eight
or nine Whig ladies who could not find room in the gallery,
after a cosy dinner, were contentedly sitting round a pool in
one of the Speaker's chambers. "Mrs. Lumm," wrote Rigby
from Dublin in 1765, "loses two or three hundred on a
night; but Mrs. Fitzroy is very angry she does not win it;"
and in the course of the next year George Selwyn was informed that the lady who had been so unlucky in Ireland
was suspected by the gossips at Bath of having taken very

practical measures to balk the spite of fortune. "Your old
friend," writes Gilly Williams, "is of the Duke of Bedford's
party; and, I believe, carries pams in her pocket to the loo-
table." But the ladies who cheated were in the long run less
dangerous associates than the ladies who could not pay. No
man of honor would expect his fair debtor to face an angry
husband with the equanimity with which he himself encountered the surliness of his banker or the remonstrances of his
steward; and to the end of his gambling days (an end which
came much earlier than popular tradition imports) it was not
in Charles Fox to be stern with a pretty defaulter, crying as
she had never cried except on the day when he resigned the
seals, at the prospect of having on her return home to confess that she had lost her pin-money three times over in the
course of a single evening.

Gambling in all its forms was then rather a profession than
a pastime to the leaders of the London world. Trite and sordid details of the racing-stables and the bill-discounter's back
parlor perpetually filled their thoughts and exercised their
pens, to the exclusion of worthier and more varied themes.
The delicate flavors of literature palled upon those depraved
palates; and even the fiercer delights of the political arena
seemed insipid, and its prizes paltry, while sums exceeding the
yearly income of a secretary of state or the yearly perquisites
of an auditor of the Exchequer were continually depending
upon the health of a horse or the sequence of a couple of
cards. "The rich people win everything," writes the Earl of
March from Newmarket. "Sir James Lowther has won
above seven thousand." "The hazard this evening was very
deep," says the Earl of Carlisle. "Meynell won four thousand pounds, and Pigot five thousand." "White's goes on as
usual" (so Rigby reports to the Duke of Bedford in 1763).
"Play there is rather moderate, ready money being established
this winter at quinze.[1] Lord Masham was fool enough to lose

---

[1] What moderate play for ready money meant between 1760 and 1780
may be judged from the standing rule at Brooks's, which enjoined "every
person playing at the new quinze table to keep fifty guineas before him."

three thousand at hazard to Lord Bolingbroke. I guess that was not all ready money." The greed of gain had no pity for the ignorance and weakness of youth, and spared neither relative nor benefactor, nor host nor guest. "My royal visitor," wrote Rigby, "stayed here from Saturday till Tuesday. We had quinze every night and all night, but I could get none of his money." A lad fresh from his public school, if he was known to have parents who loved him well enough to stand between him and dishonor, walked into a London club like a calf eyed by the butchers. "The gaming," says Horace Walpole, in 1770, "is worthy the decline of our empire. The young men lose five, ten, fifteen thousand pounds in an evening. Lord Stavordale, not one-and-twenty, lost eleven thousand last Tuesday, but recovered it by one great hand at hazard. He swore a great oath—'Now, if I had been playing deep, I might have won millions.'"

Morality was sapped, filial affection poisoned, and the confidence which existed between old and trusted companions grievously strained by the shifts to which losers were driven in order to make good their enormous liabilities. No person of ordinary prudence could venture upon a close intimacy without considering whether his new comrade was one who would assert a comrade's claim to borrow; and the pleasantest friendships, as will be seen in these pages, were sometimes the most perilous. The letters which passed between Selwyn and the partner with whom he kept a common purse, after a field-night at White's or Almack's, are dreary reading at the best; and when both the associates had been unlucky together, the tone of the correspondence became nothing short of tragic.[1] But often, in the selfishness of despair, men did far worse

---

[1] On a Saturday morning in 1765, the Earl of March writes to Selwyn, "When I came home last night I found your letter on my table. So you have lost a thousand pounds. . . . As to your banker, I will call there to-morrow. Make yourself easy about that, for I have three thousand pounds now at Coutts's. There will be no bankruptcy without we are both ruined at the same time." Then follow some communications relating to notes of hand and the endorsing of bank-bills, of a nature very fa-

than sponge upon a fellow-gamester. The second Lord Lyttelton, who, when the humor took him, was not averse to posing as a censor, and who certainly was qualified for that function by the richest experience, tells us that his contemporaries
seemed to have made a law among themselves for declaring
their fathers superannuated at fifty, and then disposed of the
estates as if already their own. He professed to know of a
peer whose sons had traded so freely on their expectations
that they were paying interest to the amount of eighteen
thousand a year between them. A still blacker case was that
of a nobleman and his brothers who, after squandering their
patrimony, cajoled their mother into mortgaging her jointure
(which was all that she had to maintain her), and sent her on
some lying pretext into the parlor of a Jew money-lender in
order to afford him an opportunity of satisfying himself that
the poor lady's life was a good one. George Selwyn had reason on his side when, on being told that a waiter at Arthur's
had been arrested for felony, he exclaimed, " What a horrid
idea he will give of us to the people in Newgate !"

Some excuse for the vices of idle and irresponsible gentlemen was to be found in the example of those elevated personages who embodied the majesty of justice and the sanctity of
religion. When Charles Fox first took rank among grown
men, the head of the law in England and the head of the
Church in Ireland were notorious as two among the hardest
livers in their respective countries; and such a pre-eminence
was then not lightly earned. " They tell me, Sir John," said
George the Third to one of his favorites, " that you love a
glass of wine." " Those who have so informed your Majesty,"

---

miliar to the student of eighteenth-century memoirs ; and, finally, before
the week is out, the earl writes again,

" My dear George, I have lost my match and am quite broke. I cannot
tell how much. I am obliged to you for thinking of my difficulties, and
providing for them in the midst of all your own."

Selwyn, when he was in his senses, bitterly cried out against the passion for cards. " It was a consumer," he said, " of four things—time,
health, fortune, and thinking." He eventually gave up high play, but not
before he had tried his hand at fleecing Wilberforce.

was the reply, "have done me great injustice; they should have said a bottle;" and in the days of Lord Chancellor Northington and Archbishop Stone very small account was taken of any aspirant to convivial honors who reckoned his progress through the evening by glasses. Philip Francis, with a motive for keeping guard upon his tongue as strong as ever man had, could not always get through an after-dinner sitting without losing his head, although he sipped thimblefuls while his companions were draining bumpers.[1] Two of his friends, without any sense of having performed an exceptional feat, finished between them a gallon and a half of champagne and burgundy—a debauch which, in this unheroic age, it almost makes one ill to read of. It is impossible to repress a feeling of undutiful satisfaction at the thought that few among our ancestors escaped the penalties of this monstrous self-indulgence, from which so many of their innocent descendants are still suffering. Their lives were short, and their closing years far from merry. "Lord Cholmondeley," wrote Walpole, "died last Saturday. He was seventy, and had a constitution to have carried him to a hundred, if he had not destroyed it by an intemperance that would have killed anybody else in half the time. As it was, he had outlived by fifteen years all his set, who have reeled into the ferry-boat so long before him." A squire past five-and-fifty who still rode to hounds or walked after partridges was the envy of the country-side for his health, unless he had long been its scorn for his sobriety; and a cabinet minister of the same age who could anticipate with confidence that, at a critical juncture, he would be able to write a confidential despatch with his own hand must have observed a very different regimen from most of his contemporaries. The memorable denunciation of our alliance with the North American savages, as splendid a burst of eloquence as ever thrilled the House of Lords, was levelled by an ex-secretary of state who never was himself except after a sharp attack of the gout against a secretary of state who, at thirty-

---

[1] Horne Tooke relates that, in his younger days, it was a usual thing for the company at a coffee-house to end by burning their wigs.

two, had been almost too gouty to accept the seals. Wine did more than work or worry to expedite that flow of promotion to which modern vice-presidents and junior lords look back with wistful regret. A statesman of the Georgian era was sailing on a sea of claret from one comfortable official haven to another at a period of life when a political apprentice in the reign of Victoria is not yet out of his indentures. No one can study the public or personal history of the eighteenth century without being impressed by the truly immense space which drinking occupied in the mental horizon of the young, and the consequences of drinking in that of the old. As we turn over volume after volume we find the same dismal story of gout, first dreaded as an avenger, and then, in a later and sadder stage, actually courted and welcomed as a friend. It is pitiful to witness the loftiest minds and the brightest wits reduced to the most barren and lugubrious of topics; talking of old age at seven and forty; urging a fellow-sufferer to stuff himself with Morello cherries, in order to develop a crisis in the malady; or rejoicing with him over the cheering prospect that the gout at length showed symptoms of being about to do its duty. It spoke well for George the Third's common-sense that he never would join in the congratulations which his ministers eagerly and unanimously bestowed upon any of their number who was condemned to list slippers and a Bath chair. "People tell me," said his Majesty, "that the gout is very wholesome; but I, for one, can never believe it."

As far as he was himself concerned, the king had no occasion to adopt any such desperate medical theory. He applied to the management of his own health a force of will and an independence of judgment which greater men than he too seldom devote to that homely but most difficult task. His imagination had been profoundly impressed by the sight of his uncle, the Duke of Cumberland, dying at forty-four of a complication of diseases aggravated or caused by an excessive corpulence, which the vigorous habits of a soldier who entertained a soldier's dislike to rules of diet had altogether failed to keep in check. From that time forward George the Third observed a rigid temperance, which might not have been mer-

itorious in a religious recluse, but was admirable when practised amidst the temptations of a court by one who husband-
ed his bodily powers for the sake of his duties. He never
allowed himself to be complimented on his abstinence. "'Tis
no virtue," he said. "I only prefer eating plain and little to
growing sickly and infirm." He would ride in all weathers
from Kew or Windsor to St. James's Palace, and dress for a
levee, at which he gave every individual present some token
of his favor or displeasure.[1] Then he would assist at a privy
council or do business with his ministers till six in the evening, take a cup of tea and a few slices of bread-and-butter
without sitting down at table, and drive back into Berkshire
by lamplight. In his recreations he was more hardy and energetic even than in his labors. On hunting-days he remained
in the saddle from eight in the morning till the approach of
night sent him home to a jug of hot barley-water, which he
in vain endeavored to induce his attendants to share with him.

---

[1] His Majesty made his state-receptions an opportunity for keeping his
subjects (or, at any rate, those among them who had not forfeited his
friendly interest by voting for Wilkes) up to his own mark in the matter
of bodily exercise. Mason was rather hard upon his innocent curiosity:

> "Let all the frippery things
> Replaced, bepensioned, and bestarred by kings,
> Let these prefer a levee's harmless talk;
> Be asked how often, and how far, they walk."

Warburton has left a most characteristic notice of a morning at St.
James's in February, 1767. "A buffoon lord in waiting was very busy
marshalling the circle, and he said to me, without ceremony, 'Move forward. You clog up the doorway.' I replied with as little, 'Did nobody
clog up the king's doorstead more than I, there would be room for all
honest men.' This brought the man to himself. When the king came
up to me, he asked why I did not come to town before. I said, I understood there was no business going forward in the House in which I could
be of service to his Majesty. He replied, he supposed the severe storm
of snow would have brought me up. I replied, 'I was under cover of
a very warm house.' You see, by all this, how unfit I am for courts."
"I see nothing," writes Macaulay on the margin of his Warburton,
"but very commonplace questions and answers; questions worthy of a
king, and answers worthy of a bishop."

His gentlemen in waiting tasted nothing of the luxury which the humble world presumes to be the reward of courtiers, and not very much of the comfort on which an Englishman of rank reckons as his birthright.   Doors and windows so habitually open that a maid of honor encountered five distinct and thorough draughts on the way from her own room to the queen's boudoir; expeditions on foot across country for ten miles on end, without shirking a ploughed field or skirting a patch of turnips; early prayers in winter, with a congregation dwindling daily as the mornings grew colder and darker, until by Christmas the king and his equerry were left to shiver through the responses together.   Nothing would have retained men of fortune and men of pleasure in such a Spartan service, except the strong and disinterested affection with which George the Third inspired all who had to do with him in his character of master of a household.

The habit and morals of that household were those which prevailed rather in the middle than the upper classes of his Majesty's subjects.   The first two hundred lines of the " Winter's Evening "—a passage as much beyond Cowper's ordinary range as it surpasses in wealth and strength of thought, and in sustained beauty and finish of execution, all the pictures of lettered leisure and domestic peace that ever tantalized and tempted a politician and a Londoner—show us what was then the aspect of a modest English home, refined by culture, and ennobled by a religious faith of which hardly a vestige can be traced in the records of fashionable and ministerial circles. Cowper has elsewhere left a reference to the astonishment with which the official world witnessed the appearance in its midst of such a phenomenon as

> "one who wears a coronet and prays"

in the person of Lord Dartmouth.   Voltaire, writing in 1766, pronounced that there was no more religion in Great Britain than the minimum which was required for party purposes. Commenting on this passage in the first blank space which he could find, as was ever his custom when he read, Macaulay remarks, "Voltaire had lived with men of wit and fashion during his visit to England, and knew nothing of the feeling of the grave part of mankind, or of the middle classes. He says in one of his ten thousand tracts that no shopkeeper in London believes there is a hell." Shopkeepers who had listened to Whitefield and the Wesleys for thirty years were not very likely to be sceptics on the question of future punishment; but men of fashion did not concern themselves about the beliefs of smaller people. There is just as much and as little trace of Christianity in Horace Walpole as in Pliny the younger. Indeed, in this very year of 1766, Walpole describes his first sight of the man who was guiding a revolution in creed and practice which has deeply and permanently modified the religion of the English-speaking race, in a letter which, if translated into good Latin, might pass muster as an extract from the familiar correspondence of Gallio.[1]

Few, indeed, among the rich and great had a relish for the quiet round of rural pursuits and family anniversaries outside which their monarch never found, or looked for, happiness. The finest of country-houses was too often regarded by its owner as a place of exile, unless he could fill it with a company large enough to keep the loo-table crowded until within an hour of daybreak, and to manufacture sufficient scandal

---

[1] "My health advances faster than my amusement. However, I have been at one opera, Mr. Wesley's. They have boys and girls with charming voices, that sing hymns to Scotch ballad-tunes, but so long that one would think they were already in eternity, and knew how much time they had before them. The chapel is very neat, with true Gothic windows; yet I am not converted, but I was glad to see that luxury was creeping in upon them before persecution. Wesley is a lean elderly man, fresh-colored, his hair smoothly combed, but with a soupçon of curl at the ends. Wondrous clean, but as evidently an actor as Garrick. He spoke his sermon, but so fast, and with so little accent, that I am sure he has often uttered it. There were parts and eloquence in it; but towards the end he exalted his voice, and acted very ugly enthusiasm. Except a few from curiosity, and *some honorable women*, the congregation was very mean." Those who have seen the "true Gothic" of Strawberry Hill will not suspect the poor Methodists of any excess in ecclesiastical decoration.

for its own consumption. "Ten miles from town," said Walpole, "is a thousand miles from truth;" that is to say, from the truth as to which of the king's brothers would first be secretly married, and what pretty lady was killing herself the fastest with white-lead. Lord Coventry was not alone among Lord Holland's friends in valuing his country-seat chiefly as a convenient pretext for a visit to Paris, where he took care to be observed at the upholsterer's "buying glasses and tapestry for a place in which he never sees himself but he wishes himself, and all belonging to it, at the devil." Even Lord Carlisle, who could paint the delights of literary retirement in sentences worthy of Montaigne, did not seek that retirement willingly. To live with a wife whom he worshipped in the most delicious palace in the three kingdoms was in his eyes a banishment to which it was necessary to submit as the penalty for past, and the preparation for future, extravagance. Castle Howard was endurable because there he could eat his own venison, burn his own firewood, and save in the course of two years enough to repair the disasters of a single ruinous evening. And yet he could enter heartily into all the enjoyments of a purer and less fevered life, and was shrewd enough to rate the pleasures of London at their proper worth. "I rise at six" (so he writes to Selwyn); "am on horseback till breakfast; play at cricket till dinner; and dance in the evening till I can scarce crawl to bed at eleven. You get up at nine; sit till twelve in your night-gown; creep down to White's and spend five hours at table; sleep till you can escape your supper reckoning; and then make two wretches carry you in a chair, with three pints of claret in you, three miles for a shilling." Such was the daily existence of the men whom Lord Holland chose as mentors to his young Telemachus.

There has been little satisfaction in dwelling upon those social allurements to which Charles Fox so readily succumbed; but it is with very different feelings that we turn to the contemplation of a scene whose enticements to evil he of all men had the greatest merit in resisting, and whose corruptions, taking his career as a whole, he of all men did the most to reform. The political world, then as always, was no better than

the individuals who composed it. Private vices were reflected
in the conduct of public affairs; and the English people suffered, and suffers still, because at a great crisis in our history
a large proportion among our rulers and councillors had been
too dissolute and prodigal to be able to afford a conscience.
The enormous expenditure which the habits and ideas of good
society inexorably demanded had to be met by one expedient
or another; and an expedient was not far to seek when the
same men who, as a class, were the most generally addicted to
personal extravagance, possessed a practical monopoly of political power. Everybody who had influence in Parliament or
at court used it for the express and avowed purpose of making
or repairing his fortune. "There is no living in this country
under twenty thousand a year—not that that suffices; but it
entitles one to ask a pension for two or three lives." So said
Horace Walpole, and he had a right to know; for he lived in
the country, and on the country, during more than half a century, doing for the country less than half a day's work in half
a year. His father, acting like other fathers who enjoyed the
like opportunities, charged the exchequer for the maintenance
of his sons, according to their several claims on him, as calmly
and systematically as a country gentleman settles an estate
upon one child and a rent-charge on another;[1] and he was
regarded, in return, by his family with precisely the same
gratitude as he would have excited had he been generous
with his own savings, instead of with the national money.
After describing how his eldest brother had been appointed
auditor of the exchequer, and his second brother clerk of the
pells; how, for his own share, his father had made him clerk
of the estreats while he was still at Eton, and usher of the
exchequer before he had left Cambridge; and how the profits
of the collectorship of customs had been carefully divided by
bequest between his second brother and himself—Horace
Walpole goes on to speak of his emoluments as a noble por-

[1] When an alteration in the routine of the exchequer business reduced
Horace's profits by ten per cent., Sir Robert, " with his wonted equity
and tenderness," at once took measures for readjusting what he looked
upon as the private fortunes of his sons by adding a codicil to his will.

tion for a third son, and calls upon his readers, sublimely ig-
noring the consideration that they were likewise taxpayers, to
join him in admiring the tenderness of a father who had lavished riches on him greatly beyond his deserts.   "Endowed,"
he says, "so bountifully by a fond parent, it would be ridiculous to say that I have been content." He might well be content; for, from first to last, his gains must have amounted to
at least a quarter of a million, in an age when a quarter of a
million was worth a great deal more than now.

We, who look upon politics as a barren career, by which few
people hope to make money and none to save it, and who
would expect a poet to found a family as soon as a prime-minister, can with difficulty form a just conception of a period
when people entered Parliament, not because they were rich,
but because they wanted to be rich, and when it was more
profitable to be the member of a cabinet than the partner in
a brewery.   And yet those who have not clearly before their
minds the nature of that vital change which has come over
the circumstances of English public life during the last hundred years will never understand the events of the eighteenth
century, or do justice to its men—men who were spurred forward by far sharper incentives, and solicited by far fiercer
temptations, than ours, and who, when they held a straight
course, were entitled to very different credit from any that we
can possibly deserve.   A minister of state in the year 1880,
while he draws from the treasury a mere pittance compared
with what, in two cases out of three, he would have made in
the open market if he had applied his talents to commerce or
to the bar, has less facilities for advancing his relatives and
connections than if he were the chief of a law court, or a
director of the Bank of England.   A merchant who belongs
to the *noblesse* of the city can put his children in the way of
making their fortunes for themselves.   A lord chancellor, or
a lord chief-justice, has still in his gift posts in which the number of hours of work compares so favorably with the number
of pounds of salary that Rigby himself would have condescended to hold one.   But a prime-minister may count on the
fingers of one hand the well-paid and lightly-worked appoint-

ments which fall vacant during his tenure of power; and he will be fortunate if he can count on the fingers of both hands the meritorious departmental officers, and the influential parliamentary supporters, who regard each of these appointments as their due. To select for such employment a candidate outside the civil service, and under thirty years of age, would be to raise a mutiny in every board-room between Thames Street and Palace Yard. The utmost that a modern statesman can do for a son or a nephew is to nominate him to the privilege of competing with a dozen other lads in history and modern languages, with the prospect that, in case of success, he will obtain an income which would not have paid the wine-bill of a placeman in the days of Weymouth and Sandwich. Even the Duke of Newcastle would have scorned to put in his claim for the disposal of such paltry patronage as that to which his degenerate successors have limited themselves.

But it was worth a man's while to be secretary of state under the Georges. At a time when trade was on so small a scale that a Lancashire manufacturer considered himself fairly well off on the income which his great-grandson now gives to his cashier, a cabinet minister, over and above the ample salary of his office, might reckon confidently upon securing for himself, and for all who belonged to him and who came after him, a permanent maintenance, not dependent upon the vicissitudes of party, which would be regarded as handsome, and even splendid, in these days of visible and all-pervading opulence. One nobleman had eight thousand a year in sinecures, and the colonelcies of three regiments. Another, as auditor of the exchequer, inside which he never looked, had eight thousand pounds in years of peace, and twenty thousand in years of war. A third, with nothing to recommend him except his outward graces, bowed and whispered himself into four great employments, from which thirteen or fourteen hundred British guineas flowed month by month into the lap of his Parisian mistress. And the lucrative places which a statesman held in his own name formed but a part, and often the least part, of the advantages that he derived from his position. All the claims on his purse were settled, and all services rendered to him, honorable and dishonorable alike, were recompensed by fresh, and ever fresh, inroads upon the exchequer. The patron of his borough, if he was a commoner; his mouthpiece in the Lower House, if he was a peer; the gentleman of the bedchamber, who stood his friend at court; the broker who, when the last loan was brought out, had got to know more than was pleasant about the allotment of the scrip; his racing friend, who had nothing left to lose; his French cook, his children's tutor, his led captain, his hired poet, and his inspired pamphleteer, were all paid with nominations, or pacified with reversions.[1] If a comfortable berth was already occupied,

---

[1] When Lord Holland went to Italy in 1763, he thought it necessary to provide for his son's tutor; so he bequeathed him as a legacy to Lord Bute, who transferred him to George Grenville. Through this recommendation he afterwards obtained a pension out of the privy purse of three hundred a year. Cowper did not exaggerate when he wrote—

> "The levee swarms, as if in golden pomp
> Were charactered on every statesman's door,
> 'Battered and bankrupt fortunes mended here.' "

The Duke of Grafton procured five hundred a year for an old Newmarket acquaintance who had squandered his fortune on the turf. A single happy Scotchman, in his character of minister's friend, enjoyed a captain's commission for his son of ten years old, an income of three thousand in hand, and the reversion of a place valued at seventeen hundred pounds a year: "I do not," said Wilkes, "mean Scottish, but English pounds." Bute's hackwriter in prose had a pension from the public of six hundred a year. His poet, one Dalrymple, who libelled Pitt in a performance entitled "Rodondo, or the State Jugglers," which is almost a literary curiosity on account of the badness of the rhymes, was gratified with the attorney-generalship of Grenada. The Earl of Sandwich, not liking to trench upon his lay patronage, found it more convenient to have his lampoons written by gentlemen in holy orders, whom he could reward with crown livings. Paul Whitehead, by using such powers of satire as he possessed against the enemies of men who had something to give, ended by getting eight hundred a year as deputy-treasurer to the chamber; whereas the trade value of his collected works might have been something under eight hundred shillings. Dr. Johnson, speaking of his own "London," the copyright of which noble poem he sold for ten guineas, said that he might, perhaps, have been content with less;

at any rate the succession to it might still be worth the having. A paymaster of the works, or an auditor of the plantations, with plenty of money to buy good liquor, and plenty of time to drink it, did not live forever; and a next appointment to the civil service in the last century might be discounted as freely as a next presentation to a living in our own.

When every desirable office was filled two deep, there still remained the resource of a pension—a resource elastic and almost unlimited under a monarch who was never afraid of appearing before his Parliament in the character of an insolvent debtor. Those recipients of what—with an irony which the taxpayer was beginning to understand—was styled the royal bounty, who were too disreputable to figure on the English civil list, were quietly and snugly quartered on the Irish establishment. Decent men were not always willing to see themselves enrolled in a column of names which, appropriately headed by the Queen of Denmark, recalled the successive scandals of three reigns; but squeamishness was not the failing of the age, and the Irish pensions were trebled in the first thirty years of George the Third. The English pension list grew steadily and silently, with occasional periods of sudden and very perceptible expansion. It was reckoned that every change of government (and changes of government were far more frequent then than now) cost the country from nine to fifteen thousand a year. A minister who was true to his order never allowed himself to be shelved, or shifted, or degraded, or even promoted, without getting something for himself, his wife, or his son-in-law. Whenever the political cards were shuffled the people paid the stakes; and a dozen pensions had generally been distributed, and half a dozen increased, before the seals, the key, and the sticks had got into the hands where they were to remain for the next twelvemonth. When Lord Northington ceased to be chancellor in order to become president of the council, he would not leave the woolsack till he had secured an immedi-

---

" but Paul Whitehead had a little before got ten guineas for a poem, and I would not take less than Paul Whitehead."

ate pension of two thousand a year, a prospective pension of
four thousand a year, and the reversion for two lives of the
clerkship of the hanaper; and this, although he had already
provided for his daughters by vesting a rich sinecure with a
trustee for their benefit.   There were times when a disagreeable man who knew his own powers of annoyance, or even a
weak man who had fathomed his own worthlessness, could
make almost any terms he chose with those who desired to
get rid of him; and there was nothing whatever which a
strong man, by watching his occasion, might not obtain as the
price of his services.   Murray, in 1756, was offered a pension
of six thousand a year, together with the first vacant tellership, which was worth at least as much again, for his nephew,
if he would remain in the House of Commons with the attorney-general's income of seven thousand, in addition to his
own enormous gains as leader of the bar.   But, almost alone
among statesmen, he refused to make his market out of the
perplexities of his colleagues.   "Good God," he said, "what
merit have I that you should load this country, for which so
little is done with spirit, with a fresh burden of six thousand
a year?"

As were the leaders, so were the followers.   "If any noble
lord challenged me to assert that there is much corruption in
both Houses, I would laugh in his face, and tell him that he
knows it as well as I."   So said Lord Chatham plainly and
openly in his place among the peers; and there were few noble lords, and not many honorable gentlemen, whose personal
experience was such that they would have had the right or
the face to contradict him.   Parliament, chosen by corrupt
constituencies, was corruptly influenced by corrupt ministers,
of whom Junius told the literal truth when he said that they
addressed themselves neither to the passions nor to the understanding, but simply to the touch.   The arguments by
which Grenville and Grafton persuaded their supporters
were bank bills for two hundred pounds and upwards, so
generously dealt about at a premier's levee that sometimes
they were slipped into a hand which was ashamed to close
upon them; tickets for state lotteries, sold to members of

Parliament in parcels of five hundred, and resold by them at
a profit of two pounds a ticket; government loans subscribed
for by the friends of government at par, and then thrown on
the city at a premium of seven, and even eleven, per cent.
Lord Bute and his adherents by one such transaction robbed
the country of nearly four hundred thousand pounds, an ample share of which (as was roundly asserted and may with no
breach of charity be believed) found its way into Henry Fox's
capacious pocket.[1]   Then there were favorable contracts for
honorable members connected with commerce, or who were
willing to be connected with commerce when they had a
chance of supplying the fleet with sailcloth and salt pork at
exorbitant rates, and of a quality which was left pretty much
to their own sense of patriotic obligation.   And a gentleman
who liked to get his price without sacrificing his ease might
have his choice of pensions, secret and acknowledged; and of
highly endowed posts, in every climate of the globe, whose
functions could be performed while seated at the whist-table
of Brooks's by any one who had proved his fitness for public
employment by buying a borough, bribing a corporation, or
swamping a county with fictitious votes.   George Selwyn,
who returned two members and had something to say in the
election of a third, was at one and the same time surveyor-
general of crown lands—which he never surveyed—registrar
in chancery at Barbadoes—which he never visited—and sur-
veyor of the meltings and clerk of the irons in the mint—

---

[1] There survives a remarkable narrative of a dinner given by the Duke
of Grafton to the favored few who were behind the scenes when a new
loan was brought upon the stage.   Nothing could exceed the cleverness
and presence of mind with which Charles Townshend, then chancellor of
the exchequer, purposely over-acted his part of a headlong and puzzle-
headed man of business in order to confuse the accounts and retain for
himself the lion's share of the booty.   When such were the guardians of
the public purse, there was point in the epigram suggested by an announcement that the precincts of the Treasury were to be patrolled after
dark.

"From the night to the morning 'tis true all is right;
But who will secure it from morning to night?"

where he showed himself once a week in order to eat a dinner which he ordered, but for which the nation paid.[1]

When offices, whose unfulfilled duties were supposed to lie
in England, had been heaped upon one individual in such
profusion as to excite, not indeed the moral disapprobation,
but the hungry jealousy, of his brethren, a judicious pluralist,
who could scent a job across the seas, was still only at the beginning of his acquisitions.   Ireland, the natural prey of the
place-hunter, had to contribute towards the bribing of our
own senate before she proceeded to satiate the rapacity of her
own.   Her richest salaries were transmitted to London, and
her most elevated functions were discharged by deputies at
Dublin, while her native politicians were fain to content themselves with the leavings which Westminster and Whitehall
disdained.   An English duke was Lord Treasurer of Ireland;
the mouth of an English orator had been effectually stopped
with the chancellorship of her exchequer;[2] Rigby was her
vice-treasurer, with three thousand five hundred a year, and
had actually contrived to become her master of the rolls as
well, at a time when a member of the Irish Parliament thought
himself lucky if he could make up his bundle of plunder out
of such incongruous materials as commissionerships of the
Linen Board, cornetcies in the dragoons, fragments of Church
preferment, odds and ends of pensions, and employments in
the revenue too humble for their fame to have crossed the
Channel.   And, when Britain had been drained dry, and there

---

[1] The liberties of England were in as much danger in 1770 through
the pocket as they had been in 1640 from the sword.   "Every man of
consequence almost in the kingdom," wrote Bishop Watson, "has a son,
relation, friend, or dependent whom he wishes to provide for; and, unfortunately for the liberty of this country, the crown has the means of
gratifying the expectation of them all."

[2] Hamilton, whose single speech has given him a sobriquet by which
he is much better known than by his Christian names of William Gerard,
was provided for out of the Irish Treasury for life; and a long life it
was.   Forty years after his famous performance he still moved in society,
haughtily measuring out precious morsels of sarcasm with the economy
which became a man who had earned a quarter's salary by every sentence that he had uttered in public.

was nothing more to be squeezed from Ireland, ministers, in an evil hour for themselves, remembered that there were two millions of Englishmen in America who had struggled through the difficulties and hardships which beset the pioneers of civilization, and who, now that their daily bread was assured to them, could afford the luxury of maintaining an army of sinecurists. The suggestion cannot be said to have originated on the other shore of the Atlantic. " It was not," said Junius, " Virginia that wanted a governor, but a court favorite that wanted a salary." Virginia, however, and her sister colonies, were not supposed to know what was best for their own interests, or, at any rate, for the interests of their masters; and plenty of gentlemen were soon drinking their claret and paying their debts out of the savings of the fishermen of New Hampshire and the farmers of New Jersey, and talking, with that perversion of sentiment which is the inevitable outgrowth of privilege, about the " cruelty" of a secretary of state who hinted that they would do well to show themselves occasionally among the people whose substance they devoured. And yet in most cases it was fortunate for America that her placemen had not enough public spirit to make them ashamed of being absentees. Such was the private character of many among her official staff that their room was cheaply purchased by the money which they spent outside the country. The best things in the colonies generally fell to bankrupt members of Parliament, who were as poor in political principle as in worldly goods; and the smaller posts were regarded as their special inheritance by the riffraff of the election committee-room and the bad bargains of the servants' hall. " In one word," we are told, and told truly, " America has been for many years the hospital of England."

The aspect of their mercenary Parliament affected all thoughtful citizens with a feeling akin to despair. There was no hope of amendment except through repentance; and repentance implied at least a rudimentary sense of shame. But a ministerial hireling cared nothing whatever for the disapproval of any one outside the House of Commons who did not happen to be a freeman in his own borough; and among those with whom he lived, and whose esteem he valued, public employment was looked upon as a sort of personalty of which everybody had a clear right to scrape together as much as he could, without inquiring whether the particular post he coveted ought to exist at all, or whether he himself was the proper man to hold it. "If," wrote Sir William Draper, "Lord Granby is generous at the public expense, as Junius invidiously calls it, the public is at no more expense for his lordship's friends than it would be if any other set of men possessed those offices;" and so self-evident did this proposition appear to Lord Granby's friends that they did not thank their champion for going out of his way to defend a system which, in the eyes of those who lived by it, needed defence as little as did the institution of private property.

"If I had a son," said a member of the House of Commons, to the House of Commons, at a moment when he was angry enough to be candid at the expense of his own past history, and that of half his hearers, "I would say to him 'Get into Parliament. Make tiresome speeches. Do not accept the first offer; but wait till you can make great provision for yourself and your family; and then call yourself an independent country gentleman.'" The picture was not overdrawn. The first lesson taught to a political apprentice, both by example and by precept, was to mock at principle, and fight for his own hand. Lord Shelburne relates how, at the coronation of George the Third, he found himself next to Lord Melcombe, against whom he had an electioneering grievance, and whom he at once proceeded to take to task. His charges were met by an impudent equivocation, which, with the innocence of one-and-twenty, he would not allow to pass unnoticed. "Well!" laughed his elder, "did you ever know anybody get out of a great scrape but by a great lie?" In the course of the next year, the young man, for want of a more promising confidant, invited Henry Fox to sympathize with the theory that "gentlemen of independent fortune should be trustees between the king and the people, and make it their vocation to be of service to both, without becoming the slaves of either;" but the only response to his aspirations which

7

Lord Shelburne could get out of the paymaster was the recommendation to come up to London, and ask for a place. "This will lead directly to what I suppose you aim at. You'll never get it from that trusteeship that you speak of; nor, to say truth, should you get it till you have got rid of such puerile notions."

It is impossible to deny that, in these cynical phrases, Henry Fox expressed the creed of five out of six of his contemporaries. The prizes within the Parliamentary arena were too tempting—the pressure from without, under a system of representation nothing better than illusory, was too fitful and feeble—for statesmen to find their interest in turning from the chase after incomes and ribbons to the pursuit of undertakings which might promote the welfare of the people. "Parties," said Lord Mansfield, in 1767, "aim only at places, and seem regardless of measures." "The cure," wrote George Grenville, "must come from a serious conviction and right measures, instead of annual struggles for places and pensions;" and the times must, indeed, have been bad when George Grenville took to preaching. Unfaithful to the nation when in office, politicians no longer pretended to be true to each other in opposition. Amidst the turmoil of selfish ambitions and rival cupidities which was seething around him, a man did not venture to rely on others, and soon ceased to merit that others should rely on him. Outside the ranks of the little band which surrounded Lord Rockingham, there were not a dozen members who could be counted upon to work in concert during a single session; and the notion of a patriotic and disinterested statesman being able to keep his followers together throughout the weary years that must pass between the hour when a great question is first mooted and the hour when its advocacy is finally crowned with success would have supplied Lord North's jovial colleagues with material for hilarity during the longest carouse that ever was remembered by the butler at the Pay-office or the Admiralty.

While the ties which united men, who professed to be acting for the public, were too often but a rope of sand, fidelity was anything but eternal between those who were bound together by the golden fetters of office. Where mutual respect did not exist, there could be little mutual loyalty; and a statesman who one year had been making out pensions to the courtiers who had obliged his colleague, and warrants against the printers who had libelled him, next year would be thundering against him in Parliament, and plotting against him in a hundred constituencies, while the temples of friendship which they had dedicated to each other at their respective country-seats were still standing unroofed as a monument to political inconstancy. It is the nature, said Bacon, of extreme self-lovers to set a house on fire if it were but to roast their eggs; and men whose device was "Every one for himself, and the Exchequer for us all," did not hesitate to undermine a government in order to bring about an absurdly small accession of dignity or emolument for themselves. During the earlier years of George the Third, administrations fell so frequently that an anonymous statistician, the very peculiar flavor of whose humor betrays Burke in disguise, calculated that five prime-ministers maintained themselves for an average of just fourteen months apiece from the day when they kissed in to the day when they were kicked out. Meanwhile, the minor constellations of the official galaxy were darting about like fragments of glass in a kaleidoscope. Five hundred and thirty placemen went in and out, or up and down, between the Great Commoner's resignation in 1761, and Lord Chatham's resumption of power in 1766. As one glittering transmutation succeeded another, with profit to the scene-shifters, but utterly barren of entertainment to the spectators, the pit and the galleries sometimes hissed, but for the most part looked on with contemptuous and silent indifference. The great mass of Englishmen had learned by repeated experience that a change of ministry brought them no economy in their expenditure, no removal of ancient abuses, no beneficent additions to their statute-book—nothing but ever-growing files of quarterly receipts signed with the least honored names in the three kingdoms. A profound distrust of public men; a discontent which afforded the matter, and suggested the title, of the most instructive, if not the most eloquent, political treatise in our language; and that sullen disbelief in a peaceful remedy which is the gravest of national maladies, were eating their way fast and deep into the hearts of the people.[1]

"Certainly great persons had need to borrow other men's opinions to think themselves happy."[2] So said a famous student who, to his cost, was likewise a minister of state; and the truth of the saying will hardly be questioned by a modern servant of the crown who knows what it is to sacrifice health and sleep, books, art, field-sports, and travel; who during four days in the week enjoys no social relaxation beyond the whispered hope of a count-out exchanged with an overworked colleague, and who looks for no material recompense over and above a precarious income, half of which is spent upon perfunctory festivities that consume the few poor evenings which the House of Commons spares, and the other half barely replaces the capital that has been lavished on the elections of a lifetime. But those received commonplaces about the sweets of office, which are little better than dreary irony when applied to the councillors of Queen Victoria, meant a great deal in the ears of a statesman who had the privilege of serving her grandfather. With no annual bill of a hundred clauses to turn into an act on pain of being pilloried as an idler by half the newspapers in the country; with a dozen bribed burgesses for constituents, and a couple of hundred

---

[1] Burke, in the first page of the "Thoughts on the Cause of the Present Discontents," sums up the nature of the present uneasiness in one sweeping and majestic sentence. "That government is at once dreaded and contemned; that the laws are despoiled of all their respected and salutary terrors; that their inaction is a subject of ridicule, and their exertion of abhorrence; that rank, and office, and title, and all the solemn plausibilities of the world, have lost their reverence and effect; that our own foreign politics are as much deranged as our domestic economy; that our dependencies are slackened in their affection, and loosed from their obedience; that we know neither how to yield or how to enforce; that hardly anything above or below, abroad or at home, is sound or entire; but that disconnection and confusion, in offices, in parties, in families, in Parliament, in the nation, prevail beyond the disorders of any former time: these are facts universally admitted and lamented."

[2] Lord Bacon's eleventh essay, "Of Great Place."

bribed supporters to cheer him as soon as he rose from the
Treasury bench; his lot included the comforts as well as the
gains of public life, while the toil and the ferment, the scheming, the declaiming, the writing of pamphlets, the framing of
resolutions, the arranging of deputations, county meetings, and
petitions, were for the opponents who labored to dislodge him.
The veriest stranger who for the first time threw his eyes
round the House of Commons could distinguish at a glance
the

> " Patriots, bursting with heroic rage,"

from the

> " Placemen, all tranquillity and smiles."

With everything to get, and nothing to trouble him, a minister of the eighteenth century regarded office as a paradise
from which no man of sense would be so infatuated as to
banish himself on any quixotic grounds of public duty. That
was the doctrine of the school in which was reared the only
English statesman who has left a reputation of the first order, acquired not in power, but while self-condemned to an
almost lifelong opposition; who manfully and cheerfully surrendered all that he had been taught to value for the sake of
principles at which he had been diligently trained to sneer.
So that to one who began his course weighted and hampered
by the worst traditions of the past we owe much of what is
highest and purest in our recent political history; and the son
and pupil of Henry Fox became in his turn the teacher of
Romilly and Mackintosh, of Earl Grey, Lord Althorpe, and
Earl Russell.

CHAPTER IV.

George the Third.—His Education.—His Assiduity in Public Business.—
His Theory of Personal Government. — The King's Friends. — The
King's Interference in the Details of Parliament and of Elections.—His
Dislike of the Whigs.—Formation of the Whig Party.—Lord Rockingham's Administration.—His Dismissal.—Lord Chatham's Government
and the Successive Changes in its Composition.—General Election of
1768.—Fox chosen for Midhurst.—His Political Opinions and Prejudices.—He selects his Party and takes his Seat.—Lord Shelburne.—
Fox as a Young Politician.

THE venality and servility of Parliament presented an irresistible temptation to a monarch who aimed at extending the
influence of the crown.   George the Second, whose solid and
unambitious intellect had taught him that the true secret of
kingcraft was to get the best ministers he could find, and then
leave them responsible for their own business, had seen England safe through immense perils, and had died at the very
height of prosperity and renown.[1]   "In times full of doubt
and danger to his person and his family," he maintained, as
Burke most truly said, the dignity of the throne and the liberty of the people not only unimpaired, but improved, for the
space of three-and-thirty years.   A different policy from his,
pursued during the next two-and-twenty years, mutilated the
empire, loaded the nation with debt, reduced the military rep-

---

[1] "What an enviable death!   In the greatest period of the glory of
this country and of his reign, in perfect tranquillity at home, at seventy-
seven, growing blind and deaf, to die without a pang before any reverse
of fortune; nay, but two days before a ship-load of bad news!" (Walpole
to Mann, October 28, 1760.)   "Upon the whole" (wrote Lord Waldegrave in his old employer's lifetime), "he has some qualities of a great
prince, many of a good one, none which are essentially bad; and I am
thoroughly convinced that hereafter he will be numbered among those
patriot kings under whose government the people have enjoyed the
greatest happiness."

utation of Britain lower than it ever stood before or since, made formidable inroads upon freedom, and rendered the crown itself so irksome a burden that its wearer thought very seriously of resigning it.   Then at last, when the disorders engendered by the system of personal government as understood by George the Third were at their height, the author of that system, most happily for his own fame, yielded himself to the domination of a stronger will even than his own.   Our politics once more flowed along the constitutional channel from which thenceforward they rarely diverged.   Events nearer to our time, and far more startling in their magnitude and more agreeable to our patriotic feelings, threw into the shade the Middlesex election and the American revolution; and one who during the best years of his life had been known as the most wilful and the least prosperous of rulers came to be remembered as a good easy man, under whose auspices, as a reward for his virtue, Trafalgar was added to the roll of our victories.   The popular impression of George the Third is derived from the period when he had Pitt for a master and Nelson for a servant, and has little in common with the impression which has stamped itself upon the minds of those who have studied him when he was as much the rival as the sovereign of Fox.[1]

It is hard to say whether the monarch or the subject suffered most from the folly of a parent.   Frederic, Prince of Wales, died when his son was twelve years old, and left him an example which he did not desire to emulate.[2]   There was no family likeness between the trifler who could see nothing in the fruitless heroism of Fontenoy except an occasion for stringing together a score of foolish couplets about Mars and

---

[1] "Here is a man," said Dr. Johnson, in 1784, "who has divided the kingdom with Cæsar; so that it was a doubt whether the nation should be ruled by the sceptre of George the Third or the tongue of Fox."

[2] "He had great virtues," said a foolish clergyman in his funeral sermon on the Prince of Wales.   "Indeed, they degenerated into vices.   He was very generous, but I hear that his generosity has ruined a great many people; and then his condescension was such that he kept very bad company."

Bacchus, and the grave and laborious administrator who always regarded the nation's misfortunes as his own. Half a dozen love-songs which lost something of their silliness in a French dress, the memory of a few practical jokes perpetrated at the expense of his own dependents, and some bad traditions of filial jealousy and undutifulness were all the teaching which George the Third inherited from his father. But the training to which he was subjected by his mother had a marked and durable effect upon his character and his actions. A narrow-minded intriguing woman, with the Continental notion of the relations between royalty and the rest of mankind, the princess did her utmost to imbue the essentially English nature of her son with the ideas that pervaded a petty German court before Europe had been traversed throughout its length and breadth by the legions of Napoleon and the doctrines of Mirabeau. Ambitious to see him governing as arbitrarily as an elector of Saxony, and forgetting that to secure the conquests of Clive and Wolfe abroad and to moderate between Pitt and Murray at home required very different qualifications from those which sufficed a potentate whose best energies were spent on settling how large a service of Dresden china was to be given as commission to a cardinal who had purchased him a Correggio, she willingly allowed his strong mind to remain uncultivated by study and overgrown with prejudices. As far as any knowledge of the duties and the position which were before him were concerned, she kept him in the nursery till within two years of the time that he mounted the throne. All that bedchamber women and pages of the backstairs could tell him about royal prerogative and popular rights she took care that he should learn ; but at that point his political education ended. There was some talk among his many tutors of having a treatise on international commerce written for his instruction ; but the work stopped with the choice of a title, and the sovereign of a nation which led, and at one conjuncture in his reign almost monopolized, the traffic of the globe went through life ignorant of everything connected with maritime trade to a degree which would have been hardly becoming

in a King of Bohemia. The Bishop of Norwich prepared him
for the task of ruling a community the individual members
of which, to an extent unknown elsewhere, had long been in
the habit of thinking for themselves in matters of religion,
by teaching him to view with suspicion and dislike all except
one of the many forms of faith which prevailed in his do-
minions. Another of his preceptors enjoyed the reputation
of being a Jacobite; and the belief that this gentleman had
contrived to instil his principles into the mind of his pupil
in part accounted for the enthusiasm with which, after the
death of George the Second, the old malcontents of '15 and
'45 hastened to transfer their allegiance from the white rose
to the white horse. It is easy to imagine the scandal that
was created among the Whig families by the intelligence that
one of the very few books which their future king was ever
authentically known to have read was a Jesuit history of
their own great and glorious Revolution.

If to be a Jacobite was to regard himself as "the great servant of the commonwealth," in the sense in which that phrase
was employed by James the First, George the Third was indeed a worthy successor of the Stuarts. He possessed all the
accomplishments which are required for doing business as
business is done by kings. He talked foreign languages like
a modern prince of the blood, and he wrote like the master
of every one with whom he corresponded. The meaning of
the brief and blunt confidential notes in which he made
known his wishes to an absent minister never failed to stand
clearly out through all his indifferent spelling and careless
grammar. Those notes are dated at almost every minute
from eight in the morning to eleven at night; for, as long as
work remained on hand, all hours were working-hours with
the king. Punctual, patient, self-willed, and self-possessed;
intruding into every department; inquiring greedily into
every detail; making everybody's duty his own, and then doing it conscientiously, indefatigably, and as badly as it could
possibly be done—he had almost all the qualities which enable a man to use or misuse an exalted station, with hardly
any of the talents by means of which such a station can be

reached from below. If he had been born a private gentleman, his intellectual powers would never have made him a
junior lord of the Treasury; but his moral characteristics
were such that, being a king, he had as much influence on the
conduct of affairs as all his cabinet together. A Frederic
the Great without the cleverness, he loved his own way no
less than his German brother, and got it almost as frequently;
with this difference in the result, that in the score of years
during which he governed according to his favorite theory
he weakened England as much as Frederic ever aggrandized
Prussia.

That theory is stated, as concisely as George the Third
stated everything, in the letter which recalled Pitt to his
councils in 1766. "I know," wrote the king, "the Earl of
Chatham will zealously give his aid towards destroying all
party distinctions, and restoring that subordination to government which can alone preserve that inestimable blessing, liberty, from degenerating into licentiousness." It certainly required self-assurance nothing less than royal to invite a statesman to re-enter the cabinet for the express purpose of bolster-
ing up a policy the first-fruits of which, five years before, had
been his own expulsion from office. To rise above faction,
to regard nothing but individual worth, to "distribute the
functions of state by rotation," to "withstand that evil called
connection," to "root out the present method of parties band-
ing together"—such were the fine words under which the
king disguised his unalterable intention to be the real as well
as the titular ruler of the nation. He had taken to heart the
fable of the bundle of sticks, the very last advice which his
own grandfather would have given him on his death-bed; and
he was firmly resolved that no combination of his subjects
should ever be powerful enough, or permanent enough, to
make head against his single will. Blind to the truth of
Burke's noble saying that private honor is the foundation of
public trust, and friendship no mean step towards patriotism,
he never scrupled to exert his authority and to expend his
own powers of persuasion and the nation's money in order
to foster disunion among politicians who had been accustom-

ed to act together in Parliament and in office, to break up alliances, to sow suspicions, to efface the recollection of past dangers surmounted in common and old services mutually rendered and received. He wished public men to transfer their fidelity as lightly as he himself transferred that which the *London Gazette* styled his "confidence." Knocking chancellors of the Exchequer and first lords of the Treasury down like ninepins, changing his advisers "as a parson changes his church-wardens," he reduced the administration of the country to such confusion and disrepute that in his more thoughtful hours he stood aghast at the success of his own performance. "How many secretaries of state have you corresponded with?" he asked an ex-Governor of Gibraltar. "Five, sire," was the reply. "You see my situation," said the king. "This trade of politics is a rascally business. It is a trade for a scoundrel, and not for a gentleman."

He had only himself to thank. Since his day, as well as before it, English monarchs have occasionally so far failed in their constitutional obligations as to show themselves partisans; but all the preference which, from time to time, the crown has displayed towards one or another of the existing parties never produced a tithe of the mischief which was brought about by this king, who set his heart upon creating a party of his own. When he first took that calamitous project in hand, he found everybody whose services as an effective and respectable supporter were worth securing already enlisted under the banner of some recognized parliamentary captain. Of what sort of materials, asked Burke, must that man have been made who could sit whole years in the House of Commons, with five hundred and fifty of his fellow-citizens, "without seeing any sort of men whose character, conduct, or disposition would lead him to associate himself with them, to aid and be aided, in any one system of public utility?" The only recruiting-ground that was left open to his Majesty's operations lay among the waifs and strays of politics; among the disappointed, the discontented, and the discredited; among those whom Chatham would not stoop to notice, and Newcastle had not cared to buy; and out

of such material as this was gradually organized a band of
camp-followers promoted into the ranks, at the head of which
no decent leader would have been seen marching through the
lobby.   These mercenaries, who dubbed themselves the king's
friends ("as if," said Junius, "the body of the people were
the king's enemies"), were the very last whom George the
Third himself would have complimented with such a title.
They were attached to him whose friendship they boasted not
by the bonds of affection and familiarity, but by a secret understanding in accordance with which they placed their conscience and their honor at his absolute disposal; while he, on
his part, undertook that they should get, and under all circumstances should keep, the best of everything that was going.   He loved to surmount himself in his privacy with kindly honest folk, not too clever to relish his garrulity, and give
him plenty of their own in return, nor so much men of the
world as to put him out of conceit with his simple habits and
homely pleasures.[1]   But while he chose the associates of his
intimacy among the best, if not the wisest, of the class from
which the companions of royalty are drawn, he was altogether
indifferent to the personal character of those whom he hired
as his tools.   Among the king's friends in the Peers, the steward of the household was an avowed profligate.   The Earl of
March, whom to call an avowed profligate would be to absolve
with faint blame, remained a lord of the bedchamber for
eight-and-twenty years, under eleven successive prime-ministers.   Another lord of the bedchamber, who received a special mark of the royal gratitude in the shape of a regiment,
which had been taken from the most respected soldier in the

---

[1] Lord Carlisle declined the bedchamber on the avowed, and most avow-
able, ground that it would not admit him to personal relations with his
sovereign.   "I have no reason," he wrote, "to expect, however long I
may continue, that either by assiduity, attention, and respect I can ever
succeed to any kind of confidence with my master.   That familiarity
which subsists between other princes and those of their servants whose
attachment they are convinced of being excluded from our court by the
king's living so much in private damps all views of ambition which
might arise from that quarter."

army as a punishment for giving an independent vote in the House of Commons, had run away from his beautiful wife with at least one girl of family. A third king's friend, after making the crown his accomplice in an impudent but unsuccessful attempt to swindle his creditors, was judged too bad to remain even in the bedchamber, and was accordingly packed off to Virginia as its governor. And as for the nobleman who had charge of the great wardrobe, it is enough to say that he and the Earl of Sandwich were the only members of the Medmenham Club whom Wilkes thought worthy of being admitted to a private reading of the "Essay on Woman."

These were very different people from the excellent, if somewhat commonplace, colonels and chaplains who, as they gossiped round her tea-table, were sketched to the life by Miss Burney in those "Memoirs" which, in their delightful prolixity (unavoidable when describing such a court as George the Third's), are a full compensation for the loss of another Cecilia, or even another Evelina. The king knew very well whom he could venture to live with after his own fashion, and had no notion of giving Lord Bottetort or Jerry Dyson the opportunity of manufacturing a good story out of the pretty playful ceremonies with which the royal household observed a princess's birthday, or of amusing a supper-table at White's with a reproduction of the wry faces they had made over his Majesty's barley-water. What he wanted from his so-called friends was not their company or their conversation, but their votes. He kept up just so much communication with them as to inform them, at second hand or at third hand, which of the measures that he had empowered his cabinet to introduce they were to impede and, if possible, to defeat; and what minister whom he had spoken fair in the closet they were to worry in Parliament and malign at the clubs. Of the politicians whom this system bred and fostered, no one who appreciates what is most valuable in our national form of government and most honorable in our national character has ever yet brought himself to speak with patience. The "immortal infamy," prophesied for them by the far-sighted among their contemporaries, has been conferred on them in overflowing measure by the greatest prose-writers of the nation which they disgraced and well-nigh ruined. But the closely reasoned and brilliantly worded invectives in which Burke and Macaulay have done for the king's friends what Tacitus did for the informers of the Roman empire are not so damaging to George the Third and his political retainers as the unstudied expressions of vexation, and even of anguish, which were wrung from the lips of statesmen who had been stabbed in the back at the instigation of a master whom they were faithfully and diligently serving. Lord Rockingham, in his quiet way, told his sovereign to his face that the efforts of his Majesty's ministers had been thwarted by the officers of his Majesty's household, "acting together like a corps." Lord North, piqued by the inspired insolence of a subordinate place-man, complained, with more of metaphor than was usual to him, that his pillow was full of thorns. And Mr. Grenville, who had a temper with which neither king nor king's favor-ite did well to trifle, declared straight out that he would not hold power at the will of a set of Janizaries who might at any moment be ordered to put the bowstring round his neck.

The king maintained his parliamentary body-guard in a state of admirable discipline. As James the Second was his own minister of marine, and William the Third his own for-eign secretary, so George the Third selected as his special de-partment the manipulation of the House of Commons. He furnished the means, and minutely audited the expenditure, of corruption. He protected and prolonged a bad system which, but for him, would have died an earlier death by at least sixteen years. Every reformer of abuses who had got hold of a thread in the web of bribery and jobbery which was strangling the commonwealth was discouraged from follow-ing up his clew by the certainty that it would lead him sooner or later to the door of the royal closet. The king knew the secret history of all the hucksters of politics—the amount at which they appraised themselves, the form in which they had got their price, and the extent to which they were earning their pay by close attendance and blind subservience. There never was a patronage secretary of the old school who might

not have sat at his feet with advantage. He had the true
Treasury whip's eye for a division, and contempt for a debate. When he had studied the list of ayes and noes, and
the names of the speakers for and against, he had sufficient
materials to decide how he was to distribute his smiles and
his cold looks—who was to be enriched, who was to be warned, and who was to be beggared. For arguments, however
unanswerable—for protestations of loyalty, however sincere
and pathetic—he cared as little as for the virtues and the
deserts of those who had the misfortune to differ with him.
He was never more inexorable than when dealing with the
officers whose courage and conduct, by sea and land, had prepared for him so extensive an empire and so splendid a throne.
Conway, whose name was a proverb for romantic daring,[1] lost
his regiment and his place in the bedchamber because, in the
debate on General Warrants, he stood by the liberties of his
country as quietly and firmly as he had confronted the clay-
mores at Culloden and the Irish bayonets at Fontenoy. Barré,
with a French bullet still in his face, begged the speaker no
longer to address him by his military title, since, by voting
for Wilkes, he had forfeited the rank and the employment
which had been bestowed on him as the brother in arms of
Wolfe. But summary dismissal, inflicted, in order to point
the example, the most ruthlessly upon those who had the
most distinguished services or the largest families, was not the
only expedient adopted in order to deter officers from doing
their duty as members of Parliament. Their sovereign had in
store for them another mark of his displeasure, which they
felt as perhaps only soldiers can feel it. " The last division,"
wrote George to his minister (and it was a specimen letter)
" was nearer than some persons will have expected, but not
more than I thought. I hope every engine will be employed

---

[1] " I don't pretend," said a sufficiently brave officer, "to be like Harry
Conway, who walks up to the mouth of a cannon with as much coolness
and grace as if he was going to dance a minuet." At the battle of Laf-
felt, the Steenkirk of the eighteenth century, Conway got so near death
that one French hussar had him by the hair while the sword-point of
another was at his breast.

to get those friends that stayed away last night to come and support on Monday. I wish a list could be prepared of those who went away, and those that deserted to the minority. That would be a rule for my conduct in the drawing-room to-morrow." When the king, amidst a circle of exultant place-men, turned his back upon men who had never turned theirs upon his enemies, and sent them home to read in the *Gazette* that some holiday hero who had never marched farther afield than Hounslow had been promoted over their heads, they would carry their grievance to the minister at whose com-mand they had sailed across the world to encounter the wounds and jungle fevers which were all that remained to them as the reward of half a score of campaigns. There is something indescribably pathetic in the little personal atten-tions by which Lord Chatham, in his helplessness and isola-tion, endeavored to repay to the slighted and injured veterans some part of that debt of gratitude which his sovereign had thought fit to repudiate.[1]

---

[1] In 1773 Chatham drafted a memorial with his own hand for an officer who had been passed over for political reasons—"a wanton species of oppression," he says, "fatal to the army or the constitution." "If the spirit of service," he writes in another place, "could be killed in an Eng-lish army, such strokes of wanton injustice would bid fair for it." In the same year his sympathy was requested for the half-pay captains in the navy who had been rudely shown the door by a ministry which was on the eve of a war that reft from England the half of Chatham's conquests. "With these men," wrote Barré, "your lordship gave law to the world. Your bungling successors are perfectly ignorant of the use or application of such valuable instruments." One method by which Chatham gratified the old partners and instruments of his renown was by hanging their portraits in a place of honor in his house at Burton Pynsent. A compli-ment of this nature, paid to Admiral Saunders, who had commanded at Quebec, called from him a letter which breathed salt in every line. "You have put," he writes, "a plain seaman under great difficulties. I assure you I find it a great deal harder to make a proper answer to your lord-ship's civilities than to execute any orders I ever received from you. Your lordship has made an exchange with me that I am a gainer by in every way. You have my picture, and I will keep your lordship's letter as a thing I am at least as proud of as of the mark I wear of the king's approbation of the services I meant to do in that time which was truly

To those who can for a moment forget the misfortunes which the perversity of George the Third entailed upon his country, there is an element of the comical in the roundness and vehemence with which he invariably declared himself upon the wrong side in a controversy. Whether he was predicting that the publication of debates would "annihilate the House of Commons, and thus put an end to the most excellent form of government which has been established in this kingdom;" or denouncing the "indecency" of a well-meaning senator who had protested against the double impropriety of establishing State lotteries, and then using them as an engine for bribing members of Parliament; or explaining the reluctance of an assembly of English gentlemen and landowners to plunder the Duke of Portland of his estates by the theory that there was no "truth, justice, and even honor" among them—he displayed an inability to tolerate, or even to understand, any view but his own which can only be accounted for by the reflection that he was at the same time a partisan and a monarch. He never could forgive a politician for taking the right course, unless it was taken from a wrong motive. When the Protestant Dissenters applied to be emancipated from the obligation of subscribing the Thirty-nine Articles, the king, at the same time that he directed Lord North to see that the bill for their relief was lost in the House of Lords, desired him not to be hard upon those well-affected gentlemen who owed their seats to the Nonconformists. Even at the risk of encouraging the advocates of a measure which his Majesty dreaded as a blow to religion and detested as an innovation, nothing must be done to diminish the majority in a future Parliament which would have to be relied upon for gagging the press in England and maintaining the tea-duty in America. For George the Third was, before everything, an electioneerer. He had the names and the figures of all the con-

---

glorious. I am more pleased with your thinking me a friend to liberty than with all the rest. I am so to the bottom, and you may depend upon it. I think the country can have no glory without it." Saunders had suffered for his opinions, and if he had lived longer would undoubtedly have suffered more.

stituencies at his fingers' ends, and the consciences of a good many of them in his pocket. He was at home in the darkest corners of the political workshop, and up to the elbows in those processes which a high-minded statesman sternly forbids, and which even a statesman who is not high-minded leaves to be conducted by others. We find him paving the way for a new contest in a county by discharging the outstanding debts of the last candidate; helping the members of a manufacturing town to keep their seats at a general election, and contributing to the expense of defending them against a petition which, no doubt, had been richly deserved; subsidizing the patron of a borough with a grant out of the privy purse, and then, on the eve of a change of government, huddling away every trace of a bargain which would not endure the inspection of an honest minister; and writing, with the pen of an English sovereign, to offer a subject some "gold pills" for the purpose of hocusing the freeholders. Never very quick to pardon, he would not hear of an excuse from those who had crossed him in his character of a parliamentary agent. Legge, during the great war with France, had directed with consummate ability the finance of the most successful government that ever took office; but he had refused his support to a Jacobite whom Lord Bute was scheming to bring in for Hampshire, and the new reign had not lasted six months before the unhappy Chancellor of the Exchequer found to his cost that the George the Third did not intend to drop the electioneering feuds of the Prince of Wales. At the interview which he obtained in order to tender his enforced resignation, the fallen minister assured his Majesty that his future life would evince the sincerity of his loyalty. "Nothing but your future life," was the ungracious reply, "can conciliate the bad impression I have received of you."

A king so formidable, so pertinacious, so insatiable of power, and so very far from particular as to the means which he employed in the pursuit of it, found little to resist him in the base and shifting elements of which public life was composed in the third quarter of the eighteenth century. As year by year he gathered strength, he grew ever bolder in the use of it, and more hostile to those who had the magnanimity to resist his seductions and the courage to thwart his will. For, among the mob of high-born self-seekers and needy adventurers who hustled each other round the throne, the dignity of English statesmanship was still upheld by a few men to whom their bitterest enemies never denied the praise of being faithful to their opinions and to each other. The nucleus of the Liberal party, as it has existed ever since, was formed during the turbid and discreditable period that intervened between the fall of Pitt in 1761 and the fall of Grenville in 1765. Loathing the corruption which was rising around them like a noisome tide, and foreseeing the perils of that deliberate warfare against the freedom of the press which began with the arrest of Wilkes, and ended, after the lapse of more than half a century, with the acquittal of William Hone, a small knot of friends found themselves drawn together fully as much by moral as by political sympathy. High in rank, with rare exceptions; young in years; and most of them too rich, and all too manly, to be purchased, their programme, as now it would be called, consisted in little more than a determination to prove to the world that there yet remained somebody who might be trusted. The opinions and aspirations of the Duke of Richmond, Lord John Cavendish, and Sir George Savile are clearly set forth in a confidential letter addressed by the Duke of Portland to their common chief, the Marquis of Rockingham: "As to the young men of property, and independent people in both Houses, it is holding out a banner for them to come to, where interest cannot be said to point out the way, and where nothing but public good is to be sought for on the plainest, honestest, and most disinterested terms." The creed up to which these men endeavored to act was embodied by Burke in a single sentence. "The principles of true politics," he said, "are those of morality enlarged, and I neither now do, nor ever will, admit of any other"—a doctrine which in our day has been repeated almost in the same words by another great spokesman of the same party.[1]

---

[1] "It is not only true in morals," said Mr. Bright, in 1877, "but true in

These sentiments might have been mistaken for the commonplaces of opposition by such as were old enough to remember how the patriots of 1740 talked while they were on the left hand of the Speaker, and how they acted after they had taken their seats on the Treasury bench; but Lord Rockingham and his followers had been in office just long enough to show that, when they crossed the floor of the House, they did not leave their principles behind them. They came to the rescue at a moment when the enforcement of the Stamp Act in America had brought the empire to the very verge of civil war, and when the violent and despotic proceedings in which the prosecution of Wilkes had involved the executive government had agitated the mind of England with alarm and disaffection. In that dark hour George the Third besought Lord Rockingham to stand between him and the resentment of his subjects, at home and across the seas. The proposal to saddle themselves with the responsibility of striving to undo the consequences of foolish and criminal measures which they had strenuously opposed had no great charms for men all of whom valued their reputation, and some their ease, a great deal more than anything which office could bring them. Nothing, said Burke, but the strongest sense of their duty to the public could have prevailed upon them to undertake the king's business at such a time. Unattractive, however, as the invitation was, it was frankly and loyally accepted. The colonies were pacified by timely conciliation; measures were taken to guard against the repetition of those encroachments on personal liberty which had set the nation in a blaze; and, as soon as his crown was once more secure, the king began to plot the destruction of the ministry which had saved him. Lord Rockingham by his wise and courageous policy had earned the confidence, and even the affection, of the people; but, in the phrase of the day, he had ruined himself in the closet. One who lived behind the scenes for twenty years was accustomed to say that a man in office who could bring

statesmanship; and, in fact, I would not dissociate them at all—what is true in morals from what is true in statesmanship."

himself to utter the simple form of words "That is wrong"
would carry his point in council though everybody was against
him. Lord Rockingham was a brief, a bad, and a most reluctant speaker ; but he had a way of listening to a questionable
proposal which was more alarming to George the Third even
than the eloquence of Pitt or the lengthiness of Grenville.
A sovereign who had it in view to appoint a young gentleman of fourteen, the heir to a pocket-borough, comptroller of
petty customs in the port of London, or to confer a secret
pension on a member of Parliament who was not yet prepared
to let it be known that he had changed his party, naturally
liked to be met half-way by his confidential adviser. But
Lord Rockingham, who to the end of his life found it difficult
enough to express his thoughts, never rose to the higher art
of concealing them ; and the monarch very soon acquired a
dread of his amiable and modest servant, the frequent manifestation of which is a high and involuntary tribute to the
power of unswerving and unassuming virtue.

The Rockinghams took office in the summer of 1765, and
by Christmas the king had made up his mind to be rid of
them. As soon as Parliament assembled after the holidays,
he set his accustomed machinery to work. The farce began
by the master of the harriers begging an audience for the
purpose of humbly acquainting his Majesty that his convictions would not allow him to support the repeal of the Stamp
Act. His Majesty, with the air of a Henry the Fourth com-
mending and forgiving a Chief-justice Gascoigne, assured his
faithful retainer that he was at liberty to follow the dictates
of his conscience. Having obtained their cue, the king's
friends voted in a body against the king's ministers ; but
the consequences of a breach with America, as expounded
by Burke and Pitt in speeches of extraordinary force, convinced a nation which still was more prudent than its sovereign, and the attempt to save the stamp-duty was defeated
by a clear majority of two to one. George the Third, in his
disgust and disappointment, at once fell intriguing in every
direction against his own cabinet. Bute, Bedford, and Grenville became in turn the object of his advances ; but none the

less did he continue to smile upon the servants whom he was eagerly making an opportunity to discharge. "The late good old king," said Chatham, in the House of Lords, "had something about him by which it was possible for you to know whether he liked you or disliked you;" but in this respect the reigning monarch did not take after his grandfather. Lord Rockingham afterwards declared that he had never enjoyed such distinguished marks of the royal kindness as during a period when the influence of Great Britain was paralyzed in every foreign capital by the knowledge that the existing prime-minister would not remain in office ten minutes after a successor could be found for him, and when all the placemen of the king's faction were openly denouncing and obstructing the government. Dyson, the king's spokesman in the Commons, and Lord Eglinton, his acknowledged agent in the Lords, carried on a persistent and vexatious opposition which would have been contemptible if maintained on their own account, but which rendered legislation next to impossible when it was notorious that they had the court behind them. Lord Strange, the Chancellor of the Duchy of Lancaster, went about everywhere asserting, with the air of one who was fresh from a confidential interview, that when they claimed the royal sanction for the repeal of the Stamp Act, the ministers had been taking a liberty with the name of their sovereign. Lord Rockingham was not the man to curry favor by passing himself off as the dupe of a perfidy which was almost insolent in its transparence. He refused to leave the presence until his Majesty had disavowed Lord Strange in his own hand on three separate scraps of paper, which are still in existence, worth exactly as much as they were on the day when they were written. He never saw the king without demanding that the mutineers should be brought to order, and never quitted him without an assurance that their conduct was shameful, and a promise that the next fault should be their last.[1] But at length the plot was ripe,

---

[1] On one occasion Rockingham came to the palace primed with a flagrant case of insubordination on the part of Lord Eglinton. "Oh," said

and its projector no longer had need to dissemble.   Early in July, 1766, Lord Chancellor Northington, ill at ease with colleagues whose public spirit was as little to his taste as the decency of their private habits, got up a quarrel with them over a proposed code for Canada, absented himself from their councils, and on hearing that the cabinet had met without him, swore roundly that it should never meet again.   Next morning he drove to Richmond, advised the king to send for Pitt, and assisted in the concoction of a letter inviting the Great Commoner to place himself at the head of "an able and dignified" government; and on the same evening George the Third dismissed his ministers without a sentence of thanks, a word of apology, or a syllable of explanation beyond the singularly timed remark that he had not two faces.   The chancellor was loaded with pensions and sinecures as the wages of his treachery; but Lord Rockingham and his friends gained nothing by their year of power except the consciousness of having done their best to serve a master who was the reverse of grateful.   Alone among all the administrations which preceded them and several which followed them, they went out of office, the poor among them as poor and the rich no richer than they had entered it; having done more for the advantage of the nation by setting its rulers an example of disinterestedness than if they had succeeded in placing half a score of useful and enlightened measures on the pages of the Statute-book.[1]

---

the king, "that is abominable; but Eglinton is angry with me too.   He says I have not done enough for him."   George the Third at last went so far as to pledge himself that if Dyson did not mend his ways he should go in the course of the next winter; but by that time his Majesty clearly foresaw that Lord Rockingham himself would not outlast the autumn.

[1] The political satire of the day swarms with passages indicating the light in which George the Third was regarded by his subjects at the period when he held the purse-strings of bribery, committed the welfare of his kingdom to Sandwich and Grafton, and conspired with Northington and Rigby against Burke and Rockingham.

"Of vice the secret friend, the foe professed;
Of every talent to deceive possessed;

And now the king's theory of what a ministry ought to be was tested under the most favorable possible circumstances as against the theory of Burke. Party, said Burke, is a body of men united to promote the national interest by their joint endeavors upon some particular principle in which they are all agreed. Party, said his Majesty, is a body of men combined to hinder a beneficent ruler from selecting for public employment the best and wisest of his subjects, wherever he can meet with them. The Earl of Chatham (for by that name Pitt was thenceforward known) had so small a personal following that his only resource was to patch up a government out of the most respectable odds and ends on which he could lay his hands. He would gladly have strengthened his cabinet by a large draft from the ranks of the late administration; but most of Lord Rockingham's friends preferred to retire with their leader, amidst the contemptuous astonishment of political mankind.[1] Conway and the Duke of Portland

---

> As mean in household savings as profuse
> In vile corruption's scandalous abuse;
> Mentally blind; on whom no ray of truth
> E'er glanced auspicious e'en in bloom of youth.
> What though inimitable Churchill's hearse
> Saved thee from all the vengeance of his verse?
> Macaulay shall in nervous prose relate
> Whence flows the venom that distracts the State."

These lines, given to the world in 1770, refer to Mrs. Catherine Macaulay, once famous as the republican chronicler of the Stuarts. Wilkes called her a noble historian. Franklin, in a letter to the newspapers, speaks of "future Livys, Humes, Robertsons, and Macaulays, who may be inclined to furnish the world with that *rara avis*, a true history." Gray thought her book "the most sensible, unaffected, and best history of England that we have had yet." The poor lady is now remembered solely as the object of some of Dr. Johnson's coarsest, but certainly not his least amusing, jokes; but the prediction contained in the couplets quoted above was fulfilled with curious completeness in Lord Macaulay's second essay on Chatham.

[1] "The Duke of Richmond, Sir George Savile, and Lord John Cavendish," said Walpole, "were devoted to their party, and from that point of honor, which did little to their judgment, remained inflexibly attached to that poor creature, Lord Rockingham." Nothing more forcibly brings

remained, bitterly to regret ere long that they had separated themselves from their former colleagues; and the Duke of Grafton, shaking himself free from associates whose influence had hitherto preserved him from himself, surrendered—little as he then knew it—his last chance of descending to posterity as a reputable statesman. Poor Charles Townshend, who as successor of Lord Holland had been revelling in the easy profits of the Pay-office, was unceremoniously thrust up into the barren and laborious duties of Chancellor of the Exchequer. From among his own adherents Chatham nominated Barré to high and Lord Shelburne to exalted office; while Lord Northington reeled down into the presidency of the council, to make room on the woolsack for Lord Camden, who had shown his independence on the bench by discharging Wilkes from imprisonment, and in the House of Lords by denying the right of Parliament to tax America.

The experiment of a government based upon what George the Third called the principle, and Burke the cant, of "Not men, but measures," could not have been more fairly tried or have resulted in more rapid and hopeless failure. An administration whose original members had ability far above the average, and characters for the most part irreproachable enough to have qualified them for sitting in a modern cabinet, passed no laws that were not bad, took no important step that was not disastrous, and in little more than two years, by the gradual elimination of its nobler elements, had degenerated into an unscrupulous and unhonored cabal. Before the end of the fourth month one of those disagreements which were of weekly occurrence in Lord Chatham's motley and ill-assorted troop led to the retirement of all who had temporarily transferred their allegiance from Lord Rockingham to his successor; all, that is to say, but Conway, whom his evil genius, Horace Walpole, persuaded to hold his ground until he

---

out the degradation into which our public life had fallen since the great days of the seventeenth century than such a sneer in the mouth of one who affected, at any rate, to admire the mutual fidelity of Pym, Hampden, and Eliot.

could no longer retreat with credit. Next, the prime-minister, under the burden of a mysterious affliction, withdrew himself from spoken and at last even written communication with his bewildered cabinet, and left the field open for Townshend's fantastic cleverness and unspeakable folly. But death carried off Townshend before the laughter which greeted his champagne speech had well died away, and while men still believed that in imposing a tea-duty on the American colonies he had done a smart stroke for the benefit of the English Exchequer; and Lord North, who had all the qualities of a public man which Townshend lacked except public spirit, took the vacant place at the Exchequer. The Duke of Grafton, who was First Lord of the Treasury, and as much the head of the government as anybody could be at a time when a good fit of the gout might at any moment restore Lord Chatham to himself, now began seriously to look about for fresh recruits to supply the places of those who had fallen or deserted. Prepared, in his distress, to offer the very best of terms, he instinctively turned to the Bedfords. With them, as every parliamentary tactician knew, it was a question of the bounty-money, and not of the banner. They were always to be had; but, as has been wittily and compactly said, they were to be had only in the lot. Their unrivalled knowledge of the market had taught them that by sticking together they would each of them get quite as much and keep it twice as long. An attempt already had been made to bring about an alliance between them and the Rockinghams; but the Duke of Bedford insisted as a preliminary condition that Conway should be displaced in order to make room for the whole of his own connection; and the negotiation was broken off because Lord Rockingham, with rare nobility of mind, declined to sacrifice an old comrade who had sacrificed him.[1] Grafton, with nothing to for-

---

[1] The accounts which have been left of this conference of July 20, 1767, forcibly illustrate the morals and manners of the Bloomsbury gang, as they were called from the London residence of their leader. The Duke of Bedford, who was worthy of better clients, made a feeble effort to arrive at an understanding with Lord Rockingham about a common policy; but he could not keep his followers for five minutes together off the

give, was less considerate; and in January, 1767, the entire
Bloomsbury contingent marched into the ministerial camp
over Conway's prostrate body. Lord Gower became president
of the Council in the room of Lord Northington, who carried
down into Hampshire for the solace of his declining years a
cellar of port and a budget of loose stories which, if he had
remained in place, would have been critically appreciated by
his new colleagues. Rigby, who had the promise of the Pay-
office and the immediate enjoyment of an Irish vice-treasurership, refused to kiss hands until Conway had ceased to be secretary of state; and the seals were accordingly at once handed
to Lord Weymouth, while Lord Sandwich took over the salary
and the patronage of the Post-office. The first Parliament of
George the Third was now fast running to an end. A dissolution was at hand, and the incoming postmaster-general
learned with dismay that the Statute-book forbade him to
make use of his official authority for the furtherance of political objects. When boroughs were in question, Sandwich cared
nothing for the spirit of the law; but as he had just enough
respect for the letter to keep within it, he resolved to see the
elections out before assuming nominal possession of a dignity
every atom of the solid influence attached to which he was
determined ruthlessly to employ in the interests of his party.

---

subject that was next their hearts. Rigby bade the two noblemen take
the court calendar and give their friends one, two, and three thousand a
year all round. Not a single member, he declared, of the present cabinet
should be saved. "What," interposed Dowdeswell, "not Charles Townshend?" "Oh," said Rigby, "that is different. He has been in opposition." "So has Conway," cried Dowdeswell. "But Conway is Bute's
man," was the reply. "Pray," was the rejoinder, "is not Charles Townshend Bute's?" "Ay, but Conway is governed by his brother, who is
Bute's." "So is Townshend by *his* brother, who is Bute's." "But Lady
Ailesbury is a Scotchwoman." "So is Lady Dalkeith." Any one who
turns from this despicable wrangle to Lord Stanhope's narrative of the
overtures made by Pitt to the Whigs in 1804, and of the spirit in which
they were received, may estimate the reformation which forty years had
wrought in the tone of English politics; and, to whatever party he may
himself belong, he will acknowledge the debt which, on that score if on
no other, our country owes to Fox.

The general election which was held in the spring of 1768 disclosed a state of things most alarming to all except the dull, the thoughtless, and the dishonest. There was nothing fanciful in the parallel which it pleased contemporary writers to draw between the England of Chatham and the Rome of Pompey and Lucullus. Once again in the course of the world's history immense foreign conquests had been made by a free and self-governing people. Once again political institutions which had served their purpose as a machinery for enabling a nation to conduct its domestic affairs were exposed to a sudden and unexpected strain by the additional burden of a vast external empire. And once again the spoils of distant provinces were brought home to purchase the votes of electoral bodies, incapable of discharging or even understanding their increased responsibilities, and altogether out of sympathy with what was most intelligent and respectable in the community. The unreformed constituencies of England and Scotland no more represented the British energy, foresight, and valor which had triumphed under Clive and Hawke than the corrupt mob which gave its suffrages to the candidate who distributed the largest doles, exhibited the most numerous pairs of gladiators, and threw open the stateliest public baths for the lowest fees had a right to speak for the Marsian farmers and Ligurian mariners whose swords and oars had reconquered Spain and conquered Asia. The offices of electioneering agents had been besieged through the winter which preceded the election by rich army contractors eager to sit in the first Parliament that had been chosen since the Peace of Paris had allowed them to wind up their accounts with the War-office; by planters who had acquired their notions of constitutional government in the management of a sugar-estate in Barbadoes; by members of council from Calcutta and Madras who, out of a nominal salary of thirty pounds a month, accumulated baronial and even ducal revenues so fast that the directors complained that none but inexperienced youths remained beyond the seas to fill the most elevated posts in the service of the Company. The country was literally deluged with money. "Without connections," said Lord Chatham, "without any natural interest in the soil, the importers of foreign gold have forced their way into Parliament by such a torrent of corruption as no private hereditary fortune could resist." The sums lavished upon bribery in the counties and the great cities exceeded all that had been heard of in the past, and the patrons of close boroughs got anything they liked to name. George Selwyn received nine thousand pounds for the double seat at Ludgershall. The Mayor and Aldermen of Oxford, with a sort of perverted public spirit, refused to elect any candidate who would not undertake to assist them in wiping off their town debt. Some boroughs were advertised in the newspapers; others were negotiated on the commercial-travelling system by attorneys who went a round of the country-houses on horseback;[1] a great change since the autumn of 1640, when Pym and Hampden rode up and down England to promote the election of stanch and trustworthy Puritans, "wasting their bodies much in carrying on the cause." Wilkes, in a piece marked by more humor than delicacy (which, to do him justice, was seldom the case with what he gave to print), challenged his readers to deny that a share in the British legislature was bought and sold as publicly as a share in the New River Company. It fared ill with those noblemen and gentlemen who had been looking forward to the dissolution as an opportunity of giving their heirs the advantage of a senatorial career. Lord Chesterfield applied betimes to a parliamentary jobber with an offer of five-and-twenty hundred pounds if a safe seat could be provided for young Mr. Stanhope, whose education had by this time been brought to as high a point as nature seemed willing to sanction; but the man told him plainly that already there was no such a thing as a borough to be had, since the East and West Indians had secured them all at the rate of three, four, and (as the market hardened) of five thousand pounds a seat.[2]

---

[1] Hickey, the most notorious of these fellows, survives in Goldsmith's "Retaliation," with the character of "a blunt pleasant creature," and in company that is far too good for him.

[2] "*Mayor.* But, after all, Master Touchit, I am not so over-fond of these nabobs. For my part, I had rather sell myself to somebody else."

There was one father who had no intention of allowing any difficulty about money to interfere with his ideas of paternal duty. Five thousand pounds were the same as five hundred to Lord Holland, when it was a question of doing something to make Charles a man before his time. Though the lad had barely turned nineteen when Parliament was dissolved, a family arrangement was made for introducing him into public life as soon as he cared to enter it. Lord Ilchester was anxious to find some serious occupation for his son, Lord Stavordale, who was very little older than Charles, and had plunged almost as deep in the pleasures of the town; so the two brothers clubbed together to hire their boys a borough, as they might have rented them a manor to shoot over in the vacation. They selected Midhurst, the most comfortable of constituencies from the point of view of a representative; for the right of election rested in a few score of small holdings, on which no human being resided, distinguished among the pastures and stubbles that surrounded them by a large stone set up on end in the middle of each portion. These burgage-tenures, as they were called, had all been bought up by a single proprietor, Viscount Montagu, who, when an election was in prospect, assigned a few of them to his servants with instructions to nominate the members and then make back the property to their employer.[1] This ceremony was performed in March, 1768; and the steward of the estate, who acted as returning officer, declared that Charles James Fox had been duly chosen as one of the burgesses for Midhurst at a time

---

" *Touchit.* And why so, Mr. Mayor?

" *Mayor.* I don't know. They do a mortal deal of harm in the country. Why, wherever any of them settles, it raises the price of provisions for thirty miles round. People rail at seasons and crops. In my opinion, it is all along with these folks that things are so scarce.

" *Touchit.* You talk like a fool. Suppose they have mounted the beef and mutton a trifle. Ain't we obliged to them too for raising the value of boroughs? You should always set one against t'other."—FOOTE, *Nabob*, act ii., scene 2.

[1] In the year 1794 the number of permanent voters for Midhurst was returned as one. By that time Lord Egremont had acquired the burgage-holds at a cost of forty thousand guineas.

when that young gentleman was still amusing himself in
Italy. He remained on the Continent during the opening
session of the new Parliament, which met in May in order to
choose a speaker [1] and transact some routine business; and it
was not until the following winter that he made his first appearance upon a stage where, almost from the moment of his
entry, he became the observed of all observers.

Charles Fox began his political course utterly unprovided
with any fixed set of political opinions. Older than his years
in nothing but his looks and his opportunities, his outfit for
the career of a statesman consisted in a few superficial prejudices, the offspring rather of taste than of conviction; a few
personal alliances which he had formed for himself; and not
a few personal dislikes which he had, for the most part, inherited from his father. Lord Holland, by this time, was the
Ishmael of English politics. By Chatham, and Chatham's following, he could not even hope to be forgiven. The unkindness, and, as he regarded it, the ingratitude, of the Bedfords
forever rankled in his memory. Against the Grenvilles he
had a grudge of a more solid nature. In November, 1764, it
was intimated to George Grenville that Charles Townshend
had his eye upon the Pay-office. "I rather understood," wrote
the prime-minister's informant, "that he would be content to
wait for Lord Holland's death. He said he wished him dead,
and so he believed did everybody." But the paymaster's
health, as we learn in a boyish letter from his son, mended
during the winter; and in May, 1765, the king, urged by
Grenville, who was urged by Townshend, commanded him to
resign the prize for the retention of which he had sacrificed
the last shred of his reputation and become embroiled in the
most disagreeable of his hundred quarrels. And, finally, when
Grenville fell and was succeeded by Rockingham, Lord Hol-

---

[1] They chose Sir John Cust, who went through the time-honored farce
of self-depreciation, and duly submitted to be forced up the steps of the
chair, expostulating with carefully graduated vehemence which grew
fainter as he ascended from the floor. The poor man had more reason
for his reluctance than he knew of at the time, for a single session of
Wilkes killed him.

land made advances, equally unexpected and unwelcome, towards a reconciliation with the party whom more than all others he had unpardonably injured—advances which the new minister received with a quiet scorn that brought painfully home to the old statesman the consciousness that he was feared as little as he was confided in, and honored even less than he was loved.

With the capacity for self-deception which is nowhere so potent as in the breast of a politician, Lord Holland contrived to regard himself as a good, easy man, upon whom the world had borne too hard. "Don't ever, Charles," he would say to his favorite boy, "make any exception, or trust as I did.

'Of all court service know the common lot:
To-day 'tis done; to-morrow 'tis forgot.'

Well! I may thank myself, and have nothing to do but to forget it." Charles was quite prepared to resent the wrongs of a father from whom he had known nothing but kindness; and, with a strange ignorance of his own nature, looked upon himself as destined to live upon bad terms with nine out of ten of his equals and contemporaries. He could see no party which he was inclined to join, and no idol which he would condescend to worship. He dutifully refused to admire Chatham, though his animosity was softened when the caprice of that great man, by oversetting the Rockingham administration, did something to expiate the slight which the Whigs had put upon Lord Holland. The Bedfords, one and all, he cordially detested. "As for politics," he writes from Florence to Macartney in 1767, "I am very little curious about them, for almost everything I hear at this distance seems unintelligible. I am ill-natured enough to be very sorry whenever I hear there is any chance of the Bedfords being pleased, and that is all I care about." "You said," he complains from Naples to another correspondent, "you would write to me if you could find anything I should like to hear. In your last to Ste., you say the Bedfords have been cruelly used. Did you not think I should be glad to hear that? But I am sadly afraid you are imposed upon, and they have not been so ill-used as I always wish them to be. Let them feel how sharper than a serpent's tooth it is to have a thankless friend. They are now, I understand, joined with Lord Rockingham, the only party whom they have not already tried at. Lord Bute, the Duke of Grafton, and Lord Chatham have sent them empty away, and I hope and believe, if the others come in, they will serve them in the same manner." The letters which Charles Fox wrote and answered during the last twelve or fifteen months of the period which (little as he would have approved the expression) must be called his boyhood show that he was already keenly alive to politics, though his interest in them was entirely of a personal and petty description. He was greatly exercised about his father's ambition to exchange his barony for an earldom, and it was at his suggestion that Lord Holland showed himself at court, in order to press his suit for a favor which was flatly and ungraciously refused.[1] When Lord Carlisle was made Knight of the Thistle, his schoolfellow expressed his delight in a sentence that would have raised high the paternal hopes of Lord Chesterfield. "I think it," he says, "one of the best things that has been done this great while." But the very enthusi-

---

[1] "Dear Charles," Lord Holland writes, "I hope I shall not mind it; but your advice has been followed with as bad success as possible. I was at court yesterday for the first, and I believe last, time. I had as much to say as any man ever had, and said it. I saw obstinate determined denial, without any reason given; nor had I any occasion to follow your advice, 'to take a shuffling answer for a denial,' for I was not flattered even by a shuffling answer, but told it would be very inconvenient to do it now, without being told why." At the time Lord Holland was learning from the royal lips how low he had fallen, his old rival was receiving, though not enjoying, the most signal homage that a sovereign ever paid to a subject. Letters in the king's hand were going thrice a week to Lord Chatham, praying him to emerge from his retirement, if it were but for the space of a single interview; entreating him to leave no means untried for restoring his invaluable health; and earnestly beseeching him, if he could give nothing else, not to deprive his Majesty's government of the protection of his name. Such were now the relative positions of a pair of statesmen who, ten years before, stood on a level in the estimation of mankind.

asm and energy with which he discoursed on coronets and
green ribbons would have indicated to a discerning judge
that Charles Fox was not the stuff out of which gold sticks
are shaped.   Making no pretension to a public spirit which
seldom springs of itself in the breast of an English lad still in
his teens, and which grows all the more healthily for not having been forced; expatiating in a free, dashing style on whatever happened to be the genuine humor of the moment;
throwing into the all-absorbing business of the private theatricals, which were the special and time-honored pastime of his
family, more heart and sense than can be found in all the Bedford and Grenville correspondence together—he gave promise
of a sincerity, an audacity, an intensity, which would some day
be unwonted and most salutary elements in the stagnant and
vitiated atmosphere of St. Stephen's.

Fox took his seat in November, 1768, and enrolled himself
without hesitation in the ranks of the ministerialists.   Lord
Holland had chosen a most opportune moment for sending
him into Parliament.   In the opinion of that veteran placeman, there was only one bench in the House on which a wise
man would care to sit; but room would easily be found there
for the son of one who had quarrelled to the death with almost every possible prime-minister.   If Chatham had still
been at the head of affairs, and Shelburne secretary of state,
Charles Fox could not have looked for office, and, indeed,
would have had too much spirit to accept it; but between the
spring and the winter sessions of 1768 a great change had been
effected in the constitution of the ministry.   Lord Shelburne
had always desired to keep the Bedfords at a distance, and
had been at daggers drawn with them ever since their introduction into the government.   His faults and his virtues alike
rendered it more than difficult for him to act with them as colleagues.   From the beginning to the end of Lord Shelburne's
life fate seemed to have ordained that things should never go
easily inside a cabinet which held him, and the key to that
fatality is no longer a mystery.   His racy and very candid
autobiography bears on every page the impress of an acute,
a forcible, and a most original intellect, which had failed to

work itself free from conceit in the most subtle of all its innumerable forms. A man who has too much sense to overrate his own qualities will often make amends to his self-esteem by underrating his neighbor's; and Lord Shelburne, while he had too strong a sense of the becoming to praise himself even in his private diary, could not endure to admit, with regard to others, that any fame was deserved, any motives pure, or any conduct meritorious. While still a youth, he occasionally put enough restraint upon himself to preserve an outward show of respect for some powerful and eminent statesman who was old enough to be his father; but there was no reverence in his composition, and in his secret thoughts he had less mercy for his patrons than a reasonably good-natured politician bestows upon his adversaries. Lord Bute gave him his unreserved confidence at a time when that confidence was well worth having, and offered him high preferment long before he had earned it by his public performances. Lord Chatham, against the wish of the king, made him secretary of state at nine-and-twenty; and, in requital for their kindness, he amused the leisure of his later years by drawing characters of Bute and Chatham less pleasing than any which can be found elsewhere than on the fly-sheet of a lampoon. A man who lived so much in the world as Lord Shelburne could not conceal from the world so marked a feature of his disposition; and his reputation for incurable treachery, for which nothing that he actually did, when judged by the standard of his age, will sufficiently account, was principally due to the consciousness from which his political associates could not free themselves that, however fair he might speak them to their faces, at the bottom of his soul he regarded them as one less honest and less capable than the other.

If Lord Shelburne (to borrow an expressive phrase from the dictionary of French politics) was a bad bedfellow under the most favorable circumstances, he was not likely to lie comfortably with his head on the same bolster as the Bedfords. Constitutionally unable even to work for the good of the nation in hearty concert with men who desired to benefit the nation as sincerely and eagerly as himself, he found his posi-

tion intolerable in the midst of intriguers who grudged him
his premature advancement, who scouted him because he was
not of their clique, and who, if they had not dreaded him for
his insight and ability, would have despised him for his public spirit; for Shelburne, in his disinterested zeal for the advantage of the commonwealth, was a generation ahead of his
time. He was too clever to be blinded when any scheme for
plundering the Exchequer was in train among those who were
paid to protect it; and there existed no means of buying the
complicity of a great nobleman who was at the time so good
a man of business that he knew how to live in style and in
comfort on one fourth of the income which he drew from his
estates.[1] This standing incompatibility in private aims was
aggravated by differences of opinion on the gravest and most
pressing matters of state. Nothing had done so much to em-
phasize and promote the antipathy between his Majesty's
ministry in London and his Majesty's subjects in America as
the accession of the Bedfords, who came into office breathing
fire and fury against the recalcitrant colonies. Shelburne, the
pupil of Chatham and the friend of Franklin, and one of the
very few English statesmen who had taken the trouble to
make himself master of a problem as intricate and momentous
as ever statesmanship was called upon to solve, had come to the
conclusion that timely and persistent measures of conciliation
would mend the breach between the mother-country and her
dependencies, without commissioning a single additional sloop
of war, or putting another soldier on board a transport. Rigby,
on the other hand, who cursed and swore when the repeal of the
Stamp Act was alluded to in his presence, and Sandwich, who
never spoke of the Americans except as rebels and cowards,
openly proclaimed that three battalions and half a dozen frig-
ates would soon bring New York and Massachusetts to their
senses. They became ministers on an express understanding

---

[1] "Lord Shelburne," said Johnson, "told me that a man of high rank
who looks into his own affairs may have all that he ought to have, all
that can be of any use or appear with any advantage, for five thousand
pounds a year."

that the British government, in its dealings with the provincial assemblies, should thenceforward employ undisguised coercion and insist upon unconditional submission; and they grasped at this congenial policy with the greater zest because they regarded it as one of the two levers which might be so wielded as to force Shelburne out of the cabinet.

They had another weapon forged to their hands in the question of Corsica. That island had long been rather a thorn than a jewel in the crown of its mistress, Genoa, who had enough ado to preserve her own independence without trenching upon the liberty of others. The Genoese, after more than one abortive negotiation, sold their intractable little dependency to Louis the Fifteenth — a bargain which ultimately proved serious for France and fatal to Genoa, inasmuch as one incident in the transaction was that Napoleon Bonaparte was born a Frenchman. The agreement between dealer and customer was signed in May, 1768; but the delivery of the goods was a less easy matter. The islanders made a stout resistance; their cause was dignified by the respectable character, and recommended to the notice of Europe by the cosmopolitan accomplishments, of their leader; and the jealousy of England was especially excited by the prospect of her ancient enemy acquiring a foothold in the Mediterranean. The attention of London society had been attracted to Corsica by a well-timed book of travels; for Boswell, who had been sent abroad to study law, had found his way to Paoli's headquarters, and, returning home with plenty to tell, had written what is still by far the best account of the island that has ever been published. Sympathy for Corsica was as much the fashion with the English Whigs as sympathy for America became, seven years later, among the more enlightened members of the French nobility. Burke lent his eloquence to the cause. The young Duke of Devonshire, then on his travels in Italy, assisted the patriots with money, and (which in his case was a much surer proof of devotion) gave himself the trouble of collecting subscriptions for their benefit. Chatham's old admirals, who had beaten the French three-deckers up and down the Channel, were wild at the notion of a fleet

of heavy-laden troop-ships being allowed to sail unmolested
between Toulon and Ajaccio. The theory that British interests would suffer by our acquiescence in the subjugation of
Corsica—a theory which was backed by the high authority of
Frederic the Great—was warmly urged by Shelburne in the
cabinet, and would have prevailed but for the strenuous opposition of the Bedfords. Right or wrong, the party of neutrality were supported by the mercantile community, who during a generation past had been fighting the French for one
year out of every two, and were in no hurry to begin again;
and by the Jacobites, who could not persuade themselves that
it was safe to encourage people like the Corsicans, with so
very much the air of insurgents about them, unless we were
prepared to give at least the appearance of approval to the
doctrine of lawful resistance. Lord Mansfield declared with
satisfaction that the ministry was too weak, and the nation
too wise, for war; and Dr. Johnson, the most pithy exponent
of the common-sense view, whenever common-sense coincided
with Toryism, shocked his ardent disciple almost out of his
allegiance by bidding him mind his own affairs and leave the
Corsicans to theirs.[1]

---

[1] How real was the effect produced by Boswell's narrative upon the
opinion of his countrymen may be gathered from the unwilling testimony of those who regretted its influence, and thought little of its author. "Foolish as we are," wrote Lord Holland, "we cannot be so foolish as to go to war because Mr. Boswell has been in Corsica; and yet,
believe me, no better reason can be given for siding with the vile inhabitants of one of the vilest islands of the world, who are not less free than
all the rest of their neighbors, and whose island will enable the French
to do no more harm than they may do us at any time from Toulon."
Horace Walpole credited Boswell with having procured Paoli his pension of a thousand a year from the British Exchequer. Gray confessed
that the work had pleased and moved him strangely, and had shown
that "any fool may write a most valuable book by chance if he will
only tell us what he heard and saw with veracity." It is difficult to understand how Gray could have failed to recognize in the volume which
delighted him the indications of that rare faculty (whose component elements the most distinguished critics have confessed themselves unable
to analyze) which makes every composition of Boswell's readable, from

If Chatham had been in a state to make himself even occasionally felt in the councils of the government, Shelburne, in spite of every species of annoyance and humiliation, would have stood to his post for the sake of preventing the terrible mischief which was sure to follow as soon as the Bedfords were in uncontested possession; but before November, 1768, the great orator was no longer a minister. For weeks past he had never addressed the king except to renew his passionate and plaintive appeals to be relieved from the unendurable position of being called the ruler of the country when he had ceased for the time to be master of himself; and he wrote to his colleagues only for the purpose of adjuring them to assist him in persuading his Majesty to accept the resignation of a useless and afflicted servant. At length George the Third humanely yielded; Chatham was permitted to send back the privy seal; Shelburne anticipated the machinations of his enemies by a voluntary retirement; and if Lord Camden and Lord Granby had been prudent enough to follow his example, the cabinet, though it could boast no other merit, would at length have been homogeneous. Grafton became prime-minister as a matter of course; and Charles Fox, whom at that age it was not easy to scandalize, readily attached himself to a leader whose bearing and address were as full of grace as his conduct was devoid of it, and whose public errors, as the event showed, were due to infirmity of purpose rather than to perverseness of disposition.[1] In the full belief that Providence had cut him out for a placeman, the young man sat himself down behind a government which he was willing to serve as a partisan, and of which he had every intention ere long to be a member.

---

what he intended to be a grave argument on a point of law down to his most slipshod verses and his silliest letters.

[1] After a parliamentary experience of seven years, Fox, who was not given to flattery, assured the Duke of Grafton that he regarded him as "a person with whom I have always wished to agree, and with whom I should act with more pleasure in any possible situation than with any one I have been acquainted with."

If he had not been so fortunate as to find a minister in power whom considerations of filial piety allowed him to support, Fox was quite prepared to head a party of his own, and, if he failed in that, to be a party by himself. It would be useless to try his proceedings during the five years of his first Parliament by the rules of criticism which govern our judgment in the case of mature statesmen. His defects and his virtues, his appalling scrapes and his transcendent performances, as with all men of exceptional vigor under four-and-twenty, were the inevitable outcome of his temperament. Those who would call Fox conceited because, at an age when he should still have been minding his Aristotle, he thought himself the match for any opponent and the man for any office, might apply the same epithet to Nelson when he announced that, if he lived, he would be at the top of the tree; to Byron when he bearded the *Edinburgh Review;* or to Shelley when he introduced himself by letter to every philosopher of reputation whom he deemed worthy of being consulted on the prospects of human perfectibility. With health such as falls to the lot of one in ten thousand, spirits which sufficed to keep in good-humor through thirty years of opposition the most unlucky company of politicians that ever existed, and courage that did not know the meaning of fear or the sensation of responsibility, there was nobody whom Charles Fox shrank from facing, and nothing which he did not feel himself equal to accomplish. He, if any one, was a living illustration of Emerson's profound remark, that success is a constitutional trait.[1] He succeeded because all the world in con-

---

[1] "We must reckon success a constitutional trait. If Eric is in robust health, and has slept well, and is at the top of his condition, and thirty years old, at his departure from Greenland he will steer west, and his ships will reach Newfoundland. But take out Eric, and put in a stronger and bolder man, and the ships will sail six hundred, one thousand, fifteen hundred miles farther, and reach Labrador and New England. There is no chance in results. With adults, as with children, one class enter cordially into the game, and whirl with the whirling world; the others have cold hands, and remain bystanders. The first wealth is health. Sickness is poor-spirited. It must husband its resources to live.

cert could not have kept him in the background; and because, when once in the front, he played his part with a
prompt intrepidity and a commanding ease that were but the
outward symptoms of the immense reserves of energy on
which it was in his power to draw.   He went into the House
of Commons, as into the hunting-field, glowing with anticipations of enjoyment, and resolved that nothing should stop
him, and that, however often he tumbled, he would always
be among the first.   And first, or among the first, he always
was, alike in the tempestuous morning of his life and in the
splendid calm of the brief and premature evening which
closed his day of unremitting ill-fortune and almost unre-
quited labor.

But health answers its own ends, and has to spare; runs over and inun-
dates the neighborhoods and creeks of other men's necessities."

CHAPTER V.

1768–1769.

Fox's Maiden Speech.—Wilkes.—His Early Life.—The *North Briton* and the "Essay on Woman."—Persecution of Wilkes.—His Exile.—Churchill.—Return of Wilkes, and his Election for Middlesex.—Disturbances in London.—Fatal Affray between the Troops and the People.—Determination of the Court to crush Wilkes.—Conflict between the House of Commons and the Middlesex Electors.—Enthusiasm in the City on Behalf of Wilkes.—Dingley.—Riot at Brentford.—Weakness of the Civil Arm.—Colonel Luttrell.—His Cause espoused by the Foxes.—Great Debates in Parliament.—Rhetorical Successes of Charles Fox.—The King and Wilkes.—Burke on the Middlesex Election.—Proceedings during the Recess.—Recovery of Lord Chatham.—His Reconciliation with the Grenvilles and the Whigs.

WHEN Fox first spoke, and on what subject, is, and will ever remain, a doubtful matter. His eldest brother, Stephen, had entered Parliament at the same time as himself, and was quite as eager to be conspicuous, until experience taught him that public life is an element in which one of a family may flounder while another swims.[1] Various paragraphs of five

---

[1] The verdict of a clever young man before he is of an age to be cynical or jealous may safely be taken about those of his coevals with whom he lives on terms of intimacy; and two sentences from a letter of Lord Carlisle's are perhaps as much notice as the second Lord Holland can claim from a posterity which has so much else to read about. The letter refers to a fire which had destroyed Winterslow House, near Salisbury, where Stephen Fox lived after his marriage. "There is something," wrote Lord Carlisle, "so laughable in Stephen's character and conduct that, though he were broke upon the wheel, or torn between four wild horses, like Damien, the persons who live the most with him would never be grave or serious upon any calamity happening to him. If Lady Mary was much alarmed, or if the birds were really burned to death, I should be very sorry. As this is the first misfortune that ever happened to Stephen which he did not bring upon himself, all compassionate thoughts and intentions may be turned from Charles to him." Charles was just

or six lines, intercalated between the more generously reported speeches of established orators, are by some authorities
ascribed to Charles, and by some to Stephen; but the inquiry
may be left to those who hold that biography should consist
in long-flowing and discursive attempts at the solution of a
series of third-rate problems. It is probable that Charles first
opened his lips in a short discussion which arose on the question whether Sir Wilfrid Lawson, late High Sheriff of Cumberland, should be examined with regard to an election petition
presented by Humphrey Senhouse, resident in that county;
and if such is the fact, he did wisely in learning the sound of
his own voice on an occasion when nothing was expected from
him except plain sense plainly put. Whatever may have been
the topic of his maiden address, his air and manner so caught
the fancy of an artist who happened to be among the audience
that in the dearth of any more suitable material (for, to guar-
antee the secrecy of debate, paper in every shape or form was
rigorously excluded from the gallery of the House of Commons), he tore off part of his shirt, and furtively sketched a
likeness of the young declaimer on which, in after-days, those
who were fondest of him set not a little store.

No sooner did he feel himself firm in the saddle than, all
on fire to win his spurs, he plunged straight into the heart of
the most obstinate and protracted affray that has raged within
the barriers of St. Stephen's. Parliament was then in one of
the acute stages of a controversy trivial in its origin, but
most memorable in its consequences; for so strong were the
passions which it aroused, and so vital the principles which
it called in question, that during its progress our two great
political parties were moulded into the shape and consistence
which they have ever since retained. At the time when
Wilkes was unknown to any but his creditors, men took sides
in the House of Commons, and at elections, on grounds that
were almost wholly personal; the good attached themselves
to a high-minded leader, and the dishonest to an unscrupulous

---

then at the very bottom of an apparently inextricable pecuniary quag-
mire.

one; while the names of Whig and Tory had altogether lost their deeper meaning, and had ceased to be valued even as convenient badges. But long before the harassed tribune, after adventures which in duration of time and variety of incident can be paralleled only by the wanderings of Ulysses, was finally admitted to the undisputed honors of the Senate, the old party titles had once more come to signify quite as much as in the days of Somers and Harley. In the dark and evil times that closed the century, the sufferer by arbitrary power knew very well in which ranks he must look for those who were always ready to vindicate the liberty of speech, pen, and person. There is nothing exaggerated in Mr. Gladstone's declaration that the name of Wilkes, whether we choose it or not, must be enrolled among the great champions of English freedom.

That name, which was seldom out of the mouth of our great-grandfathers for three weeks together, had been stained and blotted from the first. The son of a prosperous distiller, who spent money as fast as he made it in the effort to live above his station,[1] John Wilkes, before he came of age, was persuaded by his father into a marriage which he describes as a sacrifice to Plutus rather than to Venus. His wife, a rigid Methodist, half again as old as himself, he treated shamefully. Like other famous men who have been bad husbands, he has found apologists, some of whom had recourse to the astounding theory that his domestic disagreements arose from a conscientious difference in religious views—the lady being a Dissenter, while the gentleman, though he not unfrequently honored her chapel by his attendance, made a point of never communicating except with the Church of England. His more prudent defenders fell back upon the old cant which has stood greater writers than Wilkes in stead, that the wife

---

[1] Old Mr. Israel Wilkes kept a sumptuous table, and a coach and six in which (to the detriment of the proverb that a Dissenter's second horse takes him to the parish church) he was frequently drawn to meeting, although he began life a Churchman. The explanation of the anomaly is that he had taken to wife the daughter of a rich Nonconformist, who brought him Hoxton Square as part of her dowry.

was out of sympathy with the husband, and could not rise to
the level of his higher aspirations [1]—a charge which, when
brought to the proof, comes to very little more than this, that
Mrs. Wilkes did not care to see her home made notorious as
the centre of everything which was most disreputable in London society. The revels of Medmenham Abbey were rehearsed almost nightly beneath her roof in Great George
Street; and the poor lady, after a vain attempt to make her
presence respected, was driven from her own table in order to
avoid hearing her husband bandy ribaldry and blasphemy
with Lord Sandwich and Sir Francis Dashwood. Wilkes
speedily ran through her ready money and his own, and rendered her existence so intolerable that she consented to abandon to him everything that she possessed, including her paternal estate at Aylesbury, on condition that he should covenant
to let her live in peace with her mother on a separate income
of two hundred pounds a year. Wilkes cut a dash for a while
on the strength of his position as a country gentleman. He
had already offered himself unsuccessfully as a candidate at
Berwick with professions which anticipated the relations of
Burke to his Bristol constituents;[2] and in 1757, at a cost of
seven thousand pounds, he bought himself in as member for
Aylesbury during the fag-end of George the Second's last Parliament. He became lieutenant-colonel in the Bucks Militia;
the jovial brotherhood of St. Francis noticed with pleasure
that his dinners no longer bore the marks of a somewhat too
notable housewife's frugality; and his cellar would have been
the best in the county if the proximity of his borough had

---

[1] Carlyle, in his essay on Diderot, nobly rebukes those regenerators of
mankind who, while they would banish tyranny from the globe, themselves have inflicted the most cruel of all conceivable injuries upon the
rights and feelings of an individual. "A hard saying is this, yet a true
one: Scoundrelism signifies injustice, and should be left to scoundrels."

[2] "I come here," said Wilkes, "uncorrupting, and I promise you that I
shall ever be uncorrupted. As I will never take a bribe, so I will never
offer one." But the Berwick freemen rejected this preacher of purity, although he had purchased nearly a couple of hundred of their number at
forty pounds a head.

not forbidden his vintages to mature. But the enormous expense of representing a town near which he resided sent Wilkes to the Jews, and he speedily had squandered every penny which could be raised on the acres whence his social consideration was derived. Then, in his despair, he turned once more upon the wife whom he had robbed, and, after a vain endeavor to coax from her permission to mortgage her annuity, sued out a writ of habeas corpus in order to terrify her, by the threat of exerting his conjugal rights, into a surrender of the pittance which was all that his rapacity had left her. But the Court of King's Bench, having heard the story, extended its protection to the outraged woman, and bade Wilkes molest her at his peril in a decree whose legal phraseology only slightly veils the indignation which had been aroused in Lord Mansfield by the heartlessness and ingratitude of the husband.

Such was the man whom the resentment of the king and the extravagant injustice and violence of his ministers turned into a martyr and an idol. Indeed, if Wilkes had been less of a profligate, he might have missed something of his popularity; for his ill-repute as a rake and a scoffer tempted his oppressors to employ against him weapons the use of which revolted the instinct of fair play, which is one of the few national qualities that Englishmen possess in as large measure as they take credit for it.[1] When the court, intent upon crushing

---

[1] Burke has put into the best of prose the sentiments with which nine tenths of the decent and religious people of the country heard that Wilkes was to be pursued to his destruction because he had written a loose poem and an irreverent parody for the amusement of himself and of those whom he credulously imagined to be his friends. " I will not believe what no other man living believes, that Mr. Wilkes was punished for the indecency of his publications or the impiety of his ransacked closet. If he had fallen in a common slaughter of libellers and blasphemers, I could well believe that nothing more was meant than was pretended. But when I see that for years together, full as impious and perhaps more dangerous writings to religion and virtue and order have not been punished, nor their authors discountenanced, I must consider this as a shocking and shameless pretence. I must conclude that Mr. Wilkes is the object of persecution not on account of what he has done in common

its victim, had been baffled in a method of attack which, if
arbitrary and informal, was at least bold and straightforward,
it thoughtlessly seized on what appeared to be a golden opportunity of wreaking its own grudges under the pretext of
avenging insulted piety and morality. But the good sense of
the British people, shocked by the hypocrisy of a prosecution
conducted in the interests of virtue in which Sandwich played
the conscientious informer and March the austere judge, kept
steadily in view the distinction between public actions and
private vices. With the exception of the " Essay on Woman,"
which was never meant to be published, Wilkes had written
nothing that was not sound in reason and respectful in tone.
Number forty-five of the *North Briton*, if it had appeared in
the *Morning Chronicle* as a leading article at the time when
George the Third dismissed Pitt and sent for Addington, or
at the time when William the Fourth dismissed the Whigs
and sent for Peel, would have been regarded as a very passa-
ble effusion, rather old-fashioned in the tenderness with which
it treated the susceptibilities of the monarch.[1] Grave statesmen acknowledged that Wilkes in his famous paper had rendered a solid and permanent service to the cause of constitutional government by the clear and attractive form in which
he had laid down the doctrine that ministers are responsible
for the contents of the royal speech. Every one who had read
enough history to know the danger of a bad precedent in the
hands of a masterful ruler was filled with alarm when the

---

with others who are the objects of reward, but of that in which he differs
from many of them: that he is pursued for the spirited dispositions
which are blended with his vices; for his unconquerable firmness; for
his resolute, indefatigable, strenuous resistance against oppression."

[1] " The personal character of our present sovereign makes us easy and
happy that so great a power is lodged in such hands; but the Favorite
has given too just cause for the general odium. The prerogative of the
crown is to exert the constitutional powers intrusted to it in a way not
of blind favor or partiality, but of wisdom and judgment. This is the
spirit of our constitution. The people, too, have their prerogative; and
I hope the fine words of Dryden will be engraven on our hearts—Freedom is the English subject's prerogative." Such was the criticism to
stifle and to punish which George the Third set his kingdom in a flame.

house of a politician obnoxious to authority was rifled, and his person seized, under a process of flagrant illegality, and when the independence of the legislature was undermined by the shameless coercion and corruption which were put in practice in order to wring a justification of that illegality from an unwilling Parliament. The common folk, who could not appreciate the perils which lurked beneath a general warrant, did not like to see a man ruined for writing what nine people out of ten were thinking. They could understand how terrible were the odds against a private person engaged in a combat *à outrance* with a powerful ministry which, after stooping to pilfer manuscripts and suborn printer's devils, did not scruple to employ in litigation the inexhaustible resources of the Treasury for the purpose of protecting itself and its instruments from the penalties of its tyrannical deeds and its dastardly manœuvres. They could admire the dignified silence that Wilkes opposed to the clamorous and officious treachery of his former boon companions; the cheerful and polite intrepidity with which he stood before the pistol of one court bravo or House of Commons bully after another; and the easy, if somewhat impudent, pleasantry of the demeanor which, however low his heart might sink within him, he continued to maintain amidst the wreck of his crumbling fortunes.[1]

---

[1] The spirit and humor displayed in his correspondence with the secretaries of state, and the insolent stupidity of their joint answer, almost command our sympathy for the contemptuous satisfaction with which, three months afterwards, Wilkes heard that Lord Egremont, the heavier and more respectable of the pair, "had paid the debt to nature and been gathered to the dull of ancient days." One of the two noblemen who, in the case of the "Essay on Woman," had been literary accomplices before the act, turned king's evidence against the author, and the other was gratified with the lord-lieutenancy of which Earl Temple had been deprived as a punishment for refusing to abandon an old friend in his trouble. The voluble fervor with which a lord of the Admiralty who had been intimate with Wilkes in March publicly disowned him in April was too much even for the obsequious majority of the House of Commons, and involved the time-server in an altercation which very nearly ended in a hostile meeting.

Until the wrongs of Lord Bute and his pupil had been revenged, Wilkes's life was never worth a week's purchase. Dr. Johnson spoke language more moderate than that which was current in the highest circles when he declared that if he were king he would send half a dozen footmen and have the abusive scoundrel well ducked. It would have been easy to select the half-dozen, for there were volunteers in plenty. The lord steward of the household was the first to force Wilkes into a quarrel, so conducted that the very seconds of the aggressor confessed that all which was brutal and foolish in the duel was on the side of the peer, while the chivalry of the institution was admirably sustained by the commoner. When the poor fellow crossed the Channel to enjoy a short respite in the company of his daughter, a schoolgirl whom he loved with a delicacy and devotion that did much to redeem his character, he found himself dogged about Paris by a bloodthirsty Scotch captain; and after his return to England he was challenged by a Scotch colonial governor who, after the manner of his class, was playing truant from his province of West Florida. At length a member of Parliament, a hanger-on of Bute and treasurer to the princess dowager, after diligently practising at a mark on week-days and Sundays alike, dared him to a solitary and unwitnessed encounter, ignored his undoubted right to the choice of weapons, and kept on firing till Wilkes was shot through the body. As he lay on the turf of Hyde Park, his first concern was for the safety of his opponent, who had so managed the affair that if death had been the consequence, the eloquence and skill of all the ministerial lawyers together could not have persuaded a London jury to bring in any verdict short of wilful murder.

Neither his gallantry nor his misfortunes availed in the least to soften the industrious rancor of his enemies. He was turned out of the militia. He was expelled from his seat in the Commons. His writings were ordered to be burned by the common hangman—a ceremony which very nearly terminated in the hangman and the sheriffs being burned by the spectators. In an address fulsome enough to have proceeded from the Parliament of the Restoration, the two Houses joined in

10

praying his Majesty to indict the author of the *North Brit-on*. The Peers, as if not one of them had Boccaccio on an accessible shelf in his library, were not ashamed to call for a prosecution on account of the "Essay on Woman." Wilkes, as soon as he could be moved, had been carried to Paris, partly that he might be nursed by his daughter, and partly to avoid the irritating attentions of the king's surgeons, whom the House of Commons sent almost daily to his bedside in order to watch for the moment when he would be sufficiently advanced in his convalescence to be persecuted afresh. His sufferings on the journey were such as it required all his fortitude to support;[1] and when once across the Channel, he thought it better to remain in exile than to run the gantlet of two successive criminal informations, with all the estates of the realm for his prosecutors. The public, to use his own words, had no longer any call upon him. The illegality of imprisoning a man's person and seizing his private papers under color of a nameless warrant, which left it for the discretion of the tipstaff to select his prey, had been established by Pratt, then presiding in the Common Pleas, in a series of courageous and enlightened judgments; and for Wilkes to stand his trial under the old law of libel as interpreted by Lord Mansfield, would have been to sacrifice his liberty and, feeble as he then was, his life, without any prospect of gaining a point in the interest of constitutional freedom. As long as the jury were only summoned to decide on the authorship of a paper, while the judge claimed to pronounce whether it was an innocent criticism or a seditious libel, the Court of King's Bench was nothing better than a shambles where the attorney-general pinioned the victim and the chief-justice knocked him down. Wilkes, in a letter from France of January, 1764, defined the view which he took of his obligations as a citizen in language which does him honor. "The two important decisions," he wrote, "in the Court of Common Pleas and the

---

[1] "My wound," he wrote from Dover, "has been a good deal fretted by the vile jolts through the rascally towns of Stroud, Rochester, and Chatham; but to-day I recover my spirits. I think Friday and yesterday were the most unhappy days I have known."

Guildhall have secured forever an Englishman's liberty and property. They have grown out of my firmness and the affair of the *North Briton ;* but neither are we nor our posterity concerned whether John Wilkes or John à Nokes wrote or published the *North Briton* or the 'Essay on Woman.'"

He was found guilty, and on his not appearing to receive sentence, he was outlawed for contumacy. He resided four years on the Continent, much courted by Frenchmen, whose experience of *lettres de cachet* prompted them to make common cause with the agreeable martyr of general warrants. The English colony at Paris and in the Italian cities where he sojourned received him with a courteous curiosity which the first evening passed under the same ceiling with him seldom failed to convert into an admiring intimacy. The secretaries of state had carefully instructed their agents in foreign parts to frown upon him; and his natural tendency towards hot water was kept in check by the knowledge that if he got himself into a scrape it was as much as any envoy's or consul's place was worth to stir a finger to protect him. Before, however, he left the capitals to which they were accredited, our diplomatists generally contrived to procure themselves the treat of his society; and Wilkes was not the man to break his heart because he was excluded from the doubtful joys of official hospitalities. As long as David Hume, over Baron d'Holbach's burgundy, was willing to forget that he was secretary of the British embassy, Wilkes was only too glad that his reputation saved him from a banquet at the ambassador's hotel, where "two hours of mighty grave conversation" were purchased by six more of faro.

Wilkes had a real love of letters, and had he been less ambitious he might have left something that people still would care to read; but he was not exempt from the hallucination which seduces public men to attempt the historian during their fragments of leisure, with about as reasonable a chance of success as would attend a land-surveyor who turned landscape-painter in the intervals of his business. A more hopeful task than a constitutional history of England in two quarto volumes, to be commenced and ended within two years at

a distance of a thousand miles from the State-paper Office and
the British Museum, was imposed upon him by friendship,
and accepted with an alacrity which proved that he overrated
his own industry and patience.   Churchill, among whose innumerable faults ingratitude had no place, had started from
England in the late autumn of 1764 to visit his banished patron.   He got no farther than Boulogne, where he died of a
fever in the arms of Wilkes, whom he named his literary executor, and who readily undertook the charge of editing the
collective works of one who had never written more forcibly
than when he was avenging the author of the *North Briton*, and more sincerely than when he was praising him.[1]
Wilkes inscribed his sorrow, "in the close style of the ancients," upon a sepulchral urn of alabaster, the appropriate
gift of Winckelmann, and retired to a villa overlooking Naples
with the intention of not leaving it until he had erected a
more durable monument to Churchill in the shape of a volume of annotations which he fondly expected posterity to
cherish as if they had been so many scholia on Horace from
the hands of Mæcenas or Agrippa.   But when the first grief
had passed away, he began to be aware of the unusual difficulties which beset his literary project.   The letters in which
he applied to correspondents at home for information that
could throw light upon the personal allusions in the "Duellist" and the "Candidate," where Sandwich was used worse
than Wharton had been used in the "Epistle to Lord Cob-
ham,"[2] were not likely to pass unscathed through a Post-office

---

[1]   "Friends I have made whom envy must commend,
           But not one foe whom I would wish a friend.
           What if a thousand Butes and Hollands bawl?
           One Wilkes hath made a large amends for all."

[2] The most pointed lines in the "Duellist" are, indeed, those which
compare Sandwich to Wharton, and would fain suggest a rivalry between
Churchill and Pope.

               "Nature designed him in a rage
                To be the Wharton of his age;
                But, having given all the sin,
                Forgot to put the virtues in."

over which that not too scrupulous statesman ruled supreme. There was not a man in Europe, so Wilkes feelingly complained, who wrote to a friend under the same disadvantages as himself. His more bulky manuscripts and his return proofs had little chance of escaping the searchers of the English Custom-house; and though Voltaire pressed him to accept the services of his own printers, he prudently forbore to enter on business relations with the patriarch. As the work took shape, his unerring perception of the absurd and the indecorous could not allow Wilkes to remain blind to the awkwardness of appearing before the critics of Tory magazines as the commentator on poems of which he himself was the hero. And as months, and still more as years, went on, it became evident even to the partial eye of friendship that the writer whom Cowper, and thousands besides Cowper, once esteemed the poet of the century had earned but an ephemeral reputation. Churchill was inspired by both the motives which, according to the two great Latin satirists, are the parents of satire; but his indignation did not burn with the pure flame of Juvenal, and his impecuniosity, unlike the honorable poverty of Horace, was the child of his vices. Writing to live, he did not write so that his works should live after him. Dashing off a poem a month, in order to catch a perennial stream of half-crowns from his eager and insatiable readers, he vehemently declared that to blot, prune, or correct was like the cutting-away of his own flesh.

> "Little of books, and little known of men,
>   When the mad fit comes on, I seize the pen;
>   Rough as they run, the ready thoughts set down;
>   Rough as they run, discharge them on the town."

With his quiver of darts so unpolished that they could not escape the rust, tipped with venom that long ago had lost its sting, Churchill, "the scourge of bad men, and hardly better than the very worst," easily and rapidly stormed in his lifetime the citadel of Fame, but he was not of those whose names are engraved upon its bulwarks. Wilkes had reckoned upon his friend's poetry as a vehicle for conveying the story of his own wrongs to future ages. He confidently prophesied that, with the powerful aid of Churchill, he would give signal proof of the depth of his "detestation for their common enemies." But he soon discovered his mistake. After working for a while with little heart, he ceased to work at all; and the very meagre result of his labors which has found its way into print is in no sense such as to make us wish for more.

It was not long before he hit upon a method of showing his enemies that he was alive very much more efficacious than the republication of satires which were already moribund. While, down at Midhurst, Lord Montagu's grooms and gardeners, in their temporary capacity of landed proprietors, were choosing Fox to represent them in Parliament, less tranquil scenes were being enacted in the more immediate neighborhood of London. Wilkes, who pined for home, had paid a secret visit to England as early as 1766, and had addressed to the Duke of Grafton a pathetic but far from undignified prayer for leave to remain, tranquil and obscure, in his native land. His letter produced him nothing except a verbal answer framed to be evasive; and he retired once more, to use his own playful words, from stern and inexorable Rome "to the gay, the polite Athenians." But he got little comfort out of his historical parallels; and, after digesting his misery and anger for another weary twelvemonth, he appealed from the governors to the governed in a pamphlet which, even when expurgated by the caution of the booksellers, made public facts which it would have been cheap for the king to have surrendered a half-year of the civil list to suppress. A story of grievous outrage, plainly and pointedly told as only a cultivated man of the world could tell it, reminded some and informed others that there were persons in high places who did not lack the will to revive the despotic cruelties of the Star-chamber. Widely and greedily read, the narrative which Wilkes had given to the press enlisted in his behalf the ardor and indignation of his fellow-countrymen; and an opportunity was close at hand for turning those sentiments to account. A general election was coming in the midst of profound and all but universal discontent, while the discontented in vain looked around for a question in support of which they could rally, and for a public man who dared to lead whither they cared to follow. Wilkism, as has been well remarked, was a half-unconscious protest on the part of the nation against the corruption and oppression of its oligarchical rulers, and the misery and despair which their iniquitous laws entailed.[1] The state of the popular mind, and the political circumstances of the period, were much the same as when, at the beginning of the next reign, the national disaffection and dissatisfaction found vent in that outburst of hatred which went near to overwhelm the enemies of Queen Caroline; but in 1768 the people had far more to say for their choice of a favorite than in 1820. The instinct which carried them to the side of Wilkes, as Burke truly said, was justified by reason. Here, at all events, was one who had endured much in their cause; who, if he had only been thinking of what was safest for himself, might have made his peace long ago at the expense of the common liberties of all citizens; and who now was returning, poor and alone, to try conclusions with a government which had already expended ninety thousand guineas of English money on the chivalrous enterprise of overthrowing the champion of English rights.

Wilkes soon followed his manifesto, and showed himself publicly about London in February, 1768. His first proceeding was to send his footman to Buckingham House with a letter entreating his Majesty to let by-gones be by-gones, and his next to present himself as a candidate for the city. His appearance on the hustings in the Guildhall aroused an excitement that showed itself, after old English fashion, in betting so extensive and systematic that the wagers on his success were consolidated by a ring of enterprising brokers into a recognized stock, which was freely quoted on 'Change. Wilkes, however, had been too late in a field that was already occupied by four trusted and influential aldermen; and he had attained as yet only to the first stage of a popularity which, before six

---

[1] This observation is made by Mr. John Morley in his " Historical Study of Edmund Burke "—a dissertation worthy of its subject.

months had gone, would have enabled him to carry any open
constituency in the country at a moment's notice. He was
defeated in the city; but his defeat served as an advertise-
ment; and nothing could exceed the enthusiasm created by
his speech to the livery on the last day of the contest, when
he announced that, since they would not have him as freemen
of London, he should at once ask for their confidence as freeholders of Middlesex.

Brentford was the polling-place for the shire; and the incumbent of Brentford chanced at that time to be Mr. John
Horne, a young clergyman who had formed himself on Wilkes,
and had endeavored to commend himself to his model by professions of impiety too strong even for the taste of one who
had discussed religion in the cloister of Medmenham.[1] Determined to carry by storm, since he could not conciliate, the
favor of his hero, and inspired by an uncontrollable hatred of
injustice, which in the course of his wayward life led him into
much trouble and entitled him to some public gratitude,
Horne plunged over head and ears into the turmoil of the
election; pledged all that he was worth in the world to set
the best taps in Brentford running in the cause of liberty;
and rode and walked up and down the county with the praises
and sorrows of Wilkes upon his very persuasive lips. The
ministerial candidates, who very soon discovered that the tide
was against them, were in hopes that the violence of the mob
would give the House of Commons an excuse to unseat their
opponent; but they had to do with two as consummate tacticians as ever mounted a hustings or thumbed a poll-book.
Horne kept his parishioners well in hand, and Brentford itself

---

[1] A clever letter from Horne, dated the third of January, 1766, full of sincere but very obtrusive adulation which Wilkes never really forgave, affords a striking instance of the effect produced upon a man of sense when
he sees his own least-becoming features enlarged and reflected in the mirror of flattery. The indecent levity of the passage which commences, but
unfortunately does not end, with the words "You are now entering into
a correspondence with a parson, and I am greatly apprehensive lest that
title should disgust," pleased Wilkes as little as Johnson was pleased by
Boswell's apology for being born a Scotchman.

was as quiet as if the inhabitants had been choosing an over-
seer of the poor; but on the morning of the election all the
strategical points in the neighborhood were occupied in force
by the popular party.　Before daylight six thousand weavers
from Spitalfields had taken possession of Piccadilly and the
Oxford road, and allowed no man to travel into the country
without a paper in his hat inscribed "Number 45.　Wilkes
and Liberty!"　The coaches of Sir William Proctor and Mr.
Cooke, who ten days before had as fair a chance of being
made knights of the shire by acclamation as any pair of candidates in the kingdom, never got farther west than Hyde
Park Corner, and did not return to town on their own wheels;
and it was with difficulty that the occupants of the ill-fated
vehicles contrived to smuggle themselves into Brentford, only
to find that Wilkes was polling five votes for every three of
theirs.

A single day decided the election; and when night fell,
London had its first experience of scenes with which it soon
learned to be familiar.　In the absence of the constables, who
were all at Brentford, waiting for a riot which never came,
the crowd insisted on a general illumination, and enforced its
decree by the customary process.[1]　Even prompt obedience
did not save Lord Bute's windows; and others of the Scotch
nobility who could not endure the notion of wasting candlelight on Wilkes had not a pane of glass left along the street-
front of their houses.　The younger of the two most famous
beauties that Mayfair has ever seen—the lady who was Duch-
ess-dowager of Hamilton and Duchess-presumptive of Argyll,
and whom two such marriages had made more of a Scotchwoman than if she had been born in the Canongate—stood a
siege of three hours rather than have to tell her husband, on
his return from Loch Fyne, that she had burned even half a
pint of oil to the maligner of his nation.　The Austrian ambassador, the most precise and solemn of German counts, was
pulled out of his carriage by a troop of patriots, who probably

---

[1] The glaziers, so Foote tells us, swore that a single night of the Middlesex election was worth to them all our Indian victories put together.

mistook him for a recent importation from North Britain, and who deliberately proceeded to chalk " 45 " on the sole of his shoe. The English peers were treated with more good-humor than the Scotch, but with quite as little ceremony. Those who were caught on their way from a rout were ordered to huzza for Wilkes and liberty, and then were graciously permitted to drive home with glasses broken, and the magic number scratched all over the panels of their chariots. One great duke found that it was not enough to regale the populace with beer, unless he would swallow some of it himself to the health of the new member for Middlesex. The lord mayor, who was zealous for the court, thought it necessary to muster the trainbands; but his drummers were marching about at the head of the mob, and platoons of tradesmen who ten days back had been cheering Wilkes in the Guildhall could not be trusted to fire on an assemblage which was mainly composed of their own apprentices. The foot-guards were drawn out, but did not come into collision with the people, who had carried their man, and were not in a temper for martyrdom; and by breakfast-time on the third day the tumults died out of themselves, leaving the recollection as yet of no irritating severity on the one side, and of nothing more dangerous than horse-play on the other.

The disturbances hitherto had been of the nature of an election riot—on a greater scale than other election riots, as London was larger than other cities; but worse remained to come. Though once more a member of Parliament, Wilkes was none the less an outlaw; and, to the disgrace of our system, the tribunal which had outlawed him, now that it had him in its power, could not make up its mind what to do with him. Among a population so contentious in its instincts that it will always take sides on every question, from a European war to a trumped-up claim for an estate, the number of those who espouse the cause of a litigant or a prisoner is determined, not so much by the strength of his case as by the length of time during which it has been before the public; but, forgetting this marked trait in the character of their fellow-countrymen, Lord Mansfield and his colleagues wasted two live-long months,

of which every day gave Wilkes thousands of partisans, and
every week brought with it an outbreak more formidable
than the last. He surrendered himself on the twentieth of
April; but though he had given the Solicitor of the Treasury
long notice of his intention, the judges of the King's Bench
took till the twenty-seventh before they would even decide
to refuse him bail; and meanwhile the feeling in his favor
had risen to such a point that nothing but his own personal
influence, strenuously exerted, secured a quiet court in which
to commit him. After having been drawn in triumph from
Westminster to Bishopsgate, he stole away from his admirers
in disguise, and got into jail with almost as much trouble as
Grotius or Lord Nithisdale got out of it. The prison was
blockaded all day and every day by a throng which patiently
waited for the chance of his showing himself at the window.
On the morning of the meeting of Parliament the crowd,
which had assembled in larger numbers than usual in the expectation that Wilkes would be allowed to take his seat, found
itself confronted by a detachment of the Guards, who had been
marched down to keep order, and whom the Opposition writers accused of having wilfully disturbed it. After some mutual provocation the troops fired, and five or six lives were
lost; and most unfortunate it was that the first blood shed
in a quarrel which the nation persisted in regarding as Lord
Bute's was laid to the account of some Scotch soldiers, acting
under the orders of a Scotch ensign. At length, on the eighth
of June, Lord Mansfield reversed the outlawry, in a judgment
the stately eloquence of which only partially concealed a
framework of paltry technicalities; and, after another interval of ten days, Wilkes was brought up to receive sentence
on the original charges, and condemned to pay a thousand
pounds and be imprisoned for twenty-two calendar months,
because, five years before, he had written two pieces, of which
one did him nothing but credit, and the other he had never
published.

And now George the Third had his opportunity. The moment had arrived for repairing, and even for turning to profit,
the mistake which, when he was too young to know better, he

had committed at the instigation of the worst ministers that
ever advised him. A single flourish of the royal pen at the
bottom of a pardon would have endowed him with a popularity such as no monarch since William the Third had deserved, and none since Charles the Second had enjoyed. By
promptly and chivalrously remitting a sentence which shocked
everybody except Treasury pensioners and legal pedants, he
would at once attract to himself that national confidence and
affection which had long gone a-begging for an object, and
would relegate Wilkes to an obscurity whence, but for the in-
fatuation of his enemies, he could never have emerged. The
member for Middlesex would have been powerless in a House
of Commons which cared even less than it cares now for reputations acquired outside its own walls, and least of all for
such a reputation as his. He had not the gift of speaking
well, and his taste and judgment were too sound for him to
find pleasure in speaking indifferently. He would soon have
fallen back into his natural station—"a silent senator, and
hardly supporting the eloquence of a weekly newspaper."[1]
There were those about the court who were persuaded that it
was wiser to leave Wilkes alone; but already it was no light
matter to counsel George the Third against his wishes. It
was the misfortune of his life (so Junius told him, meaning
by the phrase that it was the fault of his disposition) that he

---

[1] Junius is always excellent on the *North Briton* and the Middlesex
election. Nothing can be more just than the passage in which he explains to the king how his Majesty had been the making of Wilkes.
"There is hardly a period at which the most irregular character may not
be redeemed. The mistakes of one sex find a retreat in patriotism; those
of another in devotion. . . . The rays of the royal indignation, collected
upon him, served only to illuminate, and could not consume. Animated
by the favor of the people on one side, and heated by persecution on the
other, his views and sentiments changed with his situation. Hardly serious at first, he is now an enthusiast. Is this a contention worthy of a
king?" "You have degraded," he says elsewhere to the Duke of Grafton, "the royal dignity into a base and dishonorable competition with
Mr. Wilkes." "If George the Third," wrote Franklin in his journal,
"had had a bad private character, and John Wilkes a good one, the latter might have turned the former out of his kingdom."

never became acquainted with the language of truth until he heard it in the complaints of his people. False pride carried the day; and the king would not be satisfied without throwing down his glove to one who might have been something more than an antagonist but for vices which rendered even his antagonism degrading to the crown.

The impulse that drove Parliament into a line of conduct which was saved from being criminal only by its stupidity came direct from the highest quarter. As early as the twenty-fifth of April the king, entering betimes on his vocation of managing the manager of the House of Commons, wrote to Lord North a letter, the first sentence of which contained the germ whence sprouted that rank overgrowth of scandal and sedition which was soon to deface our history. "Though entirely confiding in your attachment to my person, as well as in your hatred of every lawless proceeding, yet I think it highly proper to apprise you that the exclusion of Mr. Wilkes appears to be very essential, and must be effected; and that I make no doubt, when you lay this affair with your usual precision before the meeting of the gentlemen of the House of Commons this evening, it will meet with the required unanimity and vigor." What were the lawless proceedings to which his Majesty referred he perhaps found it difficult to define, for the only contribution which he made towards assisting Lord North to get up his case was a suggestion that, by going back forty years, a precedent might be discovered in the expulsion of a member who had been convicted of forgery. Armed with his meagre brief, the Chancellor of the Exchequer presented himself, first to his brother-ministers, and then before one of those general councils of the party which, as a link in the delicate mechanism of parliamentary government, had not yet fallen into unmerited disuse. Both in the cabinet and in the larger conclave the voice of common-sense made itself heard. Granby, Hawke, and Conway, the three men of the most approved valor in the kingdom, confessed that they had not the courage to face the consequences of a step which would make every second Englishman a rebel at heart, and convert London into a hostile capital. They succeeded so far that it was agreed to postpone action till Parliament met in the winter. As soon as the November sitting commenced, Wilkes himself was the first to take the field. His friends presented a petition calling the attention of the Commons to the harsh and arbitrary treatment which had been inflicted upon one who now belonged to their honorable selves, and praying in respectful terms for inquiry and redress. So artfully was the document drawn, and so ably were the strings pulled from within the King's Bench Prison, that, by the time the session was a month old, Wilkes had set the two Houses by the ears. By a simple and bold stratagem he had persuaded the Commons to request the attendance of Lord Sandwich and Lord March, in order to give evidence about the intrigue by which the proof-sheets of the "Essay on Woman" had come into the hands of the authorities; and those two noblemen, who knew Wilkes quite well enough to be aware that, if he once got them at the bar, he would set a mark on them that would outlast their lifetime, in an agony of apprehension prevailed upon the Lords to reject the application. The Commons, always forward to stand upon their rights, persisted in their demand; and the relations between the Houses were already at a deadlock when an event occurred which encouraged the ministry to assume the offensive, and deprived the world of an entertainment which would have surpassed anything of the sort that had taken place since Cicero's cross-examination of Clodius.

A fortnight before the fatal tumult of the previous spring, Lord Weymouth, as secretary of state, had written a letter to the magistrates urging them freely to employ their power of calling out the military. Just at the moment when the dispute between the Lords and Commons was at its height, this letter appeared at full length in the *St. James's Chronicle*, headed by a few lines of comment, the violence of which would have been inexcusable if proceeding from any pen except that of the man for love of whom the victims of the catastrophe had met their death. Wilkes, when taxed with the authorship at the bar of the Commons, told the Speaker that there was no need to call witnesses; that he avowed the act;

that he gloried in it ; and that he had other rods in pickle for
any secretary of state who should again indite " so bloody a
scroll." Bravely indeed did he on that occasion earn the fine
compliment which was paid him in the "Vision of Judgment"
by a poet who was as little of a time-server as himself ;[1] but
the mob of sinecurists and boroughmongers, who hooted down
his advocates as a preliminary to passing sentence on his cause,
had as much chivalry in them as a pack of prairie wolves
round a wounded buffalo. Stifling discussion by clamor, and
overriding all pleas of privilege and difficulties of procedure
by enormous majorities, they beat back the defenders of justice and legality from point to point until they found themselves face to face with the issue towards which their royal
employer so many months before had ordered them to direct
their efforts.

On Friday, the third of February, 1796, Lord Barrington,
the man through whose mouth the king had thanked the soldiery for shooting half a dozen of his unarmed subjects in
terms which would not have been too cold if addressed to the
survivors of the column of Fontenoy, moved to expel Wilkes
the House, on the ground that in the course of the last
six years he had published five seditious and impious libels.
The debate was powerful, but the power lay all on one side.
The good speakers on the ministerial benches played their
parts ill, and the bad vilely ; and the impiety of Wilkes was
far outdone by the place-holders and place-hunters, who in
every third sentence invoked the most awful of names as a

---

[1]　　　　　　　　　　　" That soul below
　　Looks much like George the Third, but to my mind
　　A good deal older.　Bless me ! is he blind ? "
　　" He is what you behold him, and his doom
　　　　Depends upon his deeds," the Angel said.
　　" If you have aught to arraign in him, the tomb
　　　　Gives license to the humblest beggar's head
　　To lift itself against the loftiest."　" Some,"
　　　　Said Wilkes, " don't wait to see them laid in lead
　　For such a liberty ; and I, for one,
　　Have told them what I thought beneath the sun."

sanction for the incense which they were burning to such brazen images as Rigby and Weymouth. "I had rather," cried a learned sergeant, who looked to be a learned judge, "appear before this house as an idolater of a minister than a ridiculer of my Maker. I never will believe that a man will render to Cæsar the things that are Cæsar's if he does not render to God the things that are God's." Dr. Blackstone, who knew that the production which he censured as blasphemous had been revised by two of the ministers with whom he was going to vote, was not ashamed to announce that, when he saw religion made a jest, he thought it incumbent upon him to vindicate his Creator. George Grenville, on the other hand, packing into a weighty argument his rare stores of constitutional learning, and the then unequalled experience of his varied and industrious career, convinced every hearer who was at once disinterested and intelligent that the course on which the government had embarked was in direct violation of parliamentary precedent, natural equity, and national expediency. Grenville took special care that his speech (the best, by universal consent, that he had ever made) should stand on record word for word as it was delivered ; but it is only from hasty and disjointed notes, scribbled on the knee of a weary senator, that we can piece together even a fragment of the masterly reasoning with which Burke exposed the peril and the iniquity of overwhelming a man who had committed no single crime worthy of punishment by gathering half a dozen peccadilloes, utterly disconnected in time, circumstance, and character, into one sweeping and accumulated indictment.[1]   Lord North an-

---

[1] "Accumulative crimes are things unknown to the courts below. In those courts two bad things will not make one capital offence. This is a serving up like cooks. Some will eat of one dish, and some of another, so that there will not be a fragment left. Some will like the strong solid roast beef of the blasphemous libel. One honorable member could not bear to see Christianity abused, because it was part of the common-law of England. This is substantial roast-beef reasoning. One gentleman said he meant Mr. Wilkes's petition to be the ground of expulsion ; another, the message from the House of Lords. 'I come into this resolution,' says a fourth, 'because of his censure of the conduct of a great magistrate.'

swered an oration, which it would have taken a volume to refute, with a trite and flippant repartee, such as contents a noisy majority in a hurry to be in bed before daylight; and the expulsion of Wilkes was carried by two hundred and nineteen to a hundred and thirty-seven—Lord John Cavendish, like a good Whig, telling for the noes. And so the throng of members poured homewards along Whitehall at three in the morning, the wiser among the victors acknowledging to themselves a suspicion that Burke was not far wrong when he told them that the lateness of the hour, the candlelight, and, as he probably added, the interruptions from the pit, put him in mind of a representation of a tragicomedy performed by his Majesty's servants, by desire of several persons of distinction, for the benefit of Mr. Wilkes, and at the expense of the Constitution.

The piece was fated to be run till both the author and the company were heartily tired of it. Triumphant in Parliament, the king had forgotten that he still had the country to reckon with. "Nothing," he wrote to Lord North, with an optimism as royal as his grammar, "could be more honorable for government than the conclusion of the debate, and promises a very proper end of this irksome affair this day." And

---

'In times of danger,' says a fifth, 'I am afraid of doing anything that will shake the government.' These charges are all brought together to form an accumulated offence which may extend to the expulsion of every other member of this House. The law, as it is now laid down, is that any member who, at any time, has been guilty of writing a libel, will never be free from punishment. Is any man, when he takes up his pen, certain that the day may not come when he may wish to be a member of Parliament? This, sir, will put a last hand to the liberty of the press." When it came to his turn to justify a precedent under which every prime-minister of the present century who has written anything more pointed than a queen's speech might have been excluded from Parliament, Lord North had nothing to say except that Burke, like the shepherd-boy in the fable, was always terrifying himself where there was no danger. Lord Temple, in a letter to Chatham, fully confirms Burke's description of the debate. "Every man," he says, "dwelt on the crime he most detested, and disapproved the punishment for the rest. The various flowers of their eloquence composed a most delightful nosegay."

11

yet signs were abroad which might well have shaken his confidence. Mr. Cooke, the ministerial member for Middlesex,
had only survived to enjoy his unpopularity for a few months.
The freeholders invited Wilkes to select his own colleague.
He named Sergeant Glynn, his trusty counsel, who, throughout the persecution of the press which raged in the first ten
years of George the Third maintained the independence of
the bar as gallantly as did Erskine during the judicial Reign
of Terror which disgraced the anti-Jacobin reaction; and the
recommendation secured the seat for Glynn as certainly as if
Middlesex had been a Cornish borough of which his client
was lord of the manor. In the following January Wilkes
himself was chosen alderman for the ward of Farringdon
Without, and he thenceforward fought his battles beneath
the shield of the redoubted municipality which has always
been the stronghold of liberty while liberty was yet in danger. As soon as what had happened at Westminster on the
morning of the fourth of February was known east of Temple
Bar, the City gathered itself together for an obstinate duel
with the Commons, as resolutely and briskly as ever in the
seventeenth century it made ready to resist the Stuarts. The
fiery cross at once went round all the haunts of business, and
that very evening a great gathering of the county voters was
collected in the Mile End Assembly-rooms. From that time
onward it became impossible for the bitterest enemies of
Wilkes even to pretend to regard him as a vulgar and un-
friended demagogue. The shrewdest, the most respected,
and (what the court relished least) the wealthiest men that
ever drew a bill or consigned a cargo contended for the honor
of proposing or seconding the tribune of the people. The
zeal of the meeting rose into positive enthusiasm when a City
magnate of the first order, himself a member of Parliament,
bidding farewell to the traditional politics of his family, announced that he would assert the right of constituents to the
choice of their representatives as long as he had a shilling to
contribute or a leg on which to hop to Brentford. There
was no talk of a government candidate; but, in order to guard
against a surprise, more than two thousand respectable free-

holders flocked to the hustings at their own charges, and stood in pouring rain till their favorite was again member for Middlesex, without having been called upon to write a line, to speak a sentence, or to spend a farthing.

The election took place on the sixteenth of February; and on the seventeenth Lord Strange, the most presentable adherent of the ministry (for he was a placeman who declined to draw his salary), moved that John Wilkes, having been expelled the House, was incapable of serving in Parliament. The motion was passed by two hundred and thirty-five votes to eighty-nine; and during the progress of the debate a hint was thrown out from the Treasury bench that any gentleman who had the courage to stand for Middlesex, and who could obtain a single score of supporters, should be declared by a resolution of the House of Commons to be a duly elected knight of the shire. The government electioneering agents accordingly searched the clubs for a gentleman who could poll twenty freeholders; but the only candidate whom they persuaded to come forward fulfilled neither of their conditions. The hope of a seat which, if not of roses, would at all events be a cheap one, proved sufficiently potent to attract one Dingley, an ex-private of the Guards, who had made some money by mechanical inventions which in themselves would have failed to secure him the immortality that he owes to one contemptuous epithet from the profuse repertory of Junius.[1] Wilkes was unanimously re-elected. His opponent showed himself as near the front of the hustings as he could penetrate; but he got no one to nominate him, and retired into private life, if we are to believe Junius, with a broken heart, and certainly with a broken head. As soon as the Commons met on the following afternoon, Rigby moved to annul the election.

---

[1] "Even the miserable Dingley," says Junius to the Duke of Grafton, "could not escape the misfortune of your Grace's protection." The most prominent among the evils that befell Dingley on account of his meddling with politics was his having been knocked down by an attorney, which appears to have impressed the public imagination as an inversion of the natural order of things. He died shortly after, of Grafton's friendship, as Junius would have it, but more probably from natural causes.

Burke told his brother-members that Wilkes had grown great by their folly, parodying for his purpose a fine passage from an old Roman play which eighteen centuries before had been quoted againt Pompey;[1] and Mr. Thomas Townshend, whose name one of the happiest couplets in Goldsmith's "Retaliation" has in all human probability linked with Burke's for at least as many centuries to come, reminded his hearers that a heavy account would some day be exacted from them if they continued to postpone all useful legislation for the sake of a frivolous and interminable squabble. But the House had gone too far to retrace its steps; and the leaders of the Opposition allowed the election to be declared null and void without putting friend or foe to the trouble of a division.

The temper of the popular party was just then exasperated by an untoward circumstance which had attended the recent election for Middlesex, in which Sergeant Glynn had been opposed to Sir William Proctor. Sir William had hired a gang of Irish chairmen, who would gladly have plied their cudgels gratis on either side in any quarrel; and at two in the afternoon, while the polling was going on in perfect tranquillity, and when Glynn was already well to the front, these fellows were suddenly turned loose upon the scene. Acting with the vigor and cohesion which they had learned in a hundred faction fights, they overset the tables, seized the books, knocked down everybody who had not Proctor's colors in his hat, frightened the sheriffs into a public-house, and, to use the expression of a bystander, sent the whole county of Middlesex flying before them. One poor fellow, the son of a gentleman in the neighborhood, who had been quietly watching the voters as they came and went, died beneath the bludgeon of a notorious ruffian whose most frequent alias was Macquirk. The murderer was brought to trial and condemned to be hanged; but his Majesty was advised to remit the sentence

---

[1] " Nostra *stultitia* tu es Magnus." The original line, and the use made of it by a Roman actor who was playing to the back benches over the heads of fifteen rows of disgusted knights and senators, may be read in one of the earliest letters to Atticus.

on grounds which would not have induced a jury of South
African Boers to acquit a Dutchman charged with killing a
Hottentot.   Contrasting this sinister clemency with the military execution which had lately been done upon a parcel of
shop-boys for throwing a few handfuls of mud and calling a
Scotch sergeant Sawney, the people came to the conclusion
that, in the view of their rulers, Wilkites might be butchered
with impunity.   But vengeance, which spared the humble instrument, overtook the statesman who by his culpable and interested lenity had made the crime his own; for it was the
pardon of Macquirk that first drew down upon the Duke of
Grafton the enmity of that writer who has handled his fame
after such a fashion that it would be well for him if he had
no fame at all.   Junius spoke but the sentiments of all law-
loving and law-abiding members of the community when he
asked the prime-minister how it happened that in *his* hands
even the mercy of the prerogative was cruelty and oppression
to the subject.[1]

---

[1] Those who would enjoy Junius at his best should study the earlier
letters, before his head was turned and his style debased, and while he
still confined himself to questions which were within his knowledge and
his abilities. Until he undertook to outwrite Burke and argue points of
law with Mansfield, his productions have all the merit of excellent lead-
ing-articles thrown into a personal, and therefore a more effective, form.
It is hardly to be expected that he should still be read by people who
have more than enough to do in keeping themselves conversant with the
politics of their own day; but it is easy to imagine the delight with
which a common-councilman who had subscribed his fifty pounds to the
Society of the Bill of Rights, and had run for his life at Brentford, would
find such writing as this on his breakfast-table of a morning:

"As long as the trial of this chairman was depending, it was natural
enough that government should give him every possible encouragement
and support. The service for which he was hired, and the spirit with
which he performed it, made common cause between your Grace and
him. The minister who by secret corruption invades the freedom of election, and the ruffian who by open violence destroys that freedom, are embarked in the same bottom. They have the same interests, and naturally
feel for each other. . . . But when this unhappy man had been solemnly tried, convicted, and condemned; when it appeared that he had
been frequently employed in the same service, and that no excuse for him

The antagonism between the people and their governors was the more alarming because in case of need the authorities could only keep the peace by methods which made matters worse than if the peace had been left to keep itself. The mild but irresistible weight of the law was not then represented by a body of disciplined policemen whom every respectable citizen, however angry politics might for the moment have made him, had always been accustomed to regard as his servants and protectors. The constables, untrained to work in concert, indignant at having to serve outside their own parish, and much more afraid of a rioter's fist than of a magistrate's reprimand, were of no value whatever at an emergency; and behind the constables there was nothing but the bullets and bayonets of the soldiery. An unpopular candidate who did not wish to commence his relations with his constituents by using his influence with the War-office to get them shot had nothing for it but to provide himself with a body-guard strong enough to procure him a hearing at the nomination, and to bring his voters safe and sound into the booths.

In order to carry out their scheme of usurping the representation of Middlesex, the ministers had first to look round for a champion not afraid of brickbats, and qualified by his antecedents to take the leading part in a struggle which was fast assuming the character of a private war. They discovered, or thought that they had discovered, the man they wanted in Henry Luttrell, a colonel of horse, who had the character of being somewhat too ready with his sword, and who, in the

could be drawn either from the innocence of his former life or the simplicity of his character, was it not hazarding too much to interpose the prerogative between this felon and the justice of his country? You ought to have known that an example of this sort was never so necessary as at present; and certainly you must have known that the lot could not have fallen on a more guilty object. What system of government is this? You are perpetually complaining of the riotous disposition of the lower class of people; yet when the laws have given you the means of making an example, in every sense unexceptionable and by far the most likely to overawe the multitude, you pardon the offence, and are not ashamed to give the sanction of government to the riots you complain of, and even to future murders."

dark days of Irish misery and disaffection which closed the
century, gave memorable proof that if he could have had his
will he would have made very short work of the Middlesex
electors and their privileges. He left his comfortable Cornish
borough with its eleven voters, of whom ten were officers in
the revenue, on an understanding that as soon as was decent he should be appointed to one of the best-paid posts on
the staff; and the populace firmly believed that he was to be
rewarded for his heroism by the hand of a daughter of Lord
Bute, to whose interests his father had been long and faithfully attached. A political retainer of the most hated among
Scotchmen, and the member of a family which every Irish
Catholic regarded much as a Christian in the Middle Ages
would regard a reputed descendant of Judas,[1] he destroyed all
the chance that he ever possessed of standing well in English
eyes by accepting the support of Lord Holland, whose house,
half-way between Brentford and the city, formed a convenient headquarters for electioneering. Supremely indifferent
to his threefold unpopularity, Luttrell published an advertise-
ment calling upon all who accounted themselves gentlemen
to join him in giving a lesson to the mob; but when the day
came, the dozen or two of cavaliers who responded to his appeal so little liked the aspect of the streets that they were
much relieved when their commander let them and their
horses out through a breach in his garden wall, and conducted them to Brentford along a network of back lanes, leaving
untasted a splendid breakfast which awaited them at Holland
House. He might have spared his precautions as well as his
vaunts. Though very different people to deal with from the
Connaught potato-farmers whom one day he was to hand over

---

[1] Henry Luttrell, grandfather of the candidate for Middlesex, after dis-
gracing the Irish Catholic party by his excesses, deserted it when Limer-
ick fell, and was richly rewarded at the expense of the people whom he
had betrayed, and of a brother who had scorned to join him in his treachery. There never was a more barefaced instance of that venal defection
which his countrymen have at all times found it harder to forgive than
the most flagrant acts of oppression prompted by consistent hostility to
their cause.

by droves to the mercies of the press-gang, or from the prisoner whose face he cut open with a riding-whip when the poor creature was already under the shadow of the gallows, the freeholders of Middlesex, so far from being bloodthirsty, had no inclination even to be turbulent. Certain that, unless the Constitution ceased to exist, they must sooner or later get their rights, they listened with good-humor while Stephen Fox expounded the claims of Luttrell as a fit and proper candidate for their suffrages, and then repaired to the poll and gave Wilkes a majority of nearly four to one.[1]

The election was over on Thursday, the thirteenth of April, and on Friday it was reversed by the House of Commons. Charles Fox, who had been canvassing and haranguing for Luttrell all over the county till his head was full of arguments which he was burning to try upon Parliament, got his

---

[1] The frequency of riots at this period, and the large space allotted to them by its historians, must be explained by the utter inefficiency of the machinery for preserving order—a consideration which only aggravates the fault of statesmen who so unjustly and gratuitously provoked the people. Disturbances were more rife, and the civil arm was weaker, in 1768 than at any period between the year of Sacheverell and the year of Lord George Gordon. The sheriffs, when giving evidence about Glynn's election, informed the House of Commons that as soon as the constables noticed some dangerous-looking people about, they all disappeared into the ale-houses and could not be induced to emerge until the fighting was over. A desperate and murderous battle with fire-arms, arising out of a trade dispute, was maintained in the east end of London from eight in the evening till five in the morning without a magistrate daring to show himself. Benjamin Franklin, the most trustworthy of observers, was then living in Craven Street, and has left some record of what he witnessed. Sawyers destroying saw-mills; coal-heavers pulling down the houses of coal-dealers; sailors on strike unrigging all the outward-bound merchantmen, and closing the port of London till their pay was raised; the very tailors marching down in their thousands to overawe Parliament—such was the aspect which the British capital presented to the decent and demure Philadelphian. "While I am writing," he says, on the fourteenth of May, "a great mob of coal-porters fills the street, carrying a wretch of their business upon poles to be ducked, for working at the old wages." In these days, before such a procession had got a hundred yards down the Strand, the ringleaders would be already on their way to Bow Street.

opportunity in a debate which was short, and but for him
would have been tame, inasmuch as the conclusion was fore-
gone, and the chief orators were saving themselves for the
morrow. A Saturday sitting seemed a portentous novelty in
those idle and pleasant times; but it was understood that the
government had a proposal to make of such gravity that, to
use Rigby's words, it was worth while for the merchants once
in a way to give up their villas, and the lawyers their fees.
There was little work done on that Saturday in London
either by high or low. The approaches to Westminster were
thronged far and near, and the House was crammed for thirteen consecutive hours by a crowd of eager speakers and
hearers, transported beyond themselves by emotions the trace
of which can easily be discerned beneath the conventional
phraseology of the reporter. Mr. George Onslow, amidst
a scene such as his father never witnessed during the three-
and-thirty years of his speakership, or witnessed only when
Walpole fell, rose from the Treasury bench to move that
Henry Lawes Luttrell ought to have been returned a knight
of the shire, to serve in the present Parliament for the county
of Middlesex. Alderman Beckford, expressing, as was believed, the mind of Chatham in his own headlong and fantastic language, denounced what he characterized as the rank
Tory doctrine of the ministry with an animation which called
down upon him a furious rebuke from Onslow. Onslow, in
his turn, brought George Grenville to his feet, who, waxing
eloquent in his old age, vindicated the law of the land as
against the will of the House with such vehemence that,
when he sat down, he spat blood. Mr. Ralph Payne, a
youthful rhetorician of the study, who was detected in the
act of pulling his speech out of his pocket, received from an
assembly every third member of which was panting to give
vent to the passions of the hour in the words of the moment
such a handling that he was glad to exchange his senatorial
ambition for the peaceful dignity of a colonial governorship,
and to seek in Antigua an atmosphere more endurable than
that of the House of Commons during one of its periodical
tornadoes. Another aspirant obtained, but did not merit, a

better fate. Charles Fox won the attention of all, and the admiration of most, by a fluency and a fire which promised much better things; but, in spite of his sword and his laced coat, he was still a schoolboy at heart, and his speech owed its immediate success to an impertinence that accorded only too well with the prejudices of the hot-brained partisans whom he was addressing, who wanted nothing more refined or accurate than the assurance that the contest lay between all that was respectable on the one side, and the lowest scum of Billingsgate and Wapping on the other.[1] Burke, who complimented the young aristocrat of yesterday with the honor of a rebuke, was hailed by one of those volleys of affected merriment with which the House of Commons, in its worst fits, greets an unpalatable statement that cannot be confuted from a man too eminent to be refused the semblance of a hearing. The insolent impatience, however, which harassed the undaunted and unwearied guardian of constitutional freedom throughout the whole course of a noble and unanswerable oration, could not stifle the voice of one who justly boasted that, when he was pleading the cause of the people, he feared the laugh of no man. At three in the morning of Sunday Luttrell was declared duly elected by a hundred and ninety-seven votes to a hundred and forty-three—a diminution in the

---

[1] "Stephen Fox," wrote Horace Walpole, "indecently and indiscreetly said, 'Wilkes had been chosen by the scum of the earth'—an expression after retorted on his family, his grandfather's birth being of the lowest obscurity. Charles Fox, with infinite superiority of parts, was not inferior to his brother in insolence." Henry Cavendish, who was present, which Walpole was not, gives Charles the credit of a piece of vituperation which certainly was not worth the claiming.

Stephen Fox's anxiety about the state of public affairs amused his acquaintances, and the memory of it continued to amuse them when he was no longer among the living. Lord Carlisle, writing from Castle Howard in 1777, says, "We watch with eager expectation for American news. We are very ministerial on this side of the country, but yet we want something to keep up our spirits. I protest I am like Stephen Fox, who used to write in the newspapers and sign himself 'A stander-by who has his fears.'"

majority, and a still more ominous increase in the minority, which proved that Burke had not braved his audience,
or Grenville shortened his life, for nothing; and which de-
terred Lord North from offering any resistance to a proposal that the electors of Middlesex should be allowed fourteen days within which they might petition against a decree
that reduced them to a political level with Normandy peasants.

They petitioned accordingly; and the hearing of their case
was fixed for the eighth of May. The House, as usual, commenced public business at two in the afternoon, in spite of
the remonstrances of an elderly member who entreated his
colleagues, as they valued their health, to return to the early
hours of their ancestors, little foreseeing that two in the afternoon would come to be the time for beginning what, in
compliance with the perverted habits of his descendants, is
denominated a morning sitting. Although Parliament was
on the eve of breaking up for the summer, the attendance
was the largest that had been known throughout that stirring
session. The ministers had been careful to bring back from
Paris those of their men who had anticipated the recess, and
to summon others from the North who hitherto had not
thought it worth while to leave their country-houses; and it
was an allusion which Burke made in the course of the evening to the industry of the Treasury officials that first rendered
the term "whipping in" classical. Never, to all appearance,
had there been a less favorable occasion for a very young
man who had no pretence to the stores of special knowledge
which are presumed to lurk beneath the folds of the long
robe. The debate was remembered in the Inns of Court as
the greatest field night which the profession had enjoyed for
a generation. The discussion was opened by paid advocates;
though John Lee, the counsel for the petitioners, a distinguished lawyer whom it is on record that the court tried in
vain to buy, was quite the man to have done so congenial a
piece of work for nothing; while Sergeant Whitaker, who
led on the other side, would gladly have returned his fee ten
times over to have been out of the case, when he found that

his activity against Wilkes had suggested him as a victim for the merciless mimicry of Foote.[1]

After the wigs and gowns had played their part, and the House was left to make up its mind by the aid of its own lights, few members ventured to speak, and still fewer to speak at length, except those who were learned by title, or those whose learning was so extensive and so profound that a seat on the woolsack would have added little to the authority with which they discoursed on all that related to the Constitution.   Dr. Blackstone, who had deserted the studies which have given him a fame worth twenty judgeships for the hot and sordid arena of party strife, where the richer prizes of his calling could alone be won, delivered it as his "firm and unbiassed opinion" that Mr. Wilkes was disqualified by common-law from sitting in Parliament.   He was silenced, to the delight of the profane, by a layman who, on such a point, was every whit as good a lawyer as himself; for George Grenville triumphantly cited the passage in the first and ungarbled edition of the "Commentaries" where the doctor had laid down, with the clearness which is his distin-

---

[1] Foote, who had failed as an actor in plays written by others, made a great and continuous success over a period of thirty years, from 1747 onwards, by a series of performances something between the comedies of Colman and the "At Homes" of Mathews. The central attraction in each of Foote's pieces consisted in one or more characters, which were understood to be modelled from living notabilities, whose gait, dress, tone, and gesture were reproduced with Aristophanic fidelity. After carrying his imitations through the whole gamut of respectability from Whitefield down to Dr. Dodd, Foote at length bethought himself of bringing on the stage a vulgar and dissolute fine lady whom the town should recognize as the Duchess of Kingston. That infamous virago had recourse to a nameless and horrible retaliation, against which poor Foote's holiday weapons were powerless; and he died a broken man in 1777, leaving a collection of dramas, flimsy, but not worthless, as literature, and highly valuable as a picture-gallery of manners. Whitaker was taken off in the "Lame Lover" as Sergeant Circuit; an amusing personage, but not nearly so amusing as the Lame Lover himself.

Fox, though he had suffered at his hands, thought Foote "excellent" both as a writer and an actor; and in private society, with every intention to ignore his presence, he had, like others, found him irresistible.

guishing merit, that every British subject, unless he came within certain definite categories of disqualification which did not include Wilkes, was eligible of common right.   Thurlow, soon to be solicitor-general, spoke temperately for the ministers; and Sir Fletcher Norton, who had been attorney-general until he got something better, forgetting, or more probably not caring, that the whole political and legal world knew him as the author of the celebrated apothegm that a judge who did his duty would regard a resolution of the House of Commons no more than the bluster of so many drunken porters, had now the face to maintain that such a resolution possessed the binding force of the ancient and immemorial traditions and principles on which are founded the obligation of a contract and the ownership of an estate.   Wedderburn, who had entered Parliament as one of Bute's henchmen, and who still sat for a ministerial borough, declared himself for the Middlesex electors with the elegant melancholy of a patriot who was sacrificing everything to his conscience, and the consummate art of a schemer intent upon nothing but his interests.   Those honorable and learned members who went the Northern circuit, and who knew Wedderburn's professional history, heard with surprise that one who had thought nothing of violating, to his own pecuniary profit, the unwritten custom of the bar was prepared to make himself a martyr for the sacredness of the common - law; [1] but no such unworthy scepticism troubled the Whig country gentlemen, who delivered themselves up, without suspicion or reserve, to the pleasure of applauding the eloquence and extolling the integrity of a jurist in whom they already recognized a second Somers.   Wedderburn had outdone Grenville, and Burke far outdid Wedderburn.   In a magnificent declamation, woven close with new thoughts and old facts, he urged the House to reflect upon the perils that would ensue if members were to be expelled and nominated by the majority of the day.

---

[1] Lord Campbell, in chapter clxiv. of his " Lives of the Chancellors," narrates, in a manner nothing short of thrilling, how Wedderburn, by practice sharper than sharp, got hold of the business of an attorney-general who had left circuit.

Was that assembly, he asked, a calm sanctuary of justice into which no passion or corruption entered? Or was it rather the theatre and stage on which the several factions had fought their battles, and where they had in turn exercised on each other their detestable vengeance? The ministers, in their eagerness to justify a bad deed by bad examples, had dug up the shields and helmets which showed that the House had once been the field of blood, and had gathered together an arsenal of fatal precedents from the evil years of the civil wars, when the majority expelled the minority, and was itself expelled in turn; when the Lower House was reduced to forty-six members, and the Upper House abolished by a curt and hasty resolution of the Commons; when the king was beheaded, and the standing army brought in to overawe Parliament, and injustice was heaped upon injustice, as if man would scale heaven.

Wedderburn and Burke were still unanswered when Charles Fox rose; but when he resumed his seat, the supporters of the ministers, and most of their opponents, pronounced that the lawyer and the statesman had both met their match. How commanding must have been the manner of the young speaker, how prompt his ideas, and how apt and forcible the language in which he clothed them, may be estimated by comparing the effect of his rhetoric upon those who were present, and the fame of it among those who heard it at second-hand, with the scanty morsels of his argument which have survived the evening on which it was delivered. The two or three sentences which oblivion, so kind to him as long as he needed her services, has permitted to stand in judgment against him have a flavor of boyishness about them for which nothing could have compensated except rare and premature excellence in the outward accomplishments of the orator. He had still enough of the undergraduate in him to imagine that he was speaking like a statesman when he informed the House that he should adore Colonel Luttrell to the last day of his life for his noble action, and that he would not take the will of the people from a few demagogues, any more than he would take the will of God Almighty from a few priests. But what he had to say he said in such a manner that he came unscathed out of a controversy on an intricate point of law with lawyers who were straining every nerve to make or sustain a professional reputation of the very first order. Horace Walpole, who had a grudge against Lord Holland and all that belonged to him, bears reluctant testimony to the impression produced upon the old stagers of the Commons by the appearance in their midst of one who was born a debater as Bonaparte was born a general. Mr. Henry Cavendish, the volunteer reporter of an otherwise almost unreported Parliament, was betrayed into breaking the rule of abstinence from personal criticism which is among the canons of his art, and, though himself a violent partisan of Wilkes, could not forbear from noticing that " Mr. Charles Fox spoke very well." If such was the involuntary tribute which the young man's deserts exacted from those who loved neither his cause nor his family, it is easy to conceive the satisfaction with which the fondest of parents and the most cynical of politicians learned that his son had already made good a place in the front rank of parliamentary combat by the ability that he had displayed against the most formidable exponents of doctrines which in the vocabulary of Holland House were designated as the cant of patriotism. In a letter where a father's pride shows not ungracefully through the measured and business-like phraseology of a veteran of St. Stephen's, Lord Holland refers to the discussion of the eighth of May, " in which," he says, " I am told, and I willingly believe it, that Charles Fox spoke extremely well. It was all offhand, all argumentative, in reply to Mr. Burke and Mr. Wedderburn, and excessively well indeed. I hear it spoke of by everybody as a most extraordinary thing, and I am, you see, not a little pleased with it. My son Ste. spoke too, and (as they say he always does) very short and to the purpose. They neither of them aim at oratory, make apologies, or speak of themselves, but go directly to the purpose; so I do not doubt they will continue speakers. But I am told Charles can never make a better speech than he did on Monday." [1]

---

[1] The speech which gave such delight to Lord Holland is nowhere

At two in the morning on Tuesday Luttrell's election was confirmed by two hundred and twenty-one votes to a hundred and fifty-two, and later in the same day the king prorogued Parliament. He concluded his speech by laying a solemn injunction upon the Peers and Commoners to exert themselves, each in their several counties, for the maintenance of that public peace which never needed to have been broken if he had been content to rule as his grandsire, and his grandsire's prudent and cool-headed adviser, had ruled before him. "*Quieta non movere*," said Horace Walpole, " was my father's motto, and he never found it a silly one." It was useless for the nation to pray that it might be godly and quietly governed, so long as it had ministers whose characters were such that the highest tribute they could pay to religion was to keep outside the church doors, except on the day when they took the sacrament in order to qualify for their offices, and so long as it was ruled by a sovereign who turned his realm upside-down because he could not be convinced that four years of exile were a sufficient punishment for a political lecture which George the First would have passed over with indifference, and George the Second would have accepted as deserved.[1] But the third

mentioned without some indication of the surprise that was excited by its extraordinary merit. Sir Charles Bunbury, who had been selected from among many rivals for the short-lived honor of being married to Lady Sarah Lennox, was at Paris when he received his report of what at that time he might still be supposed to view as a family triumph. " Mr. Charles Fox," writes his correspondent, " who, I suppose, was your schoolfellow, and who is but twenty, made a great figure in the debate last night upon the petition of the Middlesex freeholders. He spoke with great spirit, in very parliamentary language, and entered very deeply into the question on constitutional principles."

[1] When Parliament met in the winter of 1756, a mock king's speech was hawked about the streets. The ministers urged that the authors should be unearthed and punished, but George the Second expressed a hope that the penalty would be of the mildest, as he had read both speeches, and, so far as he could understand them, thought the spurious one the better of the two. The lords were foolish enough to press the matter, and the culprit was condemned to fine and imprisonment; but the king waited for his opportunity, and took care that, after a due interval, the fine should be remitted and the imprisonment curtailed.

George would not be satisfied without dragging his critic to the light of day, and forcing him in self-defence to assume the attitude of a rival whom a good half of his subjects preferred to himself. He could not stir abroad without meeting some evidence of his unpopularity, which he was too much of a man to shrink from facing; and the partisans of his adversary came to seek him under his very roof, sometimes in the shape of an unruly mob, and sometimes of grave and authoritative deputations, armed with a respectful but resolute protest against a policy which the petitioners, as by custom bound, attributed to his ministers, but which he and they well knew to be his own. When a counter-deputation was organized, and a hundred or so of City merchants, or people who passed for such, set forth to St. James's for the purpose of presenting a loyal address, the native Londoners, indignant at the notion of Jews and Dutchmen presuming to thank the king for having hindered Englishmen from exercising their political rights, shut the gates of Temple Bar, stopped the coaches, and so maltreated their occupants that out of the whole cavalcade hardly a dozen reached their destination, after a delay which scandalized the Presence-chamber, and in such a pickle as disturbed it out of its proprieties. The lord steward himself went down into the crowd, and, when his white staff was broken, betook himself to his hands, which in his case were noted weapons, and infused such spirit into the guard that fifteen of the rioters were arrested; but the grand-jury of Middlesex threw out the bills, and secured impunity for the most outrageous insult that any of our monarchs had endured since James the Second was hustled by the Kentish fishermen.[1]

---

[1] The ballad-makers celebrated the events of the day in an Amœbean poem entitled "A Dialogue at St. James's Gate between a Lord and the Mob." The case is very fairly put on both sides. The Mob says,

"Let elections be free, and whoever we choose,
His seat in the House you should never refuse;
And if great men were honest, the poor would be quiet;
So yourselves you may thank for this bustle and riot."

12

While George the Third, if he had listened to timid coun-
sellors, would have remained a prisoner in his own palace,
Wilkes, whether in jail or out of it, inspired a loyalty, and exerted a power which any monarch might have envied. Junius,
who, when he was dealing with dukes and commanders-in-
chief, thought a single courteous sentence a waste of ink, deluged him with private letters of advice as reverential, and, it
must be allowed, as tedious, as courtly bishop ever penned for
the edification of royal pupil. He had his flatterers and his
champions; his volunteer grand-cellarers and stewards of the
household; his inspired scribes in every newspaper, and his
laureates on every curbstone. His revenues for the time being, if not princely according to English ideas, would have
been despised by few indeed among the minor potentates who
then figured in the *Almanach de Gotha.* The Whig statesmen had for some years past subscribed among themselves to
provide him with an income—a more judicious use of their
party fund than if they had spent the same amount twenty

The Peer replies,

"You've insulted the Crown, and for these honest cits,
You've scared the poor gentlemen out of their wits.
When they mustered on 'Change they were decent and clean,
But are now so bedaubed they're not fit to be seen.
If such tumults as these were in France or in Spain,
Five hundred by this time had surely been slain:
But the king loves you all with such ardent affection
He'd lay down his life for the people's protection."

Whether or not the king loved, or could be expected to love, his people at that precise moment, he certainly was not afraid of them. His coolness then, and on a subsequent occasion when he was hooted on his way
to the House of Lords, roused the admiration even of those who themselves were most indifferent to the hostility of the populace. "He carried
himself so," wrote Lord Holland, "that it was hard to know whether he
was concerned or not. A lord who is near him told me that after the
great riot at St. James's, or rather in the midst of it, you could not find
out, either in his countenance or his conversation, that everything was
not quiet as usual." Lord Holland, who never could conceive of people
acting either wisely or foolishly from any motive but one, was absurd
enough to believe that the mob had been hired by French gold.

times over in the purchase of rotten boroughs. When these
secret supplies failed to keep pace with the manifold demands
of his public position and his somewhat generous notions of
personal comfort, a number of baronets, aldermen, and members of the House of Commons formed themselves into an association with a title which recalled the most significant historical reminiscences, and a political programme ambitious
enough to keep the liberalism of the country busily employed
for fifty years to come. But the Society for Supporting the
Bill of Rights found that it had quite as much as it could do
in supporting Wilkes; and the contributions which were to
have been devoted to impeaching ministers and restoring annual parliaments soon went in paying his outstanding debts,
and enabling him to drink claret and keep a French valet.
In the course of eighteen months, through this agency alone,
at least as many thousand pounds had been raised and dis-
bursed in his behalf.[1] He was constantly receiving less splen-

---

[1] The Society for the Bill of Rights drained a very wide area of patriotic munificence. Newcastle-on-Tyne subscribed handsomely. The Assembly of South Carolina, in a very full house, voted as much of their
paper currency as would purchase bills of exchange for fifteen hundred
pounds sterling. A great deal of money came to Wilkes direct. A nobleman presented him with three hundred pounds as late as 1778. Two
ladies of rank gave him a hundred pounds apiece; and a party of gentlemen who used a tavern near Covent Garden requested him to accept
a purse of twenty guineas and a hamper of their favorite liquor.
Nothing could exceed the adoration of which Wilkes long continued
to be the object, or the variety of the forms in which it was expressed.
In July, 1769, a clergyman pulled the nose of a Scotch naval officer for
talking disparagingly of the member for Middlesex, and then ran him
through the sword-arm in Hyde Park. The Chevalier d'Éon sent Wilkes
a dozen smoked Russian tongues on his birthday, with a wish that they
had the eloquence of Cicero and the delicacy of Voltaire, in order wor-
thily to celebrate the occasion. A gentleman of Abergavenny announced
his intention to construct a miniature Stonehenge, dedicated to Liberty,
and begged of him " a few strong words " by way of an inscription. Another correspondent wrote to offer his friendship and fortune; proposed
to marry his daughter, as an excuse for giving Wilkes himself ten or fifteen thousand pounds; and ended by leaving him a handsome legacy.
Large and frequent tribute came from an unknown person who signed

did, but very material, testimonials of sympathy from every class of his fellow-countrymen. Wine, game, fruit, and poultry reached him nearly every day, and from most counties south of the Tweed. Those who had nothing else to give placed their suffrages at his disposal. He nominated members of Parliament, sheriffs and recorders of London, and mayors of county towns at his pleasure. The theatres were his own from the first.[1] Garrick, who, when playing Hastings in " Jane Shore," had pronounced some lines derogatory to the majesty of the people with such an emphasis as would have been laid upon them by a baron and a courtier of the fifteenth century, found that it was safer to quarrel with the lord chamberlain than with the unofficial censors who watched the stage in the interests of Wilkes and liberty, and was glad to get off with nothing more severe than a friendly admonition. Captive as he might be, it was no light matter to trifle with a man whose name or symbol[2] was chalked upon every door and shutter between Paddington and Brentford, and was seldom out of the sight of a traveller between Brent-

---

himself Philo-Wilkes, and who addressed his hero as "Eximious Sir." As for poetry, or what its authors thought such, Wilkes was nothing less than the Mæcenas of the whole Churchill school until it had drunk itself into extinction. With his public fame and his long credit, the only form of opulence known in that circle, he commanded the sincere and devoted admiration of those ill-starred and ill-deserving bards. One extract from poor Robert Lloyd will more than suffice as a specimen of their encomiums:

> " Wilkes, thy honored name,
> Built on the solid base of patriot fame,
> Shall in truth's page to latest years descend,
> And babes unborn shall hail thee England's friend."

[1] During the period of his first persecution, when the king was at Drury Lane, a piece was given out for the next night called " All in the Wrong." The galleries at once saw their chance, and cried, amidst general clapping of hands, " Let *us* be all in the right. Wilkes and Liberty !"

[2] Alexander Cruden used to vary the labor of revising the third edition of the Concordance by wiping out Number 45, wherever he saw it, with a great sponge which he carried with him on his walks—a task which, as his biographer relates, defied even such industry as his.

ford and Winchester; and who hung in effigy on the sign-posts of half the ale-houses in the kingdom, swinging (so he heard, or pretended to have heard, a loyal old lady say as he walked behind her) everywhere but where he ought. When he brought his action against the Earl of Halifax, the surviv-or of the two secretaries of state who, six years before, had launched the immortal general warrant which had been the beginning of mischief, the jurymen imagined that they had established their character for patriotism by giving him dam-ages to the amount of four thousand pounds; but they had failed to make allowance for the exacting affection of the pop-ulace, who thought their champion moderate in estimating his wrongs at five times that paltry sum; and when the ver-dict was known, the gentlemen who were responsible for it had to be smuggled out of court along a back passage, and to fly, if not for their lives, at any rate for their periwigs. The most eminent statesmen, the most persuasive orators, were eager to conjure with the name of Wilkes, and the potency of the spell seldom fell short of their expectations; but when the gale was raised, and they desired to turn it to their own account, they discovered that the allegiance of the elemental forces was due to the talisman, and not to themselves. The Whigs, as Rigby justly observed, endeavored to separate the cause from the man, without perceiving that he alone had all the popularity which they were struggling to obtain. "If," said Horace Walpole, "the Parliament is dissolved, Lord Chat-ham and Lord Rockingham may separately flatter themselves, but the next Parliament will be Wilkes's." The roar of ap-plause, which deafened Walpole and Rigby, penetrated even to the ears of a recluse in whose solitude the tumult of poli-tics sounded faint and indistinct like the murmur of a distant city. "Whether the nation is worshipping Mr. Wilkes or any other idol is of little moment to one who hopes, and believes, that he shall shortly stand in the presence of the great and blessed God." So wrote poor Cowper in 1768, while he still ventured to connect eternity with hope.

History, which is very civil to the reformers who swore by Brougham and the free-traders who swore by Cobden, has

seldom any but hard or slighting words for the devotion and
fidelity of the Wilkites. But strong emotions, which prevail
among all classes, and outlast many years, are generally of a
nature which may be analyzed without bringing discredit on
the heads or the hearts of those who entertain them. The mass
of the community, which had little cause to bless or trust the
House of Commons, was firmly persuaded that no one could
be excluded from Parliament for any other reason than because he was too good to belong to it. George Grenville truly
prophesied that whenever a calamity befell the State, the multitude would account for it by a theory which satisfied all the
requirements of popular logic. " Ay," they would say, " if
Master Wilkes had been there, he would have prevented it.
They knew that right well, and therefore they would not
suffer him to come among them." [1] The sagacious instinct
which expressed itself after this homely fashion on club-night
in the tavern, and during the meal-hour at the factory, was
interpreted into the language of political philosophy in a treatise which young Englishmen destined for a public career
would do well to study with something of the attention
which they now expend on Aristotle's speculations as to
whether the citizens of a well-ordered State should all dine
at a common table. Burke's great pamphlet on the " Discontents" showed with marvellous clearness, and, considering
who was its author, with still more remarkable brevity, that
the patriots of 1769, when they protected Wilkes in his rights,
were in truth defending the commonwealth against an attack
upon its liberties more covert and less direct, but quite as determined, as that which was planned by Strafford and repelled
by the Long Parliament. The question of old had been
whether the king was to tax and govern in his own name;
but that issue had been decided on Marston Moor. There
now had arisen the equally momentous question whether he
was to tax and govern in the name of the Parliament. With
ministers whom the Crown appointed, an Upper House which
it might increase at will, and a Lower House full of men who

---

[1] Cavendish's Debates; February 3, 1769.

had bought their seats and sold themselves, there was no check
upon the excesses and follies of arbitrary authority except the
presence here and there on the benches of members endowed
with a "spirit of independence carried to some degree of enthusiasm, and an inquisitive character to discover and a bold
one to display every corruption and every error of government." Those were the qualities (so Burke reasoned) which
recommended a candidate to the few constituencies that still
could be called free and open; but they were distasteful to
the professors of this doctrine of personal government that
had been resuscitated after the lapse of a century and a quarter. These gentlemen, well aware that the deterrent force of
an example depended on other circumstances than on the
number of victims, and that the arrest of five members, if
successfully conducted, would formerly have stifled liberty as
effectually as the execution of fifty, had now resolved by the
expulsion of one to establish in the minds of all the fatal conviction that "the favor of the people was not so sure a road
as the favor of the court, even to popular honors and popular
trusts." From the Restoration onwards, and still more decid-
edly since the Revolution, the good opinion of the people had
been the avenue which led to the greatest honors and emoluments in the gift of the Crown. Henceforward the principle
was to be reversed, and the partiality of the Court was to become the only sure way of obtaining and holding even those
honors which ought to be in the disposal of the people.

To unmask this conspiracy against the nation, and to withstand it to the death, was a duty which the Whig party could
not have shirked without making Vane and Russell turn in
their graves. Lord Rockingham and his followers were a
mere handful; but when they faced the Court, they knew that
they had the country behind them. Burke, a master in the
art of putting into the most attractive form those incentives to
political action which no true-bred Whig statesman ever could
or ever will resist, explained to his leader, in a series of skilful
letters, that the Middlesex election united the two conditions
essential to a good party question, of being at once popular
and practical. "The people," he said, "feel upon this and

upon no other ground of our opposition. We never have had, and we never shall have, a matter in every way so calculated to engage them; and if the spirit excited upon this occasion were suffered to flatten and evaporate, you would find it difficult to collect it again when you might have the greatest occasion for it." And then he clenched his argument with an appeal to a maxim of policy that has earned the Whigs all the success and most of the abuse which between his day and ours have fallen to their share. "It was the characteristic," he wrote, "of your lordship and your friends never to take up anything as a grievance when you did not mean in good earnest to have it reformed."

They were in earnest now, and fully resolved not to relax their efforts until the breach in the Constitution had been securely and durably repaired. The day after Parliament was up, seventy-two members of the minority dined together at the Thatched House Tavern, and toasted the "Rights of Electors," the "Freedom of Debate," and the "First Edition of Dr. Blackstone's 'Commentaries.'" The hero of the evening was Wedderburn, who, as usage demanded, had placed his seat once more at the disposal of the patron against whose views he had voted and spoken. He was rewarded by hearing the health of the Steward of the Chiltern Hundreds drunk with three times three; and the cheering swelled into a volume which exceeded the power of convivial arithmetic to compute when, kissing the bottle, and laughing behind it at the dupes who did not know an adventurer when they saw one, he swore that he did from his soul denounce, detest, and abjure that damnable doctrine and position that a resolution of the House of Commons can make, alter, suspend, abrogate, or annihilate the law of the land.[1] Fortified by the exchange of patriotic sentiments, and primed with one-and-twenty bumpers, the Whig squires hastened down to their counties and fell to the

---

[1] Lord Clive, the leviathan of boroughmongers, who as an admirer and adherent of George Grenville was temporarily connected with the Opposition, placed another seat at the disposal of Wedderburn on the morrow of the day that he resigned his old one.

work of stirring public opinion and concentrating it upon the point at issue by such primitive and clumsy methods as suggested themselves before the Catholic Association and the Anti-Corn-law League had brought agitation to the level of an exact science. The word was passed to petition the throne for redress of grievances. Burke, who directed the movement, informed his coadjutors, as the fruit of long observation, that the people about the Court cared very little whether the occupants of the Treasury bench had a hard or an easy time of it, so long as no manifestations of popular dissatisfaction obtruded themselves upon the royal presence. A string of sulky common-councilmen or justices of the peace, filing through the rooms at St. James's with an address about their invaded birthrights and the valor of their forefathers, and expecting to be received as graciously as if they were there to congratulate the king upon the birth of a princess, would do more than a score of parliamentary debates to arouse in George the Third a suspicion that his scheme for governing the country by weak, divided, and dependent administrations might end by being as disagreeable to himself as it was distressing to his subjects.[1]

Middlesex led the way, helping herself in order that she might be helped by others. Wiltshire and Worcestershire and Surrey were not slow to follow her example. The Kentish petition bore the signatures of two thousand seven hundred freeholders; though three skins of parchment which had been going the round of the hop-districts were not forthcoming. Wedderburn drafted the Yorkshire address, and made a prog-

---

[1] "The Middlesex petition," wrote Rigby, on the twenty-fourth of May, 1769, "was brought to court to-day. The man who delivered it to the king, his name is Askew. His companions were Sergeant Glynn; an old parson, Dr. Wilson, prebend of Westminster; Messrs. Townshend, Sawbridge, Bellas, and one other ill-looking fellow, whose name I could not learn. His Majesty received it with proper contempt, not speaking to any one of them; but an impropriety seems to have been committed by their being permitted to kiss the king's hand, all of them except the old parson and Sawbridge." The reasons for appealing direct to the king are very well put in Burke's letter to Lord Rockingham of July 2.

ress through the three ridings, declaiming against placemen and turncoats with a success which is said to have inspired Wilkes with a short-sighted and most superfluous jealousy. Burke undertook the county which he had honored by choosing for his home, and arranged that the voice of Buckinghamshire should declare itself by the good old-fashioned process which had been familiar to Hampden. The grand-jury voted a county meeting, which was advertised by handbills circulated at the races. When the day came, a local member of Parliament, who had been active for Wilkes at Westminster, gave spirit to the affair by riding into Aylesbury at the head of his tenantry. The assembly was moderated by the judgment and animated by the eloquence of the greatest writer and thinker who has ever given himself wholly to politics, and who on that occasion made it his pride to forget that he was anything more than a farmer of Buckinghamshire. And the proceedings were countenanced by the presence of George Grenville's son and heir,[1] and crowned by a dinner for which every freeholder, from Lord Temple downwards, paid his shilling for himself; though the Whig landowners took care that there should be plenty of good wine in which to drink through a list of toasts that embraced the entire body of Whig principles.

It was not in every county, however, that the most powerful nobleman was an ex-lord lieutenant, still sore from his dismissal. Wherever a great Whig proprietor was not irreconcilably embroiled with the Court, the ministry worked upon his hopes with every bait that official ingenuity could devise, and upon his fears with an argument which, as things then stood, could not easily be answered. "The king," it was urged, "will regard your remonstrances and addresses as so much spoiled sheepskin. You may make fine speeches about the Bill of Rights, and drink to the immortal memory of Lord Chief-justice Holt,[2] from now till the next general elec-

---

[1] "A very sensible boy," said Burke, "and as well disposed to a little faction as any of his family."

[2] Lord Chief-justice Holt was just then enjoying an enormous posthu-

tion, and Lord Montagu's butler and Mr. Eliot's boatmen will still vote as their masters bid them. When you have appealed to the country, and have got (as in the present state of the representation you know very well that you will get) nothing for your pains, what will remain to you except an appeal to the sword? Unless you are prepared to go into rebellion against your own great and glorious settlement, you had best leave this business of petitioning to others." With such language in his mouth, Rigby made a summer tour through the east of England, and, by the admission of his opponents, checkmated the party of action in at least three counties. His patron was less successful in another quarter. The Duke of Bedford, by a freak of fortune, as his descendants dutifully maintain, but more probably from one of those subtle and indefinable external peculiarities the memory of which dies with the dead, had contrived to monopolize a share of the public hatred which, if apportioned among his followers, would have given each of them almost as much as he deserved.[1] A crack-brained

---

mous popularity on account of the spirit with which, in the reign of Anne, he maintained the authority of the Court of Queen's Bench against the arbitrary encroachments of the Commons. The Wilkites made much of an apocryphal story about his having threatened to commit the Speaker to Newgate.

[1] Walpole, who calls the Duke of Bedford "a man of inflexible honesty and good-will to his country," says that his manner was impetuous, but that he was not aware of it. "He is too warm and overbearing for the world to think well of him;" so the duke would say of a statesman whose demeanor, whatever it might be, was more to the taste of the world than his own. This single touch, to those who have noticed how it is that public men come to be liked or disliked, goes further to explain the duke's unpopularity than all the malicious and unfounded stories (the consequence of that unpopularity, and not the cause of it) which Junius garnished and dished up to the eternal dishonor of the libeller rather than of the libelled. When one who was bountiful up to the utmost limits of common-sense was reviled as a skinflint; when a rigid patriot was charged with having eaten foreign bribes; when a father as loving and far wiser than Lord Holland was held up to execration for having insulted the memory of an only son, whose death all but killed him—it may reasonably be concluded that nothing very bad could be proved against the object of such random calumnies. It is satisfactory to know that

Plymouth doctor, whose practice was not so large but that he
had plenty of leisure for politics, was canvassing Devonshire
for signatures to a petition praying the king to discard his
ministers.   The Bedfords, terrified by the threatened hostility
of a county which, if it got its rights, would have sent to Parliament five-and-twenty members, adjured their chief to help
them with his influence in a district where he exercised a
princely charity.   The duke, always ready, at any cost, to
oblige adherents who gave him nothing in return except rollicking company which he should have been ashamed of enjoying, and periodical news-letters containing more impudence than wit, went down to the West of England, and with
difficulty got back alive.   He was safe as long as he stayed in
Tavistock, where his meat was in every mouth, and cloth of
his ordering on every loom; but he was stoned in the High
Street of Honiton, and literally hunted out of the town with
a pack of bulldogs; and at Exeter the vergers tried in vain to
keep the mob out of the cathedral when it was known that
he was seated in the stalls.

While the ministers, by playing on the weakness of individuals, might hope to stifle opinion in counties which, like
Nottinghamshire as described by Sir George Savile, consisted
of "four dukes, two lords, and three rabbit-warrens," they
were powerless in the great cities, where men were afraid of
nothing except the ill-will of the multitude.   Bristol voted
contempt for its member, who had been bitter against Wilkes.
Westminster petitioned, and Newcastle; and a remonstrance
to the king, outspoken to audacity, was sanctioned at a gen-

Junius had entirely to himself the gratification which the most infamous
of all his slanders appeared to give him.   Humbler lampooners, who usually were only too glad to pick up his cast-off weapons, would have nothing to do with this poisoned shaft.   The only tolerable couplets in a dull
dialogue of the dead between Bedford and Beckford represent the duke
as speaking with feeling of his irreparable loss:

> "Though fate, my Tavistock, soon set thee free,
>   And early stole thee from the world and me,
>   Thy merits ever will that world deplore,
>   And thou wilt live when I shall be no more."

eral meeting of the Livery in Guildhall, amidst a thunder of
applause which, as Burke told Lord Rockingham, raised the
idea that he had previously entertained of the effect of the
human voice.　The word had gone forth from the headquarters of the Opposition to prepare addresses calling for an immediate dissolution, in spite of Lord North's solemn warning
that any such document would render all who signed it guilty
of a breach of privilege, to be avenged with the gravest penalties that Parliament could inflict.　But the City guilds, backed
by ten thousand Yorkshire yeomen, could afford to laugh at
the sergeant and his mace; and the demand that the Commons should be sent back to their constituents as unfaithful
stewards was soon enforced by one whose person, even when
he stood alone, was as sacred as that of royalty itself.　Lord
Chatham, in seeking emancipation from office, had obeyed one
of those intuitive and irrepressible impulses which advise better than the most experienced physician.　Within three weeks
after he had sent back the privy seal, the gout came to his
rescue in a series of attacks violent and frequent in proportion to the evil for which it was the long-expected remedy.
It left him at last, happy, hopeful, and serene; young, with
the imperishable youth of genius, as when he broke his first
lance by the side of Pulteney; his ambition satiated, but
his patriotism more ardent and more enlightened than ever.
Chastened by suffering, and taught by his own errors, he was
an humbler but a far nobler man than during the period when
his immense success, too recent even for him to bear wisely,
had made him wilful, captious, and exacting.　In different
quarters, and with very different feelings, it was recognized
that he was no longer the Chatham of 1765.　The first use
which he made of his recovered faculties was to appear at
St. James's, where the king learned, in the course of twenty
minutes' conversation, that the most punctiliously loyal of his
subjects was no longer the most obsequious.　George the
Third could scarcely believe his ears when a statesman who
had hitherto approached him with a subservience which would
have been almost too pronounced for his royal brother of
France told him plainly that his Majesty had been badly

counselled in the matter of the Middlesex election, and begged that justice might be done to his own disinterestedness in case he should find himself bound in conscience to oppose the ministerial measures.

Disinterested indeed must have been the aims of one to whom a place was a torment, and who had drunk so deep of glory that he had no relish for those periodical displays which sweeten the labors of opposition to vainer and slighter men. A fine speech could add nothing to his fame. A successful division would only surround him with importunate partisans, supplicating him, for their sake, and for the sake of the country, to tear himself from all that he prized—from the peaceful joys of a married life, the story of which reads like an idyl; from the children in whose sports he renewed his boyhood, and a share of whose studies sufficed his not very rapacious appetite for printed literature; from his planting, his riding, his long lazy excursions in search of the picturesque; from his "farmer's chimney-corner," the smoke of which might be seen from the Vale of Taunton, and his summer retreat in that lovely nook on the south coast where Devonshire marches with Dorsetshire.[1] Hope of advantage or aggrandize-

---

[1] Wilkes called Chatham the worst letter-writer of the age; which, though a terrible charge in the eyes of Gilly Williams and George Selwyn, would be regarded with indifference by one who lived a little too consciously in the spirit of Themistocles, and did not care how destitute he might be of lighter accomplishments, if only he knew how to make a small state a great empire. There is, however, something attractive in Chatham's domestic correspondence, marked, as it is, by stateliness of manner contrasting most quaintly with extreme simplicity of idea. Nothing can be prettier than his letters to his wife from Lyme Regis, where he was looking after the health of his younger, and the military studies of his elder, son. "We returned late," he writes, "from the morning's ride, as the all-exploring eye of taste, and William's ardor, led us somewhat beyond our intentions. My epistle, therefore, being after dinner, eaten with the hunger of an American ranger, will be the shorter, and I fear the duller. It is a delight to see William see nature in her free and wild compositions; and I tell myself, as we go, that the *general mother* is not ashamed of her child. The *particular loved mother* of our promising tribe has sent the sweetest and most encouraging of letters to the young Vauban. His assiduous application to his profession did not allow him

ment for himself he no longer entertained; "but without hope," as he quietly said, "there is a thing called duty." The motive that brought Chatham back into public life was the highest and purest of those which impel to action; and purity of motive produced, as it ever will produce, magnanimity of conduct. He who, when engaged in fighting his own battle, had never troubled himself to propitiate a foe or to court an ally betook himself, now that his views were no longer personal, to the work of forming and consolidating a party with as much industry as a young politician who has just begun to see his way into the cabinet. Determined that it should not be his fault if the nation remained in the slough where it then was struggling, and discerning the hurricane that was brewing beyond the seas with a glance which seldom deceived him when it swept a sufficiently wide horizon, he girded himself to the effort of withstanding those enemies of England who called themselves her servants, but who were more dangerous to her welfare than the rulers and warriors of France whom he had so often foiled and humiliated. Conscious that his one poor chance of victory in such an unequal conflict depended upon his first having conquered himself, he laid aside the haughtiness which was his besetting fault, and the affectation that was his favorite weakness, and made it a duty to practise a consideration for others which hitherto had been sadly wanting. He sought and obtained a reconciliation in form with Lord Temple, who had deserted him, and with George Grenville, who had sold him; and, having performed the easier task of pardoning those by whom he had been injured, he turned to others who, as against himself, had not a little to forgive. Doing what he might to atone for the chief, and now irreparable, mistake in his career, he made frank and

---

to accompany us. He was generously occupied in learning to defend the happy land we were enjoying. Indeed, my life, the promise of our dear children does me more good than the purest of pure air." Lord Chatham's anticipations came true at least as often as those of most fathers; but William was destined to have as little leisure for contemplating the natural beauties of his native land as his brother was successful in fighting for it.

almost humble advances to a group of statesmen who held his opinions, and who were imbued with principles as elevated as his own. Those advances were accepted with a hesitation which it is impossible to blame. It was not in human nature that the Rockinghams should forget who it was that had lent the majesty of his name to excuse and dignify the conspiracy which overthrew them. So cruel a wound could not heal at the first intention. What had taken him again to court, asked Burke, except that he might talk some "pompous, creeping, ambiguous matter in the true Chathamic style?" But Chatham had done, then and forever, with bombast and mystery. Plainly and shortly he told every one whom he met what his policy was to be—tenderness towards the American colonists; justice to the Middlesex electors. This policy he hoped to be permitted to pursue in company with those who had already made it their own, and to whom, if success crowned their common endeavors, he should cheerfully hand over the spoils of victory. "For my part," he said, "I am grown old, and unable to fill any office of business; but this I am resolved on, that I will not even sit at council but to meet Lord Rockingham. He, and he alone, has a knot of spotless friends such as ought to govern this kingdom." That was the spirit in which the greatest of England's statesmen went forth to the last and the most honorable of his labors.

CHAPTER VI.

1770.

The Effect produced upon the Political World by the Reappearance of Lord Chatham.—His Speech upon the Address.—Camden and Granby separate themselves from their Colleagues.—Savile rebukes the House of Commons.—Charles Yorke and the Great Seal.—The Duke of Grafton resigns.—David Hume.—Lord North goes to the Treasury.— George the Third, his Ministers and his Policy.—George Grenville on Election Petitions and the Civil List.—Chatham denounces the Corruption of Parliament.—Symptoms of Popular Discontent.—The City's Remonstrance presented to the King and condemned by Parliament.— Imminent Danger of a Collision between the Nation and its Rulers.— The Letter to the King.—Horace Walpole on the Situation.—The Personal Character of Wilkes, and its Influence upon the History of the Country.—Wilkes regains his Liberty.—His Subsequent Career, and the Final Solution of the Controversy about the Middlesex Election.

EVEN Chatham's love of a stage effect must have been gratified to the full by the commotion which his political resurrection excited. Nothing resembling it can be quoted from parliamentary history; though the theatre supplies a sufficiently close parallel in the situation where Lucio, in "Measure for Measure," pulls aside the cowl of the friar and discloses the features of the ruler who has returned at the moment when he is least expected to call his deputy to account for the evil deeds that had been done in his name. Grafton, the Angelo of the piece, accepted his fate as submissively and almost as promptly as his dramatic prototype. Still loyal at heart to the great man whose authority he had abused, or rather permitted others to abuse, he was dumfounded when Chatham, emerging from the royal closet, met his greeting with the frigid politeness of a redoubted swordsman who salutes before a mortal duel. The unfortunate prime-minister knew that he had sinned too conspicuously to be forgiven, and envied in his heart those less prominent members of his own

13

government who could meet their old lord and master in the confidence that he would not be too hard on the political frailties of such humble personages as a lord chancellor or a commander-in-chief of the forces. Every one who had served under Chatham was as restless as an Austerlitz veteran who had just heard of the landing from Elba. Granby, the English Murat, could hardly be kept from at once resigning his immense appointments, rendered necessary to him by a profuse and ill-ordered generosity which would have been a blot on any character but that of a brave, an uncultured, and an unassuming soldier. Lord Camden, who so little approved the policy of his colleagues that he absented himself from the cabinet whenever the business on hand related to the coercion of America or the suppression of Wilkes, and who for two years past had never opened his mouth in the House of Peers except to put the question from the woolsack, viewed the reappearance of Chatham as a tacit but irresistible appeal to a friendship which from his school-days onwards had been the ornament and delight of his life and the mainstay of his professional advancement.

And yet, though all that was best in the ministry already hankered to be out of it, the Bedfords had still fair ground for hoping that a crisis might be averted. Horribly frightened (to use Burke's energetic metaphor) lest the table they had so well covered and at which they had sat down with so good an appetite should be kicked over in the scuffle, they still could not bring themselves to believe that Chatham would adopt the cause of the Middlesex electors. For when during the first months of the late government Wilkes applied to the secretary of state for permission to live unmolested in England, the Duke of Grafton, clever in small things, had contrived to shift the odium of a refusal from himself to the prime-minister. The unhappy exile stole back to France, persuaded that he had a vindictive personal enemy in Lord Chatham, who, as a matter of fact, had never been informed of his petition, and who, if he thought about him at all, regarded him as a cosmopolitan able and willing to make himself at home in a country where claret was and sheriff's officers were not. In the an-

guish of his disappointment Wilkes attacked his fancied op-
pressor with an audacious and observant bitterness, admirably
calculated to wound a man whom just then none dared to as-
sail except with remonstrances against his overweening pride
and predominating power, which were compliments more to
the taste of their object than so many set panegyrics. The
Bedfords, in January, 1768, had been chuckling over the novel sensation which Chatham must have experienced at finding
himself described, in a pamphlet that sold like wildfire, as the
warming-pan for Lord Bute, as the first comedian of the age,
as so puffed up by the idea of his own importance that he was
blind to the superior merit of a brother-in-law with whom he
was on the worst of terms;[1] and the motives which in January, 1770, induced the great earl to stand forth in defence of
one who had never written so ingeniously as when he was
trying to hurt the feelings of his advocate were altogether
outside the range of their comprehension. To forgive those
who had something to give, and to forget where anything was
to be got, was a form of magnanimity to which they themselves were at all times equal; but not even Sandwich, writing confidentially to Weymouth, would have suggested that
Chatham had any longer an eye to office. They accounted for
his conduct after the fashion of their tribe. When it began to
dawn upon them that a statesman who, if he played a selfish
game, might have been in power for the rest of his natural
life, deliberately preferred, at the bidding of his conscience, to
brave the anger of a sovereign whom he adored on behalf of
a penniless adventurer who had libelled him, they gratified
their malice and preserved inviolate their theory of the
springs of human action by spreading a report that the most

---

[1] " A proud, insolent, overbearing, ambitious man is always full of the
ideas of his own importance, and vainly imagines himself superior to the
equality necessary among real friends. Lord Chatham declared in Parliament the strongest attachment to Lord Temple, one of the greatest
characters our country can boast, and said he would live and die with his
noble brother. He has received obligations of the first magnitude from
that noble brother; yet what trace of gratitude was ever found in any
part of his conduct?"

impassioned of speakers had at last harangued himself out of his senses. As, one after another, resolutions were laid on the table of the House of Lords expounding in correct yet stirring phrases the principles of freedom and justice for which, time out of mind, all Englishmen worthy of the name had striven ; and as each successive declaration of public right was enforced by outbursts of majestic eloquence which have had the rare fortune to obtain a place in the familiar literature of a nation that ordinarily dwells but little upon the oratory of the past ;[1] Rigby and his fellows hardened themselves against the voice of reason and the disapprobation of posterity by reminding each other that they had only to do with another " mad motion of the mad Earl of Chatham."

Till Parliament met (and the ministry, anxious to postpone the evil hour, took the unusual course of dispensing with a winter session), Lord Chatham, said Burke, kept hovering in the air, waiting to souse down upon his prey. And, indeed, nothing short of an Homeric simile could depict the panic and the scurry which ensued upon the first swoop of the eagle whose beak and talons were henceforward to be exercised on a new hunting-field. For the House of Lords had never really heard Chatham. During the short period that he sat there as prime-minister he had not been himself either in body or in intellect. With breaking health and a bad cause, he had been confronted not unsuccessfully by men who were armed for the unequal combat with no weapon except the knowledge that they were in the right. When, borrowing the jargon which was fashionable at the palace, he declaimed against the most modest and long-suffering set of statesmen that ever did the king's business as " the proudest connection in the country," he had been plainly told by the Duke of Richmond that the nobility would not be browbeaten by an insolent minister.

---

[1] Any one who has been behind the scenes during the preparations for speech-day at a public school knows that though a well-read master may insist on an extract from Canning or Grattan, a boy, if left to himself, will choose something of Chatham's, and in most cases something which Chatham spoke in the spring of 1770.

But no one ventured to rebuke him now.   On the afternoon
of the ninth of January, the first of the session of 1770, when
the king had read his speech and had returned to St. James's,
the Lords were invited humbly to assure his Majesty that they
would dutifully assist him in doing as much mischief in either
hemisphere as in his wisdom he thought advisable.   As soon
as the noble seconder had stammered through his last sentence, Chatham rose to his feet and informed the members of
the government that he was, and had the best of reasons to
be, as loyal as any of them, and that he should give substantial evidence of his loyalty by telling the truth to his royal
master.   And then, after a few sentences of good-will towards
his fellow-subjects in America, which Americans still quote
with gratitude, he discoursed briefly and calmly of the question of the day, and concluded by calling on the Peers to inform the mind of their sovereign, and pacify the just irritation
of his people, by declaring that the House of Commons, in
proceeding of its own authority to incapacitate Wilkes from
serving in Parliament, had usurped a power which belonged
to all the three branches of the legislature.[1]   He had never
spoken more quietly or with more instant and visible results.
As he resumed his seat Lord Camden started up, displaying in
word and gesture the emotion of one in whom a long and
painful mental struggle had been brought to a sudden end by

---

[1] The best point in Chatham's first speech on this occasion was his allusion to the retribution which eventually befell the nobles of Castile,
who had been cajoled by Charles the Fifth into helping him to corrupt
the popular element in the Cortes; and its literary interest is derived
from his admiring mention of Dr. Robertson, whose style was just then
the delight of all British readers, and whose profits were the envy of
most Southern authors.   "I cannot help thinking," said Walpole, "that
there is a great deal of Scotch puffing and partiality, when the booksellers have given the doctor three thousand pounds for his 'Life of Charles
the Fifth,' for composing which he does not pretend to have obtained
any new materials."   Walpole had justification for his criticism; but such
is the charm of a clear narrative by a writer who, without being dishonest, can make the most of what he knows that Robertson's work will
probably survive the productions of the industrious and very able scholars who have followed him over the same ground.

a flash of conviction. He had accepted the great seal, he said, without conditions, fully intending never to be led into courses which he could not approve; but experience taught him that he had overrated his own independence. Often had he hung his head in council, and showed in his countenance a dissent which it would have been useless to express in words; but the time had come when he must speak out, and proclaim to the world that his opinions were those of the great man whose presence had again breathed life into the State; and that if in his character of a judge he were to pay any respect to this unconstitutional and illegal vote of the House of Commons, he should look upon himself as a traitor to his trust and an enemy to his country.

The thunder-stroke of such a confession, from the keeper of the royal conscience, could not be parried by the hackneyed tricks of the parliamentary fencing-school. Lord Mansfield, whom it never took much to disconcert, began by informing his audience that his sentiments on the legality of the proceedings of the House of Commons were locked up within his own breast, and should die with him; and what he said afterwards did little to remove the bewildering impression which had been produced by this extraordinary preface. He was followed by Chatham, who, even in the more strictly kept lists of the Commons, had always treated the forms of the House as made for anybody but himself, and who positively revelled in the license of the Lords. In a second speech, which his hearers were at liberty to call a reply if they could forget that, according to every rule of debate, he was forbidden to make one, he invoked the highest traditions of our national liberty against the many-headed tyranny of an unscrupulous senate, and electrified friend and foe alike by an appeal to Magna Charta, which, as a stroke of the genius that is above and outside art, ranks with the oath that Demosthenes swore by the dead of Marathon. It was all in vain that the Peers, not flattered by being called silken barons, declined by an overwhelming majority to imitate their ancestors at Runnymede. It was all in vain that Sandwich defied the Opposition to make any sense out of the rhetoric that they had been applauding. Chatham, whose speaking was a sort of inspired conversation which affected every one who was present as if it had been addressed especially to himself, had been perfectly well understood both in the House and under the gallery. While, more than any other orator, he gained by being heard, there was always something to take away which would bear the carriage. In as short a time as was required for an eager partisan, primed with news, to cross the lobby, it was known in the Commons that Pitt had made a speech for Wilkes surpassing anything that he had done since the night when he answered Grenville about the repeal of the Stamp Act; and the fragments of his eloquence, which were soon going the round of the benches, stirred his old followers like the peal of a distant trumpet. Granby, who always argued as if he were under fire, informed the House, in half a dozen short and plain sentences, that he now saw the Middlesex election in its true light, and that he should lament the part he had taken in seating Luttrell as the greatest misfortune of his life. Sir George Savile, picking his phrases with deliberation, declared that the vote for expelling Wilkes, which he characterized as the beginning of sorrows, was the offspring of corruption, and told the majority, in so many words, that they had betrayed their constituents. Lord North, who knew the force of such an accusation from the mouth of one who has been cited by historians as the model of what a great country gentleman should be, and whose name contemporary satirists employed as a synonym for probity, took occasion on the next day to express his assurance that Sir George had spoken in warmth. "No," said Savile; "I spoke what I thought last night, and I think the same this morning. Honorable members have betrayed their trust. I will add no epithets, because epithets only weaken. I will not say they have betrayed their country corruptly, flagitiously, and scandalously; but I do say that they have betrayed their country, and I stand here to receive the punishment for having said so." Some young and foolish members, among whom it is needless to say that Charles Fox was conspicuous, talked loudly about the scandal of condoning so pointed an insult to their august assembly; but their elders judged it wiser to do by the affront as they had done by the Treasury bank-bills which had earned it for them. It was understood that if Savile were sent to the Tower, his friends would insist on going with him; and the ministers, who had quite enough trouble with a single martyr to liberty on their hands, could easily anticipate the sort of life which they would lead with the Cavendishes on one side of the prison doors, and the Yorkshire freeholders on the other.

Granby was entreated by his colleagues to remain in office; but he knew them better than to constitute them the judges of what his honor demanded. On the sixteenth of January, a week after he had made a clean breast of it in the House of Commons, he threw up the command of the army and the mastership of the ordnance, and went into poverty, as he had so often gone into the throat of death, determined that, come what might, Pitt should never say that he had flinched from his duty. No attempt was made to retain Lord Camden. The Court had never forgiven him his celebrated decision against the legality of general warrants. Prerogative kings, it has been well said, are the making of constitutional lawyers;[1] and George the Third had long chafed against the necessity of keeping about his person, in the place of honor, the earliest and most successful specimen of his own manufacture. But to dismiss the only judge who, as a judge, had acquired a European reputation—whom foreigners, after they had heard Pitt at Westminster and Garrick at Drury Lane, used to be taken to see in the Court of Common Pleas as the third wonder of England—and to dismiss him without having secured in his place a lawyer of high distinction and respectable character, would have been to strike the last prop from beneath the tottering administration. So Grafton was well aware; but his adversaries had discerned more quickly than himself where the key of the situation lay. On the very night

---

[1] This remark is made by Lord Albemarle in his "Memoirs of Rockingham," a mine of Whig tradition, admirably worked according to the good old Whig processes.

that Lord Camden had performed his memorable act of mutiny, Lord Temple and Lord Shelburne had been prompt to testify their admiration of his conduct in terms carefully framed for the purpose of gibbeting by anticipation his successor. In the teeth of their withering denunciation, the most eminent men at the bar and on the bench refused even to be tempted by the great prize of their profession. Dunning, whom Chatham, always on the search for merit, had made solicitor-general, and who was true to his patron in opinions and in affection, could not think of accepting an offer which, according to Chatham's brother-in-law, would be rejected by anybody but an obsequious hireling, and, according to Chatham's political aide-de-camp, would have no charms except for a wretch more base and mean-spirited than could be found in the kingdom. Sir Eardley Wilmot, the Chief-justice of the Common Pleas, was earnestly and frequently pressed to take the great seal into his custody, with any rank in the peerage or slice off the pension-list that he cared to name. But that simple and sincere man, who was a lawyer as Reynolds was an artist or Brindley an engineer, preferred the regular and solid work of his calling to the ambition of making, and the annoyance of enduring, party speeches in the House of Lords until a change of government should condemn him, according to his own vigorous expression, to live thenceforward on the public like an almsman. It was hardly worth while to go through the form of begging Lord Mansfield to be chancellor. He was too intelligent and too timid to be dazzled by the attractions of an office which would add nothing to his authority, and would lay him under the obligation of defending every folly of Grafton and every job of Sandwich against Camden with his hands untied, and Chatham with his brain unclouded.

There only remained a single member of the profession who, as a candidate for the chancellorship, could be mentioned in the same day with Mansfield, Wilmot, and Dunning. Charles Yorke had been in office with the Rockinghams, and, when their government fell, they were proud at being accompanied into opposition by one who would have been an ornament to any party. Grafton, whose short political life—for he was still but four-and-thirty—had coincided with a period during which mutual treachery and disloyalty among public men were preached as a gospel by the Court, and who had been accustomed to expect any politician to change sides after a month's coquetry, and any lawyer on a moment's notice, saw no reason why he should not offer Yorke the great seal as freely and as openly as to his own attorney-general. But he forgot that the man whom he counted on buying as Bute had bought Henry Fox, or as he himself had bought the Bedfords, was one of a group of statesmen who, after a long and shameful interval, had once more introduced into the relations of parliamentary life that stanch and chivalrous fidelity which is now the common quality of both our great national parties. Richmond and Portland and the Keppels had tasted the pleasures of personal intimacy, enhanced by an identity of political views and a brotherhood in political fortunes; and they were surprised and indignant when they were informed of Grafton's overtures, and deeply hurt when they detected indications that the proposal had not been without its effect. They clearly gave Yorke to understand that he must choose between the proffered dignity and their friendship; and such was the binding power of old and familiar ties, which it required a stronger and coarser hand than his to snap at the first effort, that, with a heart fluttering between scruples and desires, he mustered courage enough to go back to the Duke of Grafton with a refusal. The duke sent him on to the palace, where the unhappy man was so overcome by his perplexity and distress, which were evidently preying on his health, that the king bade him give the matter up and set his mind at ease, as, after what he had said to excuse himself, it would be cruel to press him.

Cruel indeed it was. Lord Hardwicke, throughout the wretched business, played a true brother's part, trying, by every means at his command, to make the waverer see his duty; while at the same time he sturdily, and almost angrily, insisted that Rockingham, and Rockingham's friends, should set the most favorable construction upon their old colleague's vacillation.[1] Seriously alarmed by the little that Yorke, oppressed by an unnatural and uneasy reserve, which in a sensitive man is the worst of symptoms, could be got to tell him about his interview with the king, Hardwicke declined to leave him until, with fraternal courage, he had secured from him a promise that he would take a good dose of physic and spend the next day quietly at home.

But, before many hours had passed, the fish was again at the bait. Yorke's character and circumstances conspired to render the temptation irresistible. With brilliant abilities and all the reflected advantages of the great Lord Hardwicke's high station and unstained renown, he began life possessed of every good thing that could be inherited except the stout heart which had brought his father from an attorney's drudge to be the most prosperous, if not the most famous, of chancellors. A successful author, according to the taste of his day, while yet a boy,[2] and in large practice at the bar while still a

---

[1] On the one hand, Lord Hardwicke insisted with Yorke that, before joining the government, he should see his way very clear (which he certainly could not) towards conscientiously adopting the Court view of the American difficulty and the Middlesex election. On the other hand, in his letters to Lord Rockingham, he made the best of his brother's hesitation, and the most of his sacrifices. "I thank you for your communication," he writes on Monday, the fifteenth of January, while Yorke's decision was in abeyance. "I see the times are running into great violences, and, if so, honest men must act according to their consciences. Your lordship will know to-morrow the resolution taken in the great affair. I know not what 'kennel' you allude to. I think all parties are getting deeper into the dirt." On the evening of the same day he says, "I am authorized by my brother to acquaint you that he has finally declined the seals. How far he has judged right or wrong will only be known by the consequences. I may fairly say that he, as well as his near relations, have been victims to the violence of party and their own moderation."

[2] The young Earl of Hardwicke and Charles Yorke wrote between them "The Athenian Letters," a work not inferior in merit to the best of those pseudo-classical productions which unite the dulness of a political memoir to the affectations and inaccuracies of an historical novel, and which leave on the palate a sickly taste that is perhaps the most disagreeable of all literary sensations. It is difficult to imagine how any human being who could read a translation of Thucydides should sit down to two

minor, Yorke entered Parliament at four-and-twenty, amidst the universal welcome of an assembly which confidently hoped to have reason for acknowledging

> "How sharp the spur of worthy ancestry
> When kindred virtues fan the generous mind
> Of Somers' nephew and of Hardwicke's son."

Unfortunately his was not one of those rare natures which can be petted by the world without being spoiled. He did not idle; he did not lose his balance; he deserved all that he got, and went the right way to get it: but his idea of his own merits was so extravagant that he never heartily enjoyed a success, and took the inevitable disappointments of Westminster Hall and the House of Commons as so many personal insults on the part of destiny. He thought it a grievance that he was not a judge at thirty, and induced his friends to think so too. He murmured at being nothing more than solicitor-general at thirty-three. His chagrin when Pratt, much his senior, and indubitably his superior, was made attorney-general over his head in the summer of 1757 was too deep for words; and the feeling rankled until, after the lapse of many years, it found vent in the act which was his destruction. But it was after the fall of the Rockingham administration that his egotism was seen in the most unpleasing relief as against the patriotism of better men. While Savile and Burke were planning what they could do for the country, Yorke was forever brooding over what he might have done for himself. Politicians out of office, who work hard for nothing, are always inclined mildly to wonder at the emphasis with which a thriving barrister accuses the ill-luck that condemns him to sit on the shady side of the House of Commons; but Yorke altogether overstepped the conceded limits of professional grumbling. Endowed with an ample share of his father's fortune; happily married; the heir-presumptive to an earldom; dividing with Horace Walpole the empire of polite letters, and with Wedderburn the most lucrative and

---

volumes of the correspondence of the agent to the King of Persia, supposed to be resident at Athens during the Peloponnesian war.

interesting business of the law-courts—he lived on brambles as long as somebody else was lord chancellor. The correspondence which he maintained with foreigners of talent and distinction carried his sorrows far and wide through Europe in quest of sympathy. Lord Campbell has printed the well-turned phrases in which Stanislaus Augustus, writing from Warsaw, delicately reminded Charles Yorke that it was too much to expect a King of Poland to pity anybody, and least of all a man who could command, and was framed to appreciate, a life of dignified and cultured ease. But dignified and cultured ease seemed purgatory, or worse, in the eyes of one who was perpetually tortured by the feeling that, unless he could reach the pinnacle which fortune had hitherto made inaccessible to him, his career would have been nothing better than a long *succès d'estime*. Though he had started half-way up the hill, things had so turned out that the paths which led to the summit had successively been closed to him, until one remained open, and one only. As long as Camden stayed in the government, Yorke was chancellor designate of the Opposition ; and a change of administration, which was always possible and now seemed imminent, would put him in secure possession of the great seal. But the scene of the ninth of January in the Lords had destroyed his solitary chance. Whigs and Wilkites had now a hero in Camden, for whom no praise could be too warm, and, when the day of triumph arrived, no reward could be too splendid. If the Rockinghams came in on the question of the Middlesex election, their chancellor must be the statesman whose fame as a judge was identified with the earliest, and, as a political martyr, with the latest, phase of the endless controversy, and who was in the intimate confidence and under the special protection of the great orator without whose hearty assistance they could not retain power for a fortnight.[1]

And so, with thirteen years less of life and hope before him, Charles Yorke found himself once again postponed to his an-

---

[1] It is quite clear from Lord Hardwicke's letters that the Yorkes believed that, in case of a change of government, the selection of a chancellor would lie with Chatham, and that he would choose Camden.

cient rival. Camden, after making his market by conforming
to the Court, was now at the eleventh hour to be richly recompensed for his tardy independence, while he himself was left
to the reflection, so cruel to a wordly-minded man, that he had
been disinterested gratis. The strain was too much for his
constancy. After a broken night, leaving his medicine untasted on the table, he went of his own accord to the levee.
His appearance there at such a time could have only one
meaning. The king, who saw that he wanted to have his
hands forced, drew him into the closet, and, dropping the tone
of the previous evening, told him that he must never look to
be forgiven if he failed his sovereign in such a plight. He
himself (he declared) had been unable to sleep from vexation
at the thought of Yorke's having declined to rescue him from
a " degrading thraldom."—the thraldom of submitting to see
America saved and England pacified by statesmen who were
his own devoted servants and Yorke's loving friends. Such
was the reasoning which persuaded the unhappy man to set
at naught the claims of what in any other company he would
have called duty and honor; but few have the presence of
mind to scrutinize the language of entreaty when a monarch
condescends to plead. Yorke consented to be chancellor.
The seal was taken from Lord Camden, who that night, for
the first time during many months, enjoyed the sweet and
tranquil sleep that was never to revisit his successor. He retired, not as other chancellors, loaded with multifarious spoils,
but far nearer poverty than he had been since the days when
he rode the barren round of the Western circuit, a briefless
and rather hopeless barrister, mounting himself sorrily out of
the proceeds of his college fellowship. His son, who inherited much of his capacity and all his public spirit, never could
recover for the family the favor of their sovereign. When
the second Lord Camden was invested with the Garter, in token
of eminent services which he made it his pride not to permit
the country to overpay, the courtiers noticed that George the
Third performed his part in the ceremony with an ungracious
reluctance which indicated that forty years had not obliterated
the memories of the great crisis of January, 1770.

Having yielded to the flattering violence which he had wantonly courted, Yorke left the palace undone. The Jane Shore of politics, his frailty aroused no harsher sentiment than compassion in those who, men themselves, could make allowance for his feminine nature. But the consternation with which Lord Hardwicke, who had spent the morning, by his express desire, in telling everybody that he had declined the seal, received the announcement that he had accepted it, did more than could have been done by the most poignant reproaches to disclose to him the aspect which his conduct must present to all whose good opinion he treasured. He foresaw what Barré would say, what Burke would write, and what Savile would feel, when a brother who had always evinced a more than fraternal interest in his career, and who was conversant enough with established proprieties to know the gravity of the advice that he was giving, adjured him to return forthwith to St. James's and entreat his Majesty to release him from an engagement which he ought never to have undertaken. But such an effort was far beyond Charles Yorke's courage. He could not, he said, retract. His honor was concerned. He had given his word, and the king had wished him joy. Forbearing to remind him that, according to the law of honor, promises rank by their priority in time, and not by the station of those to whom they have been made, Lord Hardwicke, now that the step was irrevocable, did his best to raise his brother's spirits and calm his increasing agitation. But a hearty quarrel would have been less terrible to Charles Yorke than the tenderness and assiduity by which the members of a family whose idol he had always been endeavored to conceal from him that he had changed their pride to shame. It was useless to appeal from his true friends to his new confederates in search of the admiring and unquestioning affection without which life was unendurable to him. Grafton sympathized with him as an unlucky climber who is sliding over a precipice sympathizes with the last piece of turf at which he clutches. The Bedfords applauded him as the one wise fellow among a party of saints and fools, and were inclined to envy him the facility of his ghastly triumph. To

Lord Holland his fate was only the matter for a heartless jest, and a text for one of his heart-felt but selfish sermons on his own sorrows.[1]

The protracted agony of the struggle had thrown Charles Yorke into a high fever, both of mind and body. Mr. John Yorke, who, though able and cultivated, and in Parliament as a thing of course, had sunk his own ambition in order to push the success of a brother whom he worshipped, took turns with Lord Hardwicke in keeping the sufferer company. Touched by his kindness, and encouraged by the recollection of his life-long devotion, the chancellor proposed to him to follow his own example and accept an office in the Admiralty. John Yorke gently put aside the offer; but no delicacy could disguise the motives of his refusal, and Charles, whose melancholy had been lightened by a gleam of hope, said gloomily that since his brother threw him over he was a ruined man. From that instant he turned his face to the wall. Wednesday, the seventeenth of January, was the day on which he grasped the prize that crowned the labors, the struggles, and the intrigues of a lifetime. On Friday he took to his bed, and by the evening his family had reasons for dreading the worst, whatever those reasons were.[2] When he was asked whether

---

[1] "I never envied Mr. Yorke while he lived," wrote Lord Holland to George Selwyn; "but I must take leave to envy him, and everybody else, when they are dead. I comfort by persuading myself it is happier to wish for death than to dread it; and I believe everybody of my age does one or the other. But I do not find myself near a natural death, nor will you see me hanged, though I verily think they will never leave off abusing me." "Yorke," he says at a subsequent date, "was very ugly while he lived. How did he look when he was dead?" Most of these letters of Lord Holland contain an allusion to the morbid fondness for death, especially in its more sensational forms, by which Selwyn is now chiefly remembered. His interest in dead men and his indifference to living women were inexhaustible topics for the audacious raillery of his cronies.

[2] "I can only tell your lordship," wrote Lord Hardwicke to Lord Rockingham on the Friday, "that my dear and unhappy brother is much worse, and that I tremble for the event. God send me and his family strength enough to bear against this too probable calamity. I abominate the Court politics, and almost those of every sort. My poor

the great seal, which lay in his chamber, should be affixed to the patent of his new peerage, he collected himself enough to express a hope that he was no longer guardian of the bauble which eight-and-forty hours before he had bought at such a price. On the Saturday morning an apparent change in his condition slightly reassured his friends; but he did not survive the week. Into the precise manner of his death history, which has been deservedly indulgent to him, has forborne curiously to inquire. It is enough that he could not endure the shame of having stooped to that which for two generations after him was done with unabashed front by some of the most celebrated statesmen whose names are inscribed on the roll of our chancellors.

Nothing was now left for the Duke of Grafton but to get himself out of the way before Junius had time to point the moral of the tragedy. It was impossible for him to continue prime-minister after the most ambitious lawyer at the bar had thought death a less evil than the disgrace of being his chancellor. The government, which, like a snowball, had been changing its composition as it was kicked along, was now dissolving fast beneath the breath of Chatham. Seven places were already vacant; and now Conway, who had of late been acting as an unpaid member of the cabinet, intimated that though he had been willing to attend as long as he sat between Camden and Granby, he would not undertake to provide respectability for the whole administration. Lord Weymouth and Lord Gower eagerly assured Grafton that, desert him who might, they would stand by him to the last; but he more than suspected that the crew of three-bottle men who had been sailing under his nominal command from one dubious adventure to another were already on the lookout for a more capable and less discredited captain with whom they might pursue during a renewed term of service their jovial

---

brother's entanglement was such as history can hardly parallel." " Oh, my unhappy brother!" he says on the Sunday. " Born (one hoped) to a most prosperous scene of life, and qualified to shine in it, had he lived in such times as his father did, or indeed in any not so disturbed as these."

and lucrative trade of political freebooters. Sick of his followers, and heartily disgusted with himself, he resigned an office
to which he would under no circumstances have been equal,
and into which he had been thrust before his character, which
developed late, had acquired the dignity and solidity which
came after his day of grace had passed. His conduct in coming years was such as to regain for him the esteem of the
few; but he had not the native force to make his repentance
and reformation so conspicuous as to redeem his credit with
the many. The time was not very far distant when, as the
subordinate member of a cabinet, he took a course which, if
he had never been prime-minister, would have established his
reputation for foresight and patriotism; but the public at
large, after paying him a momentary tribute of surprised approbation, soon relapsed into its former mental attitude, and
remembered him once again as he had appeared beneath the
fierce light that beats upon the Treasury. The portrait which
had been bitten into the national memory by the acid of Junius has never been obliterated. Thirty years after the duke
had fallen from power, a friendly writer, who was his country
neighbor, could not venture to record the thoughtful generosity by which he rescued the author of the "Farmer's Boy"
from laborious penury without an elaborate apology for praising one who was known almost exclusively as the object of
the most famous diatribes in our language. A popular conception which has lasted for a generation is likely to last for a
century; and when it has outlived a century, it may die, but
it cannot be corrected. Doing penance for the accumulated
sins and scandals of his colleagues, Grafton, while English is
read, will continue to stand in his white sheet beneath the
very centre of the dome in the temple of history.

The king and his system, in this their dire peril, had the
good wishes of one who was then the most famous among living political philosophers. As long as Grafton's resignation
appeared to threaten the collapse of the royal policy, David
Hume never knew a moment's peace. He saw in George the
Third a representative of the autocratic principles of which
he himself was the most attractive exponent, and the taskmas-

ter of a people whom he loved as little as Nelson loved the
French. Hume had suffered cruelly under the furious outbreak of prejudice against everything that was Scotch, by
which Southern patriotism avenged itself on Bute. A true
artist, he kept out of his printed books all ungraceful and obtrusive manifestations of his dislike for England and the English; but many a passage in his private correspondence shows
how deeply the iron had entered into his soul. "From what
human consideration," he asks Sir Gilbert Elliot, "can I prefer living in England than in foreign countries? Can you seriously talk of my continuing an Englishman? Am I, or are
you, an Englishman? Do they not treat with derision our
pretensions to that name, and with hatred our just pretensions
to surpass and govern them?"[1] The intimate connection between Hume's constitutional theories and his sentiments with
regard to the nation at whose expense the Charleses and the
Jameses had put those theories in practice comes out strongly
in the letters which he wrote during February, 1770. There
was little fun, and that little very grim, in the remonstrance
which he addressed to Adam Smith, who had gone south to
make his bargain for the "Wealth of Nations" with a London
publisher. What was the use, cried Hume, of wasting a book
full of reason, sense, and learning upon a tribe of wicked and
abandoned madmen? "Nothing but a rebellion and bloodshed will open the eyes of that deluded people; though, were
they alone concerned, I think it is no matter what becomes
of them." "Our government," he wrote in the same month,

---

[1] This letter was written in September, 1764. Two years afterwards,
when Smollett made the tour which is commemorated under a thin disguise in "Humphry Clinker," he found all the inn windows, from Doncaster
northwards, still scrawled with doggerel rhymes in abuse of the Scotch
nation. In 1765, Sir Gilbert Elliot made a vigorous protest in Parliament
against the international jealousy which had survived the Union, and declared that in his opinion Englishman and Scot were one. If he himself,
he said, had merit enough, he should pretend to any English place. It
certainly would have been difficult for him just then to have hit upon
any illustration less calculated to recommend his sentiments to the audience which he was addressing.

" has become a chimera, and is too perfect in point of liberty
for so rude a beast as an Englishman, who is a man (a bad
animal too) corrupted by above a century of licentiousness. I
am running over again the last edition of my ' History,' in order to correct it still further. I either soften or expunge many
villanous, seditious Whig strokes which had crept into it. I
am sensible that the first editions were too full of those foolish English prejudices which all nations and all ages disavow."
" The firm conduct" of George the Third, and his " manly
resentment " against subjects who were loath to surrender that
freedom of parliamentary election which even the Stuarts did
not contest, sent the historian to his proof-sheets fired by the
conviction that he had not yet done enough to magnify Strafford, to canonize Laud, and to whitewash Jeffreys.

After the fall of Grafton, Lord North became prime-minister; if a designation may be applied to him which he never
allowed to be used in his own family, on the theory that no
such office existed in the British Constitution. And, most
assuredly, he had little claim to any title that conveyed an
idea of predominance; for he consented to place his indolent
conscience and his excellent judgment without reserves or
conditions in the hands of his sovereign. Adopting the royal
views with a lazy docility, which, as his private correspondence
proves, was sometimes hardly short of inexcusable dishonesty,
he never hesitated about taking the royal road to a parliamentary majority. Submission in the closet and corruption in the
Commons were the watchwords of his disastrous and inglorious administration. Having obeyed where it was his duty
to have protested, he had no resource but to bribe where it
was impossible that he should ever convince. Idle and inat-
tentive in all other departments of public business, he was
vigilant and indefatigable in buying every borough, patron
of a borough, and occupant of a borough that was in the market; and he had plenty of ready wit and handy logic for
those occasions when it became necessary to give his supporters a justification for voting according to the promptings of
their pocket.[1] When his measures were so faulty or the re-

---

[1] Fox, who, with all his good-nature, was too much a born critic to

sults of his policy so glaringly calamitous that the comments
and expostulations of the Opposition could not be stifled by
the uproar of his hired *claque,* he would step on to the floor
with the air of a popular stage-manager who makes jokes in
order to gain time and pacify the audience when something
has gone hopelessly wrong behind the curtain. Speaking with
unscrupulous tact and imperturbable temper, he seldom sat
down without leaving on the minds of his followers a comfortable sense of confidence in a statesman who could see the
humorous side of a defeat or a deficit; and whose slumbers
on the Treasury bench were only deepened and sweetened by
the news that England had a province the less or an enemy
the more, or that a village full of people who a few years before were loyal subjects of the king had perished beneath the
torches and tomahawks of savages hired with the produce of a
loan in whose profits half the cabinet had gone shares with
the most favored of their supporters.

Lord North's first business was to reconstruct the administration. The influence of Chatham, acting on noble natures
as silently and irresistibly as magnet upon steel, drew to itself all the sterling metal which still lurked in any corner of
the official fabric. Lord Howe refused to stay any longer in
a government condemned by the statesman under whose inspiration he had outdone himself in valor and conduct both
by sea and land. Dunning went; and James Grenville, the
most agreeable, if the least eminent, of the brothers.[1] Lord
Cornwallis had ridden as Granby's aide-de-camp at Minden,
and was not going to desert him now. Their places were supplied by professional office-holders, who received from Buckingham House detailed instructions when and how they were
to speak, and on which side they were to go on voting until

over-praise, when regaling Samuel Rogers with a general review of the
oratory of his day, pronounced Lord North to be " a consummate debater."

[1] " The day before yesterday," wrote George Grenville from Stowe, " we
were surprised by the laughing and laughter-promoting Jemmy." Those
pleasant epithets were certainly the last which could be applied to George
Grenville himself.

further orders.[1] The great seal, at which, since Yorke's death, all prudent lawyers more than ever looked askance, was intrusted to three commissioners, who had not between them enough knowledge of equity to qualify for a taxing - master in Chancery, but whose number and insignificance diluted the unpopularity which would have been fatal to any single aspirant who should have posed as the equivalent of Camden. The privy seal went a-begging until Lord North, who had the courage of sloth in as large a measure as his royal master had the courage of energy, defied the Wilkites by bestowing it on his uncle, the Earl of Halifax, who, not three months before, had been cast in damages for having broken the law in his eagerness to persecute their hero.

To say that Halifax had ruined his estate by extravagance and his constitution by strong liquor is to say that he had lived like every one of North's colleagues who attained to mediocrity. George the Third had now reached the platform towards which he had so long been struggling, and stood there, in his own estimation, every inch a king. He had a prime-minister clever enough to do him credit as a spokesman, and so thick-skinned as to be invaluable for a whipping-boy; a cabinet containing two or three respectabilities without a will of their own, and three or four broken-down men of fashion who could not afford to throw away a quarter's salary; and a House of Commons which lent itself kindly to the process of parliamentary manipulation, the only one among all the branches of statecraft which the servants of his choice

---

[1] On the ninth of January, George the Third desired Lord North to press a member who, with some others, had, in his Majesty's opinion, taken things too easily during the previous session to exert himself in the coming debate; "and I have no objection," said the king, "to your adding that I have particularly directed you to speak to them on this occasion." On the thirty-first of the month this gentleman got an opportunity to make his tirade, and inveighed hotly against the party which was defending the freedom of election as a combination whose object was to destroy the monarchy and abolish the House of Commons. The next morning the king signified to Lord North that he was satisfied with the performance; and, before the week was out, the obedient orator had been rewarded with a good place in the new administration.

thoroughly understood. Keeping up the constitutional fiction that the king acquiesced in a vicious policy out of his affection for worthless ministers, and dutifully pretending to be ignorant that he put up with worthless ministers because none but they would consent to be the instruments of a vicious policy, Junius implored him to ask himself whether it was for his interest or his honor to live in perpetual disagreement with his people " merely to preserve such a chain of beings as North, Barrington, Weymouth, Gower, Ellis, Onslow, Rigby, Jerry Dyson, and Sandwich," whose very names were a satire upon all government, and formed a catalogue which the gravest of the royal chaplains could not school his voice to read without laughing. After a lapse of sixteen years the strictures of Junius were repeated by a far greater writer, in a " Birthday Ode " which has survived all the official verse that was laid at the foot of the throne from the first effusion of Eusden to the last of Pye. Having discovered, by the instinct of his own genius, the art of infusing the spirit of poetry into the transient topics of the newspaper—an art which Heine, who alone among moderns possessed it to equal perfection, confessed that he borrowed from the old Greek comedy—Burns traced the prostration of Britain and the loss of her colonies to her sovereign's propensity for committing the honor and welfare of the State to adventurers with a character which would not have got them a place in a decent Lowland homestead.[1] It was not that George the Third had any

---

[1] " 'Tis very true, my sovereign king,
        My skill may weel be doubted;
     But facts are chiels that winna ding,
        And downa be disputed.
     Your royal nest, beneath your wing,
        Is e'en right reft and clouted;
     And now the third part of the string,
        And less, will gang about it
                Than did ae day.

     " Far be't frae me that I aspire
        To blame your legislation,
     Or say ye wisdom want, or fire,
        To rule this mighty nation.

natural affinity for looseness of conduct or obliquity of principle.   He knew the worth of an honest man as well as any
farmer on the Carrick Border.   When there arose a question
of keeping Lord Hertford in the embassy at Paris, the king
observed to his minister that a respectable man must not be
lightly cast aside, since he was not so fortunate as to have in
his employment "too many people of decent and orderly behavior."   There was no affectation in the delight which he
expressed at the prospect of enlisting in the cabinet the Earl
of Dartmouth, who brought to his service good intentions
strengthened by religious convictions, and brought nothing
else.   But the work that he gave his agents to do was of such
a sort that, while he took the best whom he could obtain, the
best were very bad.   Burke, whose glance pierced the situation through and through, foresaw that the king's success
would be only the prelude to an entire break-up of the system
of personal government.   " The Court," he wrote, "perseveres
in the pursuit, and is near to the accomplishment, of its purpose.   But when the work is perfected, it may be nearest to
its destruction ; for the principle is wrong, and the materials
are rotten."   A vivid and correct imagination, while it sees
beneath the surface of processes, almost invariably antedates
results.[1]   Though the end arrived at last, it was slower in
coming than Burke had predicted.   For twelve successive
years the country continued to be administered in exact accordance with George the Third's theory of an ideal constitution; but the price which his subjects had to pay was too

But, faith ! I muckle doubt, my sire,
    Ye've trusted ministration
To chaps wha in a barn or byre
    Wad better filled their station
        Than courts yon day."

[1] The distinguished Frenchmen with whom Mr. Senior conversed at
Paris between 1852 and 1860 were very acute in discerning the causes
which ultimately brought about the fall of Louis Napoleon; but none of
them, in making their forecasts, would give those causes time to work.
The more sanguine among the Orleanists hardly allowed the empire four
years out of the eighteen which were its allotted portion.

heavy a fee even for so complete and conclusive a course of political philosophy, illustrated by practical experiments.

During the first months of that long period the wheels of the ministerial chariot drove heavily. George Grenville, who knew himself to be dying, and whose public conscience had been reawakened by the confidential intercourse which he once again maintained with his great relative, was in a hurry to employ the strength and time that remained to him in getting something accomplished which, if he could not be liked during his life, would cause him to be remembered with gratitude after it. A born House of Commons man, if ever there was one, he made it his last ambition to purify the only atmosphere which he had ever breathed with satisfaction. The moral degradation of that assembly, where he had been long the proud leader and always the contented drudge, aroused in him one of those tempests of indignation to which the gravest English statesmen, fortunately for their country, are occasionally liable, and which by their beneficent violence have cleared the ground for some of the best laws that grace our Statutebook. He introduced a bill constituting a select and responsible tribunal for the trial of election petitions, which hitherto had been decided in a committee of the whole House, with as much regard to justice as could be expected from a court where the most scrupulous man could not but be biassed by the reflection that the fate of the ministry, and it might well be of the nation, depended on his voting with his party against the merits of the cause—a court whose numbers were elastic; whose members might come and go at pleasure; which was thin to hear evidence, and full to pronounce sentence; and to which nineteen out of twenty among the judges brought either a mind made up, or a verdict to be sold for love or money.[1] Grenville was heard throughout his clear and in-

---

[1] The ladies, by ancient custom, always attended the trial of a petition in crowds, or, as an ungallant peer complained, in droves; and the member whose fate was at stake found it necessary to borrow from his friends, if he had not enough pretty sisters and cousins of his own. So much in earnest were the queens of beauty of these indecorous political tourna-

structive statement of the abuses that he deplored, and the remedy that he had devised, with a respectful interest which passed into willing and almost unanimous conviction as he concluded in a strain of genuine feeling that lent a touch of pathos to the close of his stern and unlovely career. The hearers whom he had lectured and wearied for thirty years were astonished, and even awed, when he entreated them to console his days, now fast running out, with the thought that he had contributed, in however small a degree, to the improvement of the House of Commons—"a house," he said, "for which I have that established affection that induces a man to die for the honor of the ship he is engaged in." When the principle of a bill which George Grenville had drafted was

---

ments that on one occasion when the Speaker ordered strangers to withdraw, it took the doorkeepers two hours to clear the gallery. Of all Grenville's arguments against the existing system, none told more than his description of the manner in which honorable gentlemen, forgetting that they ought to be giving their attention as closely as jurymen who would have no judge to direct them, absented themselves in pairs from the hearing of the case during the hours required for the carouse which then was called a dinner. And yet they were just as well away; for they could not afford to listen as men open to conviction when, as not unfrequently happened, the confirming or invalidating of an election became a stand-and-fall question. Sir Robert Walpole went out because the members of Parliament who had taken bribes from himself to vote that the burgesses of Chippenham had been bought were less numerous by one than the members who hoped to get pensions and places from his successor by voting that those burgesses were pure. Camden, as a young lawyer, had been counsel for the petitioners, and his professional conscience was hurt by the congratulations which he received on having given the death-blow to the great minister; "a compliment," he said, "which I don't desire, but am content with having served my clients faithfully." Even exceptionally high-minded men were not ashamed of allowing that they had voted about an election on party grounds; and an appeal to any other motive would have been scouted by the lower class of parliamentary tacticians as claptrap. When Lord Clive was unseated for St. Michael's, Rigby wrote to the Duke of Newcastle, analyzing and commenting on the division. "We were defeated," he says, "by the Tories going against us. The numbers were two hundred and seven against one hundred and eighty-three. I hope your Grace, nor none of your friends, will have mercy on those rascally Tories any more."

approved, its details might safely be taken on trust.   Recommended by his authority, the measure went smoothly and rapidly through all its stages; and the grosser scandals which disgraced our elections began steadily, though slowly, to abate from the day when the jurisdiction of a parliamentary committee became a terror to evil-doers, instead of a machinery which the party in power ruthlessly worked for the purpose of increasing its own majority.

Grenville, who in his worst days had never been a hypocrite or a coward, did not deceive himself, and had no intention of flattering his brother-members with the pretence that bribery, so rife in the constituencies, was unknown in the House of Commons.   He was not one of those who do either good or ill by halves.   Striking right and left among the heads of the hydra, he had hardly sat down, after calling attention to the method of trying election petitions, when he rose once more to move for an inquiry into the expenditure of the Civil List.   The unexpected proposal struck consternation far and wide.   Ministers who could not have kept their places for a day unless they had the king's purse as well as the king's favor to rely on, and ministerial supporters who, but for timely subsidies from the royal strong-box, must have exchanged the costly delights of Arthur's and of Ascot for the dull economy of their country-houses, felt their hearts low within them when an ex-first lord who knew every secret of the Treasury, and whose failing health excluded him from that prospect of a return to office which is so potent to mitigate the reforming zeal of an opposition, came forward in the character of a financial inquisitor.   How was it, asked Grenville, that the late king, spending like a king, could pay his way and leave a hundred and seventy thousand pounds as a nest-egg for his successor, while his present Majesty, though practising a personal frugality that would be most laudable if the tax-payer had benefited by it, had already, in the tenth year of his reign, been reduced to apply to Parliament for the means of discharging a debt of half a million?   The question was answered by Barré, who said, in plain English, that the money which the nation supplied to its sovereign in the loyal hope that he would employ it to gratify his private tastes and maintain his regal state had gone in debauching the House of Commons. But the frightful misfortunes arising from the subservience of Parliament and the clandestine profusion of the Crown, which ten years afterwards strengthened the arm of Burke and gave an edge to his weapon, had not as yet reached their climax; and the honor of storming the stronghold of corruption was reserved for a knight whose own shield was stainless. Lord North, an adept in all the more shallow and showy arts of parliamentary leadership, parried the attack by congratulating Grenville on having taken so kindly to the trade of an apostle of purity, for which his previous life had been but a queer apprenticeship; and when other members, whose antecedents were such that their mouths could not be closed by an epigram, pressed the prime-minister for a more courteous and adequate explanation, the dependents of the government drowned any further discussion by clamoring like a chorus of foxhounds who suspect that somebody has designs upon their porridge.

But there was one voice which they could not silence. Determined that, listen who would, the truth should be spoken, Chatham renewed in the Lords the motion that had been dropped in the Commons, and mercilessly exposed the artifices of ministers, who, by bribing lavishly out of the resources of the Civil List, and then challenging Parliament, on its loyalty, to pay the king's debts and ask no questions, obtained an unlimited power of drawing upon the nation for funds wherewith to suborn the national representatives. The jackals of the Treasury soon found an opportunity for demanding that his words should be taken down; but to take down Chatham's words was like binding over Cromwell to keep the peace on the morning of Naseby. Supremely careless whether or not the clerks at the table entered on the journals of the House phrases which, as he uttered them, took rank at once in the literature of his country, he plainly and boldly declared that he, for one, would trust no sovereign in the world with the means of buying up the liberties of his people. In a time of profound peace abroad, when no delicate negotiation for the purchase of State secrets, which publicity might hamper, was going forward at Paris or Madrid; with a virtuous king, who had no expensive vices to nourish and conceal—what reason, except the most dishonorable of all, could exist for refusing an inquiry? How had his Majesty spent the money which had been exacted in his name? Was it in building palaces worthy of his position among monarchs; in encouraging the liberal and useful arts; in rewarding veterans who, after defending his quarrel in many a rough campaign, were starving on pensions which the upper servants of a nobleman would despise as wages? Or was it not rather in procuring a Parliament which, like a packed jury, was always ready, if a minister was in the dock, to say "not guilty" in the teeth of proof, and with absolute indifference to consequences?

This grave accusation, which Chatham had forcibly but not unfairly put, was repeated almost immediately by those who were most concerned in ascertaining the truth of it. The people could not endure the thought that their House of Commons, a traditional pride in which was interwoven in every fibre of the national character, should have degenerated into a body the majority of whose members were guilty of such conduct and actuated by such motives that, even to this day, it is not easy to name individuals among them for fear of giving pain to their worthier descendants.[1] The inhabitants of Westminster and London, of Middlesex and Surrey, and all that constituted the district which then was the heart and brain of England, had long ago petitioned the king to dissolve Parliament, and leave it for the country to pronounce between

---

[1] As early as 1768 an incident occurred which showed what the public thought of its representatives, and what those representatives thought of themselves. One Thornton, a milk-seller, was at the trouble to print and placard Bond Street with the speech which Oliver Cromwell made when the Long Parliament was dissolved. Though not a word of comment was prefixed or appended to the text, every honorable gentleman who read the handbills, as soon as he reached the sentence beginning " Ye are a pack of mercenary wretches," pronounced it a libel upon the assembly to which he belonged; and Thornton was straightway committed to Newgate.

the law and its violators. When their prayers procured them no redress, and, as they complained, scanty civility, their leaders suggested to them the bold and novel expedient of approaching the throne with remonstrances upon the answers which had been returned to their petitions. The City led the way with an address which was conceived in the spirit of the famous instrument whence its title was borrowed, and the very language of which recalled the English that was spoken and written in the best days of the seventeenth century. The authors of the Grand Remonstrance might have been proud to father the sentences in which the Liverymen of London rehearsed how, though they had laid their wrongs and their desires before their sovereign with the humble confidence of dutiful subjects, their complaints still remained unanswered; their injuries had been confirmed; and the only judge removable at the pleasure of the Crown had been expelled from his high office for defending the Constitution. "We owe to your Majesty," the petitioners went on to say, "an obedience under the restriction of the laws; and your Majesty owes to us that our representation, free from the force of arms or corruption, should be preserved to us in Parliament." In the reign of James the Second, Englishmen had complained that the sitting of Parliament was interrupted because it was not corruptly subservient to the designs of the king. They complained now that the sitting of Parliament was not interrupted because it was corruptly subservient to the designs of ministers. And therefore his Majesty's remonstrants assured themselves that his Majesty would restore peace to his people by dissolving such a Parliament and removing such evil ministers forever from his councils.

Those ministers, naturally enough, would have been pleased if so formidable a document could have been encountered with the conventional reply, and consigned to the summary oblivion, which are the predestined fate of memorials to the Crown; but the sheriffs of London, who both were leading members of Parliament, insisted on the right, which the City shared with the two universities and the two branches of the legislature, of approaching the king in person, with all the train and state of royalty about him. The courtiers were thoroughly frightened ; and the cabinet began to look for precedents which might permit them to insist that the corporation should limit the numbers of the deputation, and agree to be satisfied with a private reception. But George the Third, who, with the obstinacy which endangers dynasties, was endowed with the calm resolution which seldom has failed to save them, would not let his honor out of his own keeping, and announced to Lord North that, however it might have been in the past, the present occasion was one on which he did not choose to shrink from an interview with his subjects. On the fourteenth of March the lord mayor and the sheriffs came westward, attended by an immense but not disorderly multitude. The king received them seated on his throne. The common sergeant began to read the Remonstrance ; but the poor man had over-estimated his own courage and self-command when he undertook to be the mouthpiece of such sentiments in such a presence, and he was fain to hand over the paper to the town-clerk long before he came to the concluding prayer of the petition. The king listened with patience and composure to the uncourtly doctrines which pierced through the courteous phrases in which they were thinly draped.[1] He knew very well, as Junius said, that no one ex-

---

[1] Horne furnished the *Public Advertiser* with an account of the presentation of the Remonstrance, disfigured by such vulgar spite and dishonesty as to throw some discredit upon the party which he espoused. With much reading, but less culture than Wilkes, and far less mother-wit, he was already bent on outbidding him in the estimation of the populace. "When his Majesty" (so Horne wrote) "had done reading his speech, the lord mayor had the honor of kissing his Majesty's hand; after which his Majesty instantly turned round to his courtiers and burst out a-laughing. Nero fiddled while Rome was burning." The Court was so ill-advised as to proceed against the printer of this trash; but it got no satisfaction except an apology from Horne, who inserted a paragraph to the effect that, in view of the great offence which he had given by an assertion made on a former occasion, he frankly withdrew that assertion, and admitted that Nero did not fiddle when Rome was burning. Such were the unseemly slights to which the king exposed the royal dignity in his attempt to make it more imposing than his grandfather had left it.

cept a gentleman usher would think it a season for compliments. But the petitioners must have been sanguine, indeed, if they hoped that George the Third would be either enlightened or alarmed by their free speaking. He dismissed them with a round reproof, and at once set his usual apparatus to work in order to procure them from another quarter a still severer punishment for their presumption.

The necessary arrangements were soon made for inciting Parliament to pass resolutions condemnatory of a petition which, whether or not it was, as the king had pronounced it in his reply, disrespectful to the Crown, undoubtedly could not be construed in the light of a compliment to the House of Commons. The task of calling upon that House to reprobate the audacity of those who had prayed the king to dissolve it as corrupt was, with exquisite propriety, intrusted to a member who had hitherto voted with the Opposition because he wanted nothing for himself, and who now voted with the government because he wanted something for his brother. Exhilarated by finding that there still was an untrodden corner of the field over which they had so long been battling, the ministerialists rushed to arms. At first there appeared to prevail· very nearly a unanimity of unrighteous indignation. Beckford, the lord mayor, Sheriff Townsend, and Sheriff Sawbridge, and Trecothick, who, though less of a partisan than the other Whig representatives of the City, was too much of a man to desert his brother-aldermen in the moment of adversity, rose one after the other to avow and to justify in firm but respectful terms the share they had taken in a course of action which was almost obligatory on a corporation that had always endeavored to deserve its own special liberties and privileges by jealously guarding those which were common to Englishmen. Their protests were received with jeers and interruptions, unbecoming as directed against brother-senators; but much more than unbecoming when addressed by judges to culprits who were standing upon their defence. North, speaking, as the reporter commemorates, "in a very high style," so far from remonstrating with his followers for treating their accused colleagues badly, marvelled at their lenity in

not having altogether denied a hearing to people whom he
called agitators and hinted at as bankrupts—an insinuation
which was pointless when aimed at men any one of whose
names would have been worth more on the back of a bill than
those of all his cabinet together. Inflamed by such an appeal
to their evil passions from the minister who was responsible
for the prudence of their resolves and the decency of their
proceedings, honorable gentlemen were ready and eager to
vote by acclamation that they themselves were immaculate
and their detractors calumnious; but there were those among
them who intended, however little the knowledge might affect
its decision, that at all events the House should know what it
was doing. Burke reminded his audience that they were now
entering upon another stage of the downward road; that, after
having successfully combated the right of election, they now
were on the verge of committing themselves to a campaign
against the right of petition; and that with such a prospect
before them, the least observant and the most reckless ought
at last to acknowledge that rulers could only go from bad to
worse so long as they persisted in doing violence to the sentiments of a nation. There was nothing inglorious, he entreated
them to remember, in yielding to the people of England. And
when the ignoble throng which professed to represent that
people greeted his expostulations with the noisy impertinence
from which, taking his career as a whole, he suffered in proportion as the causes which he advocated were wise and just,
he was goaded into exclaiming, in much the same words as
those which Chatham had used the day before in another
place, that while a man would be roared at inside the House
if he were to call Parliament corrupt, he would be ashamed in
any private company whatsoever to maintain the paradox that
it was pure. Burke, though brilliant as ever, was outshone by
Wedderburn, who during that spring session of 1770 made a
series of the most thoughtful, and certainly the most impressive, speeches that ever proceeded from lips which were to
unsay within a twelvemonth every syllable that they had uttered. Following, as was his wont, immediately upon the attorney-general, as if to force the government to observe the

15

contrast between its actual and its possible law - officer, he showed by historical examples that while the House of Commons had always jealously guarded the right of a subject to petition his sovereign, it had never been so precise and outspoken in its assertion of that right as in cases where the matter of the petition related to the summoning and dissolving of Parliament.[1] And then, having established his position, and proved how ancient and how firmly based was the privilege which, if the Court had its way, was thenceforward to be a dead letter, he besought them not to add folly to illegality, but, if they must test the forbearance of Englishmen, to make the experiment on some weak and solitary individual rather than on the leading city of the world—a city which, the last time that it seriously exerted itself in the cause of freedom, never ceased to bear testimony against the tyranny of the Crown until the Stuarts, passing from crime to crime, had destroyed its very existence as an organized municipality by methods which in the days of the Brunswicks no sane minister would venture to employ. But the dangers of the future weighed as lightly with Wedderburn's hearers as the precedents of the past; and Parliament by great majorities expressed, in every form that the constitution would permit, its

---

[1] After showing that the crime of not suffering others than themselves "to come near the king to advise him" had been one of the charges which cost the favorites of the feebler Plantagenets their heads; after relating how, under Charles the Second, the House had voted for impeaching Lord Chief-justice North, the ancestor of the prime-minister, and had addressed the king to dismiss Jeffreys from his offices, because that pair of worthies had contrived to get a proclamation issued for the purpose of discouraging the people from petitioning for the calling of a Parliament; after instancing how a previous House of Commons had actually expelled one of its members for taking on his own account a course precisely similar to that which the ministry was now urging the existing House of Commons to pursue—Wedderburn closed his list of cases by quoting a resolution proposed in the reign of William the Third by the Lord Hartington of the day, and carried by a majority of two to one, which declared "that it is the undoubted right of the people of England to petition or address the king for the calling, sitting, and dissolving of parliaments."

vehement and reiterated condemnation of an act which had been deliberately sanctioned, with one dissenting voice, by three thousand of the citizens of London in common hall assembled.

And now it seemed as if the unscrupulous proceedings of the cabinet and the Court were at length about to produce the consequences which, in a nation resolute to preserve the blessings of law and order, are the inevitable fruit of illegality and violence in high places. On the twenty-third of March, the two Houses elicited an assurance of gratitude from the king by informing him of the indignation with which they viewed the excesses into which his misguided subjects had been seduced by "the insidious suggestions of ill-designing men;" and the estates of the realm had hardly fulminated their joint rebuke against the citizens of London when it became abundantly evident that the spirit which prompted the remonstrance was abroad everywhere within thirty miles of Cornhill. On the morning of the twenty-eighth of March, the electors of Westminster came to a unanimous resolution to imitate the example of the Livery, and within half an hour their address was in the king's hands; so determined were they to be the first to announce that, as Chatham phrased it, they were not "frightened out of their birthrights by big words from the destroyers of them." Middlesex followed suit on the thirtieth ; and the City, with a deliberation evincing its sense of the gravity of the contest into which it had been forced, took measures for repeating an offence which, on the second occasion, could not be expected to pass without something more serious than a reprimand. In a few weeks at the latest, Lord North and his colleagues would have to say whether they were prepared to anticipate that measure against the port and town of Boston which was soon to set the mother-country and her colonies by the ears, and bring forward a bill of pains and penalties against the City of London. They were beginning to learn the truth of Burke's warning, when he told them that they must either act with the people or fight against them, since they had "no other materials to work upon but those out of which God had been pleased to form the inhabitants of this island." It was idle to explain, as their pamphleteers attempted to explain, the diffi- culties and dangers of the situation by cavils and recrimina- tions which resolved themselves into the " short but discour- aging proposition that we have a very good ministry, but that we are a very bad people." The discontent, which was now all but universal among those who were not paid to be con- tented, armed every assailant of the Court with an authority tenfold that which in quiet times he would have commanded by his own talents, and a hundredfold that which attached it- self to the pensioned scribes who defended the ministerial policy, though the acknowledged chief of British literature was conspicuous among them. Under the pressure of an ap- peal to his gratitude, which he justly regarded as a cruel wrong, and which to the day of his death he never even af- fected to forgive, Johnson submitted himself once more to the slavery which in earlier life he had endured under the pinch of necessity, and with much the same feelings towards both his employers, became the hack of North the minister, as he of old had been the hack of Osborne the bookseller—if a hack be he who writes badly and reluctantly on a theme select- ed for him by others. Those who had sat at the feet of the Rambler could not conceal their feeling of disappoint- ment, and almost of personal injury, when they were invited to search the pages of the " False Alarm " for such moral truths as that the expressions of shame and wrath with which an honest man heard that his parliamentary representative had been bought with a handful of bank-notes were " outcries ut- tered by malignity and echoed by folly," or for such jewels of political science as the proposition that the farmers and shopkeepers of Yorkshire and Cumberland need not know or care how Middlesex was represented.[1] Strong, indeed, must

---

[1] Whoever would see, in the space of a couple of pages, the difference between the work of great men when taking the right side of a question which they understand and the wrong side of a question which they do not, should compare the account of the process of getting up a county petition, which is the best, or at any rate the least feeble, passage in the " False Alarm," with the paragraph in the " Thoughts on the Discontents "

have been the party spirit of a reader who could excuse
Johnson for consenting to expose such a reputation to a venture from the consequences of which it never recovered until,
at a time of life when the world has as little right to expect
a masterpiece from an author as a brilliant campaign from a
general, he delighted every one, and astonished all but those
who were admitted to the fearful joys of his familiar talk, by
producing with matchless ease and rapidity a whole series of
biographies almost as pleasing, and quite as powerful, as any
that have appeared from Plutarch downwards.

Junius, meanwhile, at the height of a popularity which to
a calm and somewhat indifferent posterity seems at times a
more curious problem even than his identity, did not condescend to retaliate upon the disputants who challenged him
on behalf of the government. Too proud and too shrewd
to fatigue or bemire himself by charging into their highly
disciplined but faint-hearted ranks, with the true instinct of
a polemical strategist he marched straight against the key of
the hostile position. Until the end of 1769 he had flown at
no nobler quarry than a prime-minister, and had been satisfied with the amusement of smiling grimly at the flutter
caused in the higher ranks of the peerage when the *Public
Advertiser* came out with an announcement of " Junius to another duke in our next ;" but at last, on the nineteenth of December, appeared his " Letter to the King." Instead of heark-
ening to the counsels embodied in this admirable composition—counsels which no one with judgment would call inju-
dicious, and which it is a pity that a plain-spoken and stout-
hearted man like his Majesty should have regarded as disrespectful[1]—George the Third, after taking Christmas to think

which argues, no better than Burke in that marvellous production argues
everything, how it is that when the people and their rulers are at odds,
" the presumption is at least upon a par in favor of the people."

[1] " The doctrine inculcated by our laws, that the king can do no wrong,
is admitted without reluctance. We separate the amiable, good-natured
prince from the folly and treachery of his servants, and the private virtues of the man from the vices of his government. Were it not for this
just distinction, I know not whether your Majesty's condition or that of

it over, could light upon no more seasonable device for promoting peace and good-will than the prosecution of everybody who had been concerned in publishing, reprinting, or selling what he insisted upon viewing as a libel. As soon as the new year opened, the King's Bench was at work on the cases; and on the thirteenth of January, Woodfall, the editor of the *Advertiser*, was brought up for trial. Lord Mansfield, in conformity with the legal doctrine, for maintaining which he was unmercifully punished in the House of Lords by Camden and Chatham, and of which Junius did not let him hear the last until the last had been heard of Junius, charged the jury to consider whether the defendant had published the letter set out in the information, but instructed them that they had no business with the more vital point, whether that letter was a false and malicious libel or a veracious and public-spirited manifesto. The jury, however, read their duty otherwise; and their verdict of "Guilty of printing and publishing *only*" secured the liberty of the press until the period when, in the height of the anti-Jacobin panic, writers obnoxious to the Court ceased for a time to have the middle classes on their side.

While the ministry were forced to abandon the hope of getting Junius or his coadjutors into prison, they looked forward with dismay to the moment when Wilkes should be out of it. The eighteenth of April would see the tribune at large; free to go remonstrating to St. James's in his alderman's gown, at the head of as many of the Livery as could squeeze themselves into the throne-room; free to march into Palace Yard, with all Farringdon and Bishopsgate at his back, in order to place himself by force in the seat which still was his by law. With Wilkes at liberty, agitating for a new Par-

---

the English nation would deserve most to be lamented. Your subjects, sir, wish for nothing but that, as *they* are reasonable and affectionate enough to separate your person from your government, so *you*, in your turn, should distinguish between the conduct which becomes the permanent dignity of a king and that which serves only to promote the temporary interest and miserable ambition of a minister."

liament; with Junius, in letters that sold a double impression
of every journal into which they were pirated, hinting one
day that Lord North's head was growing too heavy for his
shoulders, and sneering at him the next as having no knowledge of finance except what he had gathered through George
Grenville's keyhole, and no pretensions to oratory beyond
the fact that he spoke like Demosthenes when his mouth was
full of pebbles, the prime-minister began to fear that he was
destined to have the fate of Strafford without his fame.   It
was waste of words to recommend concession to his royal
master.   At the first mention of an appeal to the constituencies, the king had laid his hand upon his sword, and had
said plainly that he would have recourse to that sooner than
be coerced into a dissolution.   The Court was murmuring because the City was let off too easily, and his Majesty was complaining that his ministers had no spirit,[1] at a conjuncture when
men whose temperament did not lead them to exaggerate the
significance of a political situation were aghast at witnessing
the Crown and the Parliament committed to a conflict with
the population not only of the capital, but of the most prosperous and thickly inhabited districts in the island.   Horace
Walpole terrified his correspondent at Florence with a striking exposition of the misgivings which possessed him while
the event was still in the future.   The crisis (so he wrote to
Mann) was tremendous.   If it became necessary to chastise
London in the person of its mayor and sheriffs, many noblemen and members of Parliament would demand to be included in their sentence.   The Tower, crammed with such proud
criminals, would be a formidable scene indeed.   The counties
would enforce their petitions by remonstrances, and their remonstrances by refusals to pay the land-tax.   Rebellion was

---

[1] Calcraft to Chatham, March 24 and 27. Junius affirms, in a foot-
note to his republished letters, that George the Third was so much affected by the unwillingness of his ministers to impeach the lord mayor
and the sheriffs that he was reduced to live upon potatoes for three weeks
in order to keep off a fever. But the foot-notes of Junius, unfortunately
for the picturesqueness of history, must not be taken as fragments of
gospel.

in everybody's mouth; and nothing could avert it unless the
prime mover of all the discord and confusion could be induced
to see that it was easier for a king of England to disarm the
minds of his subjects than their hands. "The English may
be soothed," said Walpole. "I never read that they were to
be frightened. This is my creed, and all our history supports
it." Hume predicted a revolution still more confidently than
Walpole, and very much more complacently. He watched
the march of events with an historian's eye for an effect, and
in jovial expectation of the troubles that were impending
over the nation which he detested. Party bigotry, acting
upon natures worthy of a better inspiration, has produced
some singular results; but, if it were not self-drawn, few
would regard as anything short of caricature the picture of a
humorist, so kind-hearted, tolerant, and playful that an epi-
cure in society would almost consent to have lived a century
ago for the pleasure of his company, exclaiming against his
own ill-luck in having been born a century too early to enjoy
the privilege of narrating the disruption and ruin of the community of which he was himself a citizen.[1]

The elements of a political convulsion had, indeed, long
been brewing: an obstinate court; an enraged people; a
press teased, but not restrained, by a feeble and meddling

---

[1] "I live still," Hume wrote from Edinburgh in October, 1769, "and
must for a twelvemonth, in my old house, which is very cheerful, and
even elegant, but too small to display my great talent for cookery, the
science to which I intend to addict the remaining years of my life. I
have just now lying on the table before me a receipt for making soupe
à la reine, copied with my own hand. For beef and cabbage (a charming dish), and old mutton and old claret, nobody excels me. All my
friends encourage me in this ambition, as thinking it will redound very
much to my honor.

"I am delighted to see the daily and hourly progress of madness and
folly and wickedness in England. The consummation of these qualities
are the true ingredients for making a fine narrative in history, especially
if followed by some signal and ruinous convulsion, as I hope will soon be
the case with that pernicious people. He must be a very bad cook indeed who cannot make a palatable dish from the whole. You see, in my
reflections and allusions, that I mix my old and new professions together."

censorship; a Parliament where the minority spoke with a freedom which stirred the nation, and the majority voted with a servility which exasperated it. Nothing was lacking but a leader; and that void would be supplied on the day when Wilkes, uniting in his person the most formidable and most incongruous attributes — an enemy of the governing powers, with the law on his side; an idol of the mob, with the gravest constitutional statesmen in the country for his high-priests—should walk from the prison where he had been unjustly confined to the door of the House of Commons which was illegally shut against him. A dozen supplementary numbers of the *North Briton*, and half a dozen monster meetings at Mile End and Moorfields, at York and Bristol and Newcastle, with Grenville or Savile in the chair and Wilkes on the platform, would have forced George the Third to make up his mind speedily and decisively between drawing his sword and calling a new Parliament; and in that Parliament, as every bye-election in the large constituencies proved, the ministry would not command a single unpurchased vote. With all the genuine representatives of the people on the one side, and nothing but the nominees of boroughmongers on the other—with Burke denouncing the infamies and prodigalities of the Civil List, and Chatham thundering for triennial parliaments, and for a hundred additional knights of the shire elected by household suffrage— 1832 would have been anticipated by two generations, and, the throne being filled as it then was, the triumph of popular principles could hardly have been effected without bloodshed.

But in order that history may anticipate or repeat itself, something more is required than a similarity of circumstances. The hour had come; but the hour is nothing without the man. The stage was clear for a Mirabeau; but the gentleman who was cast for the character had no fancy for the part. Both in his good and bad qualities, Wilkes stands alone among all the personages upon whom Clio has conferred an equal share of her attention. Though far from great, he was too strong and too clever to have greatness thrust upon him. His fancy must often have been tickled by the contrast be-

tween his sober estimate of himself and the more than heroic
proportions which he attained in the eyes of others. According to his admirers, there was no one since Rienzi who was
even good enough to be compared with him. He was Grac-
chus, and Drusus, and Timoleon without the dagger. He had
been elected for Middlesex as often and as deservedly as
Marius had been chosen consul. He had returned from
France, said Diderot, a nobler Coriolanus, meditating not the
ruin of his country, but her salvation. His detractors, wrote
Junius, might profess to regret that he allowed the pleasures
of life to compete with the glorious business of instructing
and directing the people; but the people loved and revered
their teacher none the less because they knew that he united
the public virtues of a Cato with the cheerful indulgence of
an Epicurus. The only acknowledgment of all this antiquated
flattery which could be extracted from the object of it (who,
if he had cared to bandy compliments out of the classics, possessed sound learning enough to repay the tinsel of his admirers with sterling coin) was a not very sincere assurance
that a line of applause from the pen which had undone Grafton made his blood run as quick "as a kiss from Chloe."
When Junius urged him not to make his presence, which
was to work such wonders for the commonwealth, too cheap
and familiar by walking so frequently in the streets, Wilkes
candidly admitted that if he took the advice and kept indoors
it would be from no loftier motive than fear of " the greatest
villains out of hell, the bailiffs." And the only project for
the repair of the violated constitution in which, as the result
of three lengthy and carefully indited appeals to his patriotism, the father of his country (for that was one of his titles)[1]

---

[1] " Johanni Wilkes, armigero :
    Qui reipublicæ restituit rem :
    Patri Patriæ ;
    Coronam hanc necti gratus
    Jussit Apollo."
Such are a few choice morsels from a hash of prose and verse, stolen from
various periods of Latin literature, with which Wilkes was flattered as a
politician, and must have been considerably diverted as a scholar, during
his visit to King's Lynn in 1771.

could be persuaded to engage, was the composition of a letter
to the lord mayor, begging him to excuse Mr. Sheriff Wilkes
from taking part in a " vain parade " on the anniversary of
the accession of a prince who would not redress the grievances of his subjects; an act of self-denial which, as the austere tribune remarked, dispensed him from "going in a ginger-
bread chariot to yawn through a dull sermon at St. Paul's." [1]

Quite unmoved by the vague and vast expectations and
alarms which he excited in every class of mind and every
grade of society, Wilkes kept steadily in sight, and continued
patiently to pursue, his own modest but very definite ambitions.
Whoever liked might regard him as the chosen instrument for
humbling the Crown and purging the House of Commons;
but seven years of fighting against almost overwhelming odds
had produced the same cooling effect upon his pugnacity as
on that of Frederic the Great. He had no notion of risking
his neck, his liberty, or even his leisure in tilting at abuses
which concerned his neighbors every bit as much as himself;
but he was at least as thoroughly determined never to renounce the modicum of personal success and advantage which
he believed to be his due. Before he died he meant to be
acknowledged as member for Middlesex; and till he died he
looked to getting his fair share in the good things of the only
world about which he interested himself, for his indifference
to the next may be estimated by his boast that he had been
his own chaplain since Churchill's death. [2] When his term of

---

[1] Junius shows poorly in his private communications to Wilkes. The
want of native humor which was at the root of his very serious literary
faults, but which is concealed by the elaborate ornamentation of his public writings, is constantly visible when he is off his guard. His letters
of advice are at times pompous to fatuity, and always dreadfully dull.
Though Wilkes did his utmost to be civil, it is evident that he soon had
enough of the correspondence.

[2] It was Wilkes's fortune to exercise a remarkable fascination over celebrated young clergymen who ended by unfrocking themselves. Churchill
was already devoted to him at the period when, as he writes,

"I kept those sheep,
Which for my curse I was ordained to keep

imprisonment was over, he took his place among his fellow-citizens as unostentatiously as their ardor and devotion would allow, and as silently as was permissible without exposing himself to the charge of surliness or ingratitude. Shunning the perilous display of a public meeting, he employed his pen to thank, in two manly and spirited addresses, the county which had done its best to make him a member of Parliament, and the ward which had made him an alderman. His municipal duties could not be performed except in person; and for weeks and months to come, whenever he appeared in Guildhall or at the Mansion House, his worse than plain features were rapturously gazed at by crowds as large as ever went to see a Miss Gunning married. "I find," he wrote to his daughter, "going about not a little troublesome, from the too great partiality of my countrymen." Indeed, it was for his daughter's sake that he chiefly valued a popularity the evidences of which he communicated to her by letter as regularly and faithfully as he divided with her the tribute in money and in kind that flowed in upon him from every quarter. Just as he put aside for his Polly the pineapple out of a hamper of fruit, and the salmon-trout out of a basket of fish, and the four "exquisitely beautiful perroquets" that had come by coach from Portsmouth, so he never failed to let her know, with a copious minuteness which in a lazy correspondent is the surest proof of affection, how he had been cheered and mobbed and stared at; how the ladies at the assembly-rooms pulled caps to dance with him; how, when he went into the Eastern counties on business, the provincial enthusiasm and curiosity turned what he intended to be a quiet jaunt into something only less noisy and fatiguing than a royal progress; how, when he visited Cambridge for his amusement, he was received both by town and gown as respectfully as if he had been a famous foreign general, and much more respectfully than if he had been an emi-

---

(Ordained, alas! to keep through need, not choice),
Those sheep which never heard their shepherd's voice;
Which did not know, yet would not learn, their way;
Which strayed themselves, yet grieved that I should stray."

nent foreign scholar;[1] how the electors of Westminster had gone like one man for a candidate who had no other claim on their suffrages except that he was an enemy of Sandwich, who was an enemy of Wilkes; how the new lord mayor was a Wilkite, and the new city member, and both the new sheriffs; and how, when he himself was sworn in as alderman, his Tory colleagues gave him the hearty welcome which so convivial a fraternity could not refuse to the pleasantest fellow in England.

He was chosen sheriff in 1771,[2] and in 1775 the news of his

---

[1] The people followed Wilkes about the colleges "in great crowds, with prodigious acclamations." In Trinity Chapel, on the Sunday evening, the anthem was from the 116th Psalm: "I am well pleased that the Lord hath heard the voice of my prayer." One of the many young Whigs who sat whispering there in their surplices came up to Wilkes, and, saying with emphasis, "I am well pleased," presented him with a book of anthems; "which," says Wilkes, "I gave to a pretty woman near me."

It was the same in the West of England. More than two years after he had come out of prison, as he was yachting along the Dorsetshire coast, he put into Swanage, and was greeted with all the honors which that "rascally dirty little town," as he ungratefully calls it, could pay him. He next went on shore at Brixham, and found the population of the neighborhood "very stanch to the cause of liberty," and much edified by the emotion which he exhibited over "the sacred spot where King William landed to rescue a wretched people from slavery and the Stuarts."

[2] At the election of sheriffs the Court made a last attempt to molest Wilkes by supporting a pair of candidates against him and his nominee. Incited by the king, who assured him that Wilkes had been "in his various struggles supported by a small though desperate part of the Livery, while the sober and major part of that body for fear kept aloof," Lord North sent word to Mr. Benjamin Smith, a leading ministerialist in the East end, that the cabinet expected all its friends to be on the alert till the poll was over. The letter was carried to the wrong Benjamin Smith, who, with the smartness of a true Wilkite, published it without any comment beyond an affidavit of its authenticity; and the only effect of the government's interference was to make Wilkes doubly sure, and to bring his man of straw in with him.

By 1771 the alienation between the government and the City had become proverbial. One of the characters in the "Maid of Bath," which

elevation to the office of lord mayor excited a profound emotion among politicians on the Continent; but Wilkes measured the worth of what he had gained more justly than the circle of famous authors and philosophers who discussed his rising greatness across Baron d'Holbach's table with a friendly interest not untinged by awe. He was gratified at hearing Miss Wilkes universally commended as the best lady mayoress that had ever done the honors of the Mansion House; but to himself his civic dignities were weary, flat, and, above all, unprofitable. To spend his mornings with the paving commissioners and his afternoons on the bench, until his days, according to his own somewhat profane expression, seemed as long as those in the last chapter of Daniel; to desert his roses at Fulham, or the book-shelves in his pleasant study near the Birdcage Walk, in order to cruise up and down the river in the City barge, exchanging dinners with the corporation of Rochester, and acting as toast-master till two in the morning at a board from which, by way of evincing a patriotic dislike of everything that was French, he had banished the only liquor that he really loved—were inflictions which it required nothing less than a handsome and a permanent salary to sweeten. At length, after a few more years of barren and irksome notoriety, he lighted upon a comfortable anchorage where he could ride securely after the storms of life. In 1779 the chamberlain of London died, and the people, whom Wilkes had so bravely and faithfully served, were proud of having a post in their gift as lucrative as anything which could have fallen to his lot if he had begun his public career by writing up Bute, and had ended it by writing down Chatham. The Liverymen hastened to install their old favorite in a situation which exactly suited his necessities and his tastes. His most important function was to deliver neat little harangues, of which he enjoyed the composition and certainly did not undervalue the merits, addressed to those successful warriors and

---

was first played in that year, expresses the idea of absolute impossibility by the phrase " You might as well expect a minister of state at the Mansion House."

statesmen who from time to time were invested with the freedom of the city. He more than once had occasion to smile
complacently when bluff seamen, fresh from exchanging broad-
sides with the French Republicans or scrambling through the
quarter-gallery window of a Spanish three-decker, reminded
him, while acknowledging his compliments, that they had
drawn their swords for the best of kings as well as for the
most perfect and glorious of constitutions. His official emoluments, which were out of all proportion to his duties, enabled
him to live with ease and style, and to keep as much ahead of
the constable as his very unambitious standard of solvency demanded. He divided his year between a mansion in Grosve-
nor Square and a cottage in the Isle of Wight with a "Tus-
can room" dedicated to Fortuna Redux, an inscription to the
filial piety of Miss Wilkes, and a Doric column commemora-
tive of Churchill in the shrubbery. In this "villakin" he
lounged away his summers, for the most part alone with a
daughter who returned the passionate affection which he lavished upon her, and who was quite capable of appreciating
the attractions of his inimitable talk, which was none the
worse for having been scrupulously expurgated for her benefit. He excused himself from any exertion less gentle than
that of occasionally reprinting for private circulation a classical
author, the accuracy of whose text he had established by the
facile process of collating previous editions; and to such a
point did he carry his economy of labor that he sent his Greek
from the press without accents—a piece of literary audacity
which, to the academic mind, is a stronger proof of his courage
even than the prefatory remarks on the letter of Lord Weymouth. But, at whatever value Brunck or Porson might rate
his contributions to learning, a fine vellum copy of his Ca-
tullus or his Theophrastus was an acceptable offering to political opponents who were half ashamed of the part they had
taken against him, and impatient at being excluded from the
privilege of listening to conversation the peculiar charm and
relish of which no good judge but Walpole ever questioned.[1]

---

[1] "Wilkes is here," wrote Walpole from Paris in 1765, "and has been

Lord Mansfield, who had long been saying behind his back that Mr. Wilkes was the politest of gentlemen, the best of scholars, and the pleasantest of companions, was glad of the opportunity of congratulating him to his face upon the elegance of the amusements which beguiled his leisure. The first amicable interview between the authors of the *North Briton* and of the "False Alarm" forms the most entertaining page in the most entertaining of books.[1] It is not on record that Wilkes was ever again in a room with Sandwich, though there is reason to believe that, in the sublimity of his good-nature, he would have made no objection to a meeting, the account of which would have thrown into the shade even the dinner at Mr. Dilly's. Reconciled to every reputable opponent, from the king downwards, he lived disliked by no one, and respected after a fashion by most, until, at the close of 1797, he died at the canonical age of threescore years and ten.

The main object of his life had long ere that been attained.

---

twice to see me in my illness. He was very civil, but I cannot say entertained me much. I saw no wit. He has certainly one merit. Notwithstanding the bitterness of his pen, he has no rancor—not even against Sandwich, of whom he talked with temper." Gibbon, on the other hand, who, in early days, had dined with Wilkes in the character of a brother-officer of militia, declared that he scarcely ever met a better companion, and recognized in him "inexhaustible spirits, infinite wit and humor, and a great deal of knowledge;" and Voltaire testified to his social qualifications in terms at least as high as those employed by Gibbon. "Nothing," said Mrs. Thrale, in Miss Burney's presence, "is so fatiguing as the life of a wit. Garrick and Wilkes are the two oldest men of their ages I know; for they have both worn themselves by being eternally on the rack to give entertainment to others." "David," said Johnson, putting the lady's remark into the shortest compass, "looks much older than he is; for his face has had double the business of any other man's."

[1] It was on a subsequent occasion that Johnson proved himself worthy of the best chance that the fortune of talk ever threw in his way. Wilkes had suggested that the House of Commons, in the teeth of an inconvenient statute, might order the pay of the army in America to be remitted in English money. "Sure, sir," said Johnson, "*you* don't think a resolution of the House of Commons equal to the law of the land." Wilkes lowered his arms at once, and wisely contented himself with ejaculating, "God forbid!"

He left prison fully resolved not to desist until he had established the principle that the choice of the people was never to be set aside in deference to monarch or minister, and that the representatives of the nation were to be elected at the polling-booth, and not inside the House of Commons. That principle, which the debates of 1770 had left in the shape of a proposition, he intended, before Lord North had done with him, to place high on the list of constitutional axioms; but what he proposed to effect for the public advantage was to be done at his own time and in his own way. His partisans urged him to assert his rights, even at the expense of a scene in Parliament and a revolution in the country. He, however, according to the saying of a book which he consulted more frequently for quotation than for edification, knew that his strength lay in sitting still. If the British Constitution was to stand, the world had nothing for it but to come round to him at last. "I have not," he wrote to his daughter in May, 1770, "been at either House, to avoid every pretence of a riot, or influencing their debates by a mob." He refused to convert a grave and weighty political ceremony into a personal insult to his sovereign by making one in the procession of aldermen who carried their periodical remonstrance to St. James's. He was not used, he said, to go into any gentleman's house who did not wish to see him. His forbearance was rewarded when Beckford (taking a course not more unprecedented and informal than the proceedings by which the cabinet had provoked him, as the representative of an injured people, to break through the well-founded etiquette of the palace) told his Majesty the wholesome truth in words as plain and free as ever one honest man used to another—words which the citizens of London may still read with profit beneath the statue of their great lord mayor in the Guildhall. It was the spirit of Old England, cried Chatham, which spoke on that never-to-be-forgotten day.

With the moral triumph on his side, Wilkes could afford to wait. At the commencement of each session the sheriffs, better Wilkites than himself, summoned him to appear in Parliament as member for Middlesex; but he remained quietly at

16

home while Luttrell, as was said with wit that had a serious
political meaning behind it, continued to vote, like a good
representative, in strict conformity with the views of his constituents ; that is to say, with the views of the majority of the
House of Commons.   At the general election of 1774 the in-
truder abandoned his untenable position ; no other government candidate was put in nomination at Brentford ; and Sergeant Glynn and his patron were returned unopposed.   The
ministers came back from the country with a stronger following than ever ; but, with Massachusetts in a flame, they did
not care to rake up the embers in Middlesex, and, with silent
prudence, they allowed Wilkes to take his seat in peace.
Thenceforward, as long as he cared to be their member, the
freeholders sent him back to each successive Parliament,
without the trouble of a contest,[1] and, for the most part, accompanied by any colleague whom he chose to name.   No
lapse of time, no difference of opinion on the public questions
of the day, could detach their loyalty from the man with
whom their own liberties and the honor of their county were
identified.   Years rolled on, and every year did something to
bring into deeper discredit the system of government that
began with Bute.   The policy of which Wilkes was the earliest victim had at length conducted the whole nation from
the summit of glory and prosperity, through the depths of
humiliation, to the very brink of ruin ; and on the third of
May, 1782, he rose to tell before a sympathetic audience his
own version of his oft-told story, and to move that the resolution of the seventeenth of February, 1769, which declared
him incapable of being elected a member of Parliament
should be expunged from the journals of the House of Commons.   Charles Fox, who then long had been, and was still
for a short while to continue, without a rival in that assembly,
thought it incumbent on him to pay a tribute to political con-

---

[1] The opposition at the contested election of 1784 was not directed
against Wilkes.   Even while his party lay prostrate beneath the load of
unpopularity which crushed the Coalition Ministry, his seat was never
for a moment in danger.

sistency in the shape of a dry and perfunctory counter-argu-
ment, very different from the rattling invectives by which,
twelve years back, he had thrown the ministerial benches into
a ferment, and turned the tables upon speakers who had been
parliamentary authorities before he was born or thought of.
Fox did not succeed in averting a decision in which he was
prepared beforehand to acquiesce. The resolution was annulled by a majority pretty nearly in proportion to that which
had originally carried it;[1] and then, going beyond what Wilkes
thought his due, the House, without a single dissentient voice,
ordered its clerk to remove from its records all traces whatsoever of its own arbitrary proceedings in the past, " as being
subversive of the rights of the whole body of electors of this
kingdom."

Historians have been blamed for giving too much of their
space to Wilkes, and to the cause which he almost reluctantly
represented; but it is difficult to say what other method could
be pursued, if it be the aim of history to relate the events
which filled the minds of people in days gone by in such a
manner as to strike the minds of people in the present. The
most random excursion or the most patient and diligent re-
search into the literature of the eighteenth century will alike
confirm the truth of a remark made by a contemporary an-
nalist of no mean authority, who pronounced that no public
measure since the succession of the Brunswicks had caused
" so general an alarm and so universal a discontent" as the
foisting of Colonel Luttrell upon an unwilling constituency.[2]
As to the legality or wisdom of that step, there has ceased to
be any diversity of judgment whatsoever. " I have constantly
observed," wrote Burke, when the quarrel was at its hottest,
" that the generality of people are at least fifty years behind-
hand in their politics. Men are wise with but little reflection,
and good with little self-denial, in the business of all times

---

[1] The famous resolution had been carried in 1769 by 235 votes to 89,
and was annulled in 1782 by 115 votes to 47.

[2] This observation occurs on page 68 of the " Annual Register " for
1769. The passage was probably written, and undoubtedly revised, by
Burke.

except their own. Few are the partisans of departed tyranny.
I believe there was no professed admirer of Henry the Eighth
among the instruments of the last King James; nor in the
court of Henry the Eighth was there, I dare say, to be found
a single advocate for the favorites of Richard the Second."
It did not take fifty years to fulfil this prophecy, so subtly
couched in the form of an historical generalization. Long
before that term had elapsed, politicians who were opposing
reforms which Richmond and Rockingham would have promoted, and walking through lobbies in which Burke and
Savile would never have been found, were one and all forward in protesting that, if they had been born a generation
earlier, they would have spoken and voted with the Whigs at
every point of the dispute about the Middlesex election.

CHAPTER VII.

The Favorable Conditions for taking Rank as an Orator under which
Fox entered Parliament.—His Early Career.—He becomes a Junior
Lord of the Admiralty.—His Father's Pride and Pleasure.—Lord Holland's Unpopularity.—The Balances of the Pay-office.—Lord Holland's
Indulgence towards his Children.—King's Gate.—Charles Fox and
his Studies.—His Passion for Poetry.—Naples.—Paris.—Intimate Relations between the Good Society of France and England.—Shopping
in Paris.—Intellectual Commerce between the Two Countries.—Feelings of Fox towards France.—Madame du Deffand.—Fitzpatrick.—
Mrs. Crewe.—Private Theatricals.—Effect of his Stage Experience on
Fox's Speaking.

If the main end of public life is to hold power as a minister, Charles Fox was of all statesmen the most unfortunate;
but, as though in compensation for the ill-luck that awaited
him, the circumstances of his early career could not have been
more favorably arranged for the purpose of educating him
into an orator. The peculiar temptations of the House of
Commons are seldom understood outside its walls; and of all
those temptations the most irresistible is that which invites a
speaker, who is still on his promotion, to acquire the fatal
habit of flattering his audience. Lofty sentiments arrayed in
burning words, stern truths embellished, but not concealed, by
the ornaments of language, and all else that constitutes high
and genuine eloquence, are not expected, and if forthcoming
are seldom readily accepted, from those who are not already
in possession of what in homely phrase is known as the ear of
the House; and an aspirant very soon discovers that the shortest and surest method of gaining the ear of the House is to say
what pleases the most numerous section of its members. And
so it often happens that a politician who begins by speaking
in manly and faithful obedience to his own beliefs and aspirations gradually learns the art of reserving himself for occa-

sions when those beliefs happen to coincide with the views, or,
it may be, the prejudices, of the assembly which he addresses;
forgetting, until it is too late, that he purchases each successive ovation at the expense of the unflinching sincerity which
is the soul of true oratory.

But with Charles Fox, most happily for himself and his
countrymen, the process was exactly reversed. Before his
character was formed; before the party with which he was
to act was deliberately and finally chosen; before, it may almost be said, he was old enough to have opinions at all; he
found himself in complete accord with all that was most violent in the passions which swayed the majority of his parliamentary colleagues, but which were shared by few of the
ablest, and none of the most earnest, statesmen of the day.
With nobody better than Rigby and Sir Fletcher Norton to
oppose to Burke and Wedderburn, the ministerialists wanted
a spokesman, while Fox was looking about for a topic; and
thus it came to pass that, with unexampled rapidity, he shot
straight to the front, and acquired the confidence which emboldened him freely to speak his mind, and the authority
which secured him a hearing. And then, when his position
was established—when he had begun to think for himself,
with the certainty that the world would listen eagerly and respectfully to the result of his reflections—there was presented
to him as fertile and elevated a theme as ever called forth the
powers of an orator; and during eight years of a ceaseless
and arduous struggle against the folly of those who first insisted on provoking, and then persisted in fighting, America,
he nobly justified the reputation that he had cheaply won by
his panegyrics on Luttrell and his denunciations of Wilkes.

But those eight years were preceded by four others during
which the public doings of Charles Fox were of a nature to
afford more amusement than profit to the student of parliamentary history. His political as well as his moral wild oats
were still to sow; and he set himself to the business of scat-
tering them broadcast with a profusion that has rarely been
equalled in the case of the latter species, and never in that of
the former. With the levity of a schoolboy, the self-reliance

of an ex-prime-minister, and a debating faculty which might be put to better uses, but could not possibly become sharper or swifter than it was already, no portent at once so formidable and so unaccountable had hitherto been witnessed in St. Stephen's. The noble lord who steered the ship of the state, and whose scientific calculations were grievously disturbed by the vagaries of such a meteor, was indefatigable, as long as he had any hope of success, in inducing it to take and keep a place among the fixed constellations. It was evident that something would have to be found for a young gentleman who, according to his own account in later days, was on his legs at least once every evening, and who, by the confession of others, never sat down without having left his mark upon the discussion. At length, on the nineteenth of February, 1770, when many hours had been spent in threshing out a question of unusual intricacy connected with the Middlesex election, Wedderburn, by a singularly ingenious and well-timed argument, had convinced even his opponents that there was no precedent for the course recommended by the government, in a matter where precedent was everything; and honorable members were just settling down to the disagreeable conviction that they would have to vote against their common-sense, or see their party defeated, when Charles Fox started up, and produced a case in point so apt and recent as entirely to cut the ground from under Wedderburn. The House "roared with applause;" the king, delighted by a majority which exceeded his most sanguine expectations, begged the prime-minister to give him the particulars of a debate which had been crowned by so brilliant a victory; and, on the very day after his Majesty had heard Lord North's report of what had passed, a new writ was moved for the borough of Midhurst in consequence of Mr. Charles Fox having been appointed a junior lord of the Admiralty.[1]

---

[1] Fox's patent as Lord of the Admiralty was made out on the twenty-eighth of February, 1770. Walpole makes Fox confute Wedderburn on the twenty-fifth of January; but a careful comparison of his narrative with reports of the debates of the twenty-fifth of January and the nineteenth of February proves almost to certainty that he confused the dates.

It is easy to imagine the feelings with which Lord Holland watched the son of his hopes, while not yet of age, fighting his way towards the enchanted portals of office, and then reaching out his hand to receive a prize which came only just too late to be a birthday present.   The father's letters abound in expressions of satisfaction so hearty and affectionate as to awaken in the reader an evanescent sympathy even for the doleful dissertations on the guile and ingratitude of mankind with which those letters are plentifully interlarded.   "The newspapers, I am told, have forgot me;" so the old gentle-man writes to Selwyn from Nice, in February, 1770.   "You, I see, remember me.   The excessive fine weather we have here, and Charles's fame, have certainly for some days past made my spirits better than they had been since I saw you; and yet the man I envy most is the late lord chamberlain, for he is dead, and he died suddenly.   If that dog Beckford should be dead, I must not envy him;" and the writer then proceeds to put forward, as the ground on which he for-bore to envy Beckford, certain gloomy probabilities which, when his own death occurred, it is to be feared that many were uncharitable enough to give as their reason for not en-vying Lord Holland.   "I told you," he says again, "that Charles's fame had made Lady Holland more curious about politics.   I would not give twopence for some people's opin-ion; but what I wish most to hear is Charles's of his own speaking."   "Your panegyric upon Charles," so runs another passage, "came about an hour after I wrote mine.   He writes word that upon February the twelfth he spoke very ill.   I do not mind that; and when he speaks so well as to be, as Lady Mary says,[1] the wonder of the age, it does not give me so much pleasure as what you, very justly, I think, tell me *de son cœur*.

By this time Walpole was no longer in Parliament, and got his House of Commons information at second-hand.

[1] Lady Mary Fitzpatrick, daughter of the first Earl of Upper Ossory, married Stephen Fox in 1766, and died four years after him, in 1778. Her own letters, and every allusion made to her in the letters of others, indicate that she was such a woman as all who knew the third Lord Holland would suppose his mother to have been.

And yet that may not signify; for, if I know myself, I have been honest and good-natured; nor can I repent of it, though convinced now that honesty is not the best policy, and that good-nature does not meet with the return it ought to do."

Lord Holland's predictions with regard to Beckford's future, and his lamentations over his own ill-requited virtue, had their origin from one and the same source. He had of late been much exercised by the conduct of certain officious individuals who had threatened him with the bailiffs in order to force him to explain what he was doing with the large sums of public money that still remained in his hands; and he was yet more seriously disturbed when Beckford, as Lord Mayor of London, presented the king with a petition from the City which, after bringing a long series of elaborate accusations against the ministry, disposed of the ex-paymaster in a single half-sentence as "the public defaulter of unaccounted millions." If he had been still in active political employment, the old statesman would not have given the charge a moment's thought; but he was not exempt from that retrospective sensitiveness which is generally observable in men of ambition and energy who have been elbowed out of the game, and reduced to live on the reminiscences of their own past. After a correspondence with Beckford, maintained on his side in a tone rather plaintive and indignant, Lord Holland published a statement which proved incontestably that the procrastination in making up his books and paying in his balances, with which he had been taunted as a crime, was neither illegal nor unusual. But in defending himself he laid bare the abuses of a system which might well make an economist shudder; for his memorandum disclosed the extraordinary fact that the country did not clear accounts with the chief of all its financial agents until those accounts were at least half a generation in arrear. The accounts of the regiments that fought for George the Second at Dettingen and Culloden were only declared a few months before George the Third ascended the throne. The accounts of the regiments that had been disbanded after the Peace of Aix-la-Chapelle during the summer of 1748 had not been declared at the time that Lord Holland was writing his

exculpation in the summer of 1769. It was therefore unrea-
sonable to call hard names, and set the sheriff's officer to
work, because the accounts of the regiments which had secured America to the British Crown at Quebec would in all
likelihood be still unsettled when Lord North and his royal
master had succeeded in losing the best part of what Wolfe
had conquered. But, having made out that part of the case
which told in his favor, the calumniated administrator did not
think it necessary to remind the tax-payers that every month
during which the audit was postponed brought into his pocket
large emoluments, such as, even in his own day, men of delicacy scrupled, and high-minded men flatly refused, to take.
It was frequently asserted in print, and has never been con-
tradicted, that, to say nothing of what he gained as paymaster, the interest on the balances which were outstanding after
he left office made Lord Holland and Lord Holland's family
richer by a quarter of a million pounds; not one half-penny
of which Chatham would have condescended to touch before
him, or Burke after him.[1]

---

[1] Proceedings against the ex-paymaster had been actually commenced
in the Court of Exchequer, and were only stayed by a warrant from the
Crown. Lord Holland addressed a pathetic, if rather irregular, communication to Baron Smith, who may probably have been the judge before
whom his cause was to come on for trial. "To be made," he wrote, "so
miserable by the undeserved abuse I meet with, your lordship says is
weakness. But if my being held up to all England as one of the greatest rascals in it should incline Mr. Baron Smith to think me so, your lordship cannot blame me if I wish he were set right. Indeed, my lord, it is
impossible to be more blameless in that article upon which Mr. Horn,
Mr. Beckford, every newspaper, and all England have accused me. Mr.
Winnington's executors were near twenty years before he could pass his
accounts. Mr. Pitt was fourteen years before he could pass his. My
Lord Kinnoul was twelve years, though he had but two years' accounts
to pass. Is it not natural to suppose that the difficulty is in the nature
of things, and no fault of the paymaster, and this cruel abuse of me is
really for not being forwarder by ten years than anybody else was?
Don't let Baron Smith, who, I hear, is a worthy man, censure me for what
I cannot help, and let him know to what an infinite degree, and your
lordship would say sillily, I feel the abuse that I meet with. Charles is
my secretary; so nobody else will know that I trouble you with this."

Lord Holland had some excuse for exclaiming against the
injustice of an unpopularity which time did not mitigate, and
which followed him into the seclusion where a disgraced minister has the right to look at least for safety.   When he appealed from the relentless hatred with which he was regarded by
people who had never seen him except through the window
of his coach, to the devoted affection which he obtained from
those who were with him the most, and who knew him the
best, he can hardly be blamed for esteeming himself a misun-
derstood man.   While the City was still demanding his impeachment as vociferously as it had demanded the impeachment of Bolingbroke and Oxford within a month of their fall;
while satirists were reproaching Charles Fox on his parentage
with a ferocity which might have scared a more timid parliamentary novice and alienated a less loving son[1]—all was well,
or, at any rate, well enough for Lord Holland, in the home
where he sought for the repose and happiness that were denied him elsewhere.   It is no wonder that he was endeared to
all who were dependent upon him for their welfare and con-
tentment.   "He had that temper which kind folks have been
pleased to say belongs to our family."   Such was the testimony of his grandson; and, over and above the Fox temper,
Lord Holland was largely endowed with the Fox tact.   Like
all who bore a name which the language of society has raised
to the dignity of a laudatory epithet, he was entirely free from
prosiness and pretension, and from that ambition in small
things which will make cleverness tiresome, and render even
genius a disagreeable inmate in a household.   Those very
qualities which have earned him a black mark in history had
their amiable side when viewed from within his own doors,
and contributed to the domestic comfort, if not to the moral

---

[1] " Welcome, hereditary worth!
  No doubt, no blush, belies thy birth,
    Prone as the infernal fiends to evil.
  If that black face and that black heart
  Be not old Holland's counterpart,
    Holland himself 's unlike the devil."
Ode to St. Stephen (in " The Foundling for Wit " of 1772).

advantage, of himself and of those with whom and for whom he lived. The cynical indifference to the character of his instruments and his allies, which had done so much to discredit him as a statesman, took within the precincts of Holland House the form of an inexhaustible tolerance which exceeds all recorded instances of paternal facility. He was not the father to quarrel with his children for being what his own carelessness had made them.[1] He asked, as he had a right to ask, that they should give him their confidence; that they should be at ease in his presence, and fight his battles behind his back; that they should share with him some of their innumerable enjoyments, and sympathize to a reasonable extent with his richly merited grievances. But he asked nothing more. As long as Charles would treat him like an elder brother (a point on which the lad indulged him without infringing on the strictest filial respect, or abating an atom of that eager and minute dutifulness which he exhibited in all his personal relations), he was welcome to do as he pleased with his own time and with Lord Holland's money. He might be the talk of London and of Paris for his irregularities and extravagances; he might stuff every bill-case in the Minories with his acceptances, and lose in a night the proceeds of a twelvemonth's jobbery at the Pay-office; he might fling away his unequalled political chances in the wantonness of every passing impulse—if only he would write to his father as he wrote to George Selwyn, and talk to him as he talked to Lord Carlisle; if only he would spare him an evening in the week to discuss the odds at Newmarket, and laugh over the faces which were pulled on the Treasury bench when the Junior Lord of the Admiralty committed ministers to a policy of which they heard for the first time from the young gentleman's lips, or when he fell tooth and nail on the attorney-

---

[1] "Who ever had children," he wrote to an old friend, "that do not, when they are young men, do what their father had rather they would not do? I have found it, dear Mr. Crawford, in a very essential instance; and, *memor illum puerum esse, me fuisse*, I acted as you do; and I dare say you applaud yourself for the success of your good-natured behavior. I do not regret mine."

general with a mutinous vigor which recalled to the delighted sire his own historical onslaught on Lord Hardwicke's Marriage Bill.

The ugliest of all the features in Lord Holland's character acquired a softer aspect by the light of his own fireside. His unsparing and unreasoning generosity to his children, in itself another fault, does something to render less odious the rapacity for which he is proverbially remembered. Without a spark of the patriotism which dignified the selfishness of Wolsey and the cupidity of Marlborough, he regarded the interests of the nation much as his namesake in the animal world regards the interest of the poultry-yard; but at any rate he was not, like the great soldier, actuated by avarice, nor, like the churchman, by a passion for personal display. He plundered the many, whom he neither hated nor loved, in order to load with wealth and surfeit with pleasure the few human beings for whose benefit he would have laid down his life as readily and as lightly as he sacrificed his conscience and his reputation. When Stephen Fox was affianced to Lord Ossory's daughter, his father addressed a striking and pathetic letter to the Duke of Bedford, whose kinswoman the lady was. "I am extremely sensible," he wrote, "of the honor done my son, and will contribute (besides dying very soon) to what may give the young people great affluence;" and there was a wish as well as a prophecy in that quaint parenthesis. "I will come," he added, "into whatever they shall propose." Few, even among the class who make the marriage of their children an opportunity for buying a step of social promotion, would bind themselves beforehand by so liberal a pledge when dealing with the settlements of their eldest son; and fewer still, at a time of life when all men feel the value of money, except those who have never made or kept it, would allow a younger son, and such a specimen of a younger son as Charles Fox, to treat his father's fortune as his own.

In February, 1770, that fortune, though not intact, was still enormous. With all the will in the world, the young man had wanted the time to make any serious impression upon the mountain of wealth out of which Lord Holland fondly expected to carve him a patrimony greater than was enjoyed by half the peerage. The Kensington estate was to go with the title; but Charles was carefully instructed to regard himself as the future master of a country retreat which his father loved with the absorbing and tenacious affection which he cherished towards everything and everybody that he loved at all, and on which, fortunately for Holland House, he had concentrated his architectural industry, and tested his theories of classical and romantic decoration. At the extreme point of the Kentish coast, a little more than half a mile from the North Foreland, there runs down to the sea a dell which in the days of the Stuarts was secured against smugglers and privateers by a rampart and a portcullis. The place owed its designation of King's Gate Stairs to a chance visit of Charles the Second, who, on his way between London and Dover, once passed a few minutes on a spot which was destined to be the nursery of an offshoot of royalty whom, both for his merits and his failings, the monarch would have been proud to acknowledge as a descendant. On this site, so exquisitely adapted to recall the languors of the Caietan Gulf, Lord Holland had built himself a habitation which purported "to represent Tully's Formian villa." He fitted up the house with genuine antiquities, which soon came to the hammer; and planted the whole neighborhood, far and near, with sham castles and abbeys which have since been converted to homely uses, and rechristened with still homelier names. King's Gate, in every particular, was exactly to its owner's taste. There (an advantage which, with much reason, he placed foremost among the attractions of the home that he had chosen) he could forget himself, and hope that he was forgotten by others. There, as he wrote to Lord Shelburne before their quarrel, sea air gave him "appetite, sleep, and spirits." There he was "very happy and amused with trifles that lead to nothing sad and serious." He never tired of riding about the country, directing the progress of undertakings that stood him instead of those rural occupations which he was too much of a Londoner to appreciate. While Burke was making money by selling his carrots, and losing it by giving them to his live-stock; while

Chatham watched his trees with the eye of a woodman, and made a shift to keep within hearing of the chase when the boys took the field with their harriers—Lord Holland was training ivy over his turrets and cloisters; mounting cannons along the cliff; raffling for statues of Flora and Bacchus, and busts of Pertinax and Crispina; excavating burial-mounds; rearing a pillar to commemorate a battle between Danes and Saxons which in all likelihood never had been fought; and erecting a tower "in the Roman style" in honor of an anti-Wilkite lord mayor of London who had probably earned his monument by throwing cold water on the demand for an inquiry into the paymaster's accounts.[1]

So absorbed had been Lord Holland in the place which he was creating that the last and heaviest blow of fortune, his ejection from the Pay-office, fell lightly upon him because he was at King's Gate when the news arrived. "It comes chiefly, I understand, from the Bedfords," so he wrote to his wife; "which is as it should be, for there is not one of them that is not greatly obliged to me. Now, my dear Caroline, let us consider how this affects us. There is an end of every view; but then there is not any we had all set our hearts on. I should have liked to be an earl; but indeed I should be ashamed if at my age I could not give up that with the utmost ease. What, then, have we to regret? You never thought of a court

---

[1] This edifice, raised, in other than the Roman style, to a height which qualifies it to serve as a sea-mark, now goes by the appellation of "Candlestick Tower." "My tower in honor of Mr. Harley," wrote Lord Holland, "is built, I believe, more for my private amusement than from public spirit; but he is really almost the only man that has not been a coward." Lord Holland embodied his gratitude to the Tory lord mayor in an inscription drawn from Horace:

> " Justum et tenacem propositi virum
>   Non civium ardor prava jubentium
>   Mente quatit solida."

It does not need a very profound scholar to detect the hiatus in the stanza, and to understand the reason of it. The same most significant omission may be observed under a bust of Lord Eldon which has been banished into an obscure corner of the Chancery offices.

life, and neither my health nor age would have admitted of
politics. It seems, then, that this only leads to the life we
must and should have led. We shall have money enough for
everything but gaming, and nothing were sufficient for that.
You'll live at your favorite Holland House a good deal, and
little more than the four hot months will suffice for me here.
How will it affect the children? I hope not at all. This does
not hinder Ste from having the world before him. Charles
will be angry, I believe; but at his age it will do him no
harm, and he may be the more egged on by it. May I not
build on him for my hours of comfort? Harry is too young
and happy ever to know of this. He is the happiest of mor-
tals, and gone to show Lords Ilchester and Bateman the Mar-
gate sands, while I am writing in a room prettier than you can
imagine. Well, Caroline, I don't think you need, or will, turn
your eyes from this prospect." Three days afterwards he
wrote: "Harry has a little horse to ride, and his whole stable-
ful to look after. He lives with the horse; stinks, talks, and
thinks perpetually of the stable; and is not a very good companion. Now the others are gone, I shall try to make him
more so. He has just found out that I am turned out, and, you
may be sure, don't care a farthing; but he has been so intent
upon his horses that though he must have heard it mentioned
a hundred times since Saturday, it was not to his purpose, and
he never heeded it. After the stable was shut up last night,
he came of his own accord, and read very prettily some
words. We shall be at a loss what to read, I find. I wish
you could advise."

This letter was written in May, 1764, and twelve years afterwards, unfortunately for his happiness and dignity, Lord
Holland was still hankering after that step in the peerage
which he had so confidently professed to have renounced. In
August, 1772, excited at seeing the prize which had so often
been refused him conferred on two of his brother-barons, he
commissioned Charles to lay his claims before the prime-minister. North dared not himself inflict a rebuff upon a member
of Parliament who just at that time was the most formidable
of free lances; but the king, who disliked the young orator

more than he feared him, sent word " that the door was now shut, and that for the present no more earldoms would be granted." Then, as a last hope, Lord Holland had recourse to Bute, and dictated a piteous letter reminding his ancient confederate of those services which, if the voice of the country had been taken, would have been rewarded by a very different sort of elevation from that which he coveted.[1] " Do you remember," he asked, " you who never deceived me, when you told me if I asked anything for my children I should see the esteem the king had for me? I see no signs of it." Bute replied kindly, but decisively. " The very few opportunities I have had for many years," he said, " of being of the least service to any person are now at an end. The sad event of this fatal year has left me without a single friend near the royal person,[2] and I have taken the only part suited to my way of thinking—that of retiring from the world before it retires from me." Lord Holland had now nothing for it but to follow the advice and example which Bute had given him; and, late and perforce, he sought consolation and employment for the evening of life in pursuits more congenial to his better nature than an unprofitable and unacceptable attendance at St. James's. He was, and always had been when he cared for it, one of those who had admission to a yet more privileged circle.

> " That place that does contain
> My books, the best companions, is to me
> A glorious court, where hourly I converse
> With the old sages and philosophers."

---

[1] Mason, in his " Heroic Epistle," proposed to construct a sort of political Chamber of Horrors, containing a row of scaffolds:

> " On this shall Holland's dying speech be read;
> Here Bute's confession, and his wooden head.
> While all the minor plunderers of the age,
> Too numerous for this contracted page,
> The Rigbys, Mungos, and the Bradshaws there
> In straw-stuffed effigy shall kick the air."

[2] The princess-dowager had died in the preceding February.

17

His letters thenceforward are marked by an unvarying tone
of serenity and resignation. "I have lost," he writes, "for
more than three months past every symptom of an asthma,
every apprehension of a dropsy. My distemper is old age;
and, good physician as you are, dear Ellis, you cannot cure me
of that." "I rise from a very good night," he tells Lady Caroline from King's Gate; "as mine almost without exception
have been here. As you truly say, life is only a reprieve."
"I talk," he remarks elsewhere, "a good deal of cheerful nonsense in a day, and in every day. The truth is that I divert
myself, yet cannot help thinking very often that it were better it were all over."

King's Gate is a standing evidence of the faint impression
which the eighteenth century has left upon the imagination
of our people. If anything connected with the worthies of the
Reformation or the heroes of the Long Parliament—anything
so absolutely unaltered and so intensely characteristic of the
ideas and manners of the time—stood sixty miles from London, and within a walk of two crowded watering-places, its
name would be a household word in every educated family of
the kingdom. And indeed the tourist, as he turns the summit
of the ascent that is crowned by the North Foreland light-
house, wonders for a moment that the striking and singular
prospect which lies below him should not have taken rank
among the noted localities of our island. But, as he continues
to gaze and begins to reflect, he is forced to confess that the
hand of man has spoiled the desolate grandeur of the scene
without adding to it the charms of association. The instinct
of the least practised antiquarian tells him at a second glance
that the castle, which rears itself in such bold relief against
the perfect whiteness of the more distant cliff, was planted
there long since the days when even so unpopular a baron as
Lord Holland wanted a castle to protect him; while the Tower of Neptune, perched on the bastion that guards the other
flank of the little bay, and the detached fragments of ruin,
thrown in wherever they are demanded by the principles of
the picturesque, give to a point of our coast which has some
claims of its own to be the most famous headland in the world,
an air of masquerading as the promontory of Sunium.

But, as we descend the hill, the absurdities of the higher ground are lost to view, and the genuine interest of the spot makes itself insensibly and irresistibly felt. Lord Holland, though bound as a man of taste to erect castles, was far too much a man of sense to inhabit them. Right across the mouth of the tiny valley, filling it from bank to bank with its square main building and formal wings—most conspicuous to seaward, but curiously invisible from the land—there spreads itself an ugly, comfortable mansion which now, together with other heterogeneous inmates, lodges a party of coast-guardsmen and their officer. The glen behind the house runs gradually up into the plain, densely overgrown with stunted windstricken timber, worthless enough to be secure even under such a master as Charles Fox; and in front a platform, fifty yards in width, separates the façade from the edge of the cliff, which just there is hardly forty feet above the level of the beach. The narrow gap in the dwarf precipice, which gives the place its name, is cut in two by an isolated curtain of chalk, of about the height and thickness of a garden wall, leaving on either side a passage, in appearance rather a chimney than a road, which affords a somewhat perilous access to the shingle beneath. Other corners of England, and perhaps many others, possess reminiscences more inspiring, but none more enlivening and authentic. Down that little pathway through the chalk has often tripped the heroine of as pleasant and innocent a royal romance as any in our history; and, pacing up and down that strip of gravel, or seated on the sills of those unsightly but hospitable windows, lounged and chatted, a hundred years ago and more, a group of friends and cousins as merry, as affectionate, as easily and, it may be, as inexcusably contented with each other and themselves as ever were gathered together for Christmas sports and summer idleness —a group of which the leader and the idol was the lad who already bade fair to be the greatest known master of the art in which, of all arts, an Englishman covets to excel.[1]   To Lord

---

[1] "Brougham is quite right about Charles Fox," said Macaulay. "He was, indeed, *a* great orator; but then he was *the* great debater."

Holland himself the situation of King's Gate had peculiar advantages. It was no slight convenience for an elderly valetudinarian to embark at his own front door on those foreign tours which, since he left office, had become the most adventurous of his enterprises; and he saved some expense, and much risk of irreparable damage, by shipping the Etruscan vases and Roman altars, which then were the spoils of travel, straight from Leghorn or the Chiaja to his own private landing-place. " All my things," he says to Charles, in July, 1767, "have come from Naples. I shall make King's Gate very pretty for you, and have almost fixed upon a plan for a new house, where I hope you will spend many happy hours after I am dead and gone. I hope to spend a few with you soon; and, upon my word, I think of none with anything like pleasure but those I love, and you most sincerely."

That part of Lord Holland's prayer which related to the immediate future was abundantly and agreeably fulfilled. Charles, during the seven years that his father still had to live, spent at King's Gate many of his most profitable and his happiest hours; if, indeed, for such a nature one hour could be perceptibly happier than another. Here he laid the foundation of his profound and extensive acquaintance with history, a department of knowledge in which he was ere long reputed to stand on a level with Burke, and (which, indeed, was not difficult) to be greatly the superior of Johnson. But the spirit in which, while still a colleague of Sandwich and of Halifax, Charles Fox imbibed his constitutional learning was very different from the spirit in which he was one day to utilize it as the vindicator of personal liberty, and the creator of our freedom of the press. " I am reading Clarendon," he writes from King's Gate to George Selwyn in 1771, " but scarcely get on faster than you did with your ' Charles the Fifth.' I think the style bad, and that he has a good deal of the old woman in his way of thinking, but hate the opposite party so much that it gives one a kind of partiality for him:" strange words to fall from the pen of one whose bust now looks down from beneath the centre of the cornice in half the Whig libraries in the kingdom. At King's Gate, too, he continued that minute and all-embracing study of the classics which enabled him to hold his own, and more than his own, with such a bookworm as Gilbert Wakefield on the most delicate points of scholarship which lurked unsolved in the least frequented nooks of ancient literature.   One of his favorite, and certainly his cheapest, amusements was to turn over Apollonius Rhodius in search of passages containing hints which had been improved upon by greater poets.[1]   And in the very lowest depths of his political misfortunes he found consolation in jesting at his own expense out of the " Cassandra " of Lycophron—a work which, in a generation of grammarians and commentators who valued books primarily for their obscurity, had obtained for its author the distinguishing epithet of " the obscure."

But Charles Fox had nothing of a pedant except the acquirements.   His vast and varied mass of erudition, far exceeding that of many men who have been famous for nothing else, was all aglow with the intense vitality of his eager and brilliant intellect.   He trod with a sure step through the treasure-house of antiquity, guided by a keenness of insight into the sentiments and the circumstances of the remote past

---

[1] Fox esteemed the " Argonautics " for their own sake, as well as for the obligations under which Ovid and Virgil lay with regard to them. " Your notion," he wrote to Wakefield, " in respect to poets borrowing from each other seems almost to come up to mine, who have often been laughed at by my friends as a systematic defender of plagiarism. I got Lord Holland, when a schoolboy, to write some verses in praise of it; and, in truth, the greatest poets have been most guilty, if guilt there be, in these matters. But there are some parts of Apollonius, such as lib. iii. from 453 to 463, and from 807 to 816, that appear to me unrivalled." "I looked," notes Macaulay, " at these passages, and was pleased to find that I had marked them both when I read Apollonius Rhodius at Calcutta. The second I had marked exactly to a line." The two Whigs read their classics with the same eyes. Macaulay's favorite morsels in Latin were the letters in which Cæsar expressed his clemency towards his conquered enemies; and those letters were quite as much to the taste of Fox. When the Duke of Enghien was arrested, Fox copied out the Epistle to Oppius, with the intention of sending it to Napoleon, but was prevented by the arrival of the fatal news.

which, in an epoch of criticism far less in sympathy with
either Athenian or Roman feeling than our own, amounted to
little short of positive inspiration. With an appetite to which
nothing came amiss, he possessed a taste that was all but infallible. He could derive pleasure and profit out of anything
written in Greek or Latin, from a philippic of Cicero or
Demosthenes to an excursus by Casaubon; but he reserved
his allegiance for the true sovereigns of literature. That
dramatist who is the special delight of the mature and the
experienced was his idol from the very first. "Euripides,"
he would say, " is the most precious thing left us—the most
like Shakespeare;" and he knew him as Shakespeare was
known to Charles Lamb and to Coleridge. "Read him," he
enjoined on young Lord Holland, "till you love his very
faults." He went through the "Iliad" and the "Odyssey"
more than once a year; and, while he counted every omitted
digamma, and was always ready to cover four sides of letter-
paper with a disquisition on Homeric prosody or chronology,
there is ample proof that, as far as feeling and observation
were concerned, he had anticipated that exquisite vein of
criticism which is the special charm of the most charming
portion of Mr. Ruskin's writings.[1] Next to Homer among

---

[1] Casual remarks which might be the text for disquisitions on Homer
resembling those which help to render the third volume of "Modern
Painters" incomparable among productions of its class are scattered
thick through Fox's talk and letters. His notice of the bard's dislike of
Hercules; of his tenderness to all women except those good-for-nothing
hussies at the Court of Ithaca who had insulted a better woman than
themselves; of the ghastly episode at the Suitors' banquet, where, as he
truly says, second-sight is treated with a power unrivalled by the poets
of the country in which that unpleasant gift is supposed to be indige-
nous; his observation of the circumstance that Homer never mentions
the singing of birds, and that Penelope cannot bring herself to speak of
Troy or of Ulysses by name—are symptoms indicative of the spirit in
which Fox studied his "Odyssey." When asked the question which all
literary people have been asking each other since the days of Pisistratus,
"I would not," he replied, "say I would rather have written the 'Odyssey,' but I know that I would rather read it. I believe it to be the first
tale in the world."

the ancients—and even above Homer, at the period to which
this chapter refers—Fox placed Virgil, whose pathos (so he
declared) surpassed that of all poets of every age and nation,
with the single exception which, as an Englishman with the
Elizabethan drama at his fingers' ends, he somewhat unwill-
ingly considered himself bound to make. "It is on that account," he continued, "that I rank him so very high; for
surely to excel in that style which speaks to the heart is the
greatest of all excellence." His favorite example of the quality that he admired in the "Æneid" was the farewell with
which the aged Evander sent Pallas forth to his last battle.
The beauty of this passage, in his years of vigor, Fox was always ready to expound and assert; and when his time came to
die, he solemnized his parting with the nephew whom he loved
as a son by bidding the young man repeat aloud, and then repeat once more, lines which, even at a less trying moment, few
who have ever cried over a book can read without tears.[1]

That was the last poetry to which Fox is known to have
listened; and the fact is worth recording, because poetry was
to him what it has been to no one who has ever played a part
at all comparable to his in the sterner and coarser business of
the world. Poetry was in his eyes "the great refreshment
of the human mind," "the only thing after all." It was by
making and enjoying it that men "first discovered themselves
to be rational beings;" and even among the Whigs he would
allow the existence of only one right-thinking politician who
was not a lover of poetry. Literature was "in every point
of view a preferable occupation to politics." Statesmanship
might be a respectable calling; but poetry claimed seven of
the Muses, and oratory none. The poets wrote the best
prose. The poets had more truth in them than all the historians and philosophers together. Much as he admired Johnson's "Lives" (and, except the Church Service, that book was

---

[1] The uncle and nephew at times almost conversed in Virgil. When
Fox was suffering under the dropsy which killed him, Lord Holland
tried to cheer him with "Dabit Deus his *quoque finem*." "Ay," he replied, with a faint smile; "but 'finem,' young one, may have two senses."

the last which was read to him), he never could forgive the author for his disloyalty to some among the most eminent of his heroes. " His treatment," cried Fox, " of Gray, Waller, and Prior is abominable; especially of Gray. As for me, I love all the poets." And well did they repay his affection. They consoled him for having missed everything upon which his heart was set, and to the attainment of which the labor of his life was directed; for the loss of power and of fortune; for his all but permanent exclusion from the privilege of serving his country and the opportunity of benefiting his friends; even for the extinction of that which Burke, speaking from a long and intimate knowledge of his disposition, most correctly called " his darling popularity." At the time when, for the crime of maintaining that the Revolution of 1688 had placed our Constitution upon a popular basis, he had been struck off the privy council, and had been threatened with the Tower; when he never went down to Westminster except to be hopelessly outvoted, or looked into a book-shop or print-shop without seeing himself ferociously lampooned and filthily caricatured, there yet was no more contented man than he throughout all that broad England for whose liberties he suffered. He could forget the insolence of Dundas, and the chicanery of Sir John Scott, while intent upon the debate which Belial and Mammon conducted in a senate-house less agreeable to its inmates even than the House of Commons of 1798 was to the Whigs; and although it was less easy to efface from his recollection the miseries which were endured by humbler patriots than himself, yet the wrongs of Muir and Palmer and Wakefield and Priestley lost something of their sting to one who could divert at will the current of his indignation against the despot who imprisoned Tasso, and the roisterers who affronted Milton. And whenever things were for a moment too hard on him—when he returned to his country home fretted by injustice and worn by turmoil—his wife had only to take down a volume of " Don Quixote " or " Gil Blas," and read to him until his mind was again in tune for the society of Spenser and Metastasio.[1]

---

[1] Fox liked one poem of Metastasio as well as anything of the century,

If, at the period when he was the greatest living master of
the plain and work-a-day English which Englishmen speak
over the conduct of their business, he continued to draw his
inspiration chiefly from the ancient fountains, it is not strange
that he should have preferred the classics to the moderns during the years when life still appears to its possessor rather a
romance than a reality.   And, in truth, he had little choice
in the matter.   It was through no prejudice against his contemporaries that, in his quest of the beautiful and the pathetic, Fox was forced to resort to Chaucer and Dante, and
Cowley and Filicaja.   Unlike some other famous Whigs, he
carried his Whig principles into his library; and, while tenacious of all that was worth preserving in the literature of the
past, he gave every possible proof of his readiness to welcome
what was good in the present.   He overrated Anstey.   He
even made the best of Hayley.[1]   He was forever quoting
frigid passages from Gray, which, if Gray had been dead a
century, he would assuredly have allowed to slumber in their
context.[2]   He tried hard to read Mickle's translation of Ca-
moens; and when his physical strength was already on the
turn, he struggled valiantly through "Madoc;" though his per-

---

and one book of Spenser as well as anything in the world.   During a
single winter, in addition to his daily and almost day-long private
studies, he read aloud to Mrs. Fox, Tasso, Ariosto, Milton, Spenser, Apollonius Rhodius, Lucretius, Virgil, and Homer, nine epic poems, according
to his own count.   Two of them, he said, whatever their other merits,
were far and away the most entertaining—the "Odyssey" and the "Or-
lando Furioso."

[1] "I think," Fox wrote to the third Lord Holland, "that you hold poor
Hayley too cheap.   His 'History of Old Maids,' and parts of the 'Trials
of Temper,' are, I think, very good."

[2] "His face brightened and his voice rose" as he repeated the descriptions of nature in Gray's "Fragment on the Alliance of Education and
Government."   But when he came to the point where

"The blue-eyed myriads from the Baltic coast"

were cheered on their southward march by the hope soon to "scent the
fragrance of the breathing rose," the master-gardener of St. Anne's Hill
could not abstain from remarking that it was rather unlucky for the
poet that the rose blew in the North of Europe.

severance in that case was the less meritorious from his being under an engagement to his nephew that, as soon as he had done with Southey, he would embark upon the shoreless ocean of Lope de Vega.[1]

But while Fox was young, not even the generous credulity of youth could beguile him into the belief that he lived in an age of poetry. It was seldom indeed that he then had a chance of displaying the discriminating ardor with which, as a boy of sixteen, he pounced upon Goldsmith's " Traveller."[2] The three great authors who were the delight of what may be called his middle period had as yet hardly set foot on the lowest slopes of Parnassus. Crabbe was still rolling bandages, and Burns had just been promoted to guide the plough. Cowper, deep in the Olney hymns, had at that time published nothing to which Fox, whose taste was almost too secular for "Paradise Regained," would ever have vouchsafed a second reading. The dearth of genius in British literature was such as to inspire Horace Walpole with the curiously unfortunate prophecy that the next Augustan age would dawn on the other side of the Atlantic, and that the country which in the coming generation was to boast a galaxy of poets which the Rome of Mæcenas might have envied would have to seek a Virgil in New York. It was no wonder that, in order to find in the sphere of letters something which answered to his own dancing and buoyant conceptions of the universe upon which

---

[1] The young peer had translated some of Lope de Vega, and gave an account of his author which staggered an enthusiast of the drama who was not easily frightened. " What can you mean," wrote Fox, " by eighteen hundred plays of Lope ? Consider, if he was thirty years at it, that would make five per month. I shall be very happy if you can spare a morning to read with me two or three, for I do not think I shall be equal to them myself." Two years afterwards the uncle was still trying to put off the evil day. " We have been so occupied with 'Madoc,' " he says, " that we have not yet looked at Lope ; but we will begin immediately."

[2] " If there were any way of sending you pamphlets," he writes to Russia, to George Macartney, in 1765, " I could send you a new poem, called the 'Traveller,' which appears to me to have a good deal of merit. I do not know anything else that I would advise you to read if you were here."

he had so lately entered, Charles Fox turned from Home's
"Douglas" and Mason's "Elfrida" and Glover's "Athenaid"
to the "Winter's Tale" and the "Maid of Honor," to the
"Rape of the Lock" and the "Flower and the Leaf." How
freely he had luxuriated in the poetry of romance during those
enchanted years when alone the memory retains without an
effort was known to every visitor at St. Anne's Hill who had
tried the easy experiment of tempting him from his desk into
his garden on a June morning. At such a time his companion might draw as copiously as he chose (for Fox had too much
of the orator's half-conscious but ever-present sympathy with
his hearers to inflict on them an unacceptable syllable) from
stores of vivid criticism and apt quotation, which sufficed for
many and many a stroll among his rhododendrons and azaleas
—past the urn inscribed with the prettiest couplets in the tale
of Dryden that he loved the best;[1] and the mass of laurus-
tinus embowering the retreat which the most intimate of his

---

[1] " The painted birds, companions of the spring,
        Hopping from spray to spray, were heard to sing.
        Both eyes and ears received a like delight,
        Enchanting music and a charming sight.
        On Philomel I fixed my whole desire,
        And listened for the queen of all the quire.
        Fain would I hear her heavenly voice to sing,
        And wanted yet an omen to the spring.

        .   .   .   .   .

        So sweet, so shrill, so variously she sung
        That the grove echoed, and the valleys rung."

The lines are from the "Flower and the Leaf; or, The Lady in the
Arbor"—a title which must have attracted the fancy of one who was not
averse to ladies, and who had probably constructed more arbors than
any son of Adam. Lord Holland's mania for building had in Charles
Fox most fortunately taken the shape of a passion for rustic architecture
on a scale that suited his slender means. He loved temples in gardens
(so he told Rogers). There was nothing he would like so much as a
Temple of the Muses; and he wished that anybody (including, and probably meaning, Mrs. Fox) would let him build one. Lord Newburgh, he
said, who had been the architect of King's Gate, was a man of great
taste, and had been good enough to build him a temple.

guests respected when he was seated there with Ariosto; and the Temple of Friendship, designed by the same hand which had planned the paternal mansion beneath whose roof he had begun to amass his treasures of learning and imagination.

What the reminiscences of King's Gate were to Charles Fox could not be better described than in the commencement of the fine soliloquy which Cowper puts into the mouth of the harassed minister of state, who is perhaps the most powerfully drawn of all his characters.[1] When the great politician had grown old enough to feel the weariness of politics, and to understand the craving for

> " that repose
> The servant of the public never knows,"

it must have been with sensations curiously compounded between honorable pride and bitter self-reproach that he first perused those touching and forcible lines.   Like the statesman in the poem, he had cultivated a " taste for ancient song" in his father's halls; but there the resemblance stopped. Fox never scorned the studies with which he once had been familiar, nor lost, by his own neglect, a single friend; and he had so behaved himself in the fiery ordeal of parliamentary life that he might have returned to the " groves " of King's Gate without the obligation of addressing to them the humiliating confession—

> " Receive me now, not uncorrupt as then,
> Nor guiltless of corrupting other men,
> But versed in arts that, while they seem to stay
> A falling empire, hasten its decay."

But by that time the home of his youth was his no longer.

---

[1] The " Retirement " was written during the summer of 1781, and published in the following winter. The story of the minister who knew the Court and the senate so much better than he knew himself is told with briskness and conciseness in the hundred-and-twenty lines which come just half-way through the poem. These are probably the verses which Cowper, as he informs Mr. Unwin in a letter of that date, had " finished and polished, and touched and retouched with the utmost care," writing them at the rate of a dozen, instead, as had been usual with him, of sixty, lines a morning. *O, si sic omnia!*

" Men of spirit," Ben Jonson tells us, "seldom keep earth long;" and the acres of King's Gate, as well as the groves that stood upon them, had long ere that gone the way of everything which Fox possessed except his public honor and his political conscience.

The earliest of those follies which stripped him of his patrimony before he had learned the importance of money, and of the solid worldly position which money gives, were committed beneath his father's eye. For some years together, about this period of the family history, Lord Holland made it a rule to spend his winter in the South of Europe; and his annual migrations, with sons, sisters-in-law, daughters-in-law, and tutors in his train, were, for the time that they lasted, more expensive than the travels of any one under an emperor.[1] A rumor that false dice were being dug up at Herculaneum had excited a faint antiquarian interest in the London clubs, and Charles had been commissioned to procure a pair for exhibition at White's. But he soon had reason to suspect that the manufacture was not obsolete in the neighborhood of Vesuvius, for, when he sailed from Naples on his homeward journey, he left his father poorer, it is said, by sixteen thousand pounds. As far as the public has been permitted to judge, no trace of vexation can be detected in the older man, or of compunction in the younger. The slightest change for the better or the worse in Lord Holland's health affected Charles far more keenly than did his own infrequent gains and stupendous losses; and an occasional letter from a former political ally, containing the particulars of the son's last eloquent impertinence in the House of Commons never failed to evoke from the father expressions of unbounded, and ·apparently uncheckered, satisfaction in a lad who was costing him, and for three years continued to cost him, a thousand guineas a week.

---

[1] Lord Holland, and Mr. Jesse, the editor of " George Selwyn and his Contemporaries," are at issue about the dates of these tours. As to the nature of the incidents, there is no discrepancy whatever between the various authorities.

Lord Holland's renunciation of his paternal authority was the more disastrous because the only other influence which could have reclaimed or restrained the prodigal was exerted, so far as it was exerted at all, on the wrong side. Charles, who dreaded nothing so much as giving pain, and who at a later date, when he had been brought to see that the effort was demanded of him by honor, proved that he had the strength of will to fling off in a moment the evil habits of a lifetime, would never have braved his mother's displeasure or hardened himself against her sorrow. But Lady Holland had been born and bred in the society which took its tone from Lord Chesterfield, who had laid it down as an eleventh commandment, to be kept much more religiously than the other ten, that a man of fashion should hold it a matter of duty to be on the best of terms with the greatest possible number of fine French ladies. And the finest French ladies, while they encouraged Hume to discuss books, and bore with Priestley while he expounded the properties of nitrogen, and could even summon the appropriate emotions when Burke reasoned with them on the terrors of religion, had no notion of selling their patronage so cheap to a young fellow who had still his name to make. These celebrated dames, whose memory owes so much to the species of intellectual canonization which has befallen every Frenchman and Frenchwoman who wrote, read, or gossiped during the generation that preceded the Revolution—who are now venerated as the enterprising and indefatigable agents of a system of free-trade in thought, always on the alert to secure for their own country the most recent ideas that had been generated across the Channel—while they could discourse by the hour about Richardson and Locke, seldom forgot that there was something in England better worth importing than sentimental novels and trial by jury. The political sympathy between the two capitals took à practical and profitable form when it brought over to Paris during the Christmas recess two or three experienced members of Parliament who could be relied upon for a confidential opinion as to the probability of Wilkes being unseated, and three or four of their youthful colleagues who were ready to

bet a thousand francs on either side of the great question at
the bidding of a pretty or witty countess who piqued herself
upon having made a special study of the British Constitution.
Nor, in order to have a share of the English money, was it
necessary to be at the pains of mastering the ins and outs of
the Middlesex election. "There was play at my house on
Sunday till five in the morning," wrote Madame du Deffand
in December, 1769. "The Fox lost a hundred and fifty
louis. I fancy this young man will not get off for his stay
here under two or three thousand louis."

In order to comprehend the history of Fox's mind, as well
as the part which he took in the most stirring events of his
own, and perhaps of all time, it is necessary to keep in view
the circumstance that during the most impressionable years
of his life he was subjected to an influence which was then
all-powerful, but which is now a tradition of the past. We
who are used to see our countrymen start to scour three continents in one long vacation, and come back more English
than ever, read with a want of interest closely approaching
incredulity the descriptions in the old novels of an eldest son
returning from his grand tour with a valet, a monkey, and a
trunkful of laced coats; shrugging his shoulders; swearing
out of the libretto of an opera; disquieting the housekeeper
by asking for made dishes, and the butler by rising from
table with the ladies. These fopperies are as dead to us as
the euphuism of Elizabeth; but a hundred and ten years ago
an ambitious young squire, who did his best to disguise his
nationality, was going the right way to pass himself off upon
his rural neighbors for a man of fashion. The genuine and
acknowledged leaders of society were then as much Parisians
as Londoners. They talked French fluently. They wrote it,
if not well, at any rate well enough to corrupt their English.
They got from France their dress, their carriages, their trink-
ets, their drink, and their morals. They knew the scandalous
chronicle of the Faubourg St. Germain as accurately as that
of Bloomsbury, and were better versed in the annals of the
French peerage than of their own. During the same fortnight in which George Selwyn was convicted of blundering

about the Howards of Naworth and the Howards of Corby, he obtained a well-merited apology from a friend who had presumed to inform him that the Duke of Havre was nephew to the Prince of Croy. "I beg pardon," writes Lord Grantham, "for telling you who any Frenchman's uncle is, as you have their genealogy by heart." And well he might; for Selwyn himself, and three out of four among his correspondents, as long as they were young enough to face the horrors of the Channel packet, and the dirt of the inns of Picardy, spent in France every odd month of their leisure and every spare guinea of their ready money.[1] In 1764, on the king's birthday, ninety-nine Englishmen of position sat down in Lord Hertford's hotel in Paris to one of those state banquets at which Wilkes thanked his reputation for saving him from making the hundredth guest. Two days after the last race had been run at Ascot, the road between Calais and Abbeville was alive with chaises and four, streaming southwards as fast as postilions could be bribed to travel; and two days before the Houses met for the winter session, a string of British legislators would be walking on board at Calais, in the brand-new satin coats and embroidered waistcoats which they dared not leave among their luggage, cursing the absurd commercial laws that they themselves had had a hand in framing, and learning more political economy in one day than they heard at Westminster in a twelvemonth. "The strictness of the custom-house still continues," wrote the Right Honorable Thomas Townshend on the eleventh of November, 1764. "Mr. Rigby brought one fine suit of clothes, which he saved by wearing it when he landed. Mr. Elliot saved a coat and waistcoat; but, not having taken the same precaution with

---

[1] The certainty of four hours between Dover and Calais, with the possibility of four-and-twenty; and the inn at Amiens, where he sat, "famished for want of clean victuals," as far away as possible from the frowsy tapestry behind which he could hear "the old fleas talking of Louis Quatorze," had convinced Walpole that he was past the age for France about the time that Fox was making himself at home there. "These jaunts are too juvenile," he writes, in 1771. "I am ashamed to remember in what year of Methusaleh I was here first."

his breeches, they were seized and burned." "I could not," said the Earl of Tyrone, "help blushing at the ridiculous figure we made in our fine clothes. You must wear your gold, for not even a button will be admitted." The ground must have been well prepared for Adam Smith when a peer as respectable as Lord Carlisle was driven to announce that he should go to Paris "if it were only to settle a smuggling correspondence."

The quantity of time that our ancestors consumed in France may be estimated by the amount of vicarious shopping which they accomplished. There is a letter in which the Honorable Henry St. John, better known as "the Baptist" among the grown-up schoolboys of St. James's Street, calmly directs George Selwyn to buy him thirty pounds' worth of books, the set of engravings from Vernet's views of the French seaports, an enamelled watch, and a half-dozen tea-cups. And when St. John, in his turn, went to Paris, he reports himself as having purchased a snuff-box, a pair of buckles, a dressing-gown, and some tables for Selwyn; chosen a silk, worked with olives, for the Earl of March; and executed a very intricate order for a parcel of gauze on behalf of an Italian marchioness in whom that worthy couple, partners elsewhere than at Newmarket, maintained a common interest. St. John's burden was no heavier than that of others; for he mentions a nobleman who had come from England loaded with commissions, though he did not know a good shop from a bad one. Walpole, whose thirty years' experience of the Paris streets qualified him to make money go as far as anybody, was provided by the ladies of his acquaintance with occupation for every day that he passed in that city. In a letter written in 1771 he gives Lord Ossory the choice of three clocks; tells Lady Ossory, prettily enough, that he has bought her canvas and silk "to the value of forty-six livres two sous, which, when the materials shall be manufactured by your ladyship, will increase a millionfold;" and laments that the trade in knick-knacks had fallen off to such an extent that he knew all the snuff-boxes and toothpick-cases in the windows as well as every succeeding administration knew the face of that typical placeman, Mr. Welbore Ellis. Wilkes, distrustful of English taste, would commit to no judgment less august than that of Baron d'Holbach the charge of selecting the shade of scarlet cloth which set off his remarkable person to the best advantage. But the most serious responsibility that could befall a tourist was to be requested by a friend at home to bring him over a carriage. The London coach-builders had then a great deal to learn; while the French were among the best in Europe, and were still improving. "In their dress and equipages," said Walpole, "they are grown very simple. We English are living upon their old gods and goddesses. I roll about in a chariot decorated with Cupids, and look like the grandfather of Adonis."

Men of a very different stamp from Lord March were frequent visitors to Paris on worthier errands than that of replenishing their wardrobes and buying presents for other people's wives. There a stranger whose name possessed any lustre, or whose conversation had any charm, was assured of meeting with a reception which gave him a comfortable sense of being famous and agreeable. To draw out the indolent, to set the diffident at ease, to tolerate vanity in others while tacitly and unobtrusively exacting deference for themselves, were then, as always, the arts of true-born Frenchwomen; and those arts were never so skilfully and willingly practised as when they were employed for the delectation of an Englishman. The British name was venerated on the Continent. Those were the days when it was a distinction to have breathed the same native air as the man "who had frightened the Great Mogul, and had liked to have tossed the Kings of France and Spain in a blanket if somebody had not cut a hole in it and let them slip through," and who had so fascinated the lively imagination of his chivalrous adversaries that a shy member of Parliament whose French had been acquired at Eton, or even at Edinburgh, might esteem himself lucky if he could escape from a Parisian supper-party without having been pressed to oblige the company with a specimen of Mr. Pitt's speaking. Gibbon has gratefully recorded the attentions which were lavished upon an author who had paid his hosts the compliment of writing his first book in the language of a people whom his own countrymen had so soundly beaten. The master and mistress of a French household (so he tells us) appeared to think that in entertaining him they were conferring a favor upon themselves. "Our opinions, our fashions, even our games, were adopted in France, and every Englishman was supposed to be born a patriot and a philosopher." And when the Parisians got hold of a real philosopher, who had a more solid claim to the title than having been bred on the same side of the water as Hobbes, there certainly was no stint in the adulation with which they regaled him. "I eat," said David Hume, "nothing but ambrosia, drink nothing but nectar, breathe nothing but incense, and tread upon nothing but flowers. Every man, and still more every lady, would think they were wanting in the most indispensable duty if they did not make a long and elaborate harangue in my praise." The very babes and sucklings joined in the chorus. At Versailles the great writer was presented to three future kings of France, of whom only one had as yet arrived at the dignity of a jacket and frills. The Duc de Berri gravely proclaimed himself an admirer of Hume, and begged to be enrolled among the number of his friends. The Comte de Provence assured him that his arrival had long been impatiently expected by Frenchmen, even by those for whom, like himself, the perusal of his fine "History" was still a pleasure to come; and the Comte d'Artois, who was six years old and looked four, mumbled some fragments of a panegyric which had been half forgotten on the way from the nursery.

English people of fashion, who were accustomed to see authors kept in their proper place, could not understand why such a fuss should be made about a man with nothing but his talents to recommend him; but the contrast between the estimation in which literature was held at home and abroad only enhanced the pleasure of so kindly a welcome to the objects of it. An author who in London had been made to feel at every turn that he was consorting with those who were wealthier and more important than himself, and was deafened by a ceaseless clatter of selfish personal politics which appealed

to the higher intelligence almost as little as the jargon of the
Stock Exchange, at Paris was as good as the very best, and enjoyed the novel luxury of being invited to dwell upon his
favorite topics, and give utterance to his most cherished
thoughts.[1] Among the factious barbarians of the British
metropolis (such was the constant burden of Hume's indignant rhetoric), men of letters had no weight with their fellows and no confidence in themselves, but were sunk and lost
" in the general torrent of the world." But Paris was a home
of culture, a nursing mother of intellect, a centre of the only
good society that merited the name. At Paris an article on
the Patriarchs by Voltaire made as much noise as an attack
upon the ministry by Charles Townshend ever made in London ; and the mere rumor that Rousseau was likely to walk in
the Luxembourg Gardens would draw larger crowds than in
England assembled at a horse-race. "People may talk of ancient Greece as they please, but no nation was ever so fond of
genius as this ;" and, in his capacity of a man of genius, Hume
fondly and frequently recurred to the idea of settling at Paris
for the remainder of his days ; while Gibbon confessed that
nothing but the necessity of earning his bread and obeying
his father could have induced him to tear himself from a residence among a people " who have established a freedom and
ease in society unknown to antiquity and still unpractised by
other nations." [2]

---

[1] Arthur Young, who, as a man of science with a specialty, was made
much of by the French nobility, gives the same explanation as Hume of
the contrast between the two countries. "I should pity," he writes, "the
man who expected to be well received in a brilliant circle in London because he happened to be a member of the Royal Society. But a member
of the Academy of Sciences at Paris is sure of a good reception everywhere. Politics are too much attended to in England to allow a due regard to anything else."

[2] Those who have read enough literary autobiography to be aware how
easy it is for authors to overrate their own social successes might suspect
that Hume was less ardently worshipped than he imagined ; but all that
he says about himself is confirmed by the envious sneers of his contemporaries, who were never tired of describing him in prose and verse as

"Drunk with Gallic wine and Gallic praise,"

While Louis the Sixteenth was a boy in the schoolroom, and De Lauzun a dashing bridegroom who would have laughed at the notion that he or his duchess would ever know either sorrow or terror, this international commerce in court-scandal and clocked stockings had nothing about it which seemed likely to engage the attention of posterity.   But a time came when the close alliance between the higher orders in the two countries was to produce results of world-wide magnitude. The sympathy excited among the families which governed England by the misfortunes of the families which were conspicuous in France before the Revolution mowed them down like a whirlwind in a grove of beeches was the most passionate emotion that the sufferings of men alien in race and blood have ever inspired in any section of our community.   That sympathy was stronger, and more practical in its effects, than the compassion which our nation felt for the Protestants of Holland in the days of the Spanish fury, or for the Huguenots in the days of the dragonnades; for the patriots of the Tyrol, of Hungary, of Naples; for the slaves of South Carolina; for the victims of Turkish cruelty in Greece, and of Russian cruelty in Poland.   The silken bonds of common pleasures and tastes, which seem trifling enough at the moment, proved

---

although, in point of fact, the second charge was as unfounded as the first.   Horace Walpole, who, both as an eclipsed man of letters and a somewhat antiquated person of fashion, could not keep his patience while Hume was talking Deism in a broad Scotch accent to a circle of duchesses with whose mothers he had himself exchanged *bouts rimés* in days when Fleury was minister, tried in vain to disguise his vexation under the cloak of a new-found and speedily dropped zeal on behalf of outraged piety.   His letters from France are full of strictures on the audacity of the fair Parisians, who discussed Genesis while the footmen were in the room; on the dreariness of their conversation, which " wanted nothing but George Grenville to be the most tiresome upon earth; " and on their bad taste in making a prophet of Rousseau, and a lion of Hume, " who is the only thing that they believe in implicitly; which they must do, for I defy them to understand any language that he speaks."   At length Hume went over to England, and, for his sorrow, carried Rousseau with him; and then Walpole began once more to enjoy himself as of old.

stronger under the test than the ties of religious faith or of
political creed; and while the democrats of Paris were appealing almost in vain to the brotherhood which, according
to the Jacobin programme, was to unite against their tyrants
all the peoples of Europe, there was nothing fictitious or shallow in the sentiment of class fraternity which instantly and
spontaneously enlisted the gentry of Great Britain in determined and implacable hostility to the French Republic. When
De Montmorencies and De Liancourts came flying over on
much more pressing business than that of engaging jockeys
or inspecting fancy cattle, their English comrades of earlier
and merrier days proved themselves no fair-weather friends.
Just as, after the fall of the Second Empire, Louis Napoleon
could count among his former subjects no partisans more sincere and loyal in their sorrow than those fashionable citizens
of New York who had resorted to his court in search of the
delights which they looked for in vain at home, so, ninety
years before, the old society of France found its chief mourn-
ers in the club-rooms and drawing-rooms of London. When
the city which had been the paradise of wits and dandies was
delivered over to a mob of porters and fishwives officered by
provincial attorneys—when to dress badly, and feed coarse-
ly, and talk an inflated jargon borrowed from third-rate trans-
lations of the classics had come to be the distinguishing
mark of a Parisian—George Selwyn and the Duke of Queensberry regarded the unattractive spectacle much as a good Mus-
sulman would regard the desecration of Mecca. And better
men than Queensberry and Selwyn were aghast at the deeds
of violence and barbarity that were perpetrated daily on the
very altar of the shrine of elegance and refinement. France,
after the emigration, was for Walpole a den of wild beasts, a
desert full of hyenas. Frenchmen were wretches who "had
destroyed the power of words" to paint their depravity; can-
nibals, scalp-hunters, wolves, tigers, a mad herd of swine that
had not the decency to make an end of themselves in the sea;
monsters, of whom until the earth was purged, peace and morality would never revisit it. Even Gibbon's blood was warmed
by the prospect of exterminating the "miscreants" whose lan-

guage he had written more easily than English, and whose country he once would gladly have adopted as his home. Our compatriots, with one bright exception, in proportion as they had formerly liked France, thenceforward hated the French people; but the clear intellect and generous heart of Fox preserved him from exhibiting in such an irrational and unworthy form his gratitude for the pleasant months which he had passed on French soil. His personal connections lay exclusively with the class which was paying so cruelly, and in many cases so undeservedly, for centuries of undisputed privilege and secure enjoyment; but he had sympathy to spare for the twenty millions of peasants and artisans who had long toiled and fasted, and who, intoxicated for the moment by unaccustomed and untempered draughts of liberty, were still, for better or for worse, the French nation. Though every hearth in Paris that had entertained him was cold, and though all his hosts were in exile or in the grave, France was there with her mighty past and her splendid future—with her rare genius, however obscured, and her high instincts, however perverted —and he could not bring himself to acquiesce in her exclusion from the pale of humanity. Burke never uttered a truer metaphor than when he likened Fox's love for France to the attachment of a cat which continues faithful to the house after the family has left it.

Fox might well retain through life a sense of having been domesticated in a country where he had made himself so thoroughly at home. He was a magnificent specimen of those young travelling Englishmen who in another generation used to excite the amused admiration of Goethe by their open and unembarrassed bearing in a society that was foreign to them; by the confidence with which they cross-examined the father of German literature in as much of his own language as they had picked up between Cologne and Weimar; by their instinctive and unaffected conviction that "they were lords everywhere, and that the whole world belonged to them." [1]

---

[1] "Whether it is," said Goethe, "the race, the soil, the free political constitution, or the healthy tone of education, the English show to great

Those English manners in which Goethe was philosopher
enough to recognize the qualities that had made England free at
home and dominant abroad, and which he was man enough to
relish and love, were not to the taste of the celebrated Frenchwoman who, having given law to one generation by her smiles
and to another by her wit, was beginning to feel doubtful of her
hold on the social allegiance of a new race of people whose ways
of thought were not hers, and whose faces she had never seen.
Madame du Deffand's notions of what a great English statesman's son should be were derived from Horace Walpole, who,
turned of fifty and chastened by gout, was never so happy as
when seated at her tea-table, gathering anecdotes of the Re-
gency, submitting to be rallied on his pronunciation of the
French diphthongs, and encouraging her to believe that, to a
right-minded devotee of the sex, high spirits at seventy-three
were as attractive as the sprightliness of one-and-twenty.   But
she was not fond of Charles Fox, nor easy in his company.
He did not fail in the outward respect which, according to
the social code then in force, was due to a lady who had sinned in such very high quarters, and so very many years before.   He diligently attended her parties, and guessed her
riddles, and consulted her, as the first living authority, on the
vexed point whether the expression *une jolie figure* related
only to the features, or "to every part of the body which is
susceptible of beauty."   But Madame du Deffand was not too
blind to perceive that he would rather have been studying
that question with his cousin the Duke of Berwick, after the
ancestral fashion of their family, at the feet of three fair
professors whose united ages fell short of hers;[1] however

---

advantage.   The secret does not lie in rank and riches.   It lies in the
courage which they have to be that for which nature has made them.
There is nothing vitiated, half-way, or crooked about them; but, such as
they are, they are complete men.   That they are also sometimes complete
fools, I allow with all my heart; but that is still something, and has some
weight in the scale of nature."

[1] "I supped last night," writes Fox, in November, 1770, "with Lauzun,
FitzJames, and some others, at what they call a *Clob à l'Anglaise*.   It
was in a *petite maison* of Lauzun's.   There was Madame Briseau and two

courageously she might toil to prove herself as young as her neighbors by running to all the puppet-shows and theatres, and making parties to drive in the Boulevard by moonlight, on the ground that it was too early to go to bed at one in the morning. The character of the young man was to her a moral and intellectual problem which afforded endless matter for discourse. He never spent an evening in her drawing-room without leaving her piqued, puzzled, and occasionally not a little frightened. Her letters to Walpole suggest the idea of a cat and a lap-dog talking over a lion's cub which had somehow found its way on to the hearth-rug. "I told you," she writes, "not long ago, that I was giving my last supper of twelve, and that I never again would have so many. Well, as a natural consequence, we yesterday were sixteen, which spoiled my evening. They set up a vingt-et-un; but I did not play. Your young people stayed to the very end; Fox, Spenser, and Fitzpatrick. I think the last is my favorite, for his soft, tractable manners; but I know him too little to judge. As for the Fox, he is hard, bold, and ready, with all the confidence of his merit. He will not spare the time to look well about him, but sees everything at a glance, and takes a bird's-eye view of the situation. I am inclined to think that one person is much the same to him as another. It is not from self-sufficiency, for he strikes me as neither vain nor supercilious; but he does not put his mind to yours, and I am satisfied that he will never form any connections except such as arise from play, and perhaps from politics; but of politics I know nothing." Fox, she says elsewhere, brought Fitzpatrick to see her; but the visit was a failure. She was tired; she did not know how to talk to young people; and, if she had been willing to confess it, such young people as Fox, or even as Fitzpatrick, had not often come within the sphere of her observation.

---

other women. The supper was execrably bad. However, the champagne and tokay were excellent; notwithstanding which the fools made *du ponche* with bad rum. This club is to meet every Saturday, either here or at Versailles. I am glad to see that we cannot be foolisher in point of imitation than they are."

As time went on, and the fame of the young statesman pervaded the Continent, Madame du Deffand made more and more desperate efforts to comprehend and to class him; but she arrived at no other result than that of producing a series of sketchy but suggestive studies of Charles Fox as he appeared at successive stages of his early manhood to an observer with whom he had as little in common as one very clever person could well have with another. At last, after watching him for seven years, she gave it up as hopeless, and allowed that he was too English for her to understand—an acknowledgment which it certainly was high time to make when she had committed herself to the psychological position that, while overflowing with wit, kindness, and sincerity, he was at the same time nothing short of detestable. She never could forgive him his carelessness as to whether the companions of his leisure hours thought him earnest or frivolous, brilliant or commonplace. A great genius is apt to fare ill at the hands of the memoir-writers, who deal with the surface of society, and who (unless, like Sully and De Ségur, they have themselves been men of action) are seldom quick in recognizing the forces that move the world. Napoleon was detected as a second-rate man by the diplomatist who overheard him inform twenty ladies in succession that it was a warm day; and of about equal value was Madame du Deffand's verdict that Fox had a good heart, but no principles—delivered at a time when he was already the life and soul of the stoutest and most disinterested struggle for principle that ever had been fought out by voice and pen[1]—and her announcement that he was perpetually drunk with high spirits, and that his head was turned without hope of recovery, during a period when he was daily convincing so acute and impartial a judge as Gibbon

---

[1] "Above all, my dear lord, I hope that it will be a point of honor among us all to support the American pretensions in adversity as much as we did in their prosperity, and that we shall never desert those who have acted *unsuccessfully* upon Whig principles, while we continue to profess our admiration of those who succeeded in the same principles in the year 1688." So wrote Fox to Rockingham when the hopes of the colonists had been, to all appearance, finally shattered on Long Island.

that "in the conduct of a party he approved himself equal
to the conduct of an empire."

It is not only in Madame du Deffand's letters that the
names of Fox and Fitzpatrick occur in close and constant
juxtaposition. With the exception of a short interval, when
the less distinguished of the two was fighting in America,
and fighting well, for a cause which they both equally disapproved, one of the young men is rarely mentioned anywhere
without the next sentence bringing an allusion to the other.
Fitzpatrick's father was the Lord Ossory whose daughter was
married to Lord Holland's eldest son, a relationship quite near
enough to turn into sworn brothers a pair who seemed made
for each other both by nature and circumstances. Equals in
rank, and virtually equals in age — for the two additional
years during which Fitzpatrick had been enjoying himself
on the earth did no more than counterbalance the amazing
precocity of his companion—the boys at once struck up an
alliance, offensive and defensive, which only death dissolved.
Wherever Fox was in difficulty or danger, whether in the
heat of debate at midnight, or at daybreak on the chill grass
of Hyde Park, Fitzpatrick was at his side to see him through
the business; and, when amusement was on foot, the friends
were inseparable. They had everything in common — pursuits, accomplishments, house-room, horse-flesh, their money, as
long as it lasted, and afterwards what they were pleased to
call their credit. They were both delightful talkers, whose
society people twice their age gladly purchased by the sacrifice of a morning's work, or the indefinite prolongation of an
after-dinner sitting. Fitzpatrick rapidly obtained, and long
kept, the reputation of being the most agreeable member of a
society so agreeable that posterity is tempted to forget how
little else it had to recommend it. Fox, on the other hand,
as his energies became absorbed, and his appetite for display
surfeited by his labors and triumphs as an orator, soon lost
the habit of exerting himself in conversation. He became
content to alternate between silent attention in the presence
of those whom he thought better worth hearing than himself,
and a lazy outpouring of whatever engaged his mind at the

moment, which his hearers drank in without consciously admiring, and most unfortunately (for the scanty samples that remain are redolent of fancy, sense, and humor) without undertaking to record.　Both the friends wrote verses, in the old
stilted manner, with a superabundance of capital letters, and
without even an elementary trace of a conception that what was
sung ought to bear some relation to what was felt.　Their most
ambitious flight was on the occasion when, in May, 1775, they
tuned their pipes to celebrate the charms of Mrs. Crewe, while
no less competent an umpire than Mason consented to play
Palæmon to the rival swains.　The palm was adjudged to
Fox.　"The young cub's" (so Mason wrote) "is certainly the
best.　It has something of character and originality about it.
The other is the most old-fashioned thing to be written by a
young man of fashion that I ever read.　He might have writ
it in a full-bottomed wig.　If my friend had not dated it,
I should have thought it printed somewhere about the last
four years of Queen Anne."　It is difficult to imagine what
could be less original, and more archaic, than the closing lines
of the successful poem :

> "If then for this once in my Life I am free,
>   And escape from a Snare might catch wiser than me,
>   'Tis that Beauty alone but imperfectly charms,
>   For though Brightness may dazzle, 'tis kindness that warms.
>   As on Suns in the Winter with Pleasure we gaze,
>   But feel not their Force, though their Splendor we praise,
>   So Beauty our just Admiration may claim;
>   But Love, and Love only, our Hearts can inflame."[1]

---

[1] It is pretty to contrast with the labored frigidity of this youthful performance the verses which Fox addressed to his wife in 1797, composed
as he was being brought home badly wounded from the shooting-field :

> "Sense of pain and danger flies
>   From the looks of those dear eyes;
>   Looks of kindness, looks of love,
>   That lift my mortal thoughts above,
>   While I view that heavenly face,
>   While I feel that dear embrace,
>   While I hear that soothing voice,
>   Though maimed or crippled, life's my choice,

But Fitzpatrick as well as Fox had better stuff in him than to waste his ingenuity in trying to write like Parnell when Parnell was trying to write like Waller. Ten years later, in the maturity of his powers, a happy chance revealed to him the quarter where his real strength lay; and as the author of half what is good, and almost all of what is best, in the "Rolliad," he has permanently connected his reputation with a literary performance which Whigs may be excused for regarding as the best political satire since Dryden.

The identity in tastes between the young kinsmen did not stop with poetry. There was hardly one of the Muses, and, sooth to say, not many earthly goddesses, whom, at one time or another, they had not worshipped together. They were both devoted to the stage; and their earlier correspondence, so far as it has any heart in it, refers to little else. There is something comical and rather taking in the eagerness with which Fox canvassed the histrionic capabilities of all his friends and relations. Every chance acquaintance whom he picked up on the Continent was forthwith enlisted in his troop, and thrust straight into the leading business, even though the unlucky recruit might never have learned ten lines of Virgil correctly all the while he was at Eton. "Your sister," he writes to Fitzpatrick from Florence, "is a very good actress. Lady Sarah's fame is well known. She acted extremely well in the comedy. In the tragedy he did not know his part. Carlisle is not an excellent actor, but will

---

> Without these, all the fates can give
> Has nought to make me wish to live.
> No, could they foil the power of time,
> And restore youth's boasted prime;
> Add, to boot, fame, power, and wealth,
> Undisturbed and certain health,
> Without thee 'twould nought avail;
> The source of every joy would fail:
> But loved by thee, by thee caressed,
> In pain and sickness I am blest."

Such lines at fifty are worth more to the subject of them than a ream of sonnets at six-and-twenty.

make a very useful one. Peter Brodie is the best manager
prompter in the world. We want another actor or two, but
much more another actress. There are few comedies that do
not require above two women." When, under the combined
excitement afforded by the prospect of an heir and of a seat
in Parliament, poor Stephen Fox allowed his dramatic ardor
to flag, the stern indignation of his younger brother was positively impressive. "He does not," exclaimed Charles, "so
much as mention acting in any of his letters; but I hope his
enthusiasm (for such it was last year) will return. Indeed, it
will be very absurd if he has built a theatre for nothing. You
may tell my brother I can get two actors for him; one good-
ish and one baddish. I have not engaged them, but I know I
can have them." "The two actors I mentioned" (so he tells
Fitzpatrick in his next) "were Price and Fitzwilliam. The
former has appeared with great success in the part of Gloucester in 'Jane Shore,' though in Alonzo in 'The Revenge' he
lost much of the credit he had gained. You will oblige me
very much if you will put him up at Almack's till he is chosen, without minding how many blackballs he has. Pray do
not blackball him yourself. As to Fitzwilliam, he says he
should like to act, but I do not believe he will, and I think he
would make a bad actor."

Fox was reckoned Fitzpatrick's superior in tragedy, but
much his inferior in genteel comedy. They made a point of
frequently exchanging their parts, and took infinite pains to
improve, and, as they at first thought, to perfect, themselves
where they were respectively deficient. But their misplaced
ambition did not outlast the time when the younger of them
was four-and-twenty, and had been a man about town for the
eight years which were the golden era of our green-room, with
the opportunity of sitting four times a week in a theatre managed as no British theatre has been managed before or since.
He was already making his way into that choice social circle
of which Garrick was an ornament, and might gather from
the comments or (more convincingly still) from the expressive
silence of the master what was the worth of amateur acting
according to the greatest actor who ever spoke the language

of the greatest of dramatists.[1]   From 1773 onwards, Fox concerned himself no more with a pastime which was at best but
an imitation of an imitation, and gave his undistracted powers
to an art in which his success had been as signal and as in-
stantaneous as the success of Garrick on the stage.   For the
pursuit of that art his long apprenticeship to the buskin was
among the most important of his qualifications.   It was no
slight advantage to a great extempore speaker to have at hand
an extensive and diversified stock of quotations from that
branch of literature which is nearest akin to oratory; and for
such a speaker it is essential that the voice, no less than the
memory and the reasoning faculty, should be under absolute
control.   That laborious discipline in the theory and practice
of elocution through which Fox was carried by his disinterested passion for the drama, but which no one who ever lived
was less likely to have deliberately undertaken with an eye to
parliamentary advancement, had gained him a command of
accent and gesture which, as is always the case with the highest art, gave his marvellous rhetoric the strength and the simplicity of nature.   The pains which he had bestowed upon

---

[1] Garrick, as oral tradition relates, was invited to witness some private
theatricals at a great country-house. After the performance he was anxiously questioned as to the merits of the actors, and, seeing that he must
say something, he gave it as his opinion that the gentleman who played
the king seemed quite at home on the stage. It turned out that his
praise had been bestowed upon a scene-shifter from his own theatre, who
had been brought down from London to superintend the mechanical arrangements, and had taken the part on an emergency.

Fox was elected at Brooks's about the same time that Garrick returned
from the protracted Continental tour on which he had resolved when,
after having kept the town at his feet for twenty years, he noticed that
the public for a while had grown weary of praising him. His Italian
journey, undertaken from the same motives as Napoleon's expedition to
Egypt, produced the same decisive effect upon his career and his reputation. London, as tired of hearing Powell rant as France of seeing Barras
misgovern, welcomed back her favorite with a succession of nightly ova-
tions, and took care that he should never again suspect her fidelity. The
critics remarked that Garrick, artist enough to be a learner at eight-and-
forty, had cured himself, by a course of study in the Parisian theatres,
of that occasional excess of emphasis which was his only fault.

learning to speak the words of others enabled him to concentrate his undivided attention upon the arduous task of improvising his own. If only he could find the thing which required to be said, he was sure to say it in the way that would produce the greatest possible effect. His variety of manner, we are told, was quite as remarkable as the richness of his matter. The modulations of his voice responded exactly to the nature of his subject and the emotions of his mind. When he was piling up his arguments, so correct in their sequence, and, as we read them now with cool and impartial judgments, for the most part so irresistible in their weight, every one of his massive sentences "came rolling like a wave of the Atlantic, three thousand miles long." If his cadences at times waxed shrill and even inharmonious, and his enunciation became almost preternaturally rapid, it was only when his hearers were so fascinated by his burning logic, and so entranced by the contagion of his vehemence, that he could hardly speak fast enough or loud enough to satisfy them. His deep tones, which occurred rarely, and then but for a moment, were reserved for occasions that necessitated a solemn appeal to the compassion or the justice of the assembly which he was addressing, and never failed to go straight to the heart of every one present. Feeling profoundly, thinking accurately and strongly, trained thoroughly in all the external graces of oratory, "Fox during the American war, Fox in his best days," was declared by Grattan to have been the best speaker that he ever heard; and Grattan, over and above his experiences in the Irish Parliament, had formed his taste on Chatham, and had lived through the great days of Burke, Pitt, and Sheridan, to hear Brougham on the "Orders in Council," and Canning on the "Emancipation of the Catholics."

CHAPTER VIII.

1770–1771.

The Law of Libel.—Great Speech by Charles Fox, and Burke's Reply.—
Final Solution of the Question.—Contest of Parliament with the Reporters.—Scene in the Lords.—Indignation of the Commons.—Artful
Conduct of Charles Fox.—Lord George Germaine's Duel.—The Onslows.—Their Warfare with the Press.—The King begins to take an Interest in the Controversy.—A Night of Divisions.—John Wheble.—Interference of Wilkes.—Miller Arrested, and Discharged by the Guildhall Bench.—Proceedings in the House of Commons against the Lord
Mayor and Alderman Oliver.—Rebellion of the King's Friends against
Lord North.—Fiery Speech of Charles Fox.—Feeling against him in
the Country.—March of the City upon Westminster.—Violent Conduct
of the Majority in the House.—Wedderburn's Defection from the Opposition.—Popular Excitement outside Parliament.—Fox and North
Maltreated.—The Lord Mayor and the Alderman Committed to the
Tower.—Their Imprisonment and Release.—Testimonial to Wilkes.—
Establishment of the Freedom of Reporting Debates in Parliament.

SUCH, in the heyday of youth, was Charles Fox, and such
was his chosen friend. Their joint stock of sagacity and folly,
of power and frailty, of sterling merits and grievous faults,
was amply sufficient to have made a score of reputations and
wrecked a hundred careers. When Lord Holland was at
King's Gate or on the Continent, the pair took up their quarters together over Mackie's Italian warehouse in Piccadilly.
Some frequenters of Brooks's were soft-hearted enough to pity
the landlord of two such seductive and unprofitable lodgers,
and predicted that his ruin would date from the day on which
he let them his rooms. "On the contrary," said Selwyn, "so
far from ruining him, they will make Mackie's fortune; for
he will have the finest pickles in his house of any man in
London;" and the phrase, unceremonious as it was, conveys a
truer notion of Fox when just out of his teens than a solemn

19

and elaborate analysis of his character and his policy. He was not all that he should have been between 1770 and 1774; but those who read his life are the last who have a right to complain of him. Politics are so grave a trade that a politician of mature years can hardly be an amusing personage unless he sinks into the absurd and the unbecoming; and there is therefore all the more reason to be thankful for those few great men who have played a foremost part at an age when high spirits and audacious actions are among the most hopeful symptoms of future excellence. During the earliest, and much the longest, portion of his first Parliament, Fox, as the spoiled child of the worst House of Commons that ever met, seemed bent upon ascertaining how much unsound argument and pert dogmatism would be tolerated from a ready and an agreeable speaker, and how often it was permissible to go in and out of place without any adequate reason for leaving office, or justification for resuming it. He did not mend his ways until even the fagot voters of Midhurst were tired of electing and re-electing him, and until he had exhausted his sauciness and his sophistry in declaiming against all the principles with which his name was thereafter to be identified, and most of the measures which he himself or the statesmen bred in his school were some day to place upon the Statute-book.

The activity and pertinacity which the ministry displayed in punishing, or attempting to punish, the printers and venders of the "Letter to the King" had gravely alarmed every one who desired that the freedom of the British press should be anything but an empty name. It was idle to hope that a nation would ever enjoy a political literature that was at the same time outspoken and respectable, while its booksellers, as Wilkes most truly said, "lived always in a state of jeopardy, like soldiers fighting for their country." Sustained and effective criticism was impossible when a writer who smartly assailed the measures of the government was sure, sooner or later, to be prosecuted at the expense of the State, on a charge of having traduced the personal character of the king or the minister. The Opposition lost no time in calling attention to so pressing a danger. On the day fortnight after Parlia-

ment met for the winter session of 1770, a debate was raised
by Captain Constantine Phipps, the member for Lincoln, an
industrious and sententious youth who, as Lord Mulgrave,
was erelong to embark on a course of tergiversation which
earned him an English peerage, a long succession of richly
paid offices, and a couplet by Fitzpatrick worth all the painfully composed and minutely revised speeches that he ever
made on either side of any controversy.[1] Captain Phipps,
always eager to prove how large a stock of law might be
laid in by a sailor, attacked the question on its most techni-
cal quarter, and moved for leave to introduce a bill limit-
ing the right of the attorney-general to file informations for
libel. But, by the time half a dozen members had spoken,
it became evident that the House was upon a wrong scent,
and that the officers of the Crown might be safely intrusted
with the power of filing what informations they chose, so
long as it was clearly established that a jury was to decide the
issue. But Lord Mansfield's doctrine, that it was for the
judge to determine whether a paper was libellous, while the
jury were only concerned with the fact of publication, had
placed at the mercy of himself and his brethren every printer
and author in the kingdom. It was true that, in the recent
trials, London juries had refused to let out of their own keeping the fortunes and liberty of their fellow-citizens. But
that bold course had been adopted under the influence of an
excited public feeling which to a large extent was temporary
and local; and the tradesmen of a provincial assize town, in
quiet times, could not be expected, in direct contradiction to
what would be told them from the bench, to insist on usurping a function which the greatest judge of modern days had
repeatedly and emphatically pronounced not to belong to
them. Accordingly, after the lapse of another fortnight,

---

[1] " Acute observers, who with skilful ken
      Descry the characters of public men,
      Exchange with pleasure Elliot, Lew'sham, North,
      For Mulgrave's tried integrity and worth.
      And all must own *that* worth completely tried
      By turns experienced on every side."

Sergeant Glynn, tutored by Shelburne, who in his turn had been inspired by Chatham, went straight to the root of the matter by moving for a committee which should inquire into the administration of justice in cases relating to the press, and clear up the doubts that had been cast upon the authority of juries.

The discussion, in quality and in duration, responded to the importance of the subject. De Grey, the attorney-general, speaking with temper and ingenuity, opposed the motion on behalf of the government; and he was supported by Thurlow, who, while he showed his sense of the gravity of the question by an unusual decency of language, made amends to himself by indulging in even more than a usual audacity of assertion. After adjuring his brother-members to protect virtue from the assaults of calumny — an appeal which, if rather trite, had at any rate the merit of being unselfish—he proceeded to enforce the proposition that in State libels it was idle to hope for fairness from jurymen, "who might justly be considered as parties concerned against the Crown." To have proclaimed the humiliating confession that the subjects of the Crown, as then worn, must be counted among its enemies, would at happier periods of our history have been the death-blow to a rising lawyer. But Thurlow was as well acquainted as any man living with the source which in those days fed the fountain of honor; and a declaration which, if made under a sovereign proud of being a constitutional monarch, would have sent him to pine on the back benches until his sin was purged and forgotten, exalted him into being George the Third's attorney-general within seven weeks after it had been uttered. The ministerial lawyers met with competent antagonists in the members of their own profession. Glynn, Dunning, and Wedderburn, as Lord Chatham thankfully acknowledged, "stood with much dignity and great abilities for the transcendent object now at stake." The day, said the old statesman, was a good and a great one for the public.

But the House, while it consented to be edified by the lawyers, looked, as its custom is, for amusement to the laymen, and did not look in vain. The contribution which Charles Fox made towards the entertainment of his colleagues is interesting as the best preserved specimen of his first manner. His early speeches were glaringly deficient on the side both of reason and morality; and although his rhetoric had a certain grace of its own, which may be described as the *beauté du diable* of oratory, he seldom was on his feet for three minutes without committing some offence against taste, and even against ordinary propriety. But his youthful efforts had this in common with his mature performances, that, while he attacked it from the wrong quarter, he never failed to go direct to the heart of the argument. The young Lord of the Admiralty, in this his third session, had already an eye for the point of a debate as sure as that of a heaven-born general for the key of an enemy's position; and the memorable debate of the sixth of December, 1770, as he clearly saw, turned on the point whether, in a trial of libel, the bench or the box should be intrusted with the duty of giving what was in truth a verdict of guilt or innocence. Choosing his ground with more skill than scruple, he undertook to maintain the preposterous thesis that to refuse to a judge, when sitting on a case of libel, a power which he did not possess when sitting on a case of murder was an insult to the ermine. And then, by a politic diversion, managed with quite sufficient adroitness to impose upon people who did not look too closely into any device which enabled them to get their opponents roundly and cleverly abused, he sallied forth into the tempting field of general politics, and in a torrent of nervous and vehement interrogatories which concealed the poverty of his matter and the ludicrous unfairness of his taunts, he reproached Glynn and his friends with having called for a dissolution of the Parliament on the plea that it no longer represented the people.

  "What are you about?" he cried to the supporters of the motion. "You have yourselves allowed that you are no legal House of Commons; that you are *de facto* and not *de jure;* and you are going to arraign the venerable judges of Westminster Hall, and enter upon a revision of the laws of the land. What have you been doing for these last two years but ringing constantly in our ears the contempt in which we are held by the people? Have you not made these walls incessantly echo with the terms of reproach which you allege to have been cast upon us by men of every degree—high and low, rich and poor, learned and unlearned? Were we not, and are we not still, according to your account, held in universal detestation and abhorrence? Does not the whole empire, from one end to the other, reckon us equally weak and wicked? How can you, then, with a serious face, desire us to undertake this inquiry in order to satisfy the people? The people, if your former assertions are to be credited, will get no good at your hands. Who do you think will pay any attention to your authority? From your former confessions, have they the right? They cannot, if they take you at your own words, hold you or your debates in any other light than the idle declamations of coffee-house politicians. I have heard a great deal of the people, and the cries of the people, but where and how am I to find out their complaints? As far as my inquiries have led me, those complaints do not exist; and as long as that is the view of the majority of this House (who themselves are the people, as being their legal representatives), I shall continue to think with them."

The first speech of a new minister, for any human nature that it shows, is apt to be on a level with the diploma picture of a Royal Academician; but such had not been the case here. Burke rose later in the evening; and, though four speakers had intervened between him and Fox, the practised statesman considered himself bound to exert all his powers in order to efface the impression which had been wrought by the orator of one-and-twenty. He treated with magnificent disdain the pretension to speak for the nation which had been put forward by one who spoke for nothing except a peer and his hay-field. "You the representatives of the people!" he exclaimed to the long rows of borough-mongers who were sitting impatient for the vote. "You are so far from being the representatives of the people that you do not know their faces." At far greater length, and with a profusion of gor-

geous imagery that is now as marvellous to the student as it
then was distasteful to hearers who disagreed with the conclusions which it adorned, he exposed the full absurdity of the
plea that to advocate a revision of the law was to cast doubts
upon the integrity of the judges. If any one will be at the
pains—the amply rewarded pains—to read aloud twenty consecutive sentences from these speeches of Burke and of Fox,
however much he may be personally convinced that the former was wholly in the right and the latter indefensibly in the
wrong, he will readily understand which of the two would be
most acceptable to a mob of gentlemen who had had too much
wine with their dinners, and saw themselves rapidly losing
the hope of getting enough sleep in their beds.[1] Quite apart
from the substance of what they respectively were saying, Fox
pleased where Burke wearied, and occasionally even repelled ;
and the merits, or rather the defects, of the cause espoused by

---

[1] "My sole object," said Burke, "in supporting the proposed inquiry
is the public welfare and the acquittal of the judges. Till this step is
taken, in vain do they pretend to superior sanctity. In vain do some gentlemen tread their halls as holy ground, or reverence their courts as the
temples of the Divinity. To the people they appear the temples of idols
and false oracles; or rather as the dwellings of truth and justice converted into dens of thieves and robbers. For what greater robbers can
there be than those who rob men of their liberties ? No man here has a
greater veneration than I have for the doctors of the law; and it is for
that reason that I would thus render their characters as pure and unsul-
lied as the driven snow. But will any of you pretend that this at present
is the case ? Are not their temples profaned ? Has not pollution entered
them, and penetrated even to the Holy of Holies ? Are not the priests
suspected of being no better than those of Bel and the Dragon, or rather
of being worse than those of Baal ? And has not the fire of the people's
wrath almost consumed them ?" Let anybody who possesses even the
rudiments of an imagination depict to himself the effect of such a string
of questions addressed to a noisy House of Commons within half an hour
of midnight. The passage which follows is still more painfully overdrawn, and might well have been regarded as blasphemous even by less
jealous defenders of religion than the gentlemen who had expelled
Wilkes for impiety. If portions of it had not been taken down at the
time by Mr. Henry Cavendish, it would be difficult to believe that it ever
could have been spoken.

the younger advocate rendered his eloquent effrontery irresistibly attractive to an assembly which was wanting alike in
the dignity of a senate and in the business-like self-respect of
a genuinely representative body. The House refused an inquiry by a great majority, which, when the question was renewed in the course of the next session, was swelled into a
very great majority indeed. The law of libel remained in a
condition of perilous uncertainty until, after the lapse of two-
and-twenty years—just in time to shield the writers of the
popular party from the most formidable judicial persecution
that had menaced it since the Stuarts—Fox, with the assistance of the aged Camden, carried through Parliament a bill
which vindicated the rights of juries as against the claims
of the bench, and secured that no critic of the government
should be arbitrarily punished on the pretext that, in the
performance of what is essentially a public service, he had inflicted a private injury.

But there was something which the members of that bad
Parliament liked even less than criticism. It was of small
avail that Publius Valerius and Mucius Scævola should be restrained from calling them tyrants and mercenaries in the
newspapers as long as their constituents had the opportunity
of reading what they themselves said in debate. Conscious
of belonging to the class with regard to whom truth is the
worst of libels, Lord North and his followers esteemed the reporter an equally dangerous enemy with the pamphleteer, and
were short-sighted enough to imagine that he could be the
more easily crushed of the two. The campaign began in the
House of Lords. On the twenty-second of November, 1770,
Chatham, in a speech of extraordinary power, had inveighed
against all who lived by the plunder of their country, from
the lofty robber of Asia drawn in his coach-and-six, or his
coach-and-eight, down to the broker who walked on foot to
'Change Alley with a scrap of secret information which had
been whispered into his ear by a minister. The Peers would
not have cared how often their distinguished colleague might
ease his soul by declaiming against peculation and corruption,
as long as they were comfortably shut up by themselves to

sneer and listen. But it was a very different matter when the one man in England whose words had real weight used the floor of their House as a platform from which to address his uncompromising philippics to the more numerous public outside, who had no part in the taxes but to pay them, and noth-to do with coaches except to count the horses. The ministers were already deliberating on the measures to be taken for damming up the eloquence of their terrible adversary behind barriers within which it could work little harm to them or to their system, when their movements were quickened by an attack of an unexpected nature from a hardly less ominous quarter. It was Philip Francis, as we now know, who had taken down from memory and given to the world the speech of the twenty-second of November; and in such hands it is needless to say that Chatham's invective had lost nothing of its terrors. And now, on the seventh of December, there appeared in Mr. Woodfall's journal a passage from a speech of the Duke of Grafton, which bore only too evident signs of having been reported with literal fidelity, accompanied by the unsparing comments of a critic who signed himself Domitian, and who was as much Junius as Junius was Philip Francis. The blow was too severe for the courage even of the boldest. It was sufficiently disagreeable for the supporters of the government to be held up to odium in the phrases of the greatest living orator, sharpened, as if they had not point enough already, by the vindictive industry of the most formidable among living writers. But that ordeal was nothing to the discovery that they themselves were liable to be denied the services of the gentle art which lends eloquence to the stammerer, and concentration to the diffuse, and something of logic and sequence to the incoherent observations of the dull. What had been uttered outright, without a thought of the morning's reckoning, might be served up on the morrow, unrevised, uncorrected, unexpurgated—punctuated with such infernal skill as to reproduce a lively image of the least admirable peculiarities in the speaker's manner—for the entertainment of a public that, in its ignorant self-conceit, had nothing of the indulgent fellow-feeling with which the House of

Commons, and still more the House of Lords, regards a minister who is summoned to discourse at a moment's notice on a question over which he has never expended a moment's study. Few, indeed, were the politicians who could face with composure the prospect of standing daily in such a pillory.

The emergency was just one of those which the government felt itself capable of meeting. On the third day after Domitian's letter had been printed, the Duke of Manchester was calling the attention of the Lords to the defenceless state of the nation, which was then in the thick of what still promised to be a very pretty quarrel with Spain. He had got into the middle of a sentence about a ship that was laid up at Gibraltar on account of her not being sufficiently water-tight to keep the sea, when Lord Gower rose, and desired that the House might be cleared of strangers. How, he asked, were their lordships to know whether there might not be emissaries of Spain under their gallery, spying out the weakness of the British navy. He had in his pocket the speech of a noble lord, printed from notes which some nameless individual had contrived to take; and what one unscrupulous person had done in order to gratify the curiosity of the London coffee-houses, another would find means to effect for the information of the Court of Madrid. There was a standing order that none should enter their doors except those who were there by right, and it was high time that such order should be enforced. The Duke of Richmond exclaimed energetically against a step the motives of which were more than suspicious; and he was in the course of suggesting that the disclosures which Lord Gower and the Bedfords anticipated with well-founded uneasiness related to the leaky condition of the Exchequer rather than of the Mediterranean fleet, when a tumult arose such as never again was heard within those walls until the famous half-hour when William the Fourth was on his way from the palace to dissolve his first Parliament. Then, as on the other rare, and almost secular, occasions when the Lords have broken bounds, the need was sorely felt of those efficacious methods for restoring order which in the last resort may be employed by the Speaker of the Commons for the coercion of what is ordinarily the more boisterous assembly. The remonstrances of the decorous and sober-minded among the Peers were drowned in an ignoble clamor. Under cover of the general confusion, Chatham was subjected to insults on which braver men than those who now hooted and jeered him would never have ventured had his voice been audible. The Court lords, determined that no one should call upon them to defend their proceedings, continued to roar, "Clear the House!" with a din through which the Scotch accent was plainly distinguishable. At length the Duke of Richmond lost his patience. "Clear the House!" he cried. "So you will, of every honest man;" and out he walked, followed by a train of peers which in character and in number bade fair to accomplish his prediction. Their departure was the signal for a fresh outburst of unmannerly violence. When it was noticed that the servants of the House seemed reluctant to drag forth by their coat-sleeves such intruders as Burke and Dunning,[1] a party of lords made a rush at those members of the Commons who were standing at the bar, and drove them helter-skelter into the lobby. The unseemly riot was headed by two peers, on the prominence of whose noses Barré afterwards descanted with an angry exaggeration which indicated how gladly, in any place where they were not protected by privilege, the fiery soldier would have pulled them. The members of the Commons, charged, as they were, with the duty of presenting a bill to the Upper House, insisted upon being allowed to return and perform their errand. Lord Mansfield, who, while the great seal was in commission, acted as Speaker in the Lords, came forward from his place to meet them. They made their three bows, and delivered their message. Lord Mansfield had got back to the woolsack, "as a cricketer," said Sir George Savile, "gets back to his wicket,"

---

[1] "When the deputy black rod," said Burke, "pulled me by this arm, I seemed not to feel any personal resentment; because the deputy black rod is no very gigantic man, and he is, besides, a friend whom for many reasons I love and honor." Dunning was among the most angry. "I went" (so he informed the Commons) "to the House of Lords, not to listen to their ridiculous debates, but to say a few words to a member of it."

when the indignant deputation was once more expelled amidst a volley of the exclamations with which the sixpenny gallery was accustomed to decide the fate of a bad actor in those days of dramatic rigor. "Such a scene," said Francis, "I never saw since the damning of the French dancers."

When the ejected members were safe within their own precincts, and had made their statement about the usage to which they had been exposed, the self-respect of gentlemen for a moment associated all parties in a common determination to resent so intolerable an affront. The first to call for a policy of retaliation was no less devoted a ministerialist than Mr. George Onslow; and he was seconded by so keen a Whig as William Burke, who had come straight from a place which he ventured to describe as a bear-garden in presence of an audience, the older among whom knew what a bear-garden really was. Such was the irritation excited among the adherents of the cabinet by the explosion of a plot which the cabinet itself had hatched that consequences very embarrassing to the government would inevitably have ensued if the House of Commons had been left for another half-hour to the guidance of its own unprompted instincts. Few would care to risk an established, and still fewer a growing, reputation by running counter to a sentiment which appeared to be as universal as it was natural; but Charles Fox had got from Lord Holland a courage and a readiness which formed almost the only portion of his inheritance, mental or material, that he retained through life.[1] The fiercer the storm, the more completely in his element was one who possessed beyond his fellows that willingness "to go out in all weathers" which Gerard Hamilton,[2] with the appreciative envy of a vain and timid speaker,

---

[1] So visible was the stamp of his paternity on all which Charles Fox said, and on his manner of saying it, that the reporters of those days could not refrain from breaking into their account of the parliamentary business to observe that the lad looked the very image of his father.— *Parliamentary History*, January 25, 1771.

[2] Hamilton used this expression to Lord Charlemont with reference to John Hely Hutchinson, whom most assuredly the dirtiest weather never kept in port as long as there was a prospect of salvage-money. Of Ham-

pronounced to be the quality of all others that made an inestimable debater. Putting himself calmly but resolutely in
the front of his flustered official superiors, the junior lord reminded the House that decisions taken in wrath were apt to
be repented at leisure; that to requite insult with insult was
not the right way of asserting its dignity; and that the blow
which, by an unlucky accident, had fallen upon members of
their honorable body was meant for the common enemies of
political mankind, the printers. When the supporters of the
government heard a young gentleman who might so safely
be trusted to adopt the illiberal view of every controversy
arguing so confidently against the prevailing opinion of the
moment, they began to perceive with consternation how nearly
they had been betrayed by their feelings into giving a vote
which would have gratified their fellow-countrymen. Their
speeches became first moderate in tone, and then ambiguous
in tendency, until the debate took a turn which provided them
with an excuse for definitely separating themselves from the
Opposition. Before the sitting was over, the ministers had
recovered their customary majority; and, to complete their
luck, the question soon passed into the hands of the most un-
desirable of champions, Lord George Sackville, or rather Lord
George Germaine; for that nobleman, along with a large accession of fortune, had recently acquired the more valuable
legacy of a new name. Lord George announced himself as
having devised a scheme for maintaining the honor of the
House; but before his plan, which was elaborate almost to
grotesqueness, had been discussed for half an evening, he had
been told that the honor of the House had better be committed to somebody who had proved that he could take care
of his own. The words were from the mouth of a noted
duellist, who seven years before had thrown down his glove
to Wilkes; and they were spoken at the instigation of Sir
James Lowther, who liked to get his quarrels fought for him,

---

ilton himself Lord Charlemont said "that he was the only speaker, among
the many he had heard, of whom he could say with certainty that all his
speeches, however long, were written and got by heart."

though, in the last resort, he never lacked the courage to fight them himself.   Lord George had at last the opportunity of showing that the fatal hesitation which lost him his chance of making Minden another Blenheim had nothing to do with the fear of a horse-pistol.   His conduct on the ground, and during the still more trying period that preceded the meeting, cleared him effectually and forever from the most painful of all imputations to the satisfaction of everybody but the king, who could not bring himself to acknowledge the courage of a politician who did not happen at the time to be voting with the Court.[1]   Parliament, meanwhile, in the rapt attention with which it invariably watches a personal incident, lost sight of its corporate grievances; and an estrangement which had nearly brought the Houses into open war settled down into an affectation of sulkiness in their mutual relations, which was not likely to be enduring in the case of two assemblies so cordially in unison as to the principles on which the nation ought to be governed.[2]

A hard frost, which kept even hunting-men in town during the Christmas holidays, enabled the supporters of the government in the Commons to enlighten themselves as to the real

---

[1] Before placing himself opposite an adversary who meant mischief, and came within a hair's-breadth of doing it, Lord George took four days to settle his affairs, and make provision for an infant son a week old; behaving all the while, as we are told by one who disliked him, with a cheerful indifference that deceived his wife and his whole family. The deliberation with which he carried through the affair was unfavorably interpreted by his sovereign. "Lord George Germaine," wrote George the Third to the prime-minister, "permitting so many days to elapse before he called Governor Johnston to an account for the words he made use of on Friday, does not give much idea of his resolution, but that he had at length been persuaded by his friends to take this step."

[2] Late in the session the Lords amended a money bill by striking out the provisions which offered a bounty upon the exportation of corn. The Commons, more mindful of their ancient privileges than of the doctrines of what was then the most recent among the sciences, resented the affront by doing that of which their better-mannered successors only talk. The Speaker tossed the bill over the table; and members of both parties, as they went out, kicked it along towards the door.

meaning and object of the course that had been pursued in
the Lords. To be told how swiftly and smoothly business
was carried on in the snug family party which the Upper
House had become ever since it had been cleared of strangers
was worth the loss of the best run which the Duke of Grafton
ever gave the sportsmen who had earned at St. Stephen's the
privilege of being invited to Wakefield Lodge in order to
show that they could ride as straight as they voted. The
ministerialists in the Peers were never tired of telling the
ministerialists in the Commons how evident were the symptoms of vexation in Chatham's countenance when he was reminded nightly, by some fresh instance of neglect or impertinence, that, without the nation for an audience, his power
was gone; how the secretary of state hardly made a pretence
of answering his questions about the evacuation of Port Eg-
mont and the attitude of his Catholic Majesty; and how the
thunder of his eloquence, as with stately playfulness he not
unfrequently confessed, fell dead against the faded hangings
on which Flemish art had portrayed the defeat of the Arma-
da—that tapestry which, " mute as ministers, still told more
than all the cabinet on the subject of Spain, and the manner
of treating with a haughty and insidious power." To see
Burke reduced to the same helpless plight was a treat which
the Tories in the Lower House were determined not to deny
themselves; and they had this additional incentive to stir in
the matter that, while the Lords had nothing to gain by closing their doors except an agreeable immunity from the censorship of general public opinion, the Commons, by the offi-
ciousness of the reporters, were exposed to the more particular and invidious supervision of their constituents. It was
intolerable (such was the catchword in the government ranks)
that gentlemen should be misrepresented to the people whom
they were chosen to represent.[1] In accordance with this one-
sided but convenient view of the case, Colonel George Ons-

---

[1] The words are those of Mr. Thomas De Grey, member for Norfolk,
brother of the future Lord Walsingham; and the substance of them was
repeated in every second speech that was made during thirteen evenings
of February and March, 1771.

low, on the fifth of February, 1771, reminded the Commons that for any person to presume to give in the newspapers an account or abstract of their debates had been declared a breach of privilege, to be visited on the offender with the utmost severity. The resolutions which embodied this imperious doctrine, passed as long back as the first twelvemonth of the late reign, had been judiciously allowed to slumber by the common-sense of six successive parliaments; but Colonel Onslow now persuaded the House to revive and enforce them by ordering them to be printed in the votes. The next move in the game was intrusted to one Sir John Turner, who, on an afternoon when Sir George Savile was to bring forward in a new shape the old question of the Middlesex election, took upon himself to desire that strangers should be excluded on the ground that the House was too full to be pleasant; a pretext which immediately afterwards the ministerialists deprived of any semblance of plausibility by crowding noisily out to their dinners the instant that Sir George was on his feet.

The London editors had begun to discover that their narratives of the proceedings of a newly established debating society, or a certain club, or the Senate of Rome, or the Senate of Lilliput, or whatever the pseudonym might be which in their prudent ingenuity they selected for the British House of Commons, attracted more, and ever more, subscribers as time went on; and they were furious at the notion of such a blow having been struck against their interests by members whose reputation for being able to speak half a dozen sentences of grammar was due to the good offices of the reporter. For a month to come the whole legion of *Gazetteers* and *Advertisers* and *Posts* and *Chronicles* brought to bear upon their puny tyrants a perfect deluge of the awkward and bombastic wit peculiar to the eighteenth-century newspaper, at which it is so difficult to imagine how the readers of "Tristram Shandy" could contrive to laugh. In every degree of false taste, and with endless variety of extravagant epithets and inapplicable similes, the world was invited to consider the intricate problem whether the colonel, who was the great

Speaker's nephew, or the squire, who was his son, had done the most to render the name of Onslow ridiculous. The Onslows, meanwhile, were busily engaged in carrying on the warfare according to their own notions of strategy—interrupting the serious concerns of the nation by complaints that one of them had been called "a sorry motion-maker," and the other "little cocking George;" and moving that paragraphs should be read at the table, and printers hauled to the bar, and royal proclamations issued in the *London Gazette* offering fifty pounds a head for the apprehension of delinquents whose crime consisted in having expressed the opinion that of two silly members of Parliament it was not easy to say which was the silliest.

During some weeks the self-appointed inquisitors of the press took very little for their trouble. Their intended victims were not so simple as to march into the lion's mouth. "You are like Glendower," said Charles Fox, who could not resist a quotation from the dramatists even when it hit his friends. "You can call spirits from the vasty deep; but the question is, will the spirits come when you call them?" The deputy sergeant, armed with the Speaker's warrant, attended eight times in one afternoon at the office of the *Middlesex Journal*, and was informed on each occasion that the master had just stepped out, but might be expected back at any moment—a farce which was repeated at intervals throughout the two following days, until the servant who answered the door could not keep his countenance while he delivered the message. The more respectable members of the Commons were heartily ashamed of seeing Parliament committed to a contest in which its cause was as indefensible as its adversaries were insignificant. "The French Court," said Mr. Seymour, "issuing forth with their jack-boots and gilt coaches to hunt a little hare was an august and rational spectacle compared with the aspect of a senate bribing shop-boys to peach upon their employer." And the loss of dignity was even a less evil than the waste of time. Since the House last met—it might almost be said, since it was first elected—nothing had been done to provide even an instalment of the legislation

20

which the ever-changing circumstances of a vigorous and growing community, then as now, unceasingly demanded. Admiral Frankland, a brave and smart seaman who, when an unexpected death had turned him into a baronet and a land-owner, thought himself bound to come up to Westminster and lend a hand in doing the business of the country ashore, told his colleagues that in their quarrels about privilege they would show ill by the side of a parcel of sailors at Wapping. "Is there a word," he cried, "ever said in this House that leads to the good of the nation? I hear so much of the honor of Parliament that I am sick of the very name." At length those who held that the honor of Parliament demanded of it to show that it could produce something besides floods of barren rhetoric, and a fresh scandal every session, prevailed so far that an entire evening was devoted to a measure which would be of some practical advantage if carried, and which it required some experience and special knowledge to discuss. Sir George Colebrooke, the Chairman of the East India Company, a man of mark in politics, and with a tincture of the learning which became hereditary in his family, presented a bill for enabling the directors to enlarge their European army, and beat up for recruits among the Roman Catholics of Ireland. With Hyder Ali parading his cavalry round the fort at Madras, the Company was likely, for some time forward, to have ample employment for bayonets of any creed. A debate ensued of high interest and importance; the committee on the bill was fixed for the thirteenth of March; and the better men of both parties were congratulating each other on the House having, at the eleventh hour, settled down to work, when a piece of folly and mischief more flagrant than any which had preceded it scattered to the winds all their hopes of getting something accomplished which would be of service to the public or of credit to themselves.

The Onslows had already been busy for some weeks before their zeal met with approval in the highest quarter. It was not that the king entertained any sympathy for the reporters, or any glimmering of a notion that their humble but arduous calling was useful, or even innocent. "It is highly necessary," he wrote to Lord North as late as the twenty-first of February, " that this strange and lawless method of publishing debates in the paper should be put a stop to. But is not the House of Lords the best court to bring such miscreants before, as it can fine as well as imprison, and as the Lords have broader shoulders to support any odium that this salutary measure may occasion in the minds of the vulgar?" But as time went on, and the incidents of the squabble thickened, his Majesty began to feel the interest of a situation resembling, in many of its leading features, that memorable affair of the *North Briton*, which had hitherto been the event of his reign. It was like old days to read how Mr. Jeremiah Dyson, a retainer of the Court, for whose benefit a job was then being perpetrated which proved too much for the patience even of the Irish Parliament, had been called " the d——n of this country " by the *St. James's Chronicle* in its account of the " Debates of the Council of Utopia ;" how a bookseller had been ordered into custody for contempt because, when he was invited to attend in the name of Mr. Speaker, he replied that he did not know any such gentleman, so that the message could not be for him ; and how Dowdeswell and Burke and Dunning had been overpowered by obedient majorities when they endeavored to recall their colleagues into the path of manliness and prudence. Scenting the familiar battle from afar, George the Third insisted with Lord North, who had never liked the business from the first, that the contest between Parliament and the press should be fought out to the end, however much the public peace might be endangered, and however many measures of public utility might have to be postponed or sacrificed.

On Tuesday, the twelfth of March, Colonel Onslow, with an apology to his brother-members for showing them poorer sport than he could wish, announced that he should bring before them three more brace of printers. His insolent levity met with a warm response from the dense ranks of the courtiers, who were present in ominous force, with Rigby for their fugleman, taking from him the word of command for their votes and the cue for their cheers ; while the prime-minister sat

helpless, silent, and miserable, watching the assembly, which
he was officially supposed to lead, disgrace itself as no House
of Commons ever disgraced itself before or since.   One such
night was known during the crisis of the great Reform Bill.
One such night will never be forgotten by the members of
the Parliament which has lately passed into history.   But on
the twelfth of July, 1831, and on the thirty-first of July, 1877,
the power of a majority was resolutely and even ruthlessly
asserted, with the object in the one case of establishing the
liberties of the people, and in the other of protecting the
business character of the House of Commons; whereas in
March, 1771, the stronger of the two parties was contending
for a cause as reprehensible as the tactics employed were violent and unusual.   From mid-day till morning the war of
words and votes went on.   The adherents of the Court (for
those among the ministers who were not king's friends by
profession confined their exertions to walking in and out of
the lobby with an air of lassitude and disgust which they took
no pains to dissemble) worked steadily through the list, moving and carrying by three to one, and five to one, and at last
by seven to one, that such and such a newspaper be read at
the table, and such and such a printer do attend at the bar;
while the Opposition, on the other side, fought every case with
a display of proficiency in the art of obstruction that was a
century in advance of their epoch, and intercalated at least
one motion for adjournment between each proposal of the
government.   Brilliant little spurts of oratory relieved the
weariness, without improving the temper, of the combatants.
Barré exclaimed against the inconsistency of setting in motion the despotic authority of Parliament because an obscure
supporter of Lord North had been called, more truly than
civilly, a paltry insect, at a time when the grossest calumnies
against so respected an opponent of the ministry as the Duke
of Portland were published day after day by an adventurer
whom the Earl of Sandwich had rewarded with a living that
was in the gift of the Crown.[1]   A dispute as to which of two

---

[1] The assailant of the Duke of Portland was the Scotchman of Gold-

members had been the first to get upon his legs drew from
Burke a withering impeachment of the novel, improper, and
irregular doctrine of the Speaker's eye; and the scruples of
the great constitutional philosopher could not be set at rest
until an honest attempt had been made to define the properties of that magic organ in a solemn declaratory resolution.
The absurdity of the enterprise to which the British senate
had stooped remains to all time reflected on the pages of its
journals.   The childish malice of this attack upon the freedom of the press, and upon the right of the nation to know
how its own affairs were managed, inspired the defenders of
those great principles with a grim humor that overflowed from
their speeches into the formal amendments on which they
challenged the decision of Parliament.   When it had been
resolved that the publisher of the *London Packet* should be
summoned to the bar, a quiet Whig member, who had never
before got nearer to a joke than an occasional stock-quotation
from Horace, proposed that the man should be ordered to attend, "together with all his compositors, pressmen, correctors,
and devils;" and Burke's ironical argument against striking
out the last of the four classes is among the happiest samples
of his lighter vein.   When it came to the turn of a newspaper
which had attempted to steer clear of the quicksands of privilege by substituting in its report of the debates the names of
constituencies for the surnames of their members, Barré moved
that "Mr. Constantine Lincoln," and "Jeremiah Weymouth,
Esquire, the d——n of this country," were not members of the
House.   Between daylight and daylight the two parties had
tested their strength in three-and-twenty divisions, each of
them preceded and followed by bitter mutual reproaches, in
which the Speaker bore his part with an emphasis such as in
our more sedate times would sound strangely from the chair.

---

smith's "Haunch of Venison," who wrote "Cinna" and owned to "Pa-
nurge." He was chaplain to Sandwich, and in January of this very year
had been presented to the rectory of Simonburn in Northumberland.
Sandwich's connection with the Church was, in more ways than one, peculiar. He had two mistresses, who were respectively married to, and
sought in marriage by, two clergymen who died on the gallows.

The government had begun the evening with a following of a hundred and forty; but when, at five in the morning, the yeas for the last time had gone forth to be counted, barely half as many haggard and angry men filed past the extended forefinger of Charles Fox, who was acting as teller with the jovial energy of one whose usual bedtime was only just approaching.

When the House met on the Thursday, three or four of the printers appeared at the bar, and were reprimanded on their knees in spite of the most piteous assurances that their sale would be ruined if they were forbidden to publish the debates. It took no less than twelve hours, and as many processions in and out of the lobby, to get this dismal ceremony accomplished in the teeth of the working members, who were irritated at being kept from the Indian Army Bill, and of the Whigs, who were full of fight ever since their recent performance, about which they showed an inclination to boast which excited the loudly expressed disgust of Charles Fox. Burke, who was never in greater force, found it necessary to make four speeches before he had said all he had to say about the satisfaction with which he looked back upon his twenty-three divisions. " Posterity," he cried, " will bless the pertinaciousness of that day." But Burke and his friends needed not to wait till another generation for a recognition of their labors. Their resolute and patriotic conduct had aroused in the hearts of their contemporaries a spirit more than a match for the unwieldy and half-hearted tyranny of a House of Commons which was divided against itself. The citizens of London, who, with their compact organization and long habits of political discipline, proudly regarded themselves as the regular army of freedom, saw that a crisis had arrived which made it their duty to take the field; and their operations were planned and directed by a general who had fought over every inch of the ground against far more formidable odds than he now was likely to encounter. Before the Speaker went to bed that night, there had been placed in his hands a packet, the contents of which could have left little doubt on the mind of one so intimately acquainted with the history of the past eight years as Sir Fletcher Norton that Wilkes had already his finger in the business.   John Wheble, the same publisher who had kept the deputy sergeant dancing attendance for three livelong days in Paternoster Row, wrote to the effect that a person who represented himself to be an officer of the House of Commons had called several times at his residence with what purported to be a warrant from the Speaker; and that, being better versed in printing than in law, he had thought it his wisest course to lay the matter before a learned counsel, a copy of whose opinion he begged to transmit for the information of the Honorable House.   This production, signed by a Mr. Morris, of Lincoln's Inn, and drawn up in strict legal form—with case, questions, and answers all complete—was from first to last a piece of solemn impertinence, on which Voltaire could hardly have improved.   It was no unlettered denizen of the Inns of Court who argued, with such abundance of subdued and apparently unconscious humor, that the paper which pretended to be the Speaker's warrant was so ridiculously worded as to deprive it of all show of authenticity whatsoever; that the paper which pretended to be a royal proclamation, offering a reward for the arrest of an English citizen, had no force in a free country; and that the gentleman whose comfort had been disturbed by these novel and unauthorized methods of annoyance would do well to institute an action against the promoters, aiders, and abettors of proceedings as oppressive in intention as they were nugatory at law.[1]

---

[1] The warrant commenced with the words: "Ordered, that J. Wheble do attend this house upon Tuesday morning next."   It was signed "J. Hatsell, Cl. Dom. Com. ;" and, being issued on a Thursday, it was dated "die Jovis," after the ancient usage of Parliament which remained sacred down to February, 1866, when Latin was exchanged for English by unanimous consent, as the first act of the first House of Commons that was led by Mr. Gladstone.   It may be imagined with what feelings worthy Mr. Hatsell, who had made out the warrant in accordance with the time-honored forms, must have read the following passages in Mr. Morris's opinion:

"2. 'J. Wheble' is a description of nobody.   It might as well have been written 'eye Wheble,' or 'nose Wheble.'   Either of them would be

Whoever might have been responsible for this harmless pleasantry, it was succeeded by a practical joke of a much more serious nature, the authorship of which was patent to the world. On the fifteenth of March, the day after he had despatched his letter to the Speaker, Wheble was arrested at his own desire by Carpenter, a brother-printer, who held that, however dubious might be the validity of a royal proclamation, there was no need to let fifty pounds go out of the trade. The captor and his victim went amicably to Guildhall, where care had been taken that Wilkes should be the sitting justice. The case was settled with a promptitude which indicated that the occurrence had been foreseen and the details minutely prearranged. Wheble was at once released from custody. Carpenter was first bound over to appear at the next quarter-sessions in answer to a charge of assault and false imprisonment, and then sent off to Whitehall to claim his reward with a certificate signed " John Wilkes, Alderman," which it is to be hoped may be still among the Treasury records. The next document thrown off by the handiest of pens was a letter to the secretary of state, reporting the steps which had been taken by the Guildhall bench to mark the illegality of an arrest made in direct violation of the rights of an Englishman and the chartered privileges of a London citizen. This effu-

---

as much the name of John Wheble as the former. Besides, a person is not legally named without a proper addition of quality and abode, which is not so much as attempted in this pretended order.

" 3. The place of attendance is not sufficiently expressed. ' This House' is more properly the house of John Wheble, where the order was left, than any other house ; for there is no date of place to the order. Mr. Wheble therefore best attended this order by staying at home.

" 4. The date of time being expressed in a foreign tongue, which an Englishman need not understand, the day of attendance became consequently uncertain ; ' Tuesday morning next' having no day, which it is next, to follow.

 . . . .

" 6. If the House of Commons had power to issue this summons, it ought to be signed by the Speaker, and not by a person using certain cabalistic expressions which may possibly be construed to mean ' Clerk of the House of Commons.' "

sion, which breathed the tone of humble confidence befitting
an inferior magistrate who has faced an unexpected difficulty
in a manner to win him gratitude in high quarters, was calculated to produce a startling effect alike by the intelligence
which it conveyed and the reminiscences which it awakened.
It was not the first envelope in that handwriting which the
secretary of state had opened; for the Minister of Home Affairs was once more the Earl of Halifax, who in 1763 had been
one of the parties in the celebrated correspondence about the
seizure of Wilkes's papers. Those had been days when to
engage in controversy with a friendless outcast required no
great courage in the master of thirty general warrants: but
times were altered; and to be addressed in a public letter by
Junius was now hardly more trying to the nerves of peer or
potentate than to be honored with a private letter by Wilkes.
Halifax would have read with less trepidation a request for an
interview from the solicitor of his largest creditor or his last
mortgagee; and, as for his royal master, it may fairly be said
that, for the first and only time in his existence, George the
Third was thoroughly frightened. Thrice in the course of
five days did his Majesty sit down at his desk for the purpose
of admonishing Lord North, whatever he did, to leave the
most awkward of customers alone. The prime-minister—who
had such painful reasons for remembering the royal letter of
April, 1768, which charged him, on his loyalty as a subject, to
see that Parliament reversed the Middlesex election—must
have perused with a respectful smile the sentence in which
his sovereign, in March, 1771, communicated to him the opportune discovery that Wilkes was below the notice of the
House of Commons.

But the tardy repentance of the king did not carry him far
along the path of caution. After another printer had been
taken into custody by collusion, in order to be set at liberty with
a flourish of municipal eloquence, a bona-fide arrest at length
was made. Miller, the publisher of the London *Evening Post*,
had been placed by Colonel Onslow on the list of proscription;
and a messenger of the House of Commons, calling at the
shop, was unlucky enough to find his man at home. As soon

as a finger had been laid upon his shoulder, Miller sent for a constable, who appeared on the scene with significant promptitude, attended by a posse comitatus of the neighbors. The Speaker's officer was given into charge for an assault; and as many of the party as could squeeze themselves into a hackney - coach started together for Guildhall. From Guildhall they were sent on to the Mansion House, where Lord Mayor Crosby was awaiting them, with Aldermen Oliver and Wilkes as his assessors. The City dignitaries, who had no intention that the thing should be done in a corner, gave time for the news to reach Westminster; and the deputy sergeant-at-arms came in state to rescue his subordinate and to claim his prisoner. The lord mayor replied by asking the Speaker's messenger whether he was a peace officer legally qualified to make an arrest within the City bounds, and whether his warrant was backed by a City magistrate; and when the man gave the only answer in his power, an order was drawn up committing him for trial on the charge of assault and false imprisonment. Crosby, whose courage was his best quality, though his character was otherwise not disrespectable,[1] begged his colleagues to leave him the entire responsibility of a step the consequences of which could not fail to be perilous; and, turning to Wilkes, he said, in the hearing of the court, "You, I think, have enough on your hands already." But Wilkes, who never cared how much paper was flying about the world under his signature, insisted on putting his name to the order of commitment; and an instrument which was nothing less than a declaration of war against the House of Commons went forth under the unanimous sanction of the magistrates who were in attendance to represent the City.

The leader of the House, if left to himself, would have al-

---

[1] Horace Walpole, who, though he approved the cause, took his customary pains to collect all the dirt which political hostility had raked up against the man, has furnished Crosby with the reputation of a low fellow who had risen by mean arts. As a matter of fact, there is nothing worse against him than that he did three times what some of the most eminent patriots in history, from Washington downwards, have done once—married a rich widow.

lowed the gage of battle to lie. There was no moment, late
or early, at which Lord North was not prepared to let the
matter drop, convinced, as he had been all along, that every
fresh stage in such an undertaking could only be more shameful and disastrous than the last. But the time was now come
for him to experience what it was to be at the mercy of a
stronger will and a weaker judgment than his own. As soon
as what had passed in the City was known in the palace, the
king despatched the first minister who entered his presence
with a commission to tell Lord North that, unless Crosby and
Oliver were sent to the Tower, nothing could save the Constitution; and the verbal message was enforced by a letter couched in the most stringent terms. But it was not George the
Third's custom, on an occasion which in his eyes was a crisis,
to rely either upon spoken or written words. Like all men
of energy who are forced to act through others, he thought
less of giving an order than of taking his own measures to
have that order obeyed. The proceedings at the Mansion
House had not been concluded until late on the Friday evening; and on the Monday, as soon as the private business was
over, the Speaker rose and, standing in front of his chair, expounded to the Commons, in a long and circumstantial narrative, the nature of the insult which had been offered to their
authority. His story met with a cold reception from a Parliament which, having hitherto spent the whole of its corporate existence in fighting the people, was not impatient to embark in a new contest that seemed likely to last until a general election reversed, most probably forever, the position of
the combatants. After a fresh series of county meetings, petitions, and remonstrances had animated the nation and disheartened the Court; after the liberty of the press had been
drunk with three times three in every assize town in the kingdom, and another score of letters by Junius, on the most fertile and stirring of themes, had been thumbed to pieces in all
the coffee-houses—to go then to the country on the question
of preventing the country from hearing what was said and
knowing what was done by the representatives of the country would be to provide Chatham with a devoted and irresist-

ible majority, to be used at will for the accomplishment of the purpose which he had nearest at heart. And what that purpose was, no one who had an insight into his mind, or a hint of the subject on which he most frequently and earnestly corresponded with the statesmen who enjoyed and deserved his confidence, could for a moment doubt. With Chatham once more dictator, and Shelburne or Barré his master of the knights, the very first session would usher in an era of such searching and sweeping economical and parliamentary reform that few indeed of those gentlemen whose seats were now so secure and so remunerative would ever handle a Treasury bank-bill or see the inside of St. Stephen's again.

When the Speaker had concluded his doleful and undignified tale, the House looked in vain for guidance from the usual quarters to which, in a case of perplexity, it was accustomed to turn. No leading minister—no private member qualified by his standing and his character to be put forward as an interpreter of the government policy—would consent to play the part of adviser at a conjuncture when the single piece of advice that was not utter folly was such as a king's minister dared not give. Only Welbore Ellis, whose name was a proverb for a hack placeman throughout the half-century when hack placemen went for the most in English history—who had done parliamentary job-work for Henry Pelham, and who lived to be a mark for the boyish shafts of William Pitt—moved, with the air of one who, having learned his lesson, was half afraid to say it, "that Brass Crosby, Esquire, Lord Mayor of the City of London, a member of this House, do attend this House in his place to-morrow morning." Very different men, speaking in far less uncertain accents, rose in rapid succession to combat the insane proposal. The assault was led by Sir William Meredith, a convert from Jacobite opinions, who had not abandoned his ancient faith in order at once to worship the rising sun of a new-fangled absolutism. Ever since the time that Wilkes had first engaged the attention of Parliament, Sir William had borne his part in defence of constitutional liberty with a scrupulous fairness and an almost pathetic candor which won the good-will of his

opponents, and were not always to the taste of the more impetuous of his allies. His influence in the House was rather
increased than lessened by his not aspiring to speak better
than became a country gentleman; but the occasion now was
such that to be an honest man was almost equivalent to being
an orator. Like a good cavalier, Sir William read a passage
from his Clarendon to illustrate the dangers of exalting the
privilege of Parliament as against the law of the realm;
but, without the help of quotation, his own downright language admirably expressed the energy of his honorable and
manly apprehensions. "I wish to God," cried the old Tory,
"that those who are involved in the labyrinths of this fatal
proposition had consulted their judgments and then made a
pause! I desire to make my pause now. I came down to the
House this day with a strong impression that I could take but
one part, which was, if human wisdom could point out the
means, to put a stop to this business. By whom this business
was brought into the House I know. By whose dexterity it
is to be got out of it I do not yet know. But this I know,
that, unless you do get rid of it, I see nothing but mischief
before you."

Meredith was followed by Henry Herbert, afterwards Lord
Portchester, and long afterwards the Earl of Carnarvon. A
young politician, as politicians go now—though in a House of
Commons which contained Charles Fox, thirty could hardly
be regarded as within the age of modesty—he had before this
been selected by his party to initiate debates for which Burke
and Dowdeswell and Dunning undertook to provide the eloquence, while Herbert himself contributed little beyond the
influence of his high position and blameless reputation. But
now, instead of repeating his wonted string of unimpeachable
Whig sentiments arrayed in staid Whig phrases, he astonished
his hearers and himself by speaking his mind in words as
plain and free as those in which his sailor namesake told
James the Second, to his face, that there was a point beyond
which even the loyalty of a Herbert would not carry him.
Seconding Meredith's proposal that the House should adjourn
till it had leisure to survey the precipice on the verge of

which it stood, the young patrician adjured his fellows not to be hurried into a course that was detrimental to the true interests of their order. "I shall be told," he said, "that our dignity is so nearly concerned that we cannot pause for a moment. Is it for our dignity to be eternally at war with the people?" Lord John Cavendish, who stood on a level with Herbert in the esteem of Parliament, and was much more at home in an atmosphere which to a Cavendish was native air, sketched with a practised hand a vivid picture of the dangers and humiliations in which the House of Commons was asked to involve itself. Nobody appeared on the other side but a few third-rate speakers, who endeavored to withdraw attention from the poverty of their arguments by taunting the Opposition into a quarrel over the very driest among the innumerable bones of contention that remained on the battle-field of the Middlesex election. At the first symptom of a riot, Charles Fox rushed joyously into the fray;[1] but his attempt to create a diversion was sternly repressed by Savile. Reduced to argue their cause on its demerits, the supporters of the motion spoke briefly, coldly, and most ineffectively. The heart appeared to be out of the business; and the prime-minister, as he watched the glum faces that surrounded him, began to feel the inward joy of a trainer who has sold a cock-fight when his bird will not come to time. It seemed impossible that the king, brave and pertinacious as he was, should insist upon the cabinet asserting a privilege of the House of Commons which the House of Commons itself was desirous to renounce.

But Lord North did not yet know the master whom he served. Because the statesman who was in official possession of the royal confidence stood aghast before the enterprise which he was commanded to undertake; because the great body of Tory county members, who hitherto had done their

---

[1] "I beg to lay in my claim," said Fox, "that I should not be called to order. I wish to know whether it is disorderly to say that persons have presented to the Crown insolent and impertinent petitions." Such was a fair specimen of the interpellations by which the young senator tempered for himself the otherwise intolerable tyranny which forbade him to speak more than once in every debate.

sovereign's bidding through evil report and good report, now
hung back from a conflict which, though their ostensible foes
were the City and the newspapers, was in truth waged against
their own constituents—it by no means followed that George
the Third was at the end of his resources. The time had come
for him to remind his minister and his minister's supporters
that he had in pay a prætorian guard of his own, led by a
captain whom nature had framed for more honorable employment. Sir Gilbert Elliot, the progenitor of a race which has
inherited his powers and applied them to worthier ends, had
been enrolled among the king's friends ever since the king
had begun to make a party; and that he was incomparably
the ablest of the band, if any one had doubted it, he was now
to prove. At the turn of the debate, when another half-hour's
hesitation would have set the tide racing towards a policy of
caution, Elliot stepped on the floor with a promise of saying
nothing that should inflame the House, and then proceeded to
pour forth a declamation which had fire enough about it to set
a Quakers' meeting in a blaze. He was there, he said, under
no control from king or minister. It was the House of Commons that he meant to stand by—that House which was not
an instrument to destroy, but to maintain, the rights and privileges of the people. The authority of Parliament, so he reminded his colleagues, had been denied. The sword had been
drawn, but not by them. Civil war had been as good as proclaimed; and the people who were so hot for it must be
taught that they were not the strongest. "If they come
against us," he said, "with all their City behind them, I will
not be the man to fall back. Are we, the Commons of England, the representatives of the people, afraid to defend the
law and custom of Parliament against the Lord Mayor of London and two of the aldermen? I never will cease to exhort
every gentleman who hears me—every man of family or estate or talent in this House—to defend its rights, and not to
defer that defence by consenting to an adjournment."

By the time that Elliot had done, the mischief was already
irrevocable. There was no mistaking the significance of his
tone, which was not so much that of the senator seeking to

persuade his colleagues as of the aide-de-camp who has
brought to an unwilling colonel the order to charge, and who
speaks loud enough for the regiment to hear.   His attitude
was understood, and was intended to be understood, by the
pensioners, who looked to the Court for their bread-and-butter; by the lawyers, who within the last two months had seen
the attorney-generalship given as a reward to one of their
number for making an impudent attack upon the first principles of liberty, and the solicitor-generalship to another as a
fee for ceasing to defend them; by the West Indians, who,
with more slaves than constituents, cared nothing for running
counter to a popular feeling with which they were not trained
to sympathize, and from which as politicians they had nothing
to fear; by the East Indians, who, ambitious of the social position which mere wealth, and, least of all, wealth with such
an origin as theirs, could not buy, were enchanted at being
addressed as men of family and estate, and having their course
pointed out by one whose own fortunes gave such solid proof
that he knew every turn of the avenues which led to worldly
honor. All the tribe, without whose suffrages no government
could then exist, enforced each of Elliot's periods with cheering which told the prime-minister that it was no longer within
his discretion to stay his hand. Burke replied in a speech full
of political wisdom, of literary beauty, of allusions to his own
history and his own personality—allusions from which the run
of speakers do well to refrain, but which in the mouth of the
very few who can venture to employ them are among the
most exquisite graces of oratory. The prompt wit and dignified humility with which he accepted a very unnecessary call
to order from Colonel Luttrell afford a model of the temper
in which a great statesman should deal with an interruption.
" The question of Middlesex," interposed Luttrell, " is not before us. I cannot sit and hear the seat which I honor myself
on holding called in question." " The honorable gentleman,"
said Burke, " has reason to honor himself. He is a greater
man than I am. He was elected in a much more honorable
manner, by greater constituents." But Burke, though he spoke
so as to carry delight and persuasion to every one who was

not a placeman or a partisan, showed nothing of the aggressive and almost elated air which had been remarkable in the
members of the Opposition who had preceded Elliot; and his
subdued manner was exhilaration itself as compared with the
despondency of the prime-minister. Never were followers
more clearly forewarned that the enterprise to which they
were summoned was a forlorn-hope, and that, whatever might
be the case with the rank and file, their leader did not pretend
to be a volunteer. In the three sentences which conveyed the
announcement that the cabinet had resolved to push the quarrel, the word "unhappy" occurred no less than three times;
and the sentiment was so deeply imprinted on Lord North's
countenance, and so evident in his demeanor, as to convince
the fighting-men of his party that peace might be made at any
moment, unless the government, through the mouth of one
among its own members, was committed beyond recall to a
policy of defiance. It was a rare chance for any minister,
small or great, who was ambitious to display himself in the
character of a mutineer and an incendiary. The opportunity
was come for which a mother's pride had long been waiting.
"I hope," wrote Lady Holland, in January, 1770, "that Lord
North has courage and resolution. Charles being connected
with him pleases me mightily. I have formed a very high
opinion of his lordship, and my Charles will, I dare say, inspire him with courage." And with the sort of courage which
animates a general in the presence of an enemy when he is
informed that a sub-lieutenant of engineers has taken upon
himself to break up the bridges in his rear, North was now to
be provided in abundance.

The lord mayor, who sat for Honiton, was well liked among
his brother-members. Even Colonel Onslow thought it a duty
to bear testimony in his favor, and solemnly took his Maker
to witness that he never should have expected such conduct
from a gentleman with whom he had frequently drunk a bottle. Barré skilfully attempted to avail himself of Crosby's
popularity in order to obtain him a reprieve on the ground
that he was out of health—a plea with regard to which the
House, it must be allowed, showed itself sufficiently sceptical.

21

Fox, who knew that the lord mayor was in all probability suffering from nothing more serious than was the matter with half the cabinet on the morning after they had dined with anybody except a bishop, began an energetic and most artful harangue by declaring that Parliament had no concern with questions of health or sickness. It was for the House to decree whether the lord mayor should be cited before it to answer for his proceedings; and then, if he was too ill to come, he must himself write and say so. Parliament (Fox went on to assert) would do well not to lend too credulous an ear to those who threatened it with the displeasure of the people of England. The people, in the language of certain gentlemen, was only another name for whatever class or group or handful of men might happen at the moment to be in rebellion against the people's representatives. One year the freeholders of Middlesex were the people of England; next year the citizens of London; and now the meaning of a term which ought to embrace the nation had been narrowed down until it had come to stand for the lord mayor and a couple of aldermen. The people (argued the young casuist) were correct in thinking that they had a stake in the contest; but their interest lay upon the opposite side from that on which they were invited to range themselves. The controversy which had been so impertinently and so needlessly provoked was not between the House of Commons and the people, but between the people and the Crown. The lord mayor rested his case upon the rights of the City; the charter which conferred those rights had emanated from the sovereign; and the point of the dispute, therefore, was whether the king could, of his own will and pleasure, invest a corporation with the power to treat as non-existent an established privilege of the English House of Commons. "That privilege," he cried, breaking into a peroration before his hearers had leisure to examine too closely this most unforeseen product of his sinister dexterity, "is recognized by the people of England, and disputed only by three of the City magistrates. Every gentleman who thinks the honor of this House insulted and its existence at stake will be for the lord mayor's coming here to-morrow. There may be, as in all ages there has been, discontent among a portion of the people; but while we act agreeably to law we are invulnerable. I am sick of our lenient mode of dealing with our enemies. There has long been a determination on the part of certain persons to bring the question of our privileges to an issue; and even if we had let the printers alone, we should have had that question forced upon us within another month, or, at latest, within another session. It is from those who in their souls abhor and detest our admirable Constitution that this plot has sprung."

The speech, which may still be read pretty nearly as it was spoken, explains the dislike and dread with which the speaker was then regarded by a multitude of politicians, humble in rank and zealous for their opinions, who ten years afterwards centred on him all their hopes, and twenty years afterwards would have died for him to a man. People of his own class —who knew what a good-hearted fellow he was, and how little he owed to his bringing-up (if, indeed, he could be said to have been brought up at all)—forgave him much; and those among them who had an insight into character looked forward confidently to the day when the true metal that was in him would

> " Show more goodly, and attract more eyes,
> Than that which hath no foil to set it off."

But the great body of tradesmen and small freeholders, who were beginning to recognize the abuses of the system under which they lived, and to talk eagerly and seriously of those reforms which between their time and ours have made England another and a better country, might be excused for regarding Charles Fox as a young Hannibal, whom his sire had pledged from the nursery to the destruction of freedom; with a forehead of brass and a constitution of iron; whom the nineteenth century would find still thundering with matured ability and undiminished vigor against the claims of reason, justice, and humanity. The impression produced by his youthful rhetoric on those against whose interests and convictions it was directed is recorded by a poor bookseller who had suffered many things of many secretaries of state, and who was constant in his attendance at the House of Commons on the frequent occasions when matters affecting his craft were under discussion. John Almon, of Piccadilly, who published for Wilkes and other members of the extreme section of the Opposition, thus describes the Fox of 1771: "He answered no arguments sensibly; but he showed some ingenuity in endeavoring to confound the reasoning of his opponents. Cunning, much life, more profligacy, some wit, and little sense is no unfair account of his performance. But he trusted to numbers, which beat all understanding." To be in the wrong and side with the strong on questions of civil liberty was the easy and agreeable apprenticeship of one whose highest title to honor is that on those same questions, from the first year of his discretion to the last of his life, he was almost always in the right and hardly ever in a majority. But so long as he was false to his future, fortune was true to him. The ardor with which the Whigs commenced the debate of the eighteenth of March had been damped by Elliot, and was fairly extinguished by Fox. The discussion, killed by his vehemence, dwindled into a desultory conversation, succeeded by a division in which the Court, by two hundred and sixty-seven votes to eighty, carried the day against the efforts of its opponents and the wishes of its ministers.

The king received intelligence of the victory in a spirit indicating that the calamities which since the year 1763 had befallen his realm had taught him as little about the nature of the people whom he governed as he had learned from history before he began to have experiences of his own.

> "Though some o' the court hold it presumption
> To instruct princes what they ought to do,
> It is a noble duty to inform them
> What they ought to foresee."

But the duty inculcated in those rugged lines was ill-performed in the circle which more immediately surrounded George the Third. So masterful that he did not love to associate with people of forcible and independent minds as his daily companions, he was so kind that the honest folks about him were all but sure to be sincere and passionate admirers of any course which he might pursue; and, even when they thought him mistaken, they could not bear to cross him. With no one to offer advice which was not the echo of his own purposes, he again forgot, as he had forgotten so lately and so frequently, that the enthusiasm of the English for the victim of a state prosecution was as certain as a fact in physics. The citizens of London, whose grandfathers had made a saint and a martyr of the most foolish clergyman that ever turned the pulpit into a rostrum—and who themselves had made a hero and a martyr, and, what was more, an alderman, of as dissolute a politician as ever looked to Parliament as a sanctuary from the bailiffs—would now (so George the Third had brought himself to believe) acquiesce in seeing their own chief magistrate tried, convicted, and punished for the crime of defending their own privileges, if only care was taken not to thrust the transaction too prominently before their notice. Writing as if it were a question of saving an informer from being hooted on his way to the witness-box, or balking a popular highwayman of his ovation in the cart, the king imagined that he had taken adequate precautions against a repetition of the scenes which had so often disgraced and disturbed his capital, when he recommended the prime-minister to conduct the lord mayor to Westminster by water "in the most private manner." With a little ordinary caution, and resolution something more than ordinary, on the part of North, the affair, according to his Majesty's forecast, would be "happily concluded;" the Liverymen, when they were tired of waiting on Ludgate Hill for a procession which never came, would go back to their work and leave the lord mayor to his reflections in the Tower; the newspapers would be silenced, the printers ruined, and the House of Commons as imperviously sealed to the public gaze as the Council of Ten at Venice.

But the English of that day were not so different from the people who defeated Walpole's Excise scheme that they would be content to pay taxes the necessity for which had not been explained to them, and to obey laws the process of making which they had been forbidden to inspect. Nor did Crosby and Oliver approve the notion of being smuggled about London in a fashion derogatory to its municipal ruler and its parliamentary representative. As they drove westwards together on their way to St. Stephen's, their coach passed between deep and serried ranks of citizens, well behaved, well dressed, and in a large proportion well educated, as might be judged from the character of the ejaculations that mingled with the huzzas which ran in one unbroken volume along street, hall, staircase, and lobby, from the steps of the Mansion House to the threshold of the Commons.[1] For three minutes after the door of the House had closed behind the lord mayor, the cheering from without continued to resound through the chamber, and brought the trial of the seven bishops to the memory of those who sat within, however little most of them might relish the parallel. But though the associations which the scene aroused reminded the members then present that they were assembled in the capacity of a court of justice, very few of them showed any sense of the obligation to adapt their temper and their manners to the judicial standard. During the three days which were consumed over the preliminaries of the case, the supporters of the government made no pretence of impartiality, and little enough of common propriety. They groaned down the first member who opened his lips on behalf of the City ; and when Dowdeswell interposed a few words before the House came to its final decision, he was received in a fashion which proved that even an ex-Chancellor of the Exchequer must expect to be roughly handled if he attempted to enlighten the minds of those numerous honorable gentlemen who were going to pronounce on a knotty point of legal procedure without having listened to the argument. What sort of trial was this (asked Burke), to which jurymen flocked in, wiping their mouths, and bawling " Question !" and " Divide !" when one of their number, who had remained in his place, undertook, before they delivered their verdict, to put them in

---

[1] " The crowd," said a writer in the *Gentleman's Magazine*, " during the whole passage to the House called out to the lord mayor as ' The people's friend,' ' The guardian of the city's rights and the nation's liberties.' "

possession of the evidence which had been adduced while they were absent at their dinners? Fox, completely in his element, enjoyed himself like an apprentice in an O. P. riot, and bore off the honors of the most scandalous among the many tumults which interrupted and inflamed the proceedings. Barré, who took him to task for calling his colleagues assassins, and for speaking of men whose guilt was still unproved as criminals, paid him as high a compliment as ever took the shape of a reproof by admonishing him that a member with his great abilities and acknowledged position as a leader might not plead inexperience even at one-and-twenty.

What was done during those evenings was at least as wanting in decorum as what was said or shouted. The Speaker refused to read the letter in which Wilkes, who had been summoned to attend at the bar, respectfully declined to appear elsewhere than in his place on the benches. The House refused to hear counsel on the question whether the lord mayor could have acted upon a warrant which was not signed by a City magistrate without infringing the charters which, at his accession to office, he had sworn to observe—a course as highhanded as if, in an action of trespass, the defendant were debarred from attempting to show that the land off which he had been warned was his own. And at length, mounting from informality to outrage, the ministerial majority ordered the clerk of the lord mayor to place upon their table the book containing the recognizance by which the Speaker's messenger was bound over to appear at Guildhall, and proceeded then and there to expunge the entry. On the very spot where the great men of the seventeenth century, in the presence of a frowning king, maintained that privilege of Parliament which was now perverted into a weapon for the discomfiture of liberty, their descendants were not ashamed to combine in a violation of the law which a tyrant who had not three hundred others to keep him in countenance would never have dared to perpetrate.[1] Nor would even that shameless throng have

---

[1] Chatham, in his review of the session, thus commented on the bad business: "These men, who had allowed the prostitute electors of Shore-

carried their audacity to such a length if there had been no defection from the small band who hitherto had remained true to the Constitution and to each other. But the most flagrant act of treachery which stands against the name of any public man eminent enough to have the incidents of his career recorded for the criticism of posterity had, for the time being, placed liberty and legality at the mercy of their adversaries.

No one conversant with the political literature of the middle of the eighteenth century would deny that the members of the House of Commons who, as a class, then enjoyed the affection and confidence of their colleagues in the least ample measure were the lawyers. Something of their unpopularity may be traced to a social prejudice against men who had worked their way from an humbler level into a sphere which, but for their intrusion, the aristocracy would have preserved almost exclusively to itself; but the small esteem in which gentlemen of the long robe were very generally held was chiefly due to what Bubb Dodington and Henry Fox would have termed moral causes. Everybody (such would be the theory of those profound observers) was greedy; but the lawyer was selfish. Everybody was ready to change sides with the rest of the connection to which he belonged; but the lawyer ratted alone, and at the moment which suited his individual interests. The Bedfords hunted in a pack; the Pelhams ran in a couple; but the lawyer pursued his peculiar prey with solitary avidity, and with a clamor which went far to spoil the

---

ham counsel to defend a bargain to sell their borough by auction, would not grant the same indulgence to the Lord Mayor of London pleading for the laws of England and the conscientious discharge of his duty." The erasure of the recognizance, he went on to say, was the act of a mob, and not of a parliament. "We have heard of such violences committed by the French king; and it seems better calculated for the latitude of Paris than of London. The people of this kingdom will never submit to such barefaced tyranny. They must see that it is time to rouse when their own creatures assume a power of stopping prosecutions by their vote, and consequently of resolving the law of the land into their will and pleasure."

sport of the entire field. It was hard enough that a barrister with a seat which he had bought cheap from some patron of a borough who had overstayed his market should talk of himself as ill-used if he did not secure a recordership in the course of his second session, and a judgeship before the end of his second Parliament; while a squire who had fought his county at every general election since he came of age was bidden by the ministers to think himself lucky, and by Junius to consider himself infamous, if in the fulness of time his fidelity was rewarded by a place which hardly paid the rent of his town house and the wages of his chairmen. But it was positively insufferable that a quiet supporter of the government who, after much study and many misgivings, had screwed himself up to the determination of showing his leaders that he could speak as well as vote should find himself forestalled at every stage of the debate by the fluency of men whose trade, as Chatham told them, was words. Whenever anything was to be said, there never was wanting an honorable and learned gentleman to say it, at five times the length of anybody else, and with the air of authority betokening a profession which earns its bread by affecting to be infallible. But the county members knew well how to take their revenge. Their ears were at the command of anybody on whom the Speaker's glance might light; but their minds were open to the advice of those, and those only, who resembled themselves in position, in antecedents, in habits of thought, and in the proportion which the number of their sentences bore to the weight of their arguments. Ten words from Conway or Savile went further than an hour of Sergeant Nares or Dr. Hay; and there was nothing more sure to take with the House of Commons than an allusion to the difference in quality of the attention which it paid to statesmen who were thinking of their subject and to aspirants for legal promotion who were thinking of themselves. "The artillery of the law," said Barré, "has been brought down on both sides; but, like artillery, it has not done much hurt;" and on a subsequent occasion he entertained an audience which, in those days of gunpowder, always welcomed a military metaphor from such as had the right to use one, by comparing the law officers of the Crown to the elephants in an Eastern army, which with their noise and dust bewilder their own troops a great deal more than they harm the enemy.

There was, however, one lawyer whom public opinion placed in a category apart from all others of his calling. Wedderburn had first been heard of in London as a dependent of Bute; but few even of those who disliked the favorite and disapproved his policy found it in their hearts to blame the young Scotchman for availing himself of patronage which he so sorely needed. A stranger amidst a people whose language he could hardly speak to be understood, and whose politics just then took the shape of ferocious hatred towards the country of his birth, he might well be excused if among the various party leaders he attached himself to the first who showed him kindness. But as soon as he felt his feet in the Court of Chancery and on the floor of the House of Commons—as soon as he had begun to think for himself with his hard North-country head, and to express his thoughts in the seductive intonation which he had learned from an Irish actor and an Irish master of elocution—he lost no time in making it known that gratitude to Bute did not blind him to the dangers of the system of government which was practised by Bute's master. Wedderburn's first act, after he was naturalized as an Englishman, was to declare for the liberties of England. So at least the Whigs, proud of their hopeful convert, were never tired of repeating, while the Tories listened with respect and admiration to an orator whose manner seemed to show that he was convinced himself, and whose matter was so carefully selected and arranged as to prove that he desired to inform, and not to mislead or dazzle, others. Both sides joined in regarding him as a forerunner of the eminent advocates who, between his day and ours, have asked for no better lot than to hold the faith of their party, to be admitted to its councils, and to take their share in its defeats, its labors, and its victories.[1]

---

[1] Lord Campbell asserts that Wedderburn's patriotism had all along

Such were Mackintosh and Romilly and Follett. Such men are not hard to name among those who now wear, and honor, the gown. But Wedderburn had other views and other ambitions. In constructing for himself a reputation for probity and public spirit, he was simply manufacturing an article to sell. Doing deliberately and completely what feebler schemers did fitfully and by halves, he made it a point to have in stock not merely such hackneyed staples of commerce as legal skill and parliamentary ability, but the more precious commodities of the confidence and affection of his countrymen, and an influence which extended into remote corners of the British empire. In March, 1770, he had lectured the House of Commons, the ministry, and the king himself on their lawless proceedings at home with a severity which forced even the objects of his rebuke to confess that here at last was one who reverenced the law for other reasons than because he lived by it. In May, 1770, in words which thousands of people in America then quoted to each other with hope, and millions have since read with contempt and aversion, he denounced as wicked and foolish the arbitrary taxation of the colonies; predicted, and all but justified, their rebellion; and told Lord North, in the only phrase which his own subsequent conduct did nothing to belie, that, until the fatal policy was abandoned, no man of honor would consent to be a minister. But by November in the same year his unerring observation warned him that he had sailed far enough on the tack of patriotism. Having taken the precaution of obtaining from the owner of the borough for which he sat free leave to make the best bargain that he could in any quarter that he chose, he contrived means for letting the ministers know that he was to be bought, and then proceeded to exalt their appreciation of his value by attacking them with more unction than

---

been regarded with suspicion. If ever it was possible to gather with certainty what men were thinking a hundred years ago, the opposite conclusion is the correct once. The evidence by which Lord Campbell supports his statement is a passage from Junius written five months after Wedderburn had changed his party.

ever. The less confiding members of the Opposition at last
saw through his game; but it is painful to reflect that he deceived Chatham, and that the efforts of the old statesman to
testify his esteem for Wedderburn by closer and more frequent personal intercourse did something to frighten Lord
North into concluding the business on the turncoat's own
terms.[1] On the twenty-fifth of January, 1771, appeared the
announcement that Alexander Wedderburn, Esquire, had become solicitor-general to his Majesty; and it may safely be
affirmed that no appointment has ever caused so profound
and unpleasing a sensation. The new law officer made a pretence of defending himself by putting it about that George
Grenville had been his leader, and that, since Grenville's
death, he was bound to no one. But it was a little too much
to expect the world to believe that the cleverest Scotchman
who had crossed the Tweed, and the sharpest lawyer that
ever hugged an attorney,[2] wanted a mentor at the age of
six-and-thirty to tell him that, if he took office, he would have
to unsay promptly and publicly everything that he had said
during the years that he had been active and austere in opposition. He might be bound to no leader, but he was bound
to himself — to his own solemn pledges; to his own well-
weighed actions; to the multitudes on either shore of the Atlantic whom he had taught to look upon him as their counsellor and protector.

While the eminent men who spent their all for the cause

---

[1] On the twenty-second of November, Chatham begged for an opportunity of exchanging sentiments with one "whose handsome conduct
and great abilities" he cordially admired. A fortnight later on he wrote,
"Mr. Wedderburn, as I hear, did, upon the matter of juries' right to judge,
speak openly and like a man. I shall ever truly honor him." Shelburne, on the other hand, had begun to suspect Wedderburn before the
end of November; and it is evident that his doubts were shared by
Camden.

[2] Boswell took the opinion of his great moralist on the question whether Wedderburn had behaved unworthily in canvassing for briefs through
the agency of a Scotch bookseller. "If I were a lawyer," said Johnson,
"I should not solicit employment; not because I should think it wrong,
but because I should disdain it."

which Wedderburn had sacrificed to the exigencies of his career did not disguise from themselves the disastrous consequences which could not fail to result from the treachery, they were mindful of their own dignity when speaking of the traitor. Camden reported the new ministerial arrangements for Chatham's information in language as dry and conventional as that of the *London Gazette.* "I make no remark upon all this," he added. "I am not surprised, but grieved." Chatham himself expressed his pain and astonishment in a single epithet. "The part of Wedderburn," he wrote, "is deplorable." But though the great judge and the great statesman showed a generous reluctance to avenge the wrongs of the public upon one who had so deeply injured themselves, there was no want of people who were both able and willing to give the solicitor-general a foretaste of what history had in reserve for him. Churchill, indeed, was gone; but the admirers of Churchill exultingly pointed to the lines in which the author of the "Rosciad," his foresight sharpened by a literary quarrel, had prophesied that Wedderburn, then obscure and respectable, would live to attain a splendid infamy.[1] Horace Walpole spoke the sentiments with which men of the world, and of a world which was anything but squeamish, regarded this act of unmatched and matchless duplicity. "I would keep a shop," he said to Mason, "and sell any of my own works that would gain me a livelihood, whether books or shoes, rather than be tempted to sell myself. 'Tis an honest vocation to be a scavenger; but I would not be solicitor-general." Plain citizens, who were not sinecurists or fine gentlemen, looked to Junius as the interpreter of their displeasure; and Junius, conscious that he did well to be angry, spiced his rhetoric during the whole spring and summer with epigrams, of which one, at least, embodied the opinion of mankind too compactly to be forgotten. "In vain," he wrote to the Duke

---

[1] "To mischief trained, e'en from his mother's womb;
Grown old in fraud, though yet in manhood's bloom;
Adopting arts by which gay villains rise
And reach the heights which honest men despise."
The "Rosciad" appeared in 1761.

of Grafton, in June, 1771, " would our gracious sovereign have
looked round him for another character as consummate as
yours.   Lord Mansfield shrinks from his principles; Charles
Fox is yet in blossom; and as for Mr. Wedderburn, there is
something about him which even treachery cannot trust." In
Parliament, the brother-members of the new law officer took
the earliest opportunity of apprising him that he must henceforward rely exclusively upon his talents, since his character
was gone.   When the writ for his re-election was moved, the
House, usually so forward to rejoice with the fortunate at that
supreme moment of political success, gave vent to its collective indignation in a deep groan.   When the day came for
him to take his seat on the Treasury bench, he walked down
the floor between the men whom he had so often denounced
as false to their country, and the men to whom he had now
proved false himself, blushing as red as fire; and years afterwards, when Lord North was declaiming against the Whigs
for talking of patriotism and justice while they meant nothing but pensions and places, all eyes were turned to the spot
where the former associate of Rockingham and Savile sat,
"pale as death," at the elbow of the prime-minister.

Abandoned by their most capable champion, and exasperated by the insolence with which a Parliament which was nom-
inally of their choice trampled at every step on some valued
law or cherished right, the people of England, never so little
like sheep as when their watch-dogs have deserted them, had
at last been wrought into the humor for meeting violence
with violence.   It was expected that the lord mayor would
learn his fate on Tuesday, the twenty-fifth of March; and, by
noon on that day, all London was in the streets.   The roar of
an enormous multitude which escorted him to St. Stephen's
and then waited at the doors to see him safe home, in a temper that foreboded worse things, was distinctly heard by the
members who were debating within, whenever their own
noise did not drown all external clamor; for the storm of
controversy, which was to rage without intermission during
thirteen livelong hours, began as soon as the last word of the
benediction was out of the chaplain's mouth.   In consequence

of the blunder of a Treasury official not accurately informed
as to which among the national representatives was in royal
pay, an independent Tory country gentleman had received a
Treasury circular intended only for the courtiers. On opening his letter, the astonished baronet found himself requested,
with the transparent decency of phrase that is customary in
such missives, to vote as a partisan on an occasion when he
was bound in conscience to discriminate as a judge.[1] The Opposition were justly furious. Sir William Meredith, remembering with pride that the sturdy resistance of the Jacobites
to the attainder of Sir John Fenwick was the best service
which his old party had ever rendered to public liberty, discoursed gravely and forcibly on the impropriety of canvassing for a judicial sentence as if it were a question of a clause
in the Customs Bill or an item in the Estimates. "It is contrary," he said, "to every notion of law and justice to try
these magistrates by a judicature three fourths of whom are
prepared to condemn them." And it soon was evident that
they were to be condemned unheard; for the lord mayor,
having been acquainted by the Speaker that his counsel would
be debarred from arguing the very point upon which the case
hinged, declined to go through the farce of allowing himself
to be defended. Having silenced the professional advocates,
the ministerialists were determined not to tolerate an amateur,
and promptly shouted down an old-fashioned Whig who was
so unnecessarily punctilious as to announce his intention of
considering the matter under its legal aspect.

But they forgot, in their impatience, that brute force was a
game at which two, and, still more, at which twenty thousand,
could play. As the afternoon wore on, every fresh member

---

[1] "You are most earnestly requested to attend early to-morrow, on an
affair of the last importance to the Constitution and the rights and privileges of the people of England." Such was the wording of the letter.
Its meaning no one who has ever received a government whip could for
an instant doubt. A young member contributed a touch of local color
to the discussion which took place over the incident by describing how
a Treasury clerk had been fetched from a ball at midnight to despatch
the circulars.

who entered the House brought a more alarming report of the tumult which reigned without. Each new comer, as he turned into Palace Yard, was asked whether he was for the lord mayor; and if he refused to answer, care was taken that he should remain in the company of the people long enough to make himself acquainted with their sympathies. One gentleman was two hours in getting through the throng. Another was squeezed up into a corner, where, if his neighbors had recognized him as a Controller of the Board of Green Cloth, he would certainly have stayed for a much longer space of time than he was accustomed to spend over the duties of his office. George Selwyn was with difficulty extricated from an encounter into which he had been provoked by the unendurable indignity of being hooted by mistake for George Onslow. The danger of the situation was increased by the mischievous conduct of Alderman Townshend, who had been brought down to the House, pale and bandaged from a recent surgical operation, in order to pour forth a diatribe against female caprice and backstairs influence—which fairly electrified even educated hearers, who could not quite get Bute and the Princess Dowager out of their heads—and the mere report of which, if it had once reached the streets, might at any moment have sent the mob across St. James's Park to Carlton House. The Speaker directed the High Constable of Westminster to clear the neighborhood; but the task was altogether beyond the limited and very unreliable force which that functionary had at his command. Forty men were not sufficient, he said; nor twice forty: and if he called out every peace officer in his district, he could only muster eighty truncheons. The magistrates, of whom six were in attendance, did something to disperse the populace; but Tories and Whigs alike were heartily relieved when the lord mayor pleaded bodily exhaustion as an excuse for retiring, and carried off his train with him. Unable to forego the delight of drawing a coach from Westminster to the Mansion House by torchlight, the crowd rolled away eastwards, and left the Commons happy in the prospect of being able to vote and go home to bed without running the gantlet of a legion of inquisitive Wilkites.

The matter which Parliament had in hand was such as it could not easily have justified to the satisfaction even of less hostile critics than those who had been besieging its portals. When the lord mayor had departed, Alderman Oliver was called upon to make his defence; and his friends replied by requiring to know the charge on which the ministry intended to arraign him. Charles Fox, who at this time in his life was always ready to do freedom the good turn of exhibiting tyranny in its most hateful colors, settled the point by laying down a new principle in criminal procedure, which the tribunal that he was addressing at once adopted by acclamation. "What we," he said, "shall move against the gentleman will depend upon what he shall say in his defence." Barré urged that midnight was not the hour for calling upon a court, so constituted and so advised, to deliver what was at once a verdict and a sentence; but Oliver himself pronounced against delay with a spirit which astonished those among whom he had hitherto passed, almost unremarked, as a young fellow of quiet and refined manners. "I am not," he said, "in the least solicitous to postpone the business. An adjournment of one day, or ten, will make no difference with this majority. I know that the punishment which I am to receive is determined upon; and I have nothing to say, neither in my own defence, nor in defence of the City of London. I expect little from the justice of this House, and I defy its power." His honorable contumacy forced the ministers to show their hand, and they answered his challenge by moving that he should be committed to the Tower.

The proposal, when seriously put forward in so many words, took aback even those who held themselves bound by their position to credit the government beforehand with the extreme of misbehavior and folly. The Opposition seemed dazed by the suddenness of the blow. Their tactics were disconcerted; all unity of action vanished; and every man took the course which his disposition prompted. The more sober Whigs were prepared to release themselves from the responsibility of the step by voting against it; but there were others who regarded the ordinary forms of protest as inadequate to

22

express the full depth and breadth of their dissent from so infatuated a policy. William Burke, civilly but significantly, wished the House good-night. Alderman Townshend took himself back to the bed which, for every reason, he ought never to have quitted. Barré began by telling his opponents that he should speak daggers, and ended with epithets such that they could with difficulty refrain from using their swords.[1] As he walked down the House, after summoning every honest man and every friend of England to follow him, voices were raised to demand that he should answer for his words at the bar; but there was that in the veteran's countenance which informed all who saw it that they had best let him go in peace. Edmund Burke, too depressed, and perhaps too fatigued, to speak loudly or at length, warned the friends who sat around him, in a tone too low for any except them to catch, that by prolonging the contest they would effect nothing but to increase the scandal. "All debate," he sadly said, "all deliberation, is at an end;" and such, if not before, most certainly was the case after Charles Fox, in a speech of almost furious vehemence and quite marvellous dexterity, had excited the enthusiasm and bewildered the conscience of his party. Clutching tight hold, as he rushed along, of whatever plausible argument his ingenuity could discover in support of the arbitrary and ignoble doctrines that he successively propounded, he never let it go until he had thrust it home with a skill and an impetuosity which for a moment persuaded that ser-

---

[1] "These walls are unholy, they are baleful, they are deadly, as long as a prostitute majority holds the bolt of parliamentary omnipotence, and hurls its vengeance only upon the virtuous. To yourselves I consign you. Enjoy your own pandemonium.

  'When vice prevails, and impious men bear sway,
    The post of honor is a private station.' "

  "I spoke, I believe, with great violence;" so Barré confessed to Chatham after he had slept, or tried to sleep, upon the occurrences of this extraordinary evening. He seemed to himself to have been only five minutes on his feet; and it is hardly to be believed that the most conscience-stricken assembly of Catilines could have sat quiet for any longer period under such a blast of vituperation.

vile and intolerant throng that, in muzzling the press and flouting the law, they were treading in the footsteps of Milton and of Somers. In a peroration which a true Whig can hardly read now without being convinced in the teeth of his common-sense—and which sent forth into the lobby the sham Whigs who then heard it in such flocks that the government carried the question by four to one, with a dozen votes to spare—he exhorted his brother-members to guard their rights and liberties, the fruit of the Long Parliament and the Revolution, against the assaults of the commonalty, as their forefathers had guarded them against the encroachments of the sovereign. Taking his text from the events of that very afternoon—which had heated his blood, as danger always heated it till his fighting-days, and all days, were over with him—he confidently and successfully appealed to the instincts of an assembly of English gentlemen who had the shouts of a defiant mob still ringing in their ears. "The business of the people," he exclaimed, "is to choose us. It is ours to maintain the independence of Parliament. Whether that independence is attacked by the people or by the Crown is a matter of little consequence. It is the attack, not the quarter it proceeds from, that we are to punish; and if we are to be controlled in our necessary jurisdiction, can it signify whether faction intimidate us with a rabble, or the king surround us with his Guards? If we are driven from the direct line of justice by the threats of a mob, our existence is useless in the community. The minority within doors need only assault us by their myrmidons without, to gain their ends upon every occasion. Therefore, as we are chosen to defend order, I am for sending those magistrates to the Tower who have attempted to destroy it. Convinced that we are here to do justice, whether it is agreeable or disagreeable, I will not be a rebel to my king, to my country, or to my own heart for the loudest huzza of an inconsiderate multitude."

Right or wrong, late or early—whether he was outraging the sentiments of the multitude or faithfully laboring for its interests—Charles Fox was never fated to enjoy much of its applause. He now received a proof (on which, in his youth-

ful eagerness to be conspicuous, he may be excused for plum-
ing himself as a sort of left-handed compliment) that, for his
age, he was the most unpopular man not only in England, but
in English history.   Within two years of his maiden speech
he had contrived to attract to himself an amount of active
dislike equal to that which a few, and only a few, great ministers have carried to the grave or the scaffold as the accumu-
lation of a lifetime.

On Thursday, the twenty-seventh of March, the case of the
lord mayor came on for a final hearing.   Fiercely resenting
the condemnation of one of their magistrates, and arguing
therefrom the measure which would be dealt out to the other,
the citizens of London attended Crosby to the place of judgment with the air of men who, if the day went against their
champion, were sternly resolved to know the reason why.   A
committee of four aldermen and eight common-councillors,
who had been unanimously appointed in a full court to assist
him with their countenance and advice, and pay his charges
out of the municipal funds, attended him as his immediate
body-guard.   Then came a long procession of merchants and
bankers, shopkeepers and brokers; while before, behind, and
all around surged the population of the great capital, glad, as
always, to make a holiday when their betters set them the example, and exulting in the anticipation of such doings as had
not been witnessed since the day when—by a combination
of circumstances and associations the like of which can never
recur—the author of the *North Briton* attained the age of
forty-five.   There was, indeed, every prospect of a glorious
riot.   The Guards, both horse and foot, were ready to turn
out under arms at a minute's notice; but there was not stand-
ing-room for a single red-coat within three hundred yards of
St. Margaret's Church, except what he could make for himself with the butt of his musket or the hoofs of his charger.
The civil guardians of the peace, of every degree, had been
posted betimes upon the ground; but there were almost more
justices at hand to read the Act than officers to enforce it.
The constables were speedily disarmed; and when Lord
North drove up, he was saluted by having one of their staves

thrust in his face through the carriage-window. After breaking the glasses, the rabble proceeded to demolish the vehicle.
They got the prime-minister out; they tore his hat into a hundred pieces; and there was a moment when the bystanders
apprehended with horror that the scene which a century before had been enacted under the archway at the Hague would
be repeated in Parliament Street. But among those bystanders was most fortunately Sir William Meredith, who dashed
in to the rescue with a courage which North generously acknowledged and handsomely repaid.[1] Sir William, from the
exclamations which he heard around him in the scuffle, gathered that the treatment experienced by the First Lord of the
Treasury was intended for the Junior Lord of the Admiralty—
a comedy, or, as it nearly turned out, a tragedy, of errors not
calculated to increase the prime-minister's affection for a subordinate who already balanced him in political weight as
much as in the corporal bulk that was the point of resemblance between them. Charles himself got off with less mortal peril than his leader, but in a still more woful plight.
The populace, infuriated by the sight of any panels exhibiting those family supporters which were as little like foxes as
the motto beneath them represented what had hitherto been
the family practice,[2] wrecked his coach, and his brother's likewise. They pelted him with oranges, with stones, and even
with handfuls of London mud. They rolled him and his fine
clothes in the kennel; the very suit, may be, that had come
safe on his back across the Channel, on the occasion when a
whole tailor's shop which he was bringing over for the yearly
consumption of himself and his friends was seized and burned
by the searchers of the Dover Custom-house.[3] The speech in

---

[1] He gave a good living to Sir William's brother.

[2] "Et vitam impendere vero."

[3] During the preceding winter a foolish paragraph went the round of
the papers to the effect that Charles Fox had been sent over to France
with five thousand guineas for the Comte du Barry, and a diamond neck-
lace for the countess, as bribes to induce the pair to prevail on the King
of Spain to come to terms with the English ministry on the matter of
the Falkland Islands. The real nature of the errand which took him to

which on the morrow he made his complaint to the House of Commons has perished unreported; and those who love to read a great orator on the stimulating topic of his own personal wrongs would exchange the "Pro Domo Sua," and almost the "Midias" itself, for a sample of such eloquence inspired by such an injury.

The Speaker very properly refused to let business be transacted under the pressure of external intimidation. When the magistrates sent in word that they were powerless, he transferred the responsibility of restoring the peace to the sheriffs of London, who luckily were also members of Parliament. Those officers (Wilkites both of them, or they never would have been sheriffs) undertook to dismiss the crowd on the understanding that it should not be called a mob; and, with the help of some leading members of the Opposition, who accompanied them into the streets, they persuaded four fifths of the people outside to go quietly home, and procured sufficient force to keep the remainder in bounds. But the zeal which the Whigs displayed in the cause of order did not deter their opponents from charging them with having planned and subsidized the riot; and the calumny was all the harder to bear because the first suggestion of it came from Wedderburn. He who had taught his countrymen to agitate — who had never been so fluent and so fervid as when he was reminding crowded and excited assemblies how their less patient forefathers had dealt with administrations not so wicked (such was his favorite adjective) as that to which he now belonged; who had publicly abjured the damnable doctrine that a resolution of the House of Commons could abrogate and annihilate the law of the land—now declared himself unable to believe that those very London citizens who had listened to and applauded his oath would have public spirit enough to array themselves on the side of the law against a resolution of the Commons, unless the statesmen whose friendship he so lately pretended to regard as his most cherished possession had

---

Paris, and its disastrous issue, as above related, have been preserved in a small volume of his *Ana*, published within a few months of his death.

hired their services with drink and silver. Savile had recourse to the only weapon with which men who are at once
proud and upright deign to encounter treachery, and walked
out of the House without bestowing a reproach on the apos-
tate. William Burke, not caring to mince his words, pronounced the accusation an egregious falsehood. Edmund,
with less heat and not less justice, desired the ministry to remember that there were two ways of raising riots—one by
paying the rioters, and the other by provoking them. But
no one was so deeply hurt as Meredith. "May I never," he
exclaimed, "find mercy if I show mercy to the man who set
that mob on to attack the noble lord in whose defence I ventured myself!"

It was amidst an audience agitated by such emotions that
North delivered a speech which, feeble as long as he confined
himself to his subject, when he referred to his own situation,
became as dramatic as anything in the third act of "Richard
the Second." "I certainly," he said, "did not come into office
by my own desire. Had I my wish, I would have quitted it
a hundred times; but as to my resigning now, look at the
transactions of this day, and say whether it is possible for a
man with a grain of spirit, with a grain of sense, to think of
withdrawing from the service of his king and his country at
such a moment. Unhappy that I am, that moment finds me
in this situation; and there are but two ways in which I can
now cease to be minister—by the will of my sovereign, which
I shall be ready to obey; or by the pleasure of the gentlemen
now at our doors, when they shall be able to do a little more
than they have done this day." But it was not fear of life or
limb that called forth the tears which were running fast down
the cheeks of one whose ordinary habit it was to trifle when
brave men were anxious, and to laugh when wise men were
grave. North, in that bitter hour, would have cheerfully accepted the fate of De Witt if he could have met death with
the consciousness that he had preserved the self-respect of an
English statesman. The least penetrating observer among all
who sat upon those crowded benches was at no loss to inter-
pret the passions which stirred and distracted that torpid and

cynical nature. It moved the pity of open and honest foes to watch the hapless minister, as by gesture, voice, and manner he confessed himself the scapegoat of a policy which he detested and disapproved; the slave of those who were in name his own servants, but who looked to another for directions and for rewards, and who, tired of maintaining the appearance of subordination, had thrown off the mask and assumed without disguise the airs of successful mutineers. At length he knew what he had done when he subjected himself, as Chatham truly said, to the insolence of a vile cabal who had made him the scourge of the country and now insulted his shame and distress. "Sir Gilbert Elliot," wrote Chatham's most regular correspondent in the Commons, "scarce restrains an absolute avowal of his power;" and even if Elliot, or others of his troop, had been touched by a feeling of compassion for their humbled chief, it was then too late to give effect to their repentance. The king's friends could not allow themselves to be softened by tears which the king was not there to see. The draught had to be swallowed to the dregs; and the prime-minister, feeling and looking rather like a culprit than an accuser, commissioned one of his more hardened colleagues to make the announcement which could no longer be averted. Welbore Ellis, who never minded what came into a day's work so long as it did not endanger the day's wages, rose to say that the crime of the lord mayor was undoubtedly heinous beyond that which had been so severely visited on the person of Oliver; but that, in consideration of his broken health, and to show the tender mercy of the House, the cabinet were of opinion that he might be spared the Tower and committed to the gentler custody of the sergeant-at-arms. Crosby, however, would have none of their indulgence, and scornfully declared that he was quite well enough to share the lodgings of his brother-alderman; so that the government had no choice but to order him to the Tower, whither, but for his active and loyal assistance, they most assuredly never could have got him. Announcing that he had obtained leave to sleep one more night in his own bed, he returned to the Mansion House, and left it again at four in the morning for his prison; but even this stratagem hardly saved the deputy sergeant from the vengeance of the mob, who would have hanged him on a sign-post as high as Porteous if it had not been for the vigorous interposition of his captive.

By the time that it was a week old, Chatham's forecast had come true to the letter. "These wretches called ministers," he wrote on the twenty-first of March, "will be sick enough of their folly (not forgetting iniquity) before the whole business is over. They have brought themselves and their master where ordinary inability never arrives, and nothing but first-rate geniuses in incapacity can reach; a situation wherein there is nothing they can do which is not a fault." And so, as they had reached the point where one additional fault might be fatal to the realm, it only remained for them to do nothing. Wilkes had been directed to attend at the bar of the Commons on Monday, the eighth of April; but by adjourning till Tuesday, the ninth, the House judiciously contrived to evade its own order. The prosecutions against the printers were dropped; and when, in contempt of a resolution which had been solemnly entered on the journals of Parliament, Wheble and his associates pursued the Speaker's messenger as a criminal for having attempted to enforce the Speaker's warrant, the government, without looking too closely into the legality of the step to which they found themselves driven, made shift to hush up the business by means of a *nolle prosequi*. Crosby and Oliver, indeed, remained in prison; but they lived there in state, and certainly in clover. The City kept them a table furnished according to civic ideas of what was necessary for men who required not only nourishment, but consolation. The Whig magnates, after a full and grave discussion, made up their minds to show them an attention which, as a compliment from peers to burgesses, meant a great deal more a hundred years ago than it does now. "We would not," wrote Lord Rockingham, "have a procession, but only a few, and those considerable ones;" and on the last day of March the journals announced to an awe-struck public that two dukes, a marquis, and an earl, with Burke and Dowdeswell as representative commoners, had waited on the lord mayor and Mr. Oliver in their apartments in the Tower. Their humbler admirers did what they could to evince their sympathy by marching twice in one week to Tower Hill, in order to behead Bute and hang the George Onslows in effigy.[1] Gold boxes and laudatory addresses from towns of every size and rank between Newcastle and Honiton showed that mayors and aldermen, all the country over, made common cause with the illustrious martyrs of municipal independence. Parliament was prorogued on the eighth of May; and at the close of the session, by a self-acting process, all House of Commons prisoners regained their liberty. To avoid a popular demonstration, the ministry purposely kept the day of prorogation secret; but by the time that the Park guns began to fire and the Tower gates were opened, a cavalcade was already in waiting to conduct Crosby and Oliver to the Mansion House, more imposing by far than that which attended the king from the Palace to the House of Lords. The aldermen in their scarlet gowns, and the Artillery Company in full uniform, escorted the lord mayor in his state-coach through roaring streets, which, as soon as night fell, honored the champions of the city and the press with an illumination so general and spontaneous that the very apprentices of Paternoster Row had no excuse for breaking windows.

While the instruments had their triumph, the master hand was not forgotten. The Court of Common Council voted Wilkes a silver cup, and left to himself the selection of the design. In commemoration of the date on which the publisher of the *Middlesex Journal* had been brought up to him for judgment, he chose the scene of the Ides of March in the Roman Senate-house, "as certainly one of the greatest sacrifices to public liberty recorded in history." On that singular piece of plate appeared the dictator "in an attitude of fall-

---

[1] "I had the honor, sir," said Colonel Onslow, addressing himself to the Speaker in February, 1774, "to be hanged in effigy on Tower Hill on the same gibbet with you. Indeed, in the dying-speeches, the patriots paid me the greater compliment; for they gave out that I died penitent, but that you, sir, remained hardened to the last."

ing," and Brutus congratulating Cicero on the recovery of freedom. Above were engraved the city arms, with a dagger in the first quarter; while below, framed in myrtle and oak leaves, ran Churchill's prayer that every tyrant might feel

"The keen deep searchings of a patriot's steel."

The subject and the inscription were in the taste of a man who exaggerated the taste of his age; but none the less was the power of Parliament to keep the country in the dark as dead as Julius Cæsar. A twelvemonth afterwards the sheriffs, in an address to the Livery, boasted with just pride that the House of Commons "tacitly acquiesced in the claim made by London citizens on behalf of the public at large, that the constituents had a right to be informed of the proceedings of their servants in Parliament." All pretence of keeping the debates secret had by that time been dropped. "Your galleries," said Burke, on the budget-night of 1772, "are like to break down with the weight of strangers, as you are pleased to call the people of England." The door, once forced, was never locked again; and if from time to time there was talk of shutting it, it was thrust wide open by a hand strong enough, if need were, to have torn it from the hinges. When Colonel Luttrell, in January, 1778, stated his intention of moving that strangers should be excluded—on the well-worn plea that he had been misrepresented in a newspaper—Fox, to whom seven years had taught some maxims of political wisdom even less obvious than that which he now rose to enforce, declared that in his view the only method of preventing misrepresentation was by giving more publicity than ever to the debates and decisions of the House, since the surest recipe for killing a lie was to multiply the witnesses to the truth. The reporters might well be at ease as to the future of their craft, when once they had taken down in black and white so sweeping and explicit a recantation from the mouth of the most formidable among their ancient enemies.

CHAPTER IX.

1771–1772.

Fox at this Period a Consistent Defender of the King's System.—The Case of New Shoreham.—The Grenville Act.—Quarrel between Fox and Wedderburn.—The Duke of Portland and Sir James Lowther.— The Nullum Tempus Bill.—Mnemon.—Pertinacity of Sir James Lowther.—Sir William Meredith introduces an Amending Bill, which is opposed, and at length defeated, by Fox. — Fox and Burke. — Fox sends a Challenge to an Unknown Adversary.—The Petition of the Clergy, and its Fate.—Story of Mr. Lindsey.—The Dissenters' Relief Bill.—Priestley and the Early Unitarians.—Courage and Independence of Charles Fox.

It must not be supposed that Charles Fox reserved all his combativeness for such far-sounding and historical controversies as those which the House of Commons maintained against the shire of Middlesex and the city of London. He loved the old political system under which his father had risen to greatness too frankly and loyally to place himself beneath its standard only on the occasion of a battle royal or a full-dress parade. Whenever there was a call to arms in the most remote outwork of that stronghold of abuses behind whose protection the country was with impunity misgoverned, Fox appeared at the threatened spot with all his artillery, almost as soon as the assailants had opened their trenches. His prowess in the cause was a theme for constant discourse and admiration among the rank and file of the ministerial party; but he never more than half pleased the managers. North and Thurlow and the Bedfords had quite wit enough to perceive that his devotion to the very peculiar institutions which Lord Holland had taught him to revere arose from the generous conservatism of youth, and not from the sordid anticipations of self-interest. They foresaw that an enthusiasm like his, when once it had detected itself to be misplaced, would

not be long before it was converted into bitter and most effectual hostility; and they looked forward uneasily to the
day when his energy and intrepidity might be directed from
the outside against those weak points in their circle of defence whither, with a promptitude which showed his all too
accurate knowledge of the ground, he now flew to post himself on the first alarm of danger.

That alarm never rang more clearly to a discerning ear
than when the first committee which had ever been appointed under George Grenville's Act for securing the purity of
the constituencies brought in its first report. In the November of 1770, there was an election in the borough of New
Shoreham, in consequence of the death of a sitting member.
The country gentlemen of Sussex, who knew what sort of a
place New Shoreham was, kept aloof from the contest, which
lay between two candidates, of whom one, in the phrase of
the day, was a Nabob, and the other a Caribbee. Mr. Purling, the West Indian, got only thirty-seven votes, as against
eighty-seven which were secured by his opponent, Mr. Rumbold. The bribery oath was administered to Mr. Rumbold's
supporters and freely taken; but it was noticed that the re-
turning-officer, Hugh Roberts by name, put to each of them
certain queries offensive to the dignity of a British citizen;
and the surprise which his conduct throughout the day provoked deepened into positive stupefaction when, at the close
of the poll, he declared Mr. Purling duly elected. When
questioned by a committee of the House of Commons, Roberts stated that he was aware that Mr. Rumbold had a legal
majority, but that he was aware also of the means by which
the majority had been obtained. There was, he said, at
Shoreham a company which, instituted with a view to the
promotion of ship-building, the most important among the
confessed industries of the town, had for some years past
been reorganized on a less worldly basis. Towards the end
of 1764, the association resolved to devote its efforts to works
of charity, called itself the Christian Club, and swore all its
members on the four Evangelists to be steadfast, true, and silent. Those members included the majority of the borough

voters; and the society, whether in the commercial or the religious phase of its existence, had, in point of fact, never been anything else than a trades-union for purposes of corruption. On the principle that no man has a right to injure his neighbor by selling his conscience below the market-price, and that the skilful and the clumsy, the impudent and the bashful, ought to share and share alike in the wages fund of bribery, the club, on the eve of an election, made its bargain for the payment of a lump sum, which was divided, after the contest was over, among men who were thus enabled to swear at the polling-booth that they had never received a farthing for their votes. Those votes had been bought by Rumbold for five - and - thirty pounds apiece; and Roberts, who had once been a Christian brother, and had left the fraternity, disgusted (according to his own story) at finding that his colleagues were quite indifferent to the nationality of their member as long as they saw the color of his money,[1] was in a position to identify seventy-six of the majority as members of the club. With these facts in his cognizance, he had made bold to take the law into his own hands, and save the expense of a petition by summarily altering a return which no election committee that ever was packed could for an instant hesitate to reverse.

These disclosures produced a wholesome though transient effect upon the opinion and the tone of Parliament. Ten years of personal government and secret influence had not yet so impaired the character of English gentlemen but that they had still the grace to hate their own faults when distorted in a vulgar mirror. Burke, for once, had the House with him, as he moralized upon the spectacle of a depravity so hypocritical, and, above all, so systematic. " I am shocked," he said, " at the wisdom to be found in these transactions. I

---

[1] "*Lord John Cavendish.*—Do you remember a meeting of the club upon a false report of Sir Samuel Cornish's death?

"*Roberts.*—Yes. They were debating upon the several gentlemen who were to represent the borough. They said they would vote for the member who would give most money. John Wood said, ' Yes, damn him, if he was a Frenchman.' "

am shocked at the virtue — at the principles of honor and
trust upon which these men acted : principles deserving a
better cause.   It is a wasp's nest—most curiously constructed,
but still a wasp's nest—and as such it must be destroyed."
A bill disfranchising the members of the Christian Club was
introduced, and an address praying his Majesty to order a
prosecution of the ring-leaders in the conspiracy was carried,
with general, but not quite with universal, acceptance.   Whatever others might do, Charles Fox was not to be fed with
grandiloquent professions of virtue, and sermonized into the
support of pharisaical measures.   He was almost beside himself with contempt and indignation at the blindness of men
who could not or would not see that, in chastising electoral
impurity, they were striking at one of the pair of pillars on
which the roof rested that sheltered them all in common.
The Christian Club was as essential a feature in the system
which claimed their allegiance and provided them with their
bread as the privy purse itself.   The policy that found favor
with the Court was one which would not have lived through
the first week in the first session of an unbought Parliament ;
and bribed representatives would never be returned a second
time by unbribed constituents.   Fox knew the political situation as exactly and thoroughly as any veteran in the cabinet ;
and, where he was sure of his ground, he never feared to act
alone.   Faithful among the faithless to the doctrines on which
his youth had been nourished, he stood, the Abdiel of corruption, firm and square against this unexpected and imposing manifestation of public virtue.   When the question of
the Shoreham election was mooted, Fox had thrown a perfect
deluge of cold water upon the proposal of an inquiry ; and,
now that the story had come to the surface in all its ugliness,
he breathed fire and fury against the advocates of a policy of
severity.   While his colleagues were crying with one voice
for the exemplary punishment of a town in which there were
not as many righteous burgesses as in Sodom,[1] he could see
nothing but the injustice and inconsequence of visiting peo-

---

[1] Cavendish, vol. ii. p. 310.

ple with a penal disfranchisement for doing once in seven years that which was done, on every quarter-day, by two out of five among the gentlemen who condemned them.   He fought the measure with all the faculties which nature had given him, and with all the weapons which the usage of Parliament, hardly less lavish than nature, had placed at his disposal.   He would have divided against the first reading, if he could have induced a single member to assist him as teller. Hampered, though not alarmed, by his isolation, he utilized the rare and brief moments which he spent in his lodgings in Piccadilly to coax and tease Fitzpatrick into joining forces with him in opposition to the bill.   The two kinsmen, by their combined exertions, succeeded in mustering for the defence of the Christian Club a small band whose strength gradually increased from six to fourteen, and from fourteen to eighteen.   But time was against Fox; and, before the number of his contingent had turned the score, the bill had passed into a law which, in an uncontrolled burst of disappointment, he pronounced to be as ridiculous and wicked an ordinance as any that deformed the Statute-book.

The proof which the fate of Shoreham afforded that the Grenville Act was an effectual engine for checking, and, in honest and willing hands, even for suppressing, bribery sharpened the zeal of Charles Fox against a reform which he had never loved.[1]   In the spring of 1770, when Grenville's scheme

---

[1] The efficacy of Grenville's plan for trying disputed elections may be tested by the different manner in which it was regarded by a Tory who loved, and a Tory who hated, corruption.   Rigby openly said in Parliament that he was against the act, because it stopped treating; and nobody objected to treating except a candidate who wanted to save his money.   Dr. Johnson, on the other hand, in his pamphlet entitled "The Patriot," approved the act, because it insured that the man who possessed the unbought confidence of the constituents should sit as their member. "A disputed election," he wrote, "is now tried with the same scrupulousness and solemnity as any other title.   A candidate that has deserved well of his neighbors may now be certain of enjoying the effect of their approbation; and the elector who has voted honestly for known merit may be certain that he has not voted in vain."   "I never neglect business," said the political jobber in Foote's "Cozeners;" "but the perpetuating this Bribery Act has thrown such a rub in our way."

first saw the light, the young politician had not yet worked his way upwards to the doubtful privilege of being reported at full length; and the "Parliamentary History" of that year contents itself with recording that Mr. Charles Fox did his part "in a lively academical manner, stating and taking off" the arguments which were adduced in favor of the bill. But in the next session, when the law was seven months old, and its author dead, Fox had already attained to that middle stage of political notoriety when a man's graver and more workmanlike speeches are still liable to be abridged and mangled, but every syllable of folly and impertinence that he utters, or that is uttered about him, is sure of being immortalized. Towards the end of November, during a conversation that was being carried on across the House about a disputed election in the borough of Scarborough, Fox, while arguing against the new method of trying petitions, dropped something which was capable of being construed as disrespectful to the memory of the statesman by whom that method had been invented. Wedderburn, who just then was eager to provide himself with a colorable pretext for the treason which he meditated by posing on all occasions as a personal follower of Grenville, emancipated from ties of party by his master's death, saw his opportunity, and, after gratifying the Whigs with a most eloquent panegyric on his own lost leader and their regretted ally, expressed his wonder that anybody could be so heartless as to cast aspersions on such a reputation. Fox, who had no notion of lending himself as a lay-figure to be exhibited in any attitude that suited Wedderburn's rhetorical purposes, was on his legs before the other was down. Stepping at once over the line which the House of Commons has always regarded as the extreme verge of the permissible, he charged the learned gentleman with having put words in his mouth which, to the learned gentleman's own knowledge, had never been spoken. Having launched his defiance, he was marching out amidst an uproar well-nigh loud enough to have awakened Grenville in his grave, when the Speaker bade him resume his seat, and ordered the sergeant-at-arms to lock the doors. Welbore Ellis, who had the formulas applicable to all possi-

23

ble parliamentary contingencies in his head, where there was
plenty of room to keep them properly sorted and ticketed,
rose on behalf of the House to require an assurance from both
parties that the affair should not go further.   Burke, pained
by the aspect of a quarrel over a name which had always commanded respect, and of late had inspired something not dis-
tantly resembling affection, in one of the most feeling and
graceful of those short speeches of the instant which are
further beyond rivalry or imitation even than his precon-
certed efforts, urged Fox and Wedderburn to reflect that consideration for the dead ought not to inflame, but to heal, the
dissensions of the living.   To shake hands upon the union of
their hearts would, he reminded them, be a worthier tribute
to the memory of Grenville than the show of reconciliation
through which, whether they liked it or not, they would be
forced to pass.   But Wedderburn's cue was to play surly fidelity even at the risk of overdoing the part; and the burden of
submission therefore fell upon his opponent, whose heat was
real, and who, in the opinion of almost every witness present,
had been more sinned against than sinning.   Fox begged pardon of the House for having used words which ought to have
been left unsaid—an apology from the benefit of which he
pointedly excepted Wedderburn; and then, making the very
unusual and uncongenial effort of dropping his voice till it
became inaudible, he muttered something which was lost even
on the greedy ears around him.   It was enough, however, for
the Speaker, who wisely pretended to have caught the sound
of the conventional sentence, which was understood to signify
that the dispute would not be transferred to that rural solitude behind Bedford House where Whigs were in the habit
of settling their differences.[1]

It was not very long before Fox gave proof that he was
ready to maintain his words with sword and pistol against
anybody whom he was allowed to fight.   His next escapade

---

[1] That was the spot where, just two months afterwards, Lord Milton
was shot through the body by Lord Poulett, Lord John Cavendish acting as one of the seconds.

arose, as usual, out of his devotion to the royal theory of government—a devotion which, most happily for himself and for
his country, was appreciated as little and requited as ill as it
deserved. If, at an age when his character was still malleable,
his premature ambition had been tempted by the offer of the
highest place in the State, he might have gone down to the execration of posterity as the Wentworth of the eighteenth century. But strong measures were more to George the Third's
taste than strong men ; and the result of the most determined
step which the king took in the track of the Stuarts indicated
unmistakably that he was leaning on the shoulder, not of a
Strafford, but of a Grafton.

The plan of Thorough on which the Court was bent might
have succeeded but for an obstacle which had saved England
from more than one such plot in earlier times, and which remained as a second line of defence against arbitrary power
after the country had grown formidable enough to save itself.
Unless the king could attract, or drive, a larger portion of the
nobility into the ranks of his adherents, he could never hope
to see his policy durably established. Protests disputing the
principles on which that policy was founded, and censuring
the acts by which it was carried into effect, were signed, when
Rockingham and Chatham had both had a hand in the composition, by forty of the most respected and redoubted names
on the roll of Peers. If a question affecting the Constitution
was at stake in the House of Lords, the government, after
they had done all that men could do, and promised more than
ministers had to give, were obliged to be satisfied if, upon a
division, they could just beat the Opposition by two to one ;
and the influence of a great peer whose heart was with the
people more than doubled that of one whose pocket induced
him to be against them. Before the king could get his purposes fully and finally accomplished, his partisans would have
some more serious work to do than the mere voting-down of
his opponents at Westminster. A system under which the
nation had been governed, and on the whole admirably governed, during four reigns, of which all were prosperous and
three glorious, could not be overset by marching a file of

lords of the bedchamber and pensioners of the Civil List in and out of a glass door. As soon as it came to the essential push, all the rotten boroughs between the Needles and the Lizard would not be worth a single great county with an Earl of Fitzwilliam or a Duke of Richmond to marshal its army of freeholders. The spirit of the contumacious aristocracy must be broken, and a notable example made; or everything that had been concocted by Bute and perpetrated by Henry Fox would have been done in vain. It was in the summer of 1768 that Grafton consented to engage in a project of confiscation and proscription. But he commenced the undertaking rashly, and pursued it timidly. He blundered alike in the choice of the accomplice who was to be gratified with the booty, and of the victim upon whom the work of spoliation was to begin.

The Duke of Portland, though he had nothing aggressive or quarrelsome in his nature, was as dangerous a man to attack as any in the kingdom. So amiable that he had no associate who was not an attached and devoted friend—and proud with the pride which leads its possessor habitually to shrink from putting himself in the wrong, or from venturing to take a liberty with others—he was framed to go through life after such a fashion that, unless by some improbable chance he became the butt of calumny or the object of persecution, the world was never likely to discover for itself the high rate at which it valued him. How much, on the other hand, it valued Sir James Lowther, the world knew very well, and has made no effort to conceal. His countrymen hated him so heartily and with so much cause that even if the worst half of the tales which they related and printed about him are to be accounted as mythical, enough remain, authentic and undisputed, to prove that in boorishness, caprice, insolence, rapacity, lawlessness, and, above all, in the practice of cruelty for cruelty's sake, he was three centuries behind the least estimable of his own generation.[1] When a man passes his life in

---

[1] An admirable full-length portrait of the Earl of Lonsdale, as he appears in history to a high-minded man of his own rank, may be seen in

evil-doing, he and his contemporaries can seldom put their finger on the particular ill-deed which in after-times will stand in judgment against him. Sir James Lowther little knew, and, if he had known, would as little have cared, that more than fifty years after his death—when the groans of the inferiors whom he oppressed, and the murmurs of the equals whom he affronted, had long died away—an extraordinary chance would bring to light a story which has settled his character, once and forever, in the opinion of all who have a spark of feeling or manliness in their disposition. The mental tortures and humiliations which, as Earl of Lonsdale, he made it his pastime to inflict upon a dependent broken in health, advanced in years, and rendered defenceless by foibles which had been viewed with indulgence by men whose shoe the graceless peer was not worthy to buckle, are told by Boswell in letters rescued, in quite recent days, from the oblivion which will befall no production of his pen that has once passed through the hands of the printer. The faithless and brutal patron could not even plead that he had a right to despise the client whom he was deluding and tormenting; for, before Lord Lonsdale began to find his pleasure in feeding Boswell with false hopes, and harassing him with real insults and injuries, the first instalment had already been published of the book which will be read by millions after Lowther Castle has shared the lot of Raglan and of Kenilworth.

Wordsworth, in a fine sonnet addressed to that "majestic pile," speaks of it as founded upon

> " Charters won and guarded by the sword
> Of ancient honor." [1]

That the compliment to the building should be a deserved

Lord Albemarle's " Memoirs of Rockingham," in the third chapter of the second volume.

[1] The family of the poet were among the innumerable creditors whom Lord Lonsdale ruined, or half ruined, by withholding from them their due, and defying them to recover it at law from a litigant as wealthy as he was unscrupulous. The young Wordsworths, left fatherless and almost penniless, " fought life's battle as well as they could for several years," until the second earl repaired the injustice of his predecessor.

one was certainly not the desire or the intention of its most
noted occupant.   Never, since the Star - chamber ceased its
sittings, has there occurred a ruder and more dangerous violation of the safeguards which protect the existence of private
property than was attempted by Grafton and his colleagues at
the instance and for the profit of Sir James Lowther.   Not
content with a fortune which, in Walpole's words, would have
enabled him to hire the Dukes of Marlborough and Bedford
as led captains — not content with a local ascendency that
placed at his beck and nod the suffrages of a region in which
(as he loved to hear from his flatterers) he was absolute master of the land, the water, and the fire [1]—he was ever on the
watch for an opportunity to rob his neighbor of territorial
possessions and political influence.   In Cockermouth and Ap-
pleby and Whitehaven, his presence was terror and his orders
were law; but in the county of Cumberland and the city of
Carlisle his dictation was resisted, and successfully resisted,
by a population emboldened by the countenance of a potentate as formidable as himself.   The leadership of the House
of Bentinck was acknowledged far and wide through the
Northwest of England, where large tracts of Crown property
had been made over to its founder by William the Third as a
recompense for the services and the affection of a lifetime.
The title of the Portlands to the lands and royalties and
manors which they assumed as a consequence of these grants
had for seventy years never been mistrusted by themselves or
contested by others.   Among the acquisitions which the family owed to royal gratitude and munificence was the Forest
of Inglewood, a district rich in natural products, and, what
was more to the purpose on the eve of a general election,

---

[1] " E'en by the elements his power confessed,
    Of mines and boroughs Lonsdale stands possessed;
    And one sad servitude alike denotes
    The slave that labors and the slave that votes."

                              Rosciad, Part ii., No. 5.

" We all know," wrote Boswell, " what HE can do; he upon whom the
thousands of Whitehaven depend for three of the elements."

swarming with small freeholders. The duke, at the period of his marriage, had included in his wife's settlements his interest in the forest—an interest which, in the eyes of the eminent conveyancers whom he employed, belonged to him and his, as Dunster Castle belonged to the Luttrells, or St. Michael's Mount to the St. Aubyns. It is not therefore difficult to imagine the consternation with which, in September, 1767, he was informed that, in the previous July, Sir James Lowther had presented a memorial to the Lords of the Treasury, stating that the Forest of Inglewood and the soccage of the Castle of Carlisle had been long withheld from the Crown without the Crown's receiving from them any benefit, and praying a lease of them for his own life and two others on such terms as should appear fitting to their lordships.

The duke had reason to be uneasy; for the petition, on the face of it, was such as never would have been presented except in a case where the petitioner had assured his ground beforehand. Son-in-law to Bute, and in Parliament the sergeant of a whole squad of members who wheeled to right or left at his bidding, Lowther found little difficulty either with the Crown or the Treasury. The peer was trifled with, blinded, thwarted at every turn, and left out in the dark and the cold; while the baronet was kept promptly and minutely informed of the silent and rapid progress which the business made under the fostering care of officials who regarded his interests as their own. Relying on a promise that no decision should be taken until both sides had been fully and fairly heard, the duke's lawyers were still preparing his title—and the duke's agent, in pursuit of leave to inspect the records, was still travelling on a fool's errand from the Treasury to the Crown-office, and from the Crown-office back to the Treasury—when a letter from Whitehall arrived at Welbeck Abbey, informing the owner of the manor of Inglewood that his property had been granted to Sir James Lowther in consideration of a quit-rent of thirteen and fourpence per annum. The misfortune was heavy, and galling out of proportion to its weight; but, as far as sympathy could lighten it, the sufferer had no reason to complain. There was a cry of shame throughout the kingdom. The inhabitants of the ceded districts, who had been accustomed thankfully to contrast their own lot with that of their luckless neighbors, foresaw the treatment which a landlord who had stunted and impoverished boroughs that were the ancient appanages of his house, for the sake of retaining his political predominance unquestioned and undiminished, might be expected to deal out to those whom he and his electioneering agents would regard as a population of subjugated aliens. Their dismay was shared by people who could make their apprehension and resentment felt much more effectively than a community of turf-diggers and small graziers whose hard lives were led two hundred miles away from the door of the Crown-office. The most powerful noblemen in England, and still more in Ireland, were conscious that those vast estates which in any European country but their own would have made them princes could not fail to melt away like water if the obsolete doctrine of " Nullum tempus occurrit regi" (in conformity with which the Duke of Portland had been evicted) was furbished up and re-established as the law of the land. And if they had been insensible to their danger, there was one awake and stirring who would not have allowed them to sleep. Writing under the signature of " Mnemon," Junius fell tooth and nail on the obnoxious maxim. He translated it, with characteristic amplification of phrase, into a shape in which it looked even more alarming than in Latin;[1] he proclaimed, in all the majesty of capital letters, that its revival had given a shock to the whole landed property of England ; and he showed with unanswerable logic that, when once its authority was recognized in the courts of justice, no ministry, however enlightened and patriotic, could restrain the Crown from existing in a state of " unremitting and immortal litigation " with those of its subjects who were worth the robbing.[2]

---

[1] " The maxim of ' Nullum tempus occurrit regi,' ' that no length of continuance, or good faith of possession, is available against a claim of the Crown,' has long been the opprobrium of prerogative and the disgrace of our law."

[2] Mnemon's letter of the fourth of March, 1768, replete with matter,

The ministers set their staff of scribes to answer Mnemon; but they had better have left it alone. On a question that touched both law and administration, the Fleet parsons, who wrote for the newspapers under the orders of Sandwich, in the hope that he might think of them the next time that a small Crown living went a-begging round the cabinet, had no chance against a publicist deeply and carefully read in jurisprudence, and trained by a varied course of service, at home and abroad, in four leading departments of the State. The most promising idea which Grub Street could muster was to ring the changes upon the origin of the Duke of Portland's wealth, and urge the Commons of England to imitate the spirit which their predecessors of 1695 displayed in reproving and moderating the prodigality with which a Dutch king rewarded his imported favorites. This invitation to trace to its source the stream of fortune which had enriched a noble family was anything but attractive in the eyes of peers and great squires whose ancestors and ancestresses had acquired land and goods by the pillage of the Church and the poor; by the attainder of unhappy patriots who had fought on what was now regarded as the right side in some historical quarrel; or by personal services, not so reputable as those of Bentinck, rendered only too freely to monarchs of merrier, if less glorious, memory than the stern Deliverer. Even political rancor was driven to confess that there were subjects too sacred for a parliamentary inquiry; and Sir George Savile had the secret or expressed good wishes of both parties with him when, in February, 1768, he rose to introduce a bill which provided that the uninterrupted enjoyment for sixty years of an estate derived from the Crown should bar the Crown from reclaiming its gift under pretence of any flaw in the grant, or other defect of title. By desperate exertions the government contrived to postpone the question till the gen-

---

clear in statement, and devoid of exaggeration, has the precise qualities in which Junius, who took the field ten months later, was defective from the first; and the gradual but total disappearance of which eventually destroyed his style and his influence.

eral election had made Sir James Lowther member for Cumberland. But the debate showed that the feeling was with Savile, and he so nearly succeeded in securing the numbers that he was only beaten by twenty in a full House. Portland thenceforward awaited the issue with a confidence which proved to be well-grounded; for the new Parliament, in its first working session, unseated Lowther for the county, and placed Savile's measure among the statutes, by majorities which the ministry had not the cash to bribe or the courage to intimidate.[1]

But the House of Commons and the freeholders of Cumberland had not yet heard the last of Sir James Lowther. Savile had drawn his bill with a view to supplement and amend a law of James the First, popularly known as the Quieting Act, which had been passed to protect the holders of property from the machinations of professional informers who lived by hunting up flaws in Crown grants of old standing, and then using their influence at Court to dispossess and supplant the rightful owner. Numerous enough formerly to have a name to themselves, these gentry were known to our ancestors, in the first quarter of the seventeenth century, by the appellation of "concealers," and were hated as the monopolists were hated in the reign of Elizabeth, and as the money-lender is now hated by the peasant of British India.[2] The most odious, and for a time the most thriving, of his class was Sir Giles Mompesson, against whom the first Quieting Act had been expressly devised, and who stood to Massinger for

---

[1] Savile's Nullum Tempus Bill was carried by 205 to 124, and the Cumberland election was overset by 247 to 95.

[2] Sir Edward Coke, who was charged with the conduct of the Quieting Bill in the Parliament of 1620, remarked that a concealer "was ever a beggar before he died." Five sorts of men, he said, in his observation, never prospered—alchemists, monopolists, depopulators, concealers, and promoters. The extent of the change which has been wrought in the constitution of society between those days and ours is strikingly illustrated by the reflection that four among these five classes have disappeared, and of the fifth nothing remains but a name which now has come to designate another branch of industry.

as powerfully over-painted a villain as ever ranted across the English stage.   Among those who lived to shudder at Edmund Kean in the most harrowing of his parts, there must have been some who remembered that, in their own younger days, they too had known a Sir Giles Overreach whose deeds emulated those of the knight in the play, though he made less noise about them.   The hero of the second Quieting Bill seemed to sleep on thorns until he had appropriated to himself the character of one who

> "Frights men out of their estates,
> And breaks through law-nets, made to curb ill men,
> As they were cobwebs."

A clause in Savile's Act had provided that the grantees of the Crown should have a twelvemonth within which to prosecute their claims.   The motive with which this proviso had been inserted was variously interpreted; but no one even affected to believe that Parliament deliberately intended a measure, specially framed for the protection of an individual land-owner and a particular district, to be so construed as to subject that very land-owner and that very district to the annoyance and expense of an appeal to the chances of the law.   Sir James Lowther, however, did not concern himself with the intentions of Parliament.   Making diligent use of what he regarded as his year of grace, he carried his dispute with the Duke of Portland into the Court of Exchequer, and, on one and the same day, served writs of ejectment upon four hundred freeholders of the Forest of Inglewood.   There was confusion and anxiety in all corners of Cumberland, where every family owned some member or connection whom a stroke as unexpected as an earthquake had rendered liable to pass the rest of his days in a series of lawsuits, the first six months of which would more than beggar him.   Fifteen bills in equity, and two hundred and twenty-five actions at common-law, were simultaneously in course of prosecution against men whose ideas of litigation had hitherto never risen above a controversy with the parson about the tenth sack of peat, or a wrangle with a brother-commoner over the parentage of a gosling.

On the eleventh of February, 1771, Sir William Meredith brought forward a bill for striking the clause under which these lamentable complications had arisen from the pages of Savile's Act. The act had found its warmest admirer in Edmund Burke, always, and in every succcessive phase of his political career, a sturdy champion of the rights of property.[1] He now adjured Parliament, as it valued its own consistency, not to disappoint one section of the community by excluding it from the operation of a healing law the benefits of which had been supposed to be universal. "The question is" (so he put the case), "whether or no you will restore the county of Cumberland to the same degree of peace, order, and security to which you have restored the rest of the kingdom." Yielding a point under pressure of disapprobation too general and pronounced even for him to despise, Sir James Lowther commissioned his friends to inform the House that he should prosecute none of his suits except that against the Duke of Portland; but by seeking to render his position less invidious, he had made it more illogical than ever. It was understood that the Duke had been willing to bargain for the safety of his less wealthy neighbors by consenting that he himself should be left, in solitary peril, outside the shelter of the act. "I will sacrifice myself" (such was stated to be his language), "provided that my insecurity makes every other

---

[1] In 1780, during the most celebrated, if not the finest, speech that a member ever made to his constituents, Burke placed Savile's Act, for the limitation of the claims of the Crown upon landed estates, on a level in importance with his act for the relief of the Roman Catholics, and pronounced that those were the two measures which would carry to posterity the most respected name in the politics of the eighteenth century. And as the member for Bristol thought then, so the member for Malton thought to the last. Burke became a Tory, not because he loved arbitrary power, but because he feared it so much that he discerned signs of it (as Whigs believe) in a wrong quarter. "Burke," said Grattan, "could not sleep on his pillow unless he thought that the king had a right to take it from under him;" but the epigram was spoken in an idle moment, to amuse and dazzle a young man whom its author did not credit with the fatal memory which was one of the most formidable gifts even of Samuel Rogers.

man in England secure;" but his friends were determined
that, if their efforts could prevent it, he should not be allowed
to suffer by his chivalry. Sir William Meredith defied the
government to produce a single argument for refusing to the
one an immunity from litigation which was extended to the
many, except that the one was rich, while the many were
poor; and, with the fervor which a just cause never failed to
arouse in him, he entreated his brother-members to reflect
whither that argument would lead them. The principle of
limitation, on which the Quieting Act was founded, seldom
(he declared) affected the interests of the poor; but it was of
all legal doctrines the most essential for the security of the
rich, unless they were to be rich no longer. It was the great
man whose influence made him formidable to the Crown; it
was the great man whose opulence made him a mark for the
informer; and to deny the great, who needed it, a safeguard
which was granted to the small, who could do without it, was
to sanction a pregnant injustice under the specious cloak of
popularity. Unless ministers could find some less dangerous
ground on which to meet him, they had nothing for it but to
support his bill.

It was never safe to challenge the Treasury bench for a
reason, with regard to any question which filled a space in the
mind of Charles Fox. Reasons, in that luxuriant soil, were
plentiful as blackberries, and changed their color at least as
often. Not when in after-days he was pleading in defence
of the poor remnants of freedom which had survived the first
fury of the anti-Jacobin reaction—not when he was deprecat-
ing the suspension of the Habeas Corpus Act, or denouncing
that elaborate net-work of repressive legislation which made
it more dangerous for an Englishman to take a citizen's part
in public affairs than to turn coiner or sheep-stealer—did he
speak in a higher strain of feeling, or rest his cause upon
more solid and time-honored considerations of natural equity
and written law, than now when he was urging Parliament to
except an individual, whose only crime was that he belonged
to one political party instead of to another, from the protection of a statute which protected every other property-holder

in the country. The discussion, in its earlier phase, had gone strongly against Lowther. His defence had been undertaken by Sir William Bagot, a rustic orator, who first made himself ridiculous by invoking against Meredith's bill the powers of earth, of heaven, and of hell; and who then blundered into an unpardonable breach of order in the shape of an appeal to the Speaker to assist the deliberations of the House by an expression of his personal opinion. Burke and Dunning had made infinite fun of the advocate, and Savile had torn the case to shreds, when Fox came forward in the character of a plain man who had nothing new or valuable to say, but whose sense of right and wrong would not allow him to give that silent vote which, as a matter of fact, he was as little capable of giving as he was likely to let the box pass him at Almack's without trying a throw. Absolutely astonished (he said) by a proposal which in appearance was totally repugnant to every principle of law and liberty, he had waited patiently, anxiously, almost hopefully, in the expectation of hearing some satisfactory justification for a bill which had statesmen of repute and integrity among its patrons. There must (he had felt sure) have been something in it which he did not understand; something which reconciled the measure with the acknowledged demands of justice. But when the debate ran its course, and the matter gradually emerged, from beneath a cloud of talk, in all its naked and genuine deformity, as he had at first been struck dumb with astonishment, so now he was impelled to speech by horror and indignation. " Who, sir," he cried, " that has a reverence for the law, a sense of liberty, or a regard for the Constitution can listen unmoved to a proposition which at one blow destroys our Constitution, our liberty, and our laws? It is under the law that every man holds his property; and I firmly believe that no one in existence has a better title to anything which he possesses than the title to Inglewood which the Crown has vested in Sir James Lowther. If that title is taken away by act of Parliament, why not bring in an act to take away any other part of his estate? Why not the estate of any landlord in the kingdom? If bills for the forcible transfer of property are thus to pass, there can be nothing sacred, nothing secure among us. Were I a party to such a transaction, my conscience would never suffer me to be at rest; and the same conscience which dictates my present opposition shall carry me on to oppose the bill in every step and through every stage. I wish that gentlemen who brought in the measure would, for their honor's sake, withdraw it. But if it succeeds here, it cannot succeed elsewhere; and I pray and trust that we may not suffer the scandal of this bill to lie at our doors, and surrender the credit of rejecting it to the other House of Parliament." [1]

St. Stephen's had never seen, and in all likelihood will never see again, such perversity of opinion combined with such acuteness of intellect and intensity of conviction. The fame of the performance outside the House of Commons betrayed Horace Walpole, who was not given to overrate his juniors, into confessing that Charles Fox was "the phenomenon of the age." A young gentleman who owned so curious a conscience, and was in the habit of appealing to it with such transcendent effect, was worth even *his* weight in bank-bills and lottery-tickets to a cabinet which could buy everything except earnestness and sincerity. The immediate result of a speech which supplied the ministerialists with the most exalted motives for continuing a course which an hour before they had been heartily ashamed of having adopted was to diminish Meredith's majority by a half; and, a week afterwards, when the time came for the bill to be committed, Fox effectually redeemed his pledge of fighting every inch of ground against a measure which (as he cleverly termed it) menaced the first principles of good government by confounding the legislative and judicial functions. From the moment that he took the affair in hand, all went well for Lowther.

---

[1] This speech, the first which Fox made on the subject, appears in the "Parliamentary History" in the debate of February the twenty-seventh; but it is the same as that which Cavendish reports as having been delivered on the twentieth. Cavendish, as always, is here clearly in the right; for, when the twenty-seventh of February came, and the motion that the Speaker should leave the chair was opposed by the friends of Lowther, Fox began by a distinct allusion to his own speech of the previous week.

By his audacious logic, and his inborn and hereditary skill in parliamentary management, Fox turned votes enough to defeat the motion that the Speaker should leave the chair; and there the matter would have ended but for the portentous discovery that a stranger had been counted in the division. The man, when brought to the bar, was recognized as a busybody who haunted the lobby, and who had been rash enough to pursue his victims into a place where they had him at a disadvantage. Gathering courage from numbers, the members whose buttons he had held, and into whose pockets he had forced his documents, revenged themselves by disowning his acquaintance, and even by throwing suspicions on his identity. One suggested that he might be a conspirator. Another, with refined malice, professed to believe that he was a reporter. A third went even further, and charged Sir William Bagot to observe what came of country gentlemen venturing to raise the devil. Burke, chafing under the sudden and, to those who had left Charles Fox out of their calculations, quite inexplicable, reverse which had befallen his party, forgot himself for a moment, and, as his nature was, showed that he had forgotten himself by becoming unreasonably and unseasonably solemn. "I do," he said, "in my soul suspect some malpractice in the coming-in of the man." This exaggeration of emphasis, which belonged to the nationality of the speaker as much as ever did Sheil's rhapsodies or O'Connell's boisterousness, called forth a smile on the countenance of Charles Fox, who was thereupon told that a gentleman capable of laughing at such a sentiment would make a laugh out of anything. The challenge, given in a flash of excusable petulance, was not accepted. Fox already admired Burke to the utmost limits of his almost immeasurable deserts. He treasured what he had been permitted to obtain of the great orator's confidence, and was ever ready to repay it with the whole of his own. While still an aspirant for office, he had not scrupled freely to tell Burke his mind about the ministers from whom alone he could hope for preferment.[1] He had introduced him into

---

[1] "Charles Fox called to see me," wrote Burke, in July, 1769. "He talks of the Bedfords in his old strain of dislike."

his family with that air of triumphant complacency which a generous young man always throws into the business of bringing together the friend of whom he is proud and the relatives whom he loves ; and he had been not a little perturbed when Lord Holland treated the claims of his hero with the scepticism which the veterans of one generation are apt to entertain for the celebrities of another.[1] Burke gratefully acknowledged that, as long as Charles Fox was in the government, he himself would never be without some one able and willing to oblige him with those services which the leaders of the party that was in were less ready then than now to do for a member of the party that was out.[2] And on the present occasion, when Fox perceived that Burke was angry, he hastened to propitiate him with an explanation of a very different sort from that which he had lately thought good enough for Wedderburn. The courteous pleasantry of his reply disarmed his adversary, and the dispute dropped—the last dispute which arose between men who were too great to be rivals until the day when, over a subject of contention that was no laughing matter, the friendship of five-and-twenty years was broken. A second division convinced the most incredulous among the Whigs that they were honestly as well as thoroughly beaten; and Fox, who had talked the House of Commons fairly round the compass, was entitled to plume himself upon a feat which any one under a prime-minister may be proud to have accomplished twice in the longest lifetime.

But though Meredith lost his bill, Sir James Lowther did not gain his cause. When, after the ensuing long vacation,

---

[1] Lord Holland remarked that he supposed Burke was a wonderful man, but that he did not like those clever fellows who could not say a plain "yes" or "no" to any question you asked them.

[2] "I hear," wrote Burke, in November, 1772, "that Charles Fox's speedy coming into the Treasury is expected. This event would not, I hope, prove sinister to a very just claim, and would prevent much oppression to individuals, and, I am quite certain, a very considerable loss to the public." The claim was on the part of Burke's brother to some land which he had purchased in Grenada, the title to which was disputed by the Crown.

his case came on for trial, the lease under which the Crown had granted him the Forest of Inglewood was found to be defective in an essential particular; and he was non-suited accordingly.   But from February to November—as long as the most popular nobleman in England was exposed without defence to all the evil consequences which might result to him from the greed of his rival and the spleen of his sovereign—public indignation was hot against the young politician who had stood between the Duke of Portland and safety.   The great writer who had constituted himself the censor of politics had up to this period shown his gratitude towards his early patron, and added one more to the innumerable evidences of his personality, by the marked forbearance which he exhibited towards the favorite son of Lord Holland.   Junius, and the cohort of Romans and Greeks who were Junius under many names, had contrived to fight Wilkes's battle without lifting their spear against the most active of his enemies. An occasional hint that the Black Boy would do well to cleanse his ways, and look to his goings in his path, was the deepest scratch from that keen and ruthless weapon beneath which Fox had hitherto smarted.   But soon after the Nullum Tempus Bill had been rejected, Lord North was addressed in the *Public Advertiser* by a correspondent who signed himself " Ulysses ;" and who, while blaming the prime-minister almost beyond his due, showed no mercy whatever to his more guilty subordinate.   " It was reserved," said the writer, "for Mr. Charles Fox, at the opening of his life, to prove how easy and irreproachable it is, under your lordship's administration, to betray his first, his nearest, and his dearest friend ; to sacrifice the interests and the honor of a young nobleman, the companion and confidant of his private hours, at the dishonorable shrine of ministerial influence."   The letter appeared on the fourth of March ; and on the fifth, by two o'clock in the afternoon, which with him was equivalent to the first thing in the morning, Fox had already called at the office of the journal in the hope of seeing the editor.   Having failed in his attempt to obtain a personal interview, he wrote to Mr. Woodfall, begging him, in firm but civil terms, to give up the

name of his contributor, as Mr. Charles Fox was anxious to
have some conversation with him on an interesting subject.
"If the author," so the invitation was worded, "either is, or
professes to be, a gentleman, he can scarcely refuse me this
request." But the much-enduring Ulysses was not to be
drawn. He was well aware that, if once he stood on the
grass beneath the sharp eyes of Richard Fitzpatrick, foot to
foot with the lad whom his own father had taught his letters,
the mystery of the epoch would be a mystery no longer.
The secret which, a generation after it had ceased to be dangerous, he carried into his grave safe from the curiosity of
domestic affection, and the promptings of his own overweening vanity, would, at a crisis when disclosure was destruction,
be known to at least three besides himself, of whom two were
hostile; and, unless the encounter proved bloodless, which between such opponents was not to be thought of, the story
would within twenty-four hours be patent to the whole
world. Ulysses would be identified with Mnemon, and Mnemon with Junius. His enormous influence over the minds
of his countrymen, of which he was silently but most justifi-
ably proud, would vanish in a day. There would be an end
to his hopes of a career in the House of Commons—hopes
very precious to him, and, as the event showed, not presumpt-
uous. His post in the department, where he was doing such
well-paid work, would be vacant as soon as the secretary at
war could get hold of a scrap of paper on which to write his
dismissal. But the loss of the means of living would be a
small matter to one at whose throat a score of swords would
at once be pointed; and when he had run the gantlet of
Bedford's friends and Lowther's trenchermen, and the broth-
er-sportsmen of Grafton, and the half-pay colonels who had
been Granby's aides-de-camp—of the Guardsmen whose military privileges he had assailed with the effective accuracy of
official knowledge, and the courtiers whose master he had
lectured with irreverence which to them was nothing short of
sacrilege—he had still before him the prospect, for years to
come, of spending in the King's Bench Prison every spare
moment that he was not in the custody of the sergeant-at-

arms. Philip Francis, as nine years later all Calcutta, and soon all London, knew, was not a whit less brave than he was quarrelsome; but Junius consistently refused to go into the field with antagonists who staked nothing but the chance of a wound against the certainty of his own utter ruin. Charles Fox, like Sir William Draper before him, was obliged to confess that he had not mastered the spell which could force that dreaded shadow to display itself in flesh and blood.[1]

While Charles Fox was consistent in his fidelity to the theory of government which Bute had invented and North perfected, he was consistent in nothing else. The ministers could always rely on him to defend any stretch of authority or abuse of patronage which the necessities of their singularly false position obliged them to commit; but when a matter which had not yet been developed into an article of party faith was before the House, no man could predict anything with regard to him except that he was quite sure to speak. The prudent and the elderly, Whigs and Tories alike, foresaw with compassion the troubles that were in store for one who, on whichever side in politics he eventually settled himself, would have so very much to unsay. But, as Burke told an author who was reckoned a prodigy because she wrote well at a time of life when Fox was already a veteran among orators, "it is vain to preach economy to those who are come young to excessive and sudden opulence."[2] It is gratifying to ob-

---

[1] Junius refused to fight Sir William Draper on the ground that Sir William, having answered him in print, had agreed to abide by the ordeal of literary combat, and was not entitled to any other form of satisfaction. Not having the same plea to urge in the case of Charles Fox, Ulysses was content to let his challenge lie unnoticed among the archives of the *Public Advertiser*. The story is told in the memoir of Sir Philip Francis which was commenced by Mr. Joseph Parkes, and completed by an author who has written only too little and too unambitiously—the late Mr. Herman Merivale. That memoir has virtually set at rest the controversy that once promised to be eternal. Mr. Merivale, it may be observed, makes the slight error of printing the *nom de plume* affixed to the letters on the Nullum Tempus Bill as "Memnon," instead of "Mnemon."

[2] Burke to Fanny Burney; July 29, 1782.

serve that the future champion of liberty and humanity gave frequent proof that the wealth with which nature had so lavishly endowed him was sterling coin. He was generally ready to make the most of every occasion on which the obligations of a partisan did not prevent his kindliness and his justice from having free play. When Sir William Meredith, anticipating the labors of Romilly, protested against the barbarity and the inefficacy of a criminal code which attached the penalty of death to a hundred and fifty separate offences, and executed that penalty upon only one criminal out of every seventy-five who were sentenced to it, his motion for an inquiry was seconded by Fox. And whenever the vexed question of religious tests was mooted in the Commons, the most ambitious aspirant for a high career who had opened his lips there since William Pitt thundered against the Spanish convention voluntarily incurred the bitter and lasting displeasure of the sovereign, whose favor was in those days indispensable to his hopes, by boldly and persistently asserting that respect for the rights of conscience was not incompatible with the duty of a servant of the Crown.

In 1768, amidst the chaos of personal rivalry and public corruption which ensued upon the dissolution of Parliament, an accurate and most experienced observer had discovered symptoms that betokened the dawn of better things. "The general election," wrote Dr. Lardner, who, in the course of his eighty-four years, had watched intelligently at least twelve general elections, "has let us know the tempers of men, and assured us of a spirit of liberty reigning in the lower rank and also in many of middle rank." Nowhere did that spirit exhibit itself in such striking and varied aspects as among the members of the denomination which looked up to Lardner as its patriarch, and which counted Price and Priestley as hardly the most distinguished amidst its many ornaments. There was not another class of the community in which the average of intellect and attainments ranged so high as among those Presbyterians who during the last half-century had been drawing ever nearer to the tenets, and more willingly answering to the name, of Unitarians. The ministers of that body were eminent in many departments of exact knowledge, and solidly but unpretentiously read in literature. They were masters of the clearest, and perhaps the most agreeable, English that ever has been written—the English of the middle class in the generation before the French Revolution, which Johnson spoke always and wrote when he was old; which Arthur Young and Benjamin Franklin possessed in its perfection; and which, after it had deservedly made his fame, William Cobbett at length carried into burlesque. The Presbyterian leaders stood valiantly to the front whenever the general interests of Nonconformity were at stake. They exercised always and in all places a freedom denied to them by statutes which the magistrate did not venture to enforce. Alone of sects they refused to be trammelled by a verbal creed. They thought as they chose; they preached as they thought; and the plenitude of their liberty aroused the admiring envy of many parish clergymen, and not a few actual and expectant dignitaries of the English Church, who, thinking with them, were ill at ease within the rigid and narrow limits of the Establishment.

The foremost of these men who felt themselves misplaced in a calling where their opinions, after every reasonable allowance and permissible reservation had been made, grievously belied the professions with which they had entered it, was Theophilus Lindsey, the Vicar of Catterick, in Yorkshire. The example and influence of Priestley, whose intimate friend he was, added point to the scruples which had long made this excellent pastor restless and uncomfortable inside a fold which he loved too well to quit until he had tried his utmost to enlarge its borders.[1] His efforts at one time seemed likely to be crowned with success. In the July of 1771, a meeting was

---

[1] It was in 1769, at Archdeacon Blackburne's rectory, that Lindsey first met Dr. Priestley, who was travelling in the company of Dr. Turner, a man of science and a layman. After the party had broken up, Mrs. Lindsey remarked on the playful talk and cheerful air of their new acquaintances, who bore their weight of knowledge and celebrity so lightly. "Ah," returned her husband; "your observation is just. But *they* are at ease."

held at the Feathers Tavern, attended by a score of clergymen, and some doctors of physic and civil law.[1] Archdeacon
Blackburne—whose arguments and expostulations, carefully
framed to soothe the sensibilities of the most unworldly and
disinterested among men, had with difficulty kept Lindsey
from seceding at any moment during the past five-and-twenty
years—was intrusted with the charge of drawing up a petition to the House of Commons, praying that clergymen of
the Church and graduates of the universities might be relieved from the burden of subscribing to the Articles, and
"restored to their undoubted rights as Protestants of inter-
preting Scripture for themselves," without being tied to any
human comment or explanation. Throughout the autumn
there was an active canvass for signatures. Lindsey visited
the country parsonages and cathedral closes that lay along
two thousand miles of road in the South of England, with
hopes that grew fainter as he became more widely acquainted
with the mental attitude of his clerical brethren. When Parr
held aloof, who tried to get preferment in the Church of Ireland for one Unitarian minister, and recommended a work
written by another as a religious manual for his own lady
friends—when Paley refused his name under the influence of
a feeling which he himself dubbed cowardice—Lindsey must
have known how little was to be expected from less independent and enlightened men. It took six months of indefatigable and ubiquitous work to collect two hundred and fifty
names, including those of the laity. Lindsey expressed his
disappointment and concern in measured and dignified terms;
but other laborers in the cause were more outspoken. "I am
verily persuaded," wrote a good man who had starved upon
a cure of forty pounds a year because he could not bring himself to purchase promotion by repeating his subscription to
the Articles, " that if the Bible was burned to-morrow, and the

---

[1] The numbers present are very differently given by different authorities. Priestley, writing to Lindsey three weeks after the event, says, "If
I have been rightly informed, you were no more than twenty-four at the
meeting, and you were in the chair, which I think more to your honor
than being at the head of any convocation or general council."

Alcoran introduced and established in its stead, we should still, provided the emoluments were the same, have plenty of bishops, priests, and deacons." To compensate him for his failure among those of his own cloth, Lindsey had reason to be proud of the quality, if not the number, of the politicians whom he converted to his views. The first impulse of a Whig was to favor a proposal which would leave one test the fewer in a world where men whose only ambition was to go quietly about their business found themselves encountered at every turn by oaths, subscriptions, and affirmations. Sir George Savile and Lord John Cavendish promised to support, though they declined to present, the petition. A still heartier adhesion was given by Thomas Pitt, who, while a student at Cambridge, had been honored by his uncle Lord Chatham with a series of letters of advice and encouragement which young men who get their rules of life from books would do well to read as an antidote to Lord Chesterfield. The care and affection of the great statesman were not thrown away; for his nephew's mind was early imbued with principles which were illustrated by his conduct and recommended by his manners throughout a career that began with an act of self-sacrifice rare in all ages, and next to superhuman in his own. To break an entail with the object of paying a father's debts was an inversion of the order of things amazing to all his contemporaries, and certainly not least so to another rising senator who, if in little else, resembled him in his repugnance to the Thirty-nine Articles. "The other day" (wrote Lindsey, quoting from one of his numerous and industrious correspondents), "Dr. Hunt went to wait upon Lord Upper Ossory at his hunting-seat, where was Charles Fox and other lively bucks. The doctor opened upon the subject of our petition, and asked if they had heard of this intention of addressing Parliament. 'Yes,' said Mr. Fox; 'and, if conducted with temper and prudence, it may not be a bad scheme.'" The doctor, who wished to keep matters as they were, reminded the young minister that, in a season of political excitement, whatever disturbed the Church must tend to embarrass the government. "If I thought so," replied Fox, "I

would oppose it. But perhaps, as there are no very considerable persons concerned in it, it will drop of itself."

A cause on behalf of which even Charles Fox did not contrive to be more than lukewarm could hardly be of a nature
to arouse any very potent or wide-spread enthusiasm. Against
the petitioners, on the other hand, was arrayed an overwhelming combination of forces which seldom, indeed, have found
themselves on the same side. Lindsey and his friends were
met by the passive resistance of all the laziness and selfishness which existed in the Church of England at a period
when her dearth of energy and devotion has passed into a
commonplace of history ; and they had to prepare themselves
for the active reprisals of a host of combatants, animated by
an earnestness as intense as their discipline was effective.
The zeal, the munificence, the spirit of organized and con-
certed effort, which in later times destroyed slavery and the
slave-trade, laid the foundation of popular education at home,
and carried the Bible far and wide throughout the inhabited
world, were now, in all the freshness of their early vigor, directed against a project that was nothing less than abhorrent
in the eyes of Evangelicals both inside and outside the Church.
They viewed that project in the light of a plausible device
for herding together, on the common ground of a cold morality, those rival denominations which kept religion alive by
the stir and fervor of their conscientious differences. Lindsey
must have been sorely disheartened by the answer that he
got when he imparted the enterprise which he and Archdeacon Blackburne had in hand to that Dissenter who, of all
others, was the most likely to bid them godspeed. "If it be
possible," wrote Priestley, "for us to act in concert with you,
I wish you would tell us how. In the present state of Christianity, I am for increasing the number of sects rather than
diminishing them. But I am only one individual. There
may be Dissenters who are just as the archdeacon would have
them."

Such were the impressions of a philosopher whose temperament and opinions inclined him to a policy of compromise,
and whose friendship for the author of that policy had led

him hitherto to strain a point in its favor. It may therefore easily be imagined how an offer so redolent of Erastianism was entertained by the old Nonconformist associations which had borne the brunt of the evil days that intervened between the Restoration and the Revolution; and by that still more formidable body of men who were so intent on higher matters that they had not yet found leisure to determine whether they were Nonconformists, or whether they were not. The disciples of Wesley laid aside for a moment their standing quarrel with the controversialists upon whom the recently dropped mantle of Whitefield had fallen, in order to unite the Arminian and Calvinistic sections of the Methodist party in a joint declaration that, however filial might be their relations with the Church of England, if, like that of Ephesus, she returned to her first love, they would have no communion, then or thereafter, with a church of Laodicea. But Lindsey's most active opponent was not of his own rank or his own sex. Wesley, who just then had upon him one of the hottest of his queer political fits, and seriously contemplated devoting himself to the confutation of Junius, was too much inclined to defend the Thirty-nine Articles from behind the old Tory lines of Church and State, and left it for the famous lady who now was his one real rival in his own field to fight the battle on firmer and higher ground. The Countess of Huntingdon had little love for those latitudinarian opinions in which her husband died, and which in her son were fast becoming something more than latitudinarian by a process of mental reaction intelligible to those who have groped their way through that memoir of his exemplary mother which will remain to all time the worst edited of printed books.[1]

---

[1] The younger Lord Huntingdon had some part in convincing the author of the Broad-Church movement of 1771 that the English Establishment was not the place for a Crypto-Unitarian. "What became of the universe," he asked of Mr. Lindsey, "when its Creator hung lifeless on a tree in Judæa?" "I am not concerned, my lord," said the other, "to answer that question; the foundation on which it rests not forming any part of my creed." "But the belief of it forms a part of the creed of

And, over and above her family grievance, Lady Huntingdon brought to the conflict a living faith which had nothing to match it among antagonists nine tenths of whom, as the issue proved, did not believe in their own cause to the point of suffering for it. Never wont to spare herself, she worked as she had never worked before. She banded together, in uncompromising hostility to the proposals of the Broad-Church party, all professors of Methodism, from the aristocratic London circles to which she of right belonged down to the humblest group who gathered weekly round a lay class-leader in a remote Cornish village. She called in person on members of Parliament who were doubtful which way they should vote, and indoctrinated those who were minded to speak on so unaccustomed a topic with ideas and phrases that were more familiar in Moorfields than at Westminster. She supplied the prime-minister, who must have been not a little amused by her unselfish importunity, with arguments of the most exalted character in favor of taking a course which he already was engaged to take by the single and simple motive for which he did everything—because the king wished it; and the king had pronounced against any tampering with the Articles, on the ground that "all wise nations have stuck scrupulously to their ancient customs." Lady Huntingdon's apprehensions were finally allayed by the assurances of a statesman whose springs of action were more complex than those of North and his master. Burke conveyed to her by letter the promise of his strenuous aid in crushing what he stigmatized as "the conspiracy of Atheism;" and in those days a measure which claimed to be a measure of reform stood but a poor chance when Burke had declared himself against it.

The petition, which Sir William Meredith presented on the sixth of February, 1772, was discussed in a manner worthy of the pains that had been taken to prime the speakers.[1] Those

---

that Church in which you weekly officiate as a minister," was Lord Huntingdon's reply.

[1] "In 1772 I published two short letters under the feigned name of 'A

giants of old, whose skill had been exercised in so many desperate and dubious conflicts, now showed of what they were capable when party feeling did not tempt them to pervert or exaggerate, and when the question which they treated had not been vulgarized by frequent handling. The problem of the obligations which may fairly and conveniently be imposed upon the ministers of a privileged church was stated and examined with a clearness and conciseness the secret of which seems to have been lost by some of our generation who choose that problem for their special study; with a frankness which makes us proud to think what courageous fellows our great-grandfathers were; and a thoroughness as exhaustive as was attainable by an assembly of men who had not yet advanced to the point of asking themselves whether it was necessary to have a privileged church at all. As long as such an institution continued in existence, it was not an agreeable task to answer the objections called forth by the proposal that a declaration of belief in the Christian religion, as set forth in the Holy Scriptures, should be the one and only test imposed upon those who aspired to obtain a share in the wealth and dignities of the Establishment, and to teach with its authority. The stout old Tory who first took up the cudgels against Meredith asked what must be thought of ecclesiastics who, having scrambled through the thorns and briers for the sake of the grapes, were now intent upon destroying the hedges and leaving the vineyard naked and defenceless. "Would you," said another member, "pay a hired laborer his wages if, instead of doing a piece of work according to order, he adopted a plan of his own perfectly inconsistent with your ideas?" A third speaker went to the root of the matter by asserting bluntly that some of the clergymen who had petitioned to be relieved from any test but the Scriptures did not find in the Scriptures

---

Christian Whig,' and put myself to the expense of giving a copy of the first to every member of the House the day before the clerical petition was taken into their consideration." So writes Bishop Watson in that book of anecdotes which a reader who respects his character and agrees with his political opinions could wish were a thought less egotistical.

that doctrine of the divinity of Christ which was held by the vast majority of the people whose souls they tended and whose substance they tithed.   Burke, by whom this idea was expanded into an oration, had seldom been finer, and never wiser.   His exposition of the insufficiency of a declaration of belief in the Bible, in place of a more defined and detailed confession of faith, may be quoted as an example of the highest performance of a man of letters who is likewise a man of the world.[1]   He would do much, he said, in order to remove a substantial grievance which could be remedied without inflicting a greater wrong upon a larger number.   But what grievance had the petitioners to show?   And what would be the consequence of granting them the concession which they craved?   Their hardship amounted to this, that the nation was not taxed two shillings in the pound to pay them for teaching their own particular fancies as divine truths; and that hardship, such as it was, could only be relieved at the expense of others whose interests and wishes had a far more legitimate claim than theirs upon the consideration of Parliament.   Among a serious people, who looked upon religion as

---

[1] "The subscription to Scripture is the most astonishing idea I ever heard, and will amount to just nothing at all.   Gentlemen so acute have not thought of answering the obvious question, what is that Scripture which they are content to subscribe.   They do not think that a book becomes of divine authority because it is bound in blue morocco and is printed by John Basket and his assigns.   The Bible is a vast collection of different treatises.   A man who holds the divine authority of one may consider the other as merely human.   What is his canon?   The Jewish?   St Jerome's?   That of the Thirty-nine Articles?   Luther's?   There are some who reject the Canticles; others six of the Epistles.   The Book of Revelation has been a bone of contention among divines.   Will those gentlemen exclude the Book of Esdras?   Will they include the Song of Songs?   As some narrow the canon, others have enlarged it by admitting St. Barnabas's Epistles and the Apostolic Constitutions, to say nothing of many other gospels.   To ascertain Scripture you must have one Article more, in order to define what that Scripture is which you mean to teach.   There are, I believe, very few who, when Scripture is so ascertained, do not see the absolute necessity of knowing what general doctrine a man draws from it before he is authorized by the State to teach it as pure doctrine and receive a tenth of the produce of our lands."

the most serious of concerns, there was a limit to the possibilities of ecclesiastical compromise; and by making a new door into the Church for a handful of men who might find a more suitable home elsewhere, at least ten times their number would be driven out of it,

Savile replied in a noble discourse which, like Mr. Bright's speech on the Irish Church Bill, suggested to all who heard it that a statesman who has his heart in the matter might beat the clergy on their own stage. "I cannot help saying," wrote John Lee, who, as one of the few lawyers then in the habit of frequenting sermons, was well qualified to judge, "that I never was so affected with, or so sensible of, the power of pious eloquence as while Sir George was speaking. It was not only an honor to him, but to his age and country." Savile's highest flight was inspired by the alluring, if chimerical, hope of a religious union with that multitude of his fellow-countrymen whose merits as citizens so devoted a Whig had the best of reasons gratefully to acknowledge. "Some gentlemen," he said, "are apprehensive that if the Scriptures are substituted in the room of the Articles, it will be a means of admitting into the Church a great number of sectaries. Sectaries, sir! Had it not been for sectaries, this cause had been tried at Rome. Thank God, it is tried here! Some gentlemen talk of raising barriers about the Church of God, and protecting his honor. They might talk as well of guarding Omnipotence, and raising barriers about the throne of heaven. Barriers about the Church of God! That Church which, if there be any veracity in Scripture, shall continue forever, and against which the gates of hell shall not prevail! It is not we who should set bars in the way of those who are willing to enter and labor in the Church of God. When the disciples came to Christ and complained that there were some who cast out devils in his name, what did our Saviour do? Did he send them tests and Articles to be subscribed? Did he ask them whether they were Athanasians, or Arians, or Arminians? No. He delivered that admirable and comprehensive maxim, 'He that is not against me is for me.' Go ye and say likewise."

Everybody who got a hearing on that occasion spoke above himself except Charles Fox. During the four days and nights that surrounded the debate he was only once in bed; he must have drunk a dozen of wine; and at one moment he had lost as many thousands of pounds. His knowledge of the subject under discussion was that of an Oxford undergraduate, clever enough to feel the absurdity of having been called upon to sign the Articles at his matriculation, and lazy enough to dislike the prospect of learning them by heart, when the time came for him to go in for his degree. But, such as it was, Fox had no notion of keeping his experience to himself; so he washed his face (a process which there is reason to believe was too often the limit of his ablutions), and went down to Westminster to inform the House of Commons, with an air which would have been all very well in a college debating society, that "religion was best understood when least talked of." At his worst, however, he had always his point to make; and the smartest thing said that evening was his allusion to the inconsistent practice of the university, which deferred the oath of allegiance and supremacy till the age of sixteen, in order that the person who had to take it might be competent to determine whether he was a loyal subject or not; while children of twelve were invited to attest the truth of a series of propositions relating to the most subtle doctrines and the most sublime mysteries that ever had bewildered the intellect and exalted the piety of mankind. His arguments, which did not even govern his own vote, sank but a very little way into the minds of an audience to whom Savile had brought delight, but not conviction. Meredith had only seventy-one supporters; whereas the members of Parliament who rejected the petition were at least as numerous as the clergy who had signed it. The question was raised again, after an interval of a year, with a somewhat more favorable result, due in part to an excellent speech from Charles Fox, who was anxious to efface the impression of a levity which he was already incapable of repeating.[1] In 1774 Sir William Meredith returned to the

---

[1] In 1772 the numbers were 71 to 217. In 1773 the minority, for which

charge for the last time; but his labored and tedious advocacy of a subject rather above his intellectual calibre, alienated hearers over whom he had lost his moral influence ever since, in an evil hour, he accepted the white wand of comptroller of the household.   Burke, with a readier perception than usual of the tactics which the situation demanded, spared his broth-er-members a serious oration, and kept them for half an hour in a continual fit of laughter at the expense of the right honorable gentleman who lacked the wisdom of Moses, although he was now possessed of the rod of Aaron.   The sense of the House was so evidently against Meredith that he did not venture to divide.   The cause was lost, and the beaten party hastened to make terms with the conqueror.   Promotion was dealt out in generous measure among the petitioning clergymen who consented to abide in the Church of England; but honors so won were not honors in the eyes of Lindsey.   Foreseeing the fate of the venture on which his peace of mind was staked, he resigned his vicarage in November, 1773; abandoned the modest luxury to whose charms he is reported to have been far from insensible; sold a library which he undoubtedly loved; and retired with his wife and daughter to a ground-floor in Holborn, on a weekly income that was counted by shillings.   His bishop confessed that the diocese had lost in him the most exemplary among its ministers; and the congregation of Catterick heard his farewell sermon with a passionate grief that was nothing less than a phenomenon at an epoch when parishes were accustomed to see their parson come and go with an indifference which was mutual.   But he did not obtain nor expect the consolation which is afforded by the praise of men.   Solitary self-sacrifice, while it arouses the tacit resentment of all who feel themselves challenged to imitate it, is no protection against the censure of such as sincerely disapprove the opinions which have prompted the act.   Lindsey survived to see four of those who had put their hands to the petition and then turned back elevated in succession to

---

Charles Fox was one of the tellers, remained at much the same figure, while the majority sank to 159.

the episcopal bench;[1] but the only distinction which fell to his own lot consisted in a few lines of grudging, and even sinister, commendation by a poet who so nobly celebrated the martyrs of faith that he might have had something better than irony to bestow upon the martyr of honesty.[2]

Lindsey would have felt less reason to despair if he could have persuaded himself that the House of Commons, in rejecting his cherished scheme, had been actuated by religious bigotry. But the earlier parliaments of George the Third, whatever might be their faults, were conspicuously free from the narrowness and timidity which blighted the understandings and perverted the actions of our public men when once Robespierre and the Convention had frightened them into intolerance. Hardly any one who spoke either for or against the petition of the clergy sat down without having said something civil to the Dissenters; and Lord North went so far as to exclaim against the injustice of the regulation which still required Nonconformist ministers and schoolmasters to sign the greater part of the Thirty-nine Articles. The State, he declared, had no right to impose conditions upon men who did not ask for emoluments. Encouraged by so plainly

---

[1] Watson, who, if he did not actually sign the petition, at least spent ink and money in canvassing for it, was the ablest of the four. The most eager to recant was Porteus, afterwards Bishop of London, and such a light of Evangelicalism that Hannah More set his bust in her garden. Lindsey, taking mild revenge in an anagram, conferred on him the nickname of Doctor Proteus.

> "They now are deemed the faithful, and are praised,
> Who, constant only in rejecting Thee,
> Deny thy Godhead with a martyr's zeal,
> And quit their office for their error's sake;
> Blind, and in love with darkness! Yet even these
> Worthy, compared with sycophants who kneel
> Thy name adoring, and then preach thee man."

The lines occur towards the end of the "Winter's Walk at Noon." They contrast painfully with the passage in the "Morning's Walk" commencing "Patriots have toiled," which, in the sweet expression of sympathy with heroic deeds and sufferings, yields to very little blank verse in or out of Shakespeare.

25

worded an invitation from so high a quarter, the Unitarians lost no time in applying to Parliament to relieve them from a position which was always precarious, and which might at any moment become intolerable. As honest men they could not pretend an assent to doctrines which they disbelieved; as thoughtful men they objected on principle to binding conscience and reason in the rigid and awkward fetters of a printed confession of faith; and their refusal to subscribe placed them outside the protection of the Toleration Act, and left their fortunes and their liberty dependent on the indulgence of their rulers and the good-feeling of their fellow-citizens. Priestley could not give a lesson to his pupils or a sermon to his congregation without coming inside the tether of the savage laws which, between 1660 and 1672, filled the jails and pillories with the brave and the innocent; those laws which, as Chatham forcibly remarked, were coupled up like bloodhounds, to be let loose at the heels of the Dissenters if ever they made themselves troublesome to the government in the pulpit or at the polling-booth. At the best of times the famous philosopher and his coreligionists were at the mercy of any justice who had a mind to play the tyrant, or any neighbor who was ill-natured enough to lay an information; and times could not always be at the best. The public opinion which kept in abeyance the Five Mile Act and the Conventicle Act was not immutable; and if ever the tide of unpopularity ran against the Nonconformists, they would assuredly find that a law which was dormant had not ceased to be dangerous. Twenty years afterwards there would have been no lack of informers among the ruffians who burned their libraries and sacked their warehouses in the name of Church and King; and the magistrates who cheered on the mob to plunder and arson would certainly not have refrained from imposing upon the objects of their dislike and suspicion those legal penalties which the Statute-book empowered them to enforce.

The Nonconformist leaders were determined that, if they still were doomed to live on sufferance, at any rate they should not have themselves to blame; and so prompt was their action that a bill for their relief was on the table of the House of Commons before the session of 1772 was past the middle of its course. They confidently relied upon the favorable dispositions which the ministry had evinced towards them; but they forgot that, behind the ministry, their sworn enemy (for, mindful of his coronation oath, George the Third insisted on so regarding himself) sat ensconced upon the throne which his ancestors owed to theirs. The king was disturbed and perplexed by the appearance of a measure which the House of Commons liked and the country demanded; but his astuteness and his resolution did not fail him, and he soon devised a system of Fabian strategy which staved off the inevitable concession for seven livelong years. There was no occasion (such was the tenor of the instructions which he laid down for Lord North's guidance) to endanger the seats of gentlemen who were returned on the Dissenting interest by obliging them to go counter to the wishes of their constituents. They might safely be allowed to get from the question what credit they could against the approaching general election; for the prime-minister (whose openly expressed concurrence with the views of the Nonconformists his Majesty quietly ignored)[1] might count upon the bill being lost in the Peers. The king was as good as his word. The measure, after passing the Lower House with flying colors, was quashed in the Upper House beneath the weight of overwhelming numbers; and the official character of the majority was indicated by the fact that the bishops, who helped to vote down the Relief Bill in the Lords, exceeded, by more than two to one, the members who vainly opposed it in the Commons.

But the question had a vitality which it required something more than the perfunctory antagonism of prelates and placemen to extinguish. It was raised afresh in the Lower House within the twelvemonth; and this time the king's friends re-

---

[1] Mr. George Onslow had actually been in communication with the Presbyterian clergy on behalf of the Treasury; had begged them to grant him the honor of bringing in their bill; and had assured them that they had the good wishes both of Lord North and Lord Mansfield.

solved not to abandon their first line of defence without a struggle. Their decision was fortified by a petition from a group of
Dissenting ministers who, fearing Socinianism more than they
loved religious liberty, entreated Parliament not to surrender
a test imposed expressly for the maintenance of those essential doctrines on which the Reformation was founded. Lady
Huntingdon, who thoroughly understood the distinction between toleration and latitudinarianism, remonstrated earnestly
with these misguided men; but they went blindly to their
fate, which was as terrible as any that oratory has within the
resources of its armory to inflict. "Two bodies of men,"
said Burke, "approach our House, and prostrate themselves
at our bar. 'We ask not honors,' say the one. 'We have
no aspiring wishes; no views upon the purple. The mitre
has no charms for us, nor aim we at the chief cathedral seats.
Content to pass our days in an humble state, we pray, for the
sake of him who is Lord of conscience, that we may not be
treated as vagrants for acting agreeably to the dictates of internal rectitude.' 'We, on the contrary,' say the Dissenters
who petition against Dissenters, 'enjoy every species of indulgence we can wish for; and, as we are content, we pray that
others who are not content may meet with no relief. We
desire that you will not tolerate these men, because they will
not go as far as we; though we desire to be tolerated—we
who will not go as far as you. Our prayer to this Honorable House is that they be thrown into prison if ever they
come within five miles of a corporate town, because they stop
somewhat short of us in point of doctrine.' What," cried
the indignant speaker, "shall we say to these reptiles except
'Arrangez-vous, canaille!'" If any one would measure the
extent of the transformation wrought in the British mind by
its recoil from the excesses of the French Revolution, he has
but to imagine the storm of fury and disgust that would have
been raised in the Parliament of 1793 by a sentence which,
a score of years before, was heard inside the same walls with
a composure very nearly akin to approbation. Even in 1773,
however, it was boldly spoken; but there was something that
evening still more boldly done. Charles Fox, who had made

it his vocation to serve his way towards that official eminence which Burke could only hope to carry by storm, planted himself at the door of the lobby as the responsible patron of a proposal every advocate of which was a marked man in the books of one who could close and open at will the road to place and power. How narrowly and attentively the king scanned the lists of those who told and voted for and against the measure which he detested was known a fortnight afterwards, when that measure once more met its annual death in the House of Lords. Alone among his brethren, Green of Lincoln ventured to assert the principle that pious and learned men ought not to be ruined and imprisoned for the crime of preaching to hearers who would reject any ministrations but theirs. "Green! Green!" exclaimed the king, when this instance of episcopal mutiny came to the royal ears; "Green shall never be translated;" and an act which betokened independence in a bishop, who could hardly hope or care to rise higher than the hill on which his cathedral stood, was nothing short of heroism in a junior lord whose ambition was as unbounded as his abilities. But could Charles Fox have foreseen the career that lay before him, he would right willingly have incurred the very extremity of Court disfavor as the price at which he laid the foundation of the strongest and most enduring sentiment that any section of the English community has ever entertained towards any statesman—the grateful veneration with which the whole body of his Nonconformist fellow-citizens adored him living, and mourned him dead.[1]

---

[1] A gentleman who sat as the first member for Manchester used to tell how the news of Fox's death affected his father, a leading merchant and citizen of that town, who had been forced to hide for his life from a mob, set on by men of his own class to punish him for his opposition to the American war; who became a Nonconformist at the time when the Church had cast in her lot with the persecutors of civil and religious liberty in the early days of the French Revolution; and who lived to treasure a Peterloo medal. The child, for he was but six years old, never forgot the scene: the untasted meal; the unaccustomed tears; the uplifted hands; the exclamation that the cause for which so much had been sacrificed and suffered had received an irreparable blow.

CHAPTER X.

1772–1774.

The Moral Danger of the Position in which Fox now stood.—He attacks Lord North on the Church Nullum Tempus Bill, and resigns
the Admiralty.—The Motives of his Conduct.—Marriages of the Dukes
of Cumberland and Gloucester.—Anger of the King.—The Royal Marriage Bill.—The Bill gets through the Lords, is strenuously opposed
in the Commons, and with difficulty passes into Law.—Strong Feeling
of Fox on the Question.—His Earnest Efforts against the Measure.—
His Sentiments with Regard to Women, and his Eager Care of their
Rights and Interests in Parliament.—His Private Life.—The Betting-
book at Brooks's.—Personal Tastes and Habits of Charles Fox.—His
Extravagance and Indebtedness.—Horace Walpole on Fox.—Influence
and Popularity of the Young Man in the House of Commons.—Fox
goes to the Treasury.—Lord Clive.—Fox and Johnson.—John Horne
Tooke.—Fox leaves the Ministry, never to return.

For the present, however, there was no love lost between
the Dissenters and their champion of the future. Ten years
of George the Third's policy had separated the nation into
two deeply marked and intensely hostile factions, which in
their composition, and even their titles, revived some of the
most ominous associations in our history. "The names of
Whig and Tory," said a political writer in the year 1774,
"have for some time been laid aside, and that of the Court
party and Country party substituted in their room;" and
when English politics took the shape that they had worn under the Stuarts, there was no doubt on which side the Nonconformists would be banded. Those were days when it was
not permitted to be friend and enemy by halves; and an occasional vote or speech in favor of religious liberty did not
make Independents and Presbyterians, who were Wilkites almost to a man, forget that Charles Fox had been foremost in
keeping the representative of Middlesex out of the House of
Commons, and in preventing the people of England from

learning what went on inside it. Here and there might be discovered an individual member of the middle or lower classes acute enough to detect that the young politician was made of different stuff from the jobbers who shared his bench and cheered his speeches.[1] But the mass of mankind judge their public men as they find them; and Fox was almost universally regarded as a bird of the same feather with the Bedfords, if, indeed, the dice-box had not rendered that metaphor inapplicable to any of the clan. To the great majority of reasonable Englishmen he seemed as desperate in his fortunes as the worst of his colleagues; as insolent in his defiance of sober political sense and legitimate popular aspirations; and superior to them in nothing except in those mental gifts which he had hitherto employed only to the detriment of the commonwealth.[2] And that which he seemed he was rapidly

---

[1] In a newspaper of the period there is a letter from a Quaker commencing with the words "Friend Charles Fox, thou seemest to be possessed of a very depraved kind of ambition," and urging him to put his talents to better purpose than "persecutions for telling the truth;" a letter conceived in a tone of respectful and hopeful remonstrance which its author would never have wasted upon Wedderburn.

[2] The reputation for mischievous ability which Charles Fox had acquired almost in boyhood would be incredible if it did not stand recorded in almost every page of the political literature of the day. There was no enemy of liberty so powerful and so highly placed that the lad's name was not coupled with his in the outbursts of public reprobation. One satirist, writing of the Barons of Runnymede, tells us that

> "Indignant from their hallow'd bed
> Each lifts a venerable head
> And casts a look of fire
> At Mansfield, chief among the band
> That deal injustice round the land,
> At either Fox, and at their sire."

Another testifies, in not ineffective verse, how the young placeman silenced those among his elders who were his betters, and outdid in impudence those who were not.

> "Hear, hear him! Peace, each hoary pate!
> While ribaldry succeeds debate,
> Learn pun and wit from youth high-mettled."

tending to become. George Herbert's proverb, "Keep not ill men company, lest you increase the number," would soon have met with its usual fulfilment had not Providence, kinder to Charles Fox than himself, made use of his own unruly impulses to work for him an escape from a contagion which must erelong have incurably poisoned even such an intellect and such a nature as his.

On the seventeenth of February, 1772, a member of Parliament, whose family estates were confiscated abbey lands, the title-deeds of which had once been nearly sold for old parchment by a discharged servant, asked leave to introduce a bill for the purpose of securing the holders of what had formerly been Church property against dormant claims of more than sixty years' standing. Lord North, at the instance of the bishops, with whose aid in the Upper House his government could not afford to dispense,[1] warmly opposed the motion, and took its author roundly to task for having omitted to place the House of Commons in possession of the details of his scheme. But roundness and warmth were not words to describe the rollicking audacity with which Charles Fox fell upon the prime-minister, charging him with having arbitrarily invented a most unparliamentary rule of procedure in order to combat a proposal against which he had not been at the pains to bring forward a single parliamentary reason. Following up his speech with his vote, he took with him into the lobby his brother Stephen, and other members upon whose allegiance Lord North was accustomed to depend; so that the ministry came nearer a serious defeat than they had ever done since the evening on which the eloquence of the same unaccountable young gentleman had preserved them from being beaten on the Nullum Tempus Bill of Sir William

---

Even Rigby is told to look to his laurels.

> "Burnish thy shining front anew.
> Shall Fox, shall Harley, Luttrell, dare
> With thine their foreheads to compare,
> Great boatswain of the Bloomsbury crew?"

[1] Lindsey to Jebb, March 3, 1772.

Meredith.   After such an exhibition, few were surprised to hear, three days later, that Fox had resigned his Commissionership of the Admiralty.   Few were surprised at his leaving office; but everybody was discussing the why and the wherefore of the oratorical ebullition which rendered it impossible for him to stay there.   The world, as its manner is, accredited him with an assortment of motives tortuous and multifarious enough to have explained the retirement of a Mazarin or a Metternich; but no one who has watched the growth to maturity of a powerful character can be at a loss to name the causes which impelled a lad of twenty-three, whose head had been turned by a run of unexampled success, towards a step which, after all, was less foolish than the world supposed it. Whenever a young minister goes out, he is influenced by the same admixture of personal and public feelings and considerations, combined in very much the same proportions.   Impatience of restraint, a not dishonorable craving for real power, a distaste for official reticence, and an indifference to official dignity and emoluments engender a state of mind in which a diversity of view on an important question with those superiors who are masters of his actions and his voice becomes a burden beyond his capacity for submission and self-effacement to endure.   One who, according to the saying of his schoolfellows, thought himself fit for the privy council while he was still at Eton[1] felt it an insufferable humiliation to be directed how he was to speak, and when he was to hold his tongue, by a leader who had the advantage of him in nothing but in years; and his injured self-esteem, always on the eve of an explosion, was kindled into flame on a sudden by a spark from a nobler and purer source.   Charles Fox's quarrel with the prime-minister had its immediate origin in his ardor on behalf of a cause curiously unlike those which ordinarily at-

---

[1] "Pray tell Charles what pleasure his promotion gives me.   As to his giving himself airs about being only in the Treasury before he is of age, I believe he thinks he ought to have been a Privy Counsellor at Eton." The quotation is from a letter of Lord Carlisle to Selwyn; written, perhaps, early in 1770, when it was certain that Fox would have office, but uncertain what that office was to be.

tract the enthusiasm of the young; but for which, young or old, he would at any moment of his life have been willing to sacrifice everything.

While George the Third, severe and conscientious beyond his years, was occupied late and early with the administrative and ceremonial business of the State, he had plenty of deputies to do, and somewhat to overdo, the lighter duties of royalty. During the jovial decade which intervened between the Seven Years' War and the American troubles, it was difficult for a fashionable gentleman to take his pleasure in public or in private without meeting one or another of the king's younger brothers. "Every place," wrote Walpole, "is like one of Shakespeare's plays: 'Flourish. Enter the Duke of York, Gloucester, and attendants.'" Death gradually thinned the illustrious group, carrying off princes whom the world pronounced hopeful and promising in exact proportion as they died young. But enough remained to provoke from the frequenters of Ranelagh and the Pantheon a revival of the witty Lady Townshend's complaint—"This is the cheapest family to see, and the dearest to keep, that ever was." The member of that family who lived at the greatest expense, moral and pecuniary, to those with whom he came in contact was Henry, Duke of Cumberland—the hero of scandals so frequent and so clumsily conducted that, as long as his Royal Highness remained a bachelor, his damages and lawcosts seemed likely to form one of the heaviest items in the Civil List. He met his fate, however, in a young widow, whose nearest kinsman had recently given proof of a courage more than equal to the task of forbidding the most childish of libertines to play the fool with his sister. The relief of fashionable society at learning that the Duke of Cumberland was safely married was nothing to the sense of epicurean enjoyment with which Whigs and Wilkites heard that the bride's brother was no other than that gallant colonel whom the Court had appointed member for Middlesex. Junius was divided between terror lest a Luttrell should succeed to the crown of England and sombre merriment over the masterstroke of irony by which destiny had avenged him and his

printer upon their implacable enemy.[1] In a public letter he
called upon the injured freeholders of Middlesex to rejoice
because a greater than themselves had now experienced what
it was to have Luttrells forced upon him against his will; and,
writing confidentially to Wilkes in terms which, even after
the lapse of a century, respect for the sceptre does not permit
to be quoted, he urged that a deputation from the City should
at once repair to St. James's with an address congratulating
his Majesty on the auspicious event that had taken place in
his family.

The king's feelings were such that the ponderous impertinences of Junius could not make him more angry than he
was already.   Just a year before, when it became necessary
that he should take notice of his brother's irregularities, he
had treated the painful subject as became a high-minded and
right-minded man;[2] but though he sternly rebuked the sin,
he had not thought it incumbent upon him to withdraw his
countenance from the offender.   The Duke of Cumberland,
however, was now to discover that little as George the Third
approved his conduct towards the wives of others, he had
committed a crime of deeper dye in procuring himself a wife
of his own.   Profligacy might be forgiven; but there was no
pardon for the step by which alone the profligate could ever
be reclaimed.   Nor can the freedom with which the king
gave vent to his irritation be explained by his contempt for
the levity of his brother, and his resentment at the designing
ambition of his brother's wife; for his wrath was still hotter
against a pair of lovers whose character gave them a claim to
respect which had been strengthened, rather than forfeited,
by their behavior under circumstances as trying as any in
which two human beings can find themselves implicated.

---

[1] Junius to the Duke of Grafton, November 23, 1771.

[2] "I cannot enough express," he wrote in November, 1770, with reference to the Duke of Cumberland's most notorious transgression, "how
much I feel at being in the least concerned in an affair that my way of
thinking has ever taught me to behold as highly improper; but I flatter
myself the truths I have thought it incumbent to utter may be of some
use in his future conduct."

The Duke of Gloucester, as far back as September, 1766, had been privately married to the widow of Lord Waldegrave —that wise and upright man who, alone among the guardians of George the Third's childhood, did anything but harm to a prince whose nature he so clearly read, and the deficiences of whose so-called education he so honestly labored to supplement. Gratitude and esteem may have' been the strongest feelings which attracted Lady Waldegrave into her first marriage; but her second was a true love-match. The natural child of Sir Edward Walpole, she was so far from coveting a royal connection, for royalty's sake, that she shrank from honors which could not fail to bring into prominence the story of her birth.¹ That misfortune apart, she was wanting in nothing which could justify the choice of her husband or mollify the displeasure of her brother-in-law. She was the favorite sitter of Sir Joshua Reynolds, by whom her portrait was seven times eagerly and carefully painted in every stage of her beauty; and when, in our own time, the papers of the great artist were brought to light, a lock of golden-brown hair marked as hers was discovered in a recess of his pocket-book. And her mind was not unworthy of its casket. The constancy, the resignation, the touching humility, with which she endured a persecution exquisitely calculated to aggravate everything that was most distressing in her situation, gave value and beauty to letters which were fondly pronounced to be inimitable by the best judge of letters that ever lived. "I have always thought," said Horace Walpole, after reading the lines in which the Duchess of Gloucester confessed the marriage to her father, "that feeling bestows the most sublime eloquence, and that women write better letters than men. I, a writer in some esteem, and all my life a letter-writer, never penned anything like this letter of my niece. How mean did my prudence appear compared with hers, which was void of all personal considerations but of her honor!" Walpole,

---

¹ "She asked me," said her uncle Horace, "if I did not approve of her signing 'Maria Gloucester,' instead of simply 'Maria,' in the royal style; 'for,' said she, modestly, 'there was a time when I had no right to any name but Maria.'"

however, in so saying, did himself scanty justice; for his
promptitude in ranging himself on the side of the weak, and
his high-bred plain-dealing with the strong, proved that age
and illness had done nothing to impair that stoutness of heart
which, as often as his sense of honor or of justice was aroused,
never failed to show that he was Sir Robert's son.[1]

From boyhood upwards, as Lord Waldegrave noted, and as
his widow was destined to feel, George the Third was never
angry without something coming of it.[2] The knowledge of
what one brother had just done, and the suspicion of what
another had done long ago, determined the king to a course
of action most characteristic of its author in boldness of conception and inflexibility of execution. There was no question but that the younger members of the royal family were
defenceless, as far as the law could defend them, against the
matrimonial schemes of adventurers and adventuresses. In
1753 they had been exempted from the protection of the Marriage Act by the special desire of George the Second; and
George the Third, correcting the omission of his predecessor,
now made up his mind to protect them with a vengeance. It
would have been a very easy matter to devise means by which
princes and princesses might be shielded from the dangers of

---

[1] "I wrote to Lord Hertford a letter which I meant he should show to
the king, couched in the most respectful terms, in which I stated my own
ignorance of the marriage till owned, but said that, concluding the new
duchess's family could not be very welcome at St. James's, I should not
presume to present myself there without leave. I mentioned having
waited on the duke as a duty, due for the honor he had done the family,
and to the tenderness I had always felt for my niece, whom were I to
abandon I should expect his Majesty's own paternal affections would
make him despise me. This letter I enclosed in a cover in which I told
Lord Hertford plainly that if it was expected I should not see my niece,
I was determined rather to give up going to St. James's."

[2] "Whenever he is displeased," wrote Lord Waldegrave of his royal
pupil, "his anger does not break out with heat and violence, but he becomes sullen and silent, and retires to his closet, not to compose his mind
by study and contemplation, but merely to indulge the melancholy enjoyment of his own ill-humor. Even when the fit is ended, unfavorable
symptoms very frequently return which indicate that on certain occasions
his Royal Highness has too correct a memory."

their own ignorance and imprudence till they had reached the age of discretion, and by which, if they then persisted in ruining themselves, the nation might be preserved from suffering by their folly. A short act, giving their parents and guardians power over the actions of those among them who were not yet of age, and requiring the consent of Parliament to the marriage of all who came within a reasonable distance of the throne, would not have needed a Mansfield to draft or a Thurlow and a Wedderburn to expound and advocate. But the aim which George the Third had in view was not to assure the succession to the crown, but to extend the authority of the individual who wore it. The preamble of the bill—which he had resolved to turn into a statute, even if he stood alone as its sincere supporter—asserted (or, as the Whigs maintained, invented) the doctrine that the right of approving or forbidding marriages in the royal family had always been intrusted to the reigning monarch; and the substance of the enactment was of a piece with its exordium. The occupant of the throne, whatever his age, whatever his inexperience, might follow his own fancy in the selection of a consort. The occupant of the throne, whatever his character, whatever his antecedents, was appointed confidant and arbiter of the love-affairs of scores and hundreds of people, the rank and status of whose wives and husbands, in the vast majority of instances, concerned the public interests no more than if they had been so many tradesmen or mechanics. No descendant of George the Second, to the end of time, unless he were by birth a foreigner, might marry before six-and-twenty without the consent of the sovereign, unless he was prepared to see his children stamped as illegitimate, and their mother excluded from the recognition of society.[1] And where "the king's poor

---

[1] The pleasantest thing said or written on the most unpleasant of subjects was the answer to Dowdeswell's objection that a prince, who might reign at eighteen, was not allowed to marry as he liked till six-and-twenty. The obvious retort that it was easier to rule a kingdom than a wife made matter for an epigram, in the shape of a conversation between the Dick and Tom whom the rather vulgar taste of our ancestors had adopted as representatives of the Rufus and Cæcilianus of Martial.

cousin" was a woman, a consequence was threatened which George the Third, when he insisted on transmitting to his successors the privilege that he claimed for himself, can hardly have foreseen. Nothing but the good-fortune of our royal house has spared it a state of things under which girls would have had no choice but to disclose their fondest affections and their most cherished hopes to the inquisition of a voluptuary whose threshold no respectable matron would submit to cross. The bill, which never could have been popular, had the additional misfortune of being introduced on the morrow of a domestic catastrophe with which Europe was ringing. Those horrible tidings which arrived from Denmark on the twenty-ninth of January, 1772, were strange data on which to ground the necessity for a law framed with the express object of insuring that, thenceforward and forever, royalty should only mate with royalty. The most hardened men of the world confessed to being shocked when, with such news barely three weeks old, the wretched Caroline's brother invited his Parliament to consider a scheme of legislation under which British princesses might have to choose between a lifetime of celibacy and an ill-assorted official union like that which just then was dissolving amidst a scene of blood and misery such as could be paralleled only in the imagination of the dramatist.[1]

Harder men of the world than the members of his government the king must have gone far afield to seek; and even they quailed at the work which lay before them. Lord Mansfield, who had drawn the bill, was the only ministerialist leader who did not hint dislike of it when on his legs and openly abuse it in his cups;[2] but his share of the task was compara-

---

[1] Surprise was expressed in society that so good a courtier as Garrick had given "Hamlet" within a twelvemonth of the real tragedy at Elsinore. "It is difficult," wrote Sir James Mackintosh, in his essay on Struensee, "to contain the indignation which naturally arises from the reflection that at this very time, and with a full knowledge of the fate of the Queen of Denmark, the Royal Marriage Act was passed in England for the avowed purpose of preventing the only marriages of preference which a princess, at least, has commonly the opportunity of forming."

[2] "One thing remarkable is," wrote Lord Shelburne to Chatham, "that the king has not a servant in either House, except the Chief-justice of

tively a light one. The Marriage Bill had an easy journey through a House of Peers from which Chatham was detained by a " winter account of gout, to be balanced after a summer of health " such as he had not known for twenty years, and where the Episcopal bench supplied a casuist who had the nerve to descant volubly and minutely upon those features in the controversy which such laymen as Sandwich and Weymouth avoided as indelicate.[1] But the debating in the Lords was not altogether unproductive of good; for an admirable protest, with the names of Richmond and Fitzwilliam at the head of the signatures, served as a brief to indicate the lines on which the question was subsequently fought in the Commons. The skilled constitutional speakers of the Lower House dwelt with unanswerable force on the confusion that might ensue if the power of altering the order of succession, by annulling a marriage and declaring its issue illegitimate, fell into the hands of a monarch who had favorites among his sons; on the untenable character of the assumption that such a power had always belonged of right to the wearer of the crown; and on the certainty that Englishmen would prefer the offspring of a prince who, with or without leave, had married an Englishwoman to the offspring of a princess who had been duly and solemnly handed over to the nephew of an

---

the King's Bench can be called so, who will own the bill, or who has refrained from every public insinuation against it." A few days before the measure finally passed the Commons, Wedderburn was dining with Fox and other senatorial dandies. " They got drunk, and Wedderburn blabbed that he and Thurlow had each drawn the plan of an unexceptionable bill, but that Lord Mansfield had said they were both nonsense, had rejected them, and then himself drew the present bill. 'And, damn him,' added Wedderburn, ' when he called my bill nonsense, did he think I would defend him ?' "

[1] The Bishop of Oxford's exposition of the moral danger of preventing men of high rank from making marriages of inclination was answered by his brother of Gloucester in a strain which awakened the disgust of all who remembered the almost blasphemous fervor of his invectives against the " Essay on Woman," and pleased nobody except a few loose-lived peers. Now that he had the bishop's sanction, said an earl who had more wit than grace, he should drive with his chariot and liveries to places whither he had hitherto been in the habit of going incognito.

elector or the younger son of a landgrave, even if that preference could only be vindicated at the expense of a revolution. "Laws," said Burke, "have till now been passed for
the purpose of explaining doubts; but this is a law made to
create them;" and then he turned from the perils in which
the proposed measure would involve the State to the hardship which it would inflict upon the individual. Proudly
conscious that the truest proof of loyalty was to save the king
from himself, and resolved that, if in after-years the sons of
George the Third were driven into courses like those from
which their uncle had just been rescued by a marriage such
as they themselves would be forbidden to make,[1] their father
should only have himself to blame, the orator, who had so
often withstood the prerogative in its encroachments upon
liberty, now exclaimed against its exaltation at the cost of our
common humanity. Amidst the breathless attention of friend
and foe, he closed a magnificent rhapsody with a stroke of
histrionic effect more spontaneous, and therefore more impressive, than the dagger scene which was the most famous,
but far from the most happy, example of his later manner.
Making as if he saw the lord-chief-justice himself, pen in
hand, on the floor before him—"He has no child," he cried,
"who first formed this bill. He is no judge of the crime of
following nature."

The ministers, few of whom had lived after a fashion which
gave them a sense of security at a time when such personali-
ties were flying about, maintained, for the most part, a prudent
silence; and even the king's friends could with difficulty be
got to say a word in favor of a measure which, except in a
speech, no man ever called by any other name than the King's
Bill. Conway, who was so far a minister that he acted as mas-
ter-general of the ordnance—though he had declined to accept
the salary and the title of an office the work of which he was
doing in a spirit worthy of a purer age—refused to flatter the

---

[1] The objects sought by the Marriage Act, and its consequences to the
next generation of the royal family, are stated by Mr. Massey, with excellent taste and feeling, in the sixteenth chapter of his "History of England
under George the Third."

House of Commons by pretending that in entertaining the
proposal of the cabinet it was actuated by a feeling of public
duty. "Were I capable," he cried, "of paying compliments
on this occasion, I should think my tongue would wither in
my mouth." And, indeed, the temper of his audience was
such that anything might have been spoken with impunity.
The supporters of the government, as fathers and husbands,
were in a mood to pardon the most extreme violence of language that could be directed against a law for which, as placemen, they were prepared to vote. When Lord North, by
turning the debate on to a point of order, attempted to evade
an attack which his boldest colleagues could not be prevailed
on to face, so decorous an ex-official as Mr. Thomas Townshend
was heard to shout, "Let us have no dirty tricks." In the
dearth of oratorical courage which seemed likely to endanger
the fortunes of the bill, and possibly of the ministry, the
Speaker, whose faults were not in the direction of timidity, was
induced to descend into the lists; but he was no sooner back
beneath his canopy than he found himself pelted with sarcasms against which his character afforded him the scantiest
protection. "Consider, sir," said Burke, "that the bill will
operate when you shall be enjoying in another world the rewards of a life well spent in this"—a glance into the future
much appreciated by an assembly which had observed nothing in Sir Fletcher Norton's parliamentary career inconsistent
with the reputation for taking fees from both sides that he
had acquired during his practice at the bar. And the House
cheered like a parcel of insubordinate schoolboys when Barré,
availing himself still more freely of the form of addressing
the chair, in order to talk at its occupant, gave vent, with a
breadth of phrase in which the contemporaries of Smollett
saw nothing amiss, to the most astounding impertinence that
the member of a senate ever ventured to level against its
president.[1]

But the reluctance of the cabinet was not proof against the
determination of the Court. The author of the Royal Mar-

---

[1] Last Journals of Walpole, March 11, 1772.

riage Bill would as soon have withdrawn it because his ministers were afraid of the House of Commons as his uncle of Cumberland would have altered his tactics at Culloden for fear lest his colonels should be nervous under fire. In thirteen letters, brief and peremptory as the slips of paper which an aide-de-camp carries along the line of battle, George the Third, throughout the whole duration of the contest, dictated to Lord North the orders of the day. Nothing could be better adapted to the purpose which they were intended to effect than the king's exhortations to sustained and vigorous action, than the clear and practical suggestions with which he met every change of strategy on the part of the Opposition leaders, and than the threats against deserters and sluggards from which the prime-minister was permitted to draw a salutary warning for his own guidance. "Lord North's attention," wrote his Majesty, "in correcting the impression I had that Colonel Burgoyne and Lieutenant-colonel Harcourt were absent yesterday is very handsome to those gentlemen; for I certainly should have thought myself obliged to have named a new governor in the room of the former, and to have removed the other from my bedchamber." Conway was pitilessly bullied through his brother, the lord chamberlain; and less formidable defaulters were punished by his Majesty in person at a drawing-room which was held while the fate of the bill was still uncertain. But no stress of discipline could keep the ministerial ranks from melting away at a rate of decrease that terrified the drill-sergeants of the Treasury. A measure which had passed the second reading by two hundred and sixty-eight votes to one hundred and forty was hustled through its final stage by a bare majority of eighteen; while among the knot of members who stood grumbling on the wrong side of the door, no less than twelve out of fourteen had missed by a minute the satisfaction of yet further swelling the numbers of the Opposition.

The discussion had all along been conducted in the utmost secrecy. Peers begged in vain for admittance; and reporters were so rigidly excluded that a debate of ten hours hardly provided the newspapers with material for a score of lines.

The danger to liberty of concealing the proceedings in Parliament from the public gaze was forcibly illustrated by the apathy displayed by a high-spirited people towards a controversy which stirred a submissive House of Commons to the verge of revolt. The unpopularity of the Marriage Bill was confined to London society; and the sentiment, strong everywhere within those narrow limits, had the focus of its intensity in Lord Holland's domestic circle. For there the family traditions were all against arbitrary restrictions upon the freedom of marriage, and the family character was instinctively opposed to any restraint being placed upon the impulses of human nature. The offspring of a runaway match with a descendant of royalty, Charles Fox was not the man to prescribe by statute the level above which a lad of spirit was forbidden to lift his eyes. The nephew of one who, but for the interference of Bute and the Princess Royal, would at that moment have been Queen of England, he scorned to vote in obedient silence for a measure inspired (so the world believed) by the influence of that very pair who had stood between his kinswoman and the throne. That the suitor of Lady Sarah Lennox should make it a crime for his own sons to marry a subject was regarded at Holland House as an act of treason against reminiscences which ten years should have been too short to profane. "I should not," Fox wrote to the Earl of Upper Ossory, "have resigned at this moment merely on account of my complaints against Lord North, if I had not determined to vote against this Royal Family Bill, which in place I should be ashamed of doing. Upon the whole, I am convinced I did right; and I think myself very safe from going into opposition, which is the only danger. I am convinced, if you were to know the whole state of the case, I should have your approbation, which, I can assure you, would make me very happy." But, however much he might covet the esteem of his relative, the young fellow did not choose to make himself out more disinterested than he was. His letter was embedded in a mass of prefaces, postscripts, and comments from the pen of Mr. John Crawford, his confidant and sworn admirer, who very frankly disclosed to Lord Ossory those views and feelings, of a personal

rather than a public nature, which were among the forces that
contributed their weight towards driving Fox from the Admiralty. "Charles," wrote Crawford, in a passage which Fox
had read and allowed to stand, "has this day resigned. He
had not any one particular reason for this step; but, upon the
whole, he thought Lord North did not treat him with the confidence and attention he used to do. It is better to err by too
much spirit than by too little; and as Charles does not mean
to go into opposition, and is always worth a better place than
what he had, it is my opinion that what he has done will do
him credit, and turn out to his advantage every way."

That opinion was not shared by Lord Holland. It was believed in the clubs that the father had urged the son to quit
the government, in order that he might be free to devote himself to the advancement of a legislative crotchet which the
two cultivated in common; "and Charles" (observed Gibbon,
in one of those sentences which render his "Memoirs" the favorite book of readers who hold the secret of good writing to
lie in saying the most with the least show of effort and expenditure of type) "very judiciously thought that Lord Holland's
friendship imported him more than Lord North's." But the
town had not got the right story. The old statesman loved
the ministry, and had reason to love it, as little as the world
had loved him when he was himself a minister; but he came
of a school which did not make politics an affair of sentiment.
"Whatever cause of ill-humor," said the third Lord Holland,
"my grandfather might have, it was not probable from the
habits of his life that he would indulge it by going into opposition." As a matter of fact, Lord Holland's dissatisfaction at
the step which his son had taken came as near displeasure as
was possible with Charles for the object of it. But his annoyance was nothing to Lord North's alarm. If it had been a
secretary of state, with half a dozen cousins in the House of
Lords and a score of clients in the Commons, threatening to
take himself and his connection into the camp of the enemy,
the prime-minister could not have been more perturbed than
at the desertion of a junior lord whose property was a great
deal less than nothing, and whose party consisted of a brother

and a couple of schoolfellows. North was instant with Fox
to withdraw his resignation, and profuse in such apologies for
his own real or fancied incivility as are seldom offered by the
head of the Board of Treasury to the lowest on the Board of
Admiralty. But the young gentleman, before he went to the
interview, had announced his intention of leaving office to
those among his acquaintance whom he deemed worthy of
the information ; and his self-respect would not allow him to
surrender himself to the unfamiliar process of being talked
over. As soon as it became plain that there was no hope of
keeping him, a panic ensued in the higher circles of the State.
Lord Temple, who had wished to get rid of the Marriage Bill
without upsetting the cabinet, went three times to Court for
the purpose of assuring his Majesty that, much as he disliked
the proposed law, he would do nothing to weaken a ministry
which had received so paralyzing a shock ; and Lord Mansfield hastened to expunge the most objectionable feature in
his original draft of a measure which was within twenty-four
hours of being submitted to Parliament, in order to provide
the large contingent of peers whom the defection of Charles
Fox had frightened back into their allegiance with a decent
excuse for supporting the government.[1]

The sacrifice did something towards reconciling the Marriage Act with the laws of humanity ; but it entirely failed to
propitiate Fox. His first speech was in so moderate, and even
subdued, a tone that Burke remarked that the dissent of some
gentlemen was the opposition of half an hour. But the young

---

[1] The bill, as it was drawn, made the consent of the sovereign a
necessary condition for the validity of a marriage contracted by any
descendant of George the Second during the term of his or her
natural life. The first fruit of Fox's resignation was, that members of
the royal family were allowed to marry at the age of six-and-twenty,
unless both Houses of Parliament interfered with an express vote of disapproval.

Till Fox, by going out, made the Marriage Bill a stand-and-fall question, few expected that it would ever become law. According to a paragraph in the newspapers, a peer had laid five thousand guineas to one
thousand against its passing.

ex-official belonged to a class in whom self-control is, for their
adversaries, the most dangerous of symptoms. Long before
the bill left the Commons, Fox, by a succession of attacks
upon Sir Fletcher Norton, had proved that he possessed in
the highest excellence two supreme qualifications of the orator—the art of assailing a bad cause in the person of a questionable individual, and the art of bringing home to the mind,
without inflicting the forms of a moral lecture upon the ear,
a clear notion of the connection between the passing controversy of the day and those eternal principles of right and
wrong which men of all parties profess to venerate. He soon
established over the ministerial speakers the marked superiority in questions of detail which a disputant who has mastered
principles never fails to obtain over antagonists who have
begged them. Following Thurlow and Wedderburn, closely
and warily, from point to point; enticing them into indefensible positions, and suddenly turning and pushing them fiercely
until they yielded in confusion; eliciting from them contra-
dictory admissions and assertions, and then warning a silent
and all but repentant House that this was the first penal law
which had ever been passed with the lawyers differing; forcing the attorney-general to take refuge in a vague but humble confession that the bill would need to be altered "according as exigencies should arise"—Fox honestly and laboriously
earned the enthusiastic applause that greeted his fine rhetorical
description of the "glorious uncertainty which always attends
the law." There was joy in Kensington and at King's Gate
over the notable success with which this chip of the old block
had taken up the paternal quarrel with the gentlemen of the
long robe, who had enjoyed an easy time in the Commons
ever since Henry Fox had succumbed to gout and unpopularity. And patriots of a very different cast from Lord Holland rejoiced to observe that the young statesman spoke better in proportion as his cause was good; and that, as an exponent of the feelings and convictions of the wiser and more
thoughtful among his fellow-countrymen, he rose quietly and
naturally to a strain which he had never compassed in the
days when he obeyed the bent of his own humors and preju-

dices. It was generally and willingly admitted that, as a force
in politics, " Fox's logic " was equivalent to Burke's power of
moving the passions, and to the persuasive influence of Conway's example and character; and the veterans of the House,
employing the most valued and envied compliment which in
the seventeenth and eighteenth centuries one English gentleman could bestow upon another, declared that, as " a Parliament man," Charles Fox at three-and-twenty excelled Charles
Townshend in his maturity.

The feeling which inspired the most prominent opponent
of the Royal Marriage Bill was no hasty or isolated impulse.
It was intimately allied to a sentiment which, springing naturally in such a disposition as that of Fox, profoundly affected
his literary judgment, altered the whole current of his later
life, and at this particular period directed, and almost monopolized, his political energies. The member and the idol of a
society whose mode of talking on the most delicate of topics
was such as it is more seemly to condemn in general terms
than to illustrate by selected quotations—and credited, as a
young man, with living after the fashion in which an unmar-
ried associate of March and Selwyn might not uncharitably
be assumed to live—he never caught the tone of cynicism
which was the fashion among the men of his circle; and still
less was his secret and unspoken creed akin to theirs. He had
been brought up in a home where intense and tender conjugal
affection was rendered doubly attractive by the presence of
good sense, and that perfect good-breeding which is unconscious of its own existence; and his favorite books, from childhood upwards, were those in which the image of such a home
was painted in the brightest colors and gilded by the noblest
associations. He loved Homer, because Homer "always spoke
well of women." In the teeth of Athenian prejudice, which
so good a scholar respected more than the prejudices of his
own day, he could hardly venture to give the same reason for
loving Euripides; but probably no one ever praised, read, re-
cited, analyzed, and translated any piece of poetry so frequently, for the benefit of so many different individuals, as did Fox
the passage where Alcestis, before her act of self-sacrifice, takes

leave of her bridal-chamber.[1] And his romance was of the heart, and not of the fancy. There have been few better husbands than Fox, and probably none so delightful; for no known man ever devoted such powers of pleasing to the single end of making a wife happy. When once he had a home of his own, the world outside, with its pleasures and ambitions, became to him an object of indifference, and at last of repugnance. Nothing but the stings of a patriotic conscience, sharpened by the passionate importunity of partisans whose fidelity had entitled them to an absolute claim upon his services, could prevail upon him to spend opposite, or even on, the Treasury bench an occasional fragment of the hours which were never long enough when passed at Mrs. Fox's work-table with Congreve or Molière as a third in company.[2]

---

[1] In 1806 he lent the "Alcestis" to his young secretary without telling him that there was anything exceptionally touching in it, and then covertly watched the countenance of the reader for an indication of the manner in which the lines would affect one who came upon them unexpectedly. Macaulay, in the margin of his Euripides, marked the passage as "the most beautiful narration that I remember in the whole Attic drama;" and, as his annotations show, he liked it all the better because Fox had liked it before him.

[2] In 1800 Fox came up from St. Anne's Hill at an important crisis, on the understanding that he would have to remain only two nights in town. "When," said Lord Holland, "he heard that the debate was postponed in consequence of Mr. Pitt's indisposition, he sat silent and overcome, as if the intelligence of some great calamity had reached his ears. I saw tears steal down his cheeks; so vexed was he at being detained from his garden, his books, and his cheerful life in the country." "Never did a letter," wrote Fox, in 1801, "arrive at a worse time, my dear young one, than yours this morning. A sweet westerly wind, a beautiful sun, all the thorns and elms just budding, and the nightingales just beginning to sing; though the blackbirds and thrushes would have been quite sufficient to have refuted any arguments in your letter. Seriously speaking, I cannot conceive what you mean by everybody agreeing that something may be *now* done. I beg, at least, not to be included in the holders of that opinion. I would, nevertheless, go to town if I saw any chance of my going being serviceable to the public, or (which, in my view of things, is exactly the same thing) to the party which I love both as a party and on account of many of the individuals who compose it." "I wish I were member for Westminster," said Lord Lauderdale. "I

Fox, from twenty to twenty-five, had doubtless not the air of a rigid moralist. The world could not believe that the king of the macaronis wore the most audacious costumes, and carried the largest nosegay in London, for nothing; and the suspicions of the world were freely expressed by the verse-writers of society.

> " Here Charles his native eloquence refined,
> Pleased at the toilet, in the senate shined ;
> And North approved, and Amoret looked kind."

But he was involved in no overt scandal. He broke up no man's home. He did not add a paragraph to the chronicle of sin and misery in which companions and relatives of his own conspicuously figured. A Lovelace never would have won or valued the enthusiastic friendship with which Fox was honored by so many high-minded women, whose loyalty to his interests at a great crisis has furnished some of the most agreeable among the stock anecdotes of English history. The secret of the certainty with which he pleased those of the other sex who were best worth pleasing is clearly revealed in the letters addressed by the Duchess of Devonshire to her mother, and still more clearly in the letters which Fox addressed to the duchess herself. His notion of true gallantry was to treat women as beings who stood on the same intellectual table-land as himself; to give them the very best of his thought and his knowledge, as well as of his humor and his eloquence; to invite and weigh their advice in seasons of difficulty; and, if ever they urged him to steps which his judgment or his conscience disapproved, not to elude them with half-contemptuous banter, but to convince them by plain-spoken and serious remonstrance.[1] The arts by which Fox

wish I were a Scotch peer," replied Fox; "for then I should be disqualified."

[1] " My dear Duchess," Fox wrote, in February, 1806, when the Whig ministry was forming, " your note has distressed me to the greatest degree. I told Lord —— explicitly that it was very doubtful whether I should have anything to propose to him; and, indeed, it is quite impossible now, unless your brother would give up Lord Althorpe's having a place at one of the boards. Can I give up Jack Townshend, or Courte-

retained the affectionate regard of the Duchess of Devonshire, until it was elevated into a devotion honorable to herself and to him, belong to a later and graver period of their lives ; but allusions to the qualities which first recommended him to her admiration and esteem are scattered, only too sparsely, through the earlier portion of her familiar correspondence. "We returned to Chatsworth this morning," she wrote on the fourteenth of August, 1777. "Mr. Fox came in the evening from town—Charles Fox *à l'ordinaire*. I have always thought that his great merit is his amazing quickness in seizing any subject. He seems to have the particular talent of knowing more about what he is saying, and with less pains, than anybody else. His conversation is like a brilliant player at billiards : the strokes follow one another, piff! paff! And what makes him more entertaining is his being here with Mr. Townshend and the Duke of Devonshire; for their being so much together in town makes them show off one another. Their chief topics are politics and Shakespeare. As for the latter, they all three have the most astonishing memory for it. I suppose I shall be able in time to go through a play as they do."

But Charles Fox's chivalry did not stop with the great and the fortunate.

> "Then gently scan your brother man,
> Still gentler sister woman,"

was the saying of a poet with whom, for good and evil, he

---

nay, or Fitzpatrick, or Lord Robert for any of these young lords? Indeed, indeed, my friends are hard upon me."

That was the strain in which, on occasion, Fox would write to the Duchess of Devonshire. How she wrote of him is prettily exemplified in a letter of hers to Lord Hartington, dated the twenty-third of the previous month. "Mr. Fox was with your father to-day, and pleased him much by his manner about Pitt. Your father said it was impossible not to feel shocked at the death of a person of such importance and former consideration. Mr. Fox agreed, and said that to him it appeared as if there was something missing in the world. The more you know of Mr. Fox's character, the more you will admire the great features of his mind—the vast comprehension that takes in any subject, united to a candor and benevolence that render him as amiable as he is great."

had much in common;[1] and it was the precept which, of all others, he honored by his observance. " Do you not hate that fellow ?" he was once asked, with reference to a member of Parliament who irritated the Whigs by the virulence of his speaking, and bored them by its prolixity. " Ah, well!" replied Fox, " I am a bad hater." And though, during his first half-dozen sessions, he could sometimes work himself up into the illusion that he detested political opponents whom he would never have voluntarily and deliberately injured, his indulgence towards the weaker half of humanity was already without stint or limit. Whenever, rich or poor, blameless or erring, a woman was in trouble, she always was sure of a champion in Fox. The spring sitting of 1772 was, as far as he was concerned, one long effort for the protection of the helpless and the unhappy. He advocated, without success, an alteration of the laws which rendered the mother of an illegitimate child liable to a degrading punishment if she confessed the birth, and which condemned her to the gallows if she was shamed or terrified into concealing it. He successfully opposed a bill framed to forbid the marriage of a divorced wife with her seducer—an ordinance which would have made sad havoc with the prospects of some of the most famous ladies of the day. But he was never so much in earnest as when inveighing against that penal legislation which he regarded as a standing insult to his own parents, whose love-story it desecrated by linking it with the idea of the constable, the dock, and the jail. He denounced the statute which refused the benefit of clergy to any one who carried off a woman with the intention of forcing her into marriage, on the ground that an angry father or guardian would not be in a temper to discriminate very nicely between an elopement and an abduction; while the wife, as no longer a legal witness, might see her husband hanged for a crime against herself in which she had been an accomplice before the act. And, eager to show that he could legislate with the wisest as

---

[1] " Burns," he said, " was about as clever a man as ever lived. Lord Sidmouth thought him a better poet than Cowper. I cannot say but he had a better understanding."

well as speak with the cleverest, he would not be satisfied until he had himself introduced a bill for the repeal of that Marriage Act of Lord Hardwicke's devising to which nineteen years had not reconciled Henry Fox or Henry Fox's son. His handling of the question was signalized by extraordinary dexterity, and quite as extraordinary heedlessness and caprice. On the seventh of April, by an easy and extemporaneous display of ability, the circumstantial and well-attested narrative of which reads like a miracle, he steered his enterprise safely through its first perils, under the fire of Burke's best oratory from one side of the House and Lord North's emphatic disapproval on the other. The impetus of that night's debate carried smoothly and silently, into the last stage but one, a measure upon which its author was too busy with his amusements to bestow any further trouble, while the Treasury managers kept on it a watchful and malevolent eye. On the nineteenth of May, Fox drove in from Newmarket just in time for a division which, by a majority of three to one, extinguished his hopes when they seemed to have reached the very edge of fruition; and with that catastrophe ended, for the present at least, his schemes for improving the relations between the sexes.

Erratic and abnormal as was the public career of Fox, his private life was just as little conformed to ordinary rules and precedents. No one thought of classing him among the common rakes and spendthrifts of the day, and still less among its respectabilities. So exceptional a personage did he appear to his own contemporaries that, in search of a comparison for him, they were in the habit of going back to Julius Cæsar; and it is not easy, even for a generation which thinks less about the Romans and knows more of the people who have come since them than the readers of the eighteenth century, to find any parallel for Charles Fox more recent than the young patrician who was worth proscribing at eighteen; who was a renowned orator at two-and-twenty; who led fashion almost from the moment that he assumed the toga; and who owed more money than Crassus ever gathered or Apicius squandered.

There exists at Brooks's Club a curious memorial of the society in which Fox lived, and of the constant and minute attention which that society bestowed upon all his proceedings. As far back as the reign of William the Third, foreigners had observed that, on matters great and small, the only sure test of English opinions was the state of the odds. Our ancestors were men of their hands—more ready with sword and purse than with word and pen—who regarded a duel as the natural issue of a quarrel, and a bet as the most authoritative solution of an argument. To drag through newspapers and law-courts the lengthening scandal of a dispute which a single interview in one of the parks would settle with credit, if not with satisfaction, to both parties was not more repugnant to their idea of what was becoming and convenient than to spend twenty minutes in confuting a man who had so little faith in his own view that he would not back it with twenty guineas. But, by the time George the Third was on the throne, persons of rank and position were tired of being challenged to stake their money by frequenters of public coffee-houses whose capacity to pay was doubtful, and about whose anticipations as to the date of the coming dissolution and the destination of the next blue ribbon they did not care a farthing. The first London clubs of the model to which that name is now exclusively applied were instituted, among other kindred purposes, with the object of providing the world of fashion with a central office for making wagers, and a registry for recording them. And so it comes about that the betting-book at Brooks's has an interest of its own which resembles nothing in any library or museum in the country. The entries in its pages, most characteristic of the time and the men, standing, each in their proper order, between the covers within which they were originally written—uniform in their general character, but with variety of detail as inexhaustible as the circumstances of our national history and the changes in our national manners —form a volume which is to an ordinary collection of autographs what the "Liber Veritatis" of Claude is to a portfolio of detached sketches by the great masters. Fifty guineas that Thurlow gets a tellership of the Exchequer for his son; fifty guineas that Mademoiselle Heinel does not dance at the opera-house next winter; fifty guineas that two thousand people were at the Pantheon last evening; fifty guineas that Lord Ilchester gives his first vote in opposition, and hits eight out of his first ten pheasants; three hundred to fifty from a nobleman who appreciated the privileges of a bachelor that the Duke of Devonshire, Lord Cholmondeley, and two given commoners are married before him; five guineas down, to receive a hundred if the Duke of Queensberry dies before half an hour after five in the afternoon of the twenty-seventh of June, 1773; a hundred guineas on the Duke of Queensberry's life against Lord Palmerston's; a hundred guineas that Lord Derby does not see the next general election; and a hundred guineas, between two unusually discreet members of the club, that some one in their eye does not live ten years from the present date.[1] The betting was hottest in war time, and during the period while a notorious criminal remained untried or unhanged; for the disciples of George Selwyn were never tired of calculating the chances of people dying elsewhere than in their beds. The old yellow leaves are scored thick with bets that one of the Perreaus would be hanged; that neither of them would be hanged, and that Mrs. Rudd would be admitted to bail; that Dr. Dodd would be executed within two months; that he would anticipate the gallows by suicide; and that if he killed himself, it would be by pistol, and not by poison. Fitzpatrick, flying at higher game, laid five hundred guineas to ten that none of the cabinet were beheaded by that day three years; and another gentleman, who believed the melancholy contingency to be not only possible, but probable, was free-spoken enough to name his minister. Still bolder spirits did not shrink from placing their money upon prophecies which the delicacy of a later age has taken effectual care to

---

[1] There is nothing in the book at Brooks's (or, at any rate, nothing which has been left unblotted) equal to the wager laid elsewhere by two men of family on the survivorship of their respective fathers—a wager which, as it happened, fate had already decided. Before the news arrived, the heart of one of the pair failed him, and he had made over his bet to Lord March.

render illegible; for, indeed, there was no event or experience in the whole compass of human existence which March and his friends thought it necessary to exclude from the field of legitimate speculation. It was in allusion to quite the most innocent class of these personal and domestic wagers that Lord Mountford, when asked whether his daughter was going to present him with a grandchild, replied, " Upon my word, I do not know. I have no bet upon it."

For ten years, from 1771 onwards, Charles Fox betted frequently, largely, and judiciously on the social and political occurrences of the time. He laid two hundred guineas that Lord North would be First Lord of the Treasury in March, 1773, and twenty guineas that he would still be First Lord in March, 1776, " bar death;" a hundred and fifty to fifty that the Tea Act was not repealed in the winter session of 1774; twenty guineas that Lord Northington, who took more kindly to water than his father, did not swim one mile the next time he went into the Thames or any other river; ten guineas down, to receive five hundred whenever Turkey in Europe belonged to a European power or powers; and a guinea down, to receive fifty " whenever Mr. Croft forgets two by honors in Mr. Fox's presence." He was fond of wagers the settlement of which was dependent upon an antecedent condition. " Lord Ossory betts Mr. Charles Fox 100 guineas to 10 that Dr. North is not Bishop of Durham this day 2 months, provided the present Bishop dies within that time." " Mr. E. Foley betts Mr. Charles Fox 50 guineas England is at war with France this day two years, supposing Louis the Fifteenth dead." And Mr. Charles Fox himself bets a hundred guineas against the Duke of Devonshire having the Garter within seven years, "the Duke to live, or no bet." When the Perreaus were on their trial for forgery, Fox was concerned in five bets out of a consecutive group of six; and it is pleasant to remark that, even in his hours of sport, the young reformer of the penal code was on the side of mercy.[1] Many pages together during

---

[1] "The town," said Walpole, with a hit at the patronage which the Court so freely bestowed upon Jacobite writers, " is very busy about a

1774 and 1775 are half covered by his unformed but frank, resolute, and most readable handwriting; and no single name appears anything like so often as his, until, at the outbreak of the Revolutionary war, under the excitement of the downward and upward rush of consols, and of defeats on land alternating with victories at sea, Sheridan brought forth from its retirement the almost neglected volume, and turned it into something very like a private betting-book of his own.[1] But the wagers made by Fox are not so suggestive as the wagers made about him. The club, which was so helpful to him in later life, and which is still so faithful to his memory, seems to have watched him, from the very first, with a sort of paternal intentness. "Lord Bolingbroke gives a guinea to Mr. Charles Fox, and is to receive a Thousand from him whenever the debt of this country amounts to 171 millions. Mr. Fox is not to pay the 1000 till he is a member of His Majesty's Cabinet." "Lord Clermont has given Mr. Crawfurd 10 guineas upon condition of receiving £500 from him whenever Mr. Charles Fox shall be worth £100,000, clear of debts." Such are two among those allusions to the opening of his political prospects and the waning of his pecuniary fortunes which fill a larger space in the records of Brooks's even than prognostications about the length of Lord North's first Parliament and the health and life of a Certain Great Person.

Mr. Crawford must have spent his ten guineas with a safe conscience. There was quite as much likelihood that Great Britain would grow solvent under Lord North and Sandwich as that Charles Fox would ever be worth his plum. Brilliant

---

history of two Perreaus and a Mrs. Rudd, who are likely to be hanged for misapplying their ingenuity. They drew bills, instead of rising from the pillory to pensions by coining anecdotes against the author and friends of the Revolution."

[1] In 1794 Sheridan was responsible for eight bets running, on subjects which varied in importance from the question of the French having failed or succeeded in occupying Amsterdam to the question of the shortest way from one house to another being by Sackville Street or Bond Street. Fox entered his last wager in 1795; but for years previously he had almost disused the practice.

at whist, quinze, and piquet, and almost invariably successful
in wagers where he backed his knowledge of the world or his
insight into politics, he never could resist the attractions of
that table where skill could not protect him from the influence of his terrible ill-luck; and he too often matched himself against antagonists who made hazard a game of chance
only in name. A half-century afterwards, Lord Egremont
told Lord Holland that mature reflection, aided by enlarged
experience, had convinced him that the constant and im-
moderate superiority which certain players maintained over
Charles Fox and other young men was not to be explained
by the fortune of the dice; but if any one, he added, had
dared to hint such a suspicion at the time, the losers themselves would have torn him in pieces. The highest play ever
known in London took place during the three years that preceded the American war.[1] Five thousand pounds were staked
on one card at faro, and seventy thousand pounds changed
hands in a single evening. Stephen Fox once sat down with
thirteen thousand pounds, and rose without a farthing; and
his brother was quoted daily, in prose and verse, as the type

---

[1] "The young men of quality," wrote Horace Walpole, with reference
to the year 1772, "had a club at Almack's, where they played only for
rouleaux of fifty pounds each; and generally there was ten thousand
pounds in specie on the table. Lord Holland had paid above twenty
thousand pounds for his two sons. Nor were the manners of the game-
sters, or even their dresses for play, undeserving of notice. They began
by pulling off their embroidered clothes, and put on frieze great-coats, or
turned their coats inside outwards for luck. They put on pieces of leather,
such as are worn by footmen when they clean the knives, to save their
laced ruffles; and, to guard their eyes from the light, and to prevent
tumbling their hair, wore high-crowned hats with broad brims, and
adorned with flowers and ribbons."

The account would be incredible but for a stage direction in Foote's
"Nabob," which was played in 1773: "Act the Second. Sir Matthew Mite
in his gaming dress, a waiter attending." The waiter was a servant at
one of the clubs, who gave the Nabob lessons in the art of playing with
style and losing with grace. "Well, Dick," said Sir Matthew at the end
of the interview, "you will go down to my steward and teach him the
best method of making a rouleau. And, d'ye hear, let him give you one
for your pains."

of the unlucky gamester. Walpole, enumerating the things in
the world that were best worth finding, bracketed together
the longitude, the philosopher's stone, the certificate of the
Duchess of Kingston's first marriage, the missing books of
Livy, " and all that Charles Fox had lost." And from among
the countless allusions to the prodigal that occur in the satires
of the day, it may be permitted to cull a few rhymes, the jovial ring of which makes amends for their lack of point and
elegance:

> " At Almack's of pigeons I am told there are flocks,
> But it's thought the completest is one Mr. Fox;
> If he touches a card, if he rattles the box,
> Away fly the guineas of this Mr. Fox.
> He has met, I'm afraid, with so many hard knocks
> That cash is not plenty with this Mr. Fox.
> In gaming, 'tis said, he's the stoutest of cocks—
> No man can play deeper than this Mr. Fox;
> And he always must lose, for the strongest of locks
> Cannot keep any money for this Mr. Fox.
> No doubt such behavior exceedingly shocks
> The friends and acquaintance of this Mr. Fox;
> And they wish from their souls they could put in the stocks,
> And make an example of, this Mr. Fox.
> He's exceedingly curious in coats and in frocks;
> So the tailor's a pigeon to this Mr. Fox.
> He delights much in hunting, though fat as an ox.
> I pity the horses of this Mr. Fox:
> They are probably most of them lame in the hocks;
> Such a heavy-made fellow is this Mr. Fox."

In defiance of nature, which seemed to have modelled him
for any other class of pursuits, Fox was an ardent, a many-
sided, and, in some departments, a most accomplished sports-
man. If it was possible for him to enjoy himself more at one
time than at another, he was most actively alive to the charms
of existence when behind his pointers or his spaniels; and, like
all men of his temperament, he shot better after advancing
years had taken off the first edge of his keenness. But he
did not require a gun to tempt him abroad. He prided himself on his endurance as a pedestrian, and on the steadiness of
pace which enabled him almost infallibly to calculate the dis-

tance that he traversed by the time that he spent over it. The friends of his later life could not please him better than by disputing whether this or that village was nine or eleven miles from St. Anne's Hill, in order to give him the opportunity of solving the problem by a walk. When a lad at Oxford, he trudged the fifty-six miles between Hertford College and Holland House in the course of a summer's day, and only broke the journey for a lunch of bread and cheese and porter, in payment for which, observing the usual proportion between the market-value of his pleasures and the price that they cost him, he left his gold watch in pawn with the innkeeper. During a tour in Kerry he swam twice round the Devil's Punchbowl, as if in the West of Ireland he had not enough water from overhead.[1] He was a cricketer; and would have been famous as a batsman if he had taken the game as seriously as he took chess and tennis. "My love to Carlisle," he wrote to Selwyn from King's Gate in August, 1771; "and tell him we have a cricket party here, at which I am very near the best player; so he may judge of the rest." In and out of his ground as freely as if it had been a Lordship of the Admiralty or the Treasury, it may well be imagined that, in the heat of youth, he was an unreliable partner at the wicket. When past five-and-fifty, and as much older than his years in body as he was younger in all else, he never failed to run himself out amidst the reproachful cries of spectators to whom it seemed almost a miracle that he could run at all. Trap-ball he played in his chair to the very last, and so skilfully as to deprive him of all excuse for the barefaced advantages which he took over the very small Whigs in whose company he was as much at home as ever he had been with their grandfathers.

The health which he began with was wonderful. A spoonful of rhubarb, he cheerfully boasted, cured all the ills to which his flesh was heir; although the maladies which his careless but laborious mode of life too early brought upon him ere long

---

[1] When he next met Herbert of Muckross in London, "Pray tell me," he said, "is that shower at Killarney over yet?"

required sterner remedies. He would gladly have been thinner. But he was too much of a man to be ashamed of a misfortune which he did his utmost to correct;[1] for, in whatever pastime he was engaged, he always contrived to get out of it the greatest practicable amount of bodily exercise. "When his horse ran," we are told, "he was all eagerness and anxiety. He placed himself where the animal was to make a push, or where the race was to be most strongly contested. From this spot he eyed the horses advancing with the most immovable look; he breathed quicker as they accelerated their pace; and, when they came opposite to him, he rode in with them at full speed, whipping, spurring, and blowing as if he would have infused his whole soul into his favorite racer. But when the race was over, whether he won or lost seemed to be a matter of perfect indifference to him, and he immediately directed his conversation to the next race, whether he had a horse to run or not." There is a passage in the Chatsworth correspondence which, while it apparently alludes to the almost inconceivable circumstance of Fox having been in the habit of riding his own matches, more probably refers to his vicarious exertions near the winning-post. "Mr. Fox returned this morning. He travelled all night, and yet won one or two races, which, considering his not having been abed, and his size, is doing a great deal." In 1772 he netted sixteen thousand pounds by laying against the favorite, who was beaten by half a neck; but, as the owner of a stable, he did not escape the fate which has so often befallen more cautious and less busy men. His own explanation of his frequent defeats was that his horses were as good as those of his neighbors, but that they never would gal-

---

[1] Lord Holland's eldest son was fatter than his brother, and minded it even less. When a bill to abolish the observance of the thirtieth of January was introduced into the Commons, Stephen Fox raised a laugh by urging that it was very hard to impose abstinence upon the world in general, when the descendants of the martyred monarch, to look at them, so evidently never fasted. At a fancy ball in the Pantheon he was followed about by a Smithfield butcher, feeling him in the ribs, and guessing at his weight in stones, until two very Merry Wives of Windsor claimed him as their Falstaff, and fastened themselves upon him for the rest of the evening.

lop fast enough to tire themselves. Of these prudent animals he had at one time thirty in training; and how fairly he ran them, and how much he lost by them from first to last, may be conjectured from what is known about his racing partner, Lord Foley—who, when he gave up the turf, left behind him a reputation for honor and good-fellowship which is still a tradition of the Jockey Club, and a fortune which had once included above a hundred thousand pounds of ready money.

The world, never tired of gossiping about the young man's extravagance, was not in the dark as to the source which fed it. "Ask Foley," said Lord Lyttelton, "ask Charles Fox what they think of modern infidelity; and they will tell you that the Jews themselves, that unbelieving race, have deserted the standard of scepticism, and, having borne the stigma of spiritual unbelief for upwards of sixteen hundred years, are at this moment groaning beneath the effects of temporal credulity." And, indeed, to an heir-apparent who had experienced the difficulties of borrowing on the reversion of a peerage, the all but unlimited credit which Lord Holland's younger son was unfortunate enough to obtain must have appeared nothing less than a prodigy. The poets of society attributed his success with the money-lenders to those powers of oratorical seduction which had so often beguiled the House of Commons into a scrape; and the golden youth of the day spoke with envy of one who had at his command

> "Soft words to mollify the miser's breast,
> And lull relenting Usury to rest;
> Bright beams of wit to still the raging Jew,
> Teach him to dun no more and lend anew."

But it was not the charm of eloquence that drew together the crowd of bill-discounters who kicked their heels till three in the afternoon in the waiting-room which Charles Fox was accustomed to call his Jerusalem Chamber. It was the knowledge that only one very bad life stood between their client, whose own vitality was so unquestionable, and an estate which was still among the richest in the kingdom. But even those capitalists of St. Mary Axe who counted the years during which Lord Holland had manipulated the Exchequer balances, and who had watched Stephen Fox as he panted up the steps by which the pavement of St. James's Street ascended from Pall Mall to Piccadilly, would at length have shaken their heads over the young man's reiterated demands for cash, unless he had brought with him other guarantees than his expectations. " The macaronis," wrote Walpole, in July, 1773, " are their *ne plus ultra*. Charles Fox is already so like Julius Cæsar that he owes a hundred thousand pounds. Lord Carlisle pays fifteen hundred and Mr. Crewe twelve hundred a year for him ;" and Walpole underrated the sacrifices that Charles Fox's friends had made to an attachment which no misconduct on his part could sever, or even strain.

> " A love from me to thee
> Is firm, whate'er thou dost,"

was the text for every letter that Lord Carlisle wrote to or about Fox from the country - seat which the good - natured young peer could not afford to leave, on account of the pecuniary distress in which the improvidence of his comrade had involved him. Each fresh instance of prodigality that was reported to him from London or Newmarket affected that generous heart with anxiety for the character, the health, and the happiness of his friend before he found time to compute and lament its calamitous influence upon his own fortunes.

" It gives me great pain," he wrote to Selwyn, " to hear that Charles Fox begins to be unreasonably impatient at losing. I fear it is the prologue to much fretfulness of temper; for disappointment in raising money, and serious reflections upon his situation, will occasion him many disagreeable moments. They will be the more painful when he reflects that he is not following the natural bent of his genius; for that would lead him to serious inquiry and laudable pursuits. I believe there never was a person yet created who had the faculty of reasoning like him. His judgments are never wrong; his decision is formed quicker than any man's I ever conversed with ; and he never seems to mistake but in his own affairs. When he tells you that he will not talk to you upon his circumstances, he is certainly right; for, if your head is not so much heated with chimerical schemes as his own, or if you are not prepared to hear of enchantment and miracles, you will never enter into his manner of reasoning, or derive any comfort from those resources which he brings into his picture. Adieu, my dear George! I have written a very dull letter. I sometimes am determined never to think about Charles's affairs, or his conduct about them; for they are like religion—the more one thinks, the more one is puzzled." "I hear," he says, later on, "Charles cannot go to perform his part at the Winterslow play on account of his eyes. I am afraid his eyes are otherwise employed. When you see him, pray press him to write to Lord Stavordale. If you are serious with him, he must sacrifice two minutes and a half to writing, folding up, and sealing. The more I live, the more I think I shall alter my way of life very essentially for the future. I feel more ambitious here than at Almack's, among a set of people who seem to have none, except Charles, and he seems to have as much in ruining himself as in any other pursuit." "Indeed," he urges on a third occasion, "Charles must take care of himself. He has very bad humors which require great attention, or they will make his life miserable. As he is so careful in every other part of his conduct, he will not be consistent with himself to neglect his health. If there should be any change for the better in his circumstances, Hare will not lose that opportunity of speaking seriously to him about that business. But what he says is true. It would be useless to torment him about it when he has not a guinea: so there it ends for the present."

This letter was written in the early spring of 1773; and, before the year had run out, the crash came. The signal for it was the birth of the boy whom Charles Fox loved with more than a father's love; the false rumor of whose death was the most poignant sorrow that he ever knew; and who, in the absence of children of his own, repaid him in full measure that attention and affection in which his parents had never found him wanting. The first service which the future Lord Holland rendered to his uncle was that of checking him in his career of senseless profusion. Gibbon has recorded the comment with which the young minister received the interesting tidings. "My brother Ste's son," said Charles, "is a second Messiah, born for the destruction of the Jews;" but, as a matter of fact, the happy event proved to be the making of his professional and the salvation of his private creditors. The flood of unpaid accounts and renewed acceptances which at once poured in from every quarter enlightened Lord Holland on the desperate position into which Charles had floundered. Lord Carlisle, most reluctantly obeying his bounden duty as a husband and father, laid his claim before the parents of his friend in a letter which, if nothing else remained from his pen, would of itself stamp him as everything that a true nobleman should be. Lord Holland confronted the portentous situation like the man of honor and courage which, with all his faults, he was. High or low, exacting or considerate, grasping Jew or good Samaritan, no one was a penny the worse for having helped and trusted his favorite boy. Much was paid on the spot; much was extinguished by annuities which gradually fell in; and by the time that all was clear the Fox property was less by a hundred and forty thousand pounds as the consequence of three years of childish giddiness and misbehavior. Charles was ready enough to do anything that his father would sanction towards alleviating the burden which he had imposed upon the family. There are symptoms in the book at Brooks's that he was not unaffected by a touch of the only generous envy—that sense of self-abasement with which a man who lives upon others regards those among his contemporaries who owe everything to their own exertions. "Lord Northington betts Mr. Charles Fox 20 guineas that he (Mr. Fox) is not called to the barr before this time four years." "Mr. Burgoyne betts Mr. Charles Fox 50 guineas that four members of the club are married or dead before Charles Fox is called to the bar." But, while he himself had got as far as laying money that he would turn his extraordinary gifts to some remunerative purpose, the public, and perhaps his friends, had other and easier schemes for his maintenance. It was said that he was to marry one of the greatest heiresses in the country, on the condition that he should never lose more than a hundred pounds in one bet or at one sitting.

Lord Holland was asked whether the report was true. "I earnestly hope so," he replied; "for then he will be obliged to go to bed on at least one night in his life." But even if there had been anything in it, the match never came off; and Fox was exposed, fleeced and unmated, to the compassion of the world—" the world" (said Horace Walpole), "which talks of Wilkes at the top of the wheel, and of Charles Fox at the bottom. All between is a blank."

Fox was unfortunate in having Walpole for the chronicler of his follies, but not of his achievements. The great memoir-writer was daily hearing some fresh story of the doings at Almack's—which he had full leisure to transcribe and little disinclination to over-color—while he had no opportunity of seeing the younger man on his best, or at any rate his strongest, side; for just as Fox entered Parliament, Horace Walpole left it. He had always hated electioneering. To dine with two hundred burgesses amidst bumpers, songs, and tobacco; to lead off at the town ball; "to hear misses play on the harpsichord, and to see an alderman's copies of Rubens and Carlo Maratti," were tortures to which nothing would have induced him to submit, except a feeling of gratitude towards the constituency which had stood bravely and faithfully by Sir Robert in the darkest hour of his checkered life.[1] But five-and-twenty years of late nights and bad air and dull speeches at length cured Horace Walpole of all desire to remain in a place the method of entering which was so shocking to his tastes and deranging to his habits; and at the dissolution of 1768 he did not again court the suffrages of his electors. "The comfort I feel," he wrote from Arlington Street, "in sitting peaceably here, instead of being at Lynn in the high fever of a contested election, which at best would end in my being carried

---

[1] "My ancient aunt," he wrote, in 1761, "came over to Lynn to see me. The first thing she said to me, although we have not met these sixteen years, was, 'Child, you have done a thing to-day that your father never did in all his life. You sat as they carried you. He always stood the whole time.' 'Madam,' said I, 'when I am placed in a chair, I conclude I am to sit in it. Besides, as I cannot imitate my father in great things, I am not ambitious of mimicking him in little ones.'"

about that large town like a pope at a bonfire, is very great.
I do not think, when that function is over, that I shall repent
my resolution.   Could I hear oratory beyond my Lord Chatham's?   Will there ever be parts equal to Charles Townshend's?   Will George Grenville cease to be the most tiresome
of beings?"   Nor was the sober exultation with which he threw
off his political fetters damped by a longer experience of freedom.   "Ambition," he told Sir Horace Mann in 1771, "should
be a passion of youth; not, as it generally is, of the end of
life.   What joy can it be to govern the grandchildren of our
contemporaries?   It is but being a more magnificent kind of
schoolmaster.   I was told that I should regret quitting my
seat in Parliament; but I knew myself better than those
prophets did.   Four years are past, and I have done nothing
but applaud my resolution."   He lived in the great world,
but outside the busy world, contented, tranquil, and occupied;
concerning himself with the conflict of parties as little as the
country gentleman who was out with his hounds between the
armies on the morning of Edgehill; matching china; storing
anecdotes; keeping the anniversary of the day on which he
found Count Grammont's miniature; and holding up Strawberry Hill and its owner as the model and example for the
possessors of lordlier palaces and more turbulent ambitions.
"Oh! if my Lord Temple knew what pleasures he could create for himself at Stowe, he would not harass a shattered car-
cass, and sigh to be insolent at St. James's.   For my part, I
say with the Bastard in "King John"—though with a little
more reverence, and only as touching his ambition—

> 'Oh, old Sir Robert, father, on my knee
> I give Heaven thanks I was not like to thee.' "

Walpole, like a wise man, did not mistake where his happiness lay.   He never wished himself back in the lobbies, and
still less on the benches of St. Stephen's; but what he gained
by his retirement from politics was as nothing to the loss
which that step inflicted upon the readers of our day and the
orators of his.   It is difficult to say whether Fox and Burke
would have profited more in fame, or we in pleasure, if the

artist—who at four-and-twenty sketched for us with such
vividness and fidelity every changing phase of the Titanic
party conflict which raged for months before and after the
Christmas of 1741—had left us a picture of the debates on
the Middlesex election and the prosecution of the printers,
painted in the full maturity of his rare and remarkable powers.   Once, and once only, on the seventh of April, 1772, did
Walpole show himself again in his ancient haunts. "Though
I had never," he wrote, "been in the House of Commons since
I had quitted Parliament, the fame of Charles Fox raised my
curiosity, and I went this day to hear him. He made his
motion for leave to bring in a bill to correct the old Marriage
Bill; and he introduced it with ease, grace, and clearness, and
without the prepared and elegant formality of a young speaker. He did not shine particularly; but his sense and facility
showed that he could shine. Lord North, who had declared
that he would not oppose the introduction of a new bill, now
unhandsomely opposed it to please the Yorkes and the Peers,
and spoke well. Burke made a fine and long oration against
the motion. He spoke with a choice and variety of language,
a profusion of metaphors, and yet with a correctness in his
diction that were surprising. His fault was copiousness above
measure, and he dealt abundantly too much in establishing
general positions. Charles Fox, who had been running about
the House talking to different persons, and scarce listening to
Burke, rose with amazing spirit and memory; answered both
Lord North and Burke; ridiculed the arguments of the former, and confuted those of the latter, with a shrewdness that
as much exceeded that of his father, in embracing all the arguments of his antagonists, as he did in his manner and delivery. Lord Holland was always confused before he could clear
up the point; fluttered and hesitated; wanted diction; and
labored only one forcible conclusion. Charles Fox had great
facility. His words flowed rapidly; but he had nothing of
Burke's variety of language or correctness, nor his method.
Yet his arguments were far more shrewd. Burke was indefatigable, learned, and versed in every branch of eloquence.
Fox was dissipated, dissolute, idle beyond measure. He was

that very morning returned from Newmarket, where he had
lost some thousand pounds the preceding day. He had stopped at Hockerel, where he found company; had sat up drinking all night; and had not been in bed when he came to move
his bill, which he had not even drawn up. This was genius
—was almost inspiration. The House dividing, Lord North
was beaten by sixty-two to sixty-one—a disgraceful event for
a prime-minister."

The result must have satisfied Fox, who held the only true
crown of rhetoric to be a good division. He was no holiday
declaimer. His eloquence, like that of Sir Robert Walpole,
"was for use, and not for show." There probably never was
such a famous and attractive orator who gave so much care
to the substance of his discourse, and so little to the trappings.
His speaking, like that of all men who can speak to any purpose, was the full and exact expression of his true self. "I
do not believe it, sir," said Johnson to a critic who opined that
Burke was of the school of Cicero. "Burke has great knowledge, great fluency of words, and great promptness of ideas,
so as to speak with great illustration on any subject that comes
before him. He does not speak like Cicero or like Demosthenes. He speaks as well as he can." And in like manner
Fox charmed and moved and persuaded because his oratory
was the faithful reflection of his ardent and sagacious nature.
"Mr. Pitt," Porson used to say, "conceives his sentences before he utters them. Mr. Fox throws himself into the middle
of his, and leaves it to God Almighty to get him out again."
"Pitt," said Fox, "is never at a loss for *the* word, and I am
never at a loss for *a* word," and (he might have added) for
an idea. Circling round and about the point, but never leaving it; composing at the moment, and for the moment, and,
as he laughingly confessed, forgetting every line of every
speech which he had ever uttered; bringing out a thought or
a circumstance the very instant that it occurred to him with
the certainty that, in the impetuous rush of his declamation,
he never would recover it again if he once allowed it to fall
for half a minute into the rear—he almost seemed as if, in
the words of Sterne, he was catching the ideas which Heaven

intended for another man. He repeated himself freely, frequently, and emphatically ; obeying, as he declared, his theory of the art, but more probably acting on the instinct of the orator, who will never leave his hearers alone until he has talked them over. And how willingly those hearers, at every period of his life, submitted themselves to the process of having the hard facts and clinching arguments in which he dealt dinned and pounded into their ears is evident from allusions which lie thick in every corner of the literature of his epoch. At one-and-twenty he had already been dubbed "the flower of oratory" by a poet far too thick-witted to do anything but reproduce the accepted judgment of the world; and in 1780 an acute and impartial observer bore witness how little he had wearied Parliament by ten years of perpetual speaking. A Prussian clergyman who had the courage to walk on foot through a country the inhabitants of which in those days treated nobody so badly as a foreigner, except a pedestrian, came in the course of his arduous journey to London, and went forthwith to see Fox in the House of Commons. "It is impossible for me," he writes, "to describe with what fire and persuasion he spoke, and how the Speaker in the chair incessantly nodded approbation from beneath his solemn wig, and innumerable voices incessantly called out 'Hear him! hear him!' And when there was the least sign that he intended to leave off speaking, they no less vociferously exclaimed, 'Go on!' and he continued to speak in this manner for nearly two hours."

So it was at the outset, and so it continued to the end. But, although his brother-senators heard him more and more willingly as years went on, Fox never turned so many votes as during his first half-dozen sessions, when party limits were still undefined, and party obligations far less strict than they afterwards became. "It is very well worth while," said Burke, in 1776, "for a man to take pains to speak well in Parliament. The House of Commons is a mixed body. It is by no means pure; but neither is it wholly corrupt, though there is a large proportion of corruption in it. There are many members who generally go with the minister, but who will

not go all lengths. There are many honest well-meaning country gentlemen who are in Parliament only to keep up the consequence of their families, and upon most of these a good
speech will have influence."[1] Such people were open to conviction, but they preferred to be convinced by one of their
own order. How closely allied was the feeling in Parliament
to the tone of society, every list of the House, and, still more,
every list of the Whig minority, shows. Lascelleses and
Townshends and Damers and Keppels and Cavendishes
come almost as thick as Campbells and Macphersons on the
old regimental rolls of the East India Company. Lord Hardwicke had four of his sons in the Commons together. Lord
Hertford was a disappointed man because he could only seat
five of his. But while ready to welcome any number of a family which they recognized, the well-born politicians of 1770
knew the secret of making public life uncomfortable to the
vulgar herd; and their less fastidious descendants must acknowledge with awe that they drew the line of demarcation
very high. A report that Sir Joshua Reynolds was to stand
for Plympton excited the mirthful resentment of fashionable
London to a height which encouraged Selwyn to punish the
offender with the most obvious of all his jokes.[2] And when
Selwyn himself was threatened by an influential timber-mer-
chant with an opposition in his own borough, the indignation
and contempt of St. James's Street passed the very utmost
bounds of decency. "My dear George," wrote Gilly Williams, "I am heartily sorry that this damned carpenter has
made matters so serious with you." "What can a man mean,"
asked Lord Carlisle, "who has not an idea separated from the
foot-square of a Norway deal plank, by desiring to be in Par-

---

[1] Bishop Watson has preserved the analysis of a division on a question
where the views of the court were on one side and the interests of the nation on the other. The Cornish boroughs furnished twenty-seven members
to the majority which voted with the ministers; the Cinque Ports, thirteen; and all the counties of England and Wales together, only twelve.

[2] "He is not to be laughed at," said Selwyn. "He may very well succeed in being elected; for Sir Joshua is the ablest man I know on a canvass."

liament? Perhaps if you could have got anybody to ask his reasons for such an unnatural attempt, the fact of his being unable to answer what he had never thought about would have made him desist. But these beasts are monstrously obstinate, and about as well-bred as the great dogs they keep in their yards. I hope to hear soon that you have chained this animal and prevented him from doing you much harm."

Gibbon (who, as a needy squire seeking to mend his fortune by politics, was at once admitted within the pale) found the Commons "a very agreeable coffee-house," with this advantage over the Lords, that its frequenters could go there in undress. Rigby, indeed, always appeared on the Treasury bench in a court suit of purple cloth, "with his sword thrust through the pocket;" but the great body of the members pursued their business with that disregard of ceremony which, as compared to people of his class in other countries, has long been a distinguishing mark of the English gentleman. "They come into the House," wrote the German pastor who has been quoted above, "in their great-coats, and with boots and spurs. It is not at all uncommon to see a member lying stretched out on one of the benches while others are speaking. Some crack nuts; others eat oranges, or whatever else is in season. There is no end to their going in and out; and as any one wishes to go out he places himself before the Speaker and makes his bow like a schoolboy asking his tutor's permission." Meeting just as the first touch of winter suggests to mankind the wisdom of getting together in cities to keep one another warm, breaking off in December for a month's hunting at some great nobleman's seat in the home counties, and finally dispersing to their country-houses in time for the last of the lilacs and the laburnums, the members of George the Third's second Parliament had little to complain of.[1] That easy-going assem-

---

[1] Fox's first Parliament was up in May four years out of the six. Official people grumbled wofully because the Birthday kept them in town till after the fourth of June. And yet Burke found it no easy matter to get his flock to London, even for so short a session. "I would wish," wrote the Duke of Richmond to him from Goodwood in November, 1772, "not to stir from hence till after Christmas, as I have engaged a large

bly, in its character of an aristocratic debating society, at once acknowledged Charles Fox as its hero; and in its social capacity it almost as soon accepted him as a favorite. The greatest master of the art of reply that Parliament ever saw, his colleagues all but unanimously pronounced him the best fellow that ever lived. The qualities by which he acquired that reputation are pleasantly indicated in an undated letter, probably of the year 1772, from his friend Crawford—who was a man of parts and vivacity, but too self-absorbed and affected ever to have made a successful politician. "You will be delighted," this gentleman wrote to Stephen Fox, "to hear that I had the misfortune to speak a few days ago in the House of Commons. If I was the oldest and dearest friend you had in the world, you could not have wished me to succeed worse than I did. It was a prepared speech; ill-timed, ill received, ill delivered, languid, plaintive, and everything as bad as possible. Add to all this that it was very long; because, being pompously begun, I did not know how the devil to get out of it. The only thing I said which was sensible or to the purpose was misrepresented by Burke. Charles was not ashamed to acknowledge me in my distress. He explained and defended what I had said with spirit, warmth, and great kindness to me. I am really more pleased at receiving a proof of kindness from Charles, whom I admire and love more and more every day, than I am hurt at not succeeding in a thing in which I had no right to succeed." Such was an early sample of the generous acts and genial words by which through thirty years of hopeless opposition Fox recompensed the services of the trusty body-guard who never deserted him for all that king or minister had to give. "I am much of opinion," wrote Lord Bathurst to Lady Suffolk when Walpole was in power, "that a cer-

---

party to come here on the first of December and stay a month to fox-hunt." "To act with any sort of effect," so Burke urged on Lord Rockingham, "the principal of your friends ought to be called to town a full week before the meeting. Lord John ought not to be allowed to plead any sort of excuse. He ought to be allowed a certain decent and reasonable portion of fox-hunting to put him in wind for the parliamentary race he is to run; but anything more is intolerable."

tain man, who has now by far the greatest levees of any subject in England, would find it difficult, after laying down his post, to make up a party at quadrille if he resolved to play only with three personal friends." Very different was the compliment paid to the Whigs, both leader and followers, at the most desperate, but in the eyes of every true member of the party the most memorable, period of their history. " There are only forty of them," it was said in 1794 ; " but every man of them would be hanged for Fox." [1]

People who in February, 1772, were told that Lord North had lost a subordinate, at once took it for granted that Lord Rockingham had gained a follower. " Charles Fox," wrote Gibbon, " is commenced patriot, and is already attempting to pronounce the words 'country,' 'liberty,' 'corruption,' with what success time will discover." But when he assured Lord Ossory that he was safe from the danger of going into opposition, Fox knew himself better than did any of his critics. His conduct during the spring and winter sessions of 1772 was the model for a young politician who has left the ministry on a point of conscience. After he had liberated his soul about the question, or rather the group of questions, which had banished him from office, he preserved a modest silence ; interfering

---

[1] What Fox must have been for Adam and Fitzpatrick, for Lord Derby, Lord John Townshend, and Lord Lauderdale may be judged from his behavior towards people whom he did not even know by name. When Pitt was doubtful about a face, he would look hard at its possessor until he came within speaking distance, and then would look uneasily away ; but Fox nodded to everybody who appeared to recognize him, or whom he fancied that he had seen before. The parish schoolmaster of Clapham —a strong Tory, as may well be supposed—went to the House of Commons to hear a debate, but could not make his way inside. A stout member who happened to be passing perceived that he was in difficulties ; rescued him from the tyranny of the doorkeepers ; carried him into the gallery ; pointed out Dundas, Whitbread, and Sheridan ; and answered all his questions about the business of the day. After a while the Speaker named Mr. Fox, and the awe-struck visitor beheld his protector rise from his seat and commence a furious attack upon the ministry. The young people at Clapham, among whom the man was something of an oracle, noticed that he never said a word against Fox from that time forward.

mildly and briefly on matters relating to the department in which he had served before his retirement. But he had given the ministers too marked a sample of his quality in the debates on the Marriage Bill for them to delude themselves into the belief that he would be content to sit forever among the army contractors and retired Anglo-Indians below the gangway, helping his former colleagues when they were in a difficulty over their Navy estimates, and telling for them in a division when a Treasury whip happened to be away at his dinner. North trusted him as the man in the story trusted the leopard's cub which had tasted his blood; and since Charles Fox could not be shot, there was nothing for it but to muzzle him with all despatch. The year which commenced with his resignation ended with a reconstruction of the government devised for the sole object of recovering his services and insuring the ministry against his possible hostility. A king's friend was thrust up-stairs into an Irish vice-treasurership; a nobleman who had been a friend of Lord Chatham was thrust down-stairs, and a large bag of public money flung after him; and the chair at the Treasury table, which had been emptied with so little ceremony towards individuals and at so great an expense to the taxpayer, was respectfully offered to Fox. The salary, poor for those days, did not amount to half of the thirty-five hundred a year which was paid to a Vice-treasurer of Ireland for living idle in London; but Charles had set his affections upon a post where he could learn the work and entitle himself to the reversion of the Chancellorship of the Exchequer. Fame he regarded as a prize more enticing, and certainly in his case less evanescent, than money. His father was supremely contented at seeing him once more settled in life; and the delight of the old peer was reflected in the letters of his correspondents. "I am much obliged," wrote a trusty friend of the family, "by your kindness in acquainting me of the arrangement made in favor of Charles. I congratulate you and Lady Holland upon it most sincerely, as I am persuaded that this event will be attended by many circumstances which must give you both pleasure. I make no doubt that his present position will soon make a great change in other things, much to your satisfaction and my most ardent wishes."

The prediction was kindly meant and speedily falsified. It needed more than the possession of a small place and the hope of a great one to effect a radical change in the nature of Charles Fox. At whatever Board he might have been doing business in the daytime, when evening came he appeared in the House of Commons as headstrong, as unbridled, as impulsive as ever. In the historical debates of May, 1773—when the House of Commons first gravely and sedately condemned the rapacity of Lord Clive, and then balanced the accounts of patriotism and morality by putting on record its gratitude for his great and meritorious services to the country—Fox furiously declaimed against the conqueror of India as "the origin of all plunder, and the source of all robbery." His impetuosity, which arose from feelings honorable to him as a man, was not inconsistent with his obligations as an official; for the matter at issue was admittedly an open question, where the king differed from the prime-minister, while the attorney-general led for the attack, and the solicitor-general for the defence. But in the subsequent month, when the controversy was over and done with, and the glorious criminal had been censured, thanked, and pardoned—when Parliament had agreed to condone the past, and, intent upon securing Hindostan from oppression in the future, was calmly engaged upon the details of a bill for the better government of our Eastern dependencies—Fox interpolated in the discussion an invective hurled straight into Clive's face with such pointed and unsparing vehemence that the audience seemed to recognize an imitation of the apostrophe to Catiline in the mouth of a speaker who had too much of his own to borrow from any one. It does not require a Sallust to depict the consternation with which Lord North, the year before a general election, saw the most powerful Commoner in England, with ten votes in his pocket,[1] making his exit from the House in an

---

[1] "We shall come very strong into Parliament," wrote Clive, in 1768; "seven without opposition, and probably one more. Lord Clive, Shrews-

agony of rage and shame beneath the withering rhetoric of a Commissioner of the Treasury.

As long as the ministry was responsible for the proceedings of one who viewed his fellow - creatures in the light of so many subjects for a philippic, it was never likely to want enemies either in Parliament or without it. At the end of the first month of the session of 1774, Charles Fox detected in the corner of his newspaper a letter, purporting to be written by "A South Briton," which traced back the prevailing corruption and immorality of the age to the date of the rebellion against James the Second. He pounced upon the opportunity of reviving the laurels that he had won, and possibly of obtaining the crown of martyrdom that he so narrowly missed, in the course of that broil between the House of Commons and the printers, to which he still looked back as the most enlivening fortnight of his existence. So seductive was his tongue, and so inveterate the senatorial habit of regarding the daily press as a criminal organization, that he actually persuaded the collective wisdom of the country to pass a resolution ordering the attorney - general to proceed against the author and publishers of a performance which was as absolutely unexceptionable as it was detestably dull, on the farcical plea that it was a libel " on the era of the glorious Revolution." But, before the debate was concluded, Fox revealed a glimpse of that better self which was never out of sight for many hours together. Mr. Thomas Townshend, with some reason, but more ill-nature, taunted the government with their inconsistency in prosecuting an anonymous scribbler— who, in the poverty of his intellect and a temporary dearth of gossip, had earned a dinner by lampooning the Whigs of 1688—when they had pensioned notorious and virulent Jacobites like Dr. Shebbeare and Dr. Johnson. Fox, who was

---

bury; Richard Clive, Montgomery; William and George Clive, Bishop's Castle; John Walsh, Worcester; Henry Strachey, Pontefract; and Edmund Maskelyne, probably either for Whitechurch or Cricklade." "He has terminated at fifty," said Horace Walpole, in November, 1774, "a life of so much glory, reproach, art, wealth, and ostentation. He had just named ten members for the new Parliament."

just then in the first flush of pride and satisfaction at the
privilege of being admitted to dine twice a month with Johnson,[1] and who would as soon have thought of sitting at table
with Shebbeare as of standing by him on the pillory, rose in-
dignantly to protest against the unfairness of publicly coup-
ling two such names in the same indictment. " I should," he
went on to say, " be very much against persecuting a man of
great literary abilities for any opinions which he may happen
to drop in works not professedly political. It would be very
far from encouraging literature, which is ever best encouraged
in a free government." The sentiment was just ; though it
could be reconciled with the proposal which was before the
House only on the theory that any one who attacked the
government in print must expect to be punished unless he
could bring evidence that he was a great writer. But the
generous warmth of the young man redeemed the inconsequence of his arguments. Three years before, in the debates
on the arrest of the printers, Townshend had made an attack
upon Johnson and his pension precisely similar to that by
which he had on this occasion indulged his spleen ; and Wedderburn had replied with a pointed and elaborate panegyric
upon the author of the " Dictionary" and the " Rambler,"
which might be supposed to have been more gratifying to the
object of it than the brief and general terms in which Fox
paid his tribute to literature. Wedderburn left the Whigs
for the Tories, and Fox the Tories for the Whigs ; but their
common client, the most famous Tory outside Parliament between Swift and Scott, would never allow party spirit to mod-
ify the very different measure of respect which he entertained

---

[1] The Club was formed early in 1764. "After about ten years," said
Boswell, "instead of supping weekly, it was resolved to dine together
once a fortnight during the meeting of Parliament." Fox was elected
in the spring of 1774, and made the best of listeners. Johnson was much
exercised by his not taking his share of the talk, and charged him with
not caring to row unless, as in the House of Commons, he pulled first oars.
But Fox knew what a treat he was enjoying ; and his silence was the
measure of his respect for a company whose names would be remembered when three fourths of the cabinet had been forgotten.

for his two defenders. Towards Lord Loughborough he observed a cold neutrality, which all who knew their man recognized as the thin veil of profound contempt; while for Fox he cherished a lively and willing gratitude, which grew all the firmer as the political gulf between them was agitated by fiercer and ever fiercer tempests. The heartiest expression of his gratitude and regard was uttered in the very throes of the mortal duel that sent to the wall for half the century the principles which Fox represented and which Johnson made it his duty to hate. "I am for the king against Fox," he would say to those who asked him how he was affected towards the Coalition Ministry; "but I am for Fox against Pitt. The king is my master, but Fox is my friend."

At no time would the ministers have liked their young colleague the better for thrusting them into a quarrel with the newspapers; but in February, 1774, they were less inclined than ever to rejoice at having upon their hands another Wheble, and possibly another Wilkes. The House of Commons was already deep in a mess which Charles Fox had been the most active in stirring, though it was originally compounded by one who was almost as troublesome to sober and unwarlike people as himself. All London was talking of a man whose fame as a politician is now dim almost to extinction, and who, as a writer on philology, has shared the fate of specialists who start upon their discoveries before science has ascertained what is the necessary outfit for an explorer. But John Horne had a great and varied reputation while he lived, and long enough afterwards to be honored with the most florid, and far from the least amusing, of those biographies of sixty years ago, which were adulatory, but never uncandid; absurd, but never dull. There we learn that though, like Pericles, he rarely laughed, like Alcibiades he could suit himself to the humors of other men; that he could enjoy his wine with Homer and Ennius, could draw a character with Tacitus, and was as ready to accept money from his friends as Pliny and Cicero; that during his career he was as artful in counsel as Ulysses, as cool in action as the Duke of Marlborough, and as self-confident as Michael Angelo; and that, when the end came, he was as ready to die, and as desirous to have a simple funeral, as Titus Pomponius Atticus.[1] But, in truth, his character and powers were not of the heroic order; and the people who had parallel histories and similar dispositions with Horne were to be found in his own country and his own half-century. He was the earliest, and for practical business by far the ablest, of a class of men to whom Englishmen owe a debt of gratitude which they are, not inexcusably, somewhat unwilling to acknowledge. Among the most lamentable results of a system of coercion and repression is the deteriorating effect which it produces upon those who brave it. When to speak or write one's mind on politics is to obtain the reputation, and render one's self liable to the punishment, of a criminal, social discredit, with all its attendant moral dangers, soon attaches itself to the more humble opponents of a ministry. To be outside the law as a publisher or a pamphleteer is only less trying to conscience and conduct than to be outside the law as a smuggler or a poacher; and those who, ninety years ago, placed themselves within the grasp of the penal statutes as they were administered in England and barbarously perverted in Scotland were certain to be very bold men, and pretty sure to be unconventional up to the uttermost verge of respectability. As an Italian Liberal was sometimes half a bravo, and a Spanish patriot often more than half a brigand, so a British Radical under George the Third had generally, it must be confessed, a dash of the Bohemian. Such, in a more or less mitigated form, were Paine and Cobbett, Hunt, Hone, and Holcroft; while the same causes in part account for the elfish vagaries of Shelley and the grim improprieties of Godwin. But when we recollect how these, and the like of these, gave up every hope of worldly prosperity, and set their life and liberty in continual hazard for the sake of that personal and political freedom which we now exercise as unconsciously as we breathe the air, it would

---

[1] The only worthy whom we are distinctly told he did not resemble was John Wesley, who held, as did not Horne, "that without fasting and early rising it is impossible to grow in grace."

be too exacting to require that each and all of them should have lived as decorously as Perceval, and died as solvent as Bishop Tomline.

At the commencement of 1774, Horne's fortunes, which seldom were overflowing, had come to their lowest ebb. Honest, impracticable, insatiably contentious, and inordinately vain, he had thrown away almost all his chances and his friends.[1] He had lately quitted the Church (which he entered as a youth under strong instigation from his father), and had exchanged the vicarage of Brentford for a cottage where he was studying jurisprudence in the vain hope that the benchers of the Inner Temple would admit him to the bar. Sanguine, indeed, must he have been to spend six years of such industry as his on the labor of preparing himself for a profession the gate to which was easily defended by the members of the most jealous of guilds against an interloper who had no partisans at his back to help him in forcing an entrance; for, as his biographer expressly states, Horne was at this period "one of the most odious men in the kingdom." The same peculiarities of temper which in after-years brought him into violent and simultaneous hostility with both Pitt and Fox had now landed him in the singular position that he was reading law with the object of worrying Mansfield, and writing reams of correspondence filled with small-minded and grandly phrased abuse of Wilkes. The pair of patriots had abundance of mutual secrets connected with the money-lender, the vintner, the horse-dealer, and even the old-clothes man, which Horne did not scruple to unpack and display before the eyes of a laughing public; and Wilkes retaliated by extracting, from the parson of Brentford's letter of January, 1776, that sentence which, unluckily for its author, is the only passage in his works that any living man, except a lecturer on etymology, can repeat by heart. And while everybody with leisure for such a problem was discussing whether it was worse to apol-

---

[1] "You," said John Horne to his brother Benjamin, the most prosperous market-gardener of the day, "have risen by your gravity, while I have sunk by my levity."

ogize for having submitted to "the infectious hand of a bishop" or to have shirked paying for three chintz dressing-gowns and twenty - five bottles of old Jamaica rum, Junius infused a spark of common-sense and high feeling into the ignoble altercation by reminding Horne that the Wilkes whom he formerly worshipped was the same man as the Wilkes whom he now reviled, and that the sincere friend of a great cause should find some other means to evince his love for it than by gloating over the frailties of its most prominent advocate.

Horne's wayward and haughty spirit was shocked, but not tamed, by a sense of his isolation. The only reward, he feelingly complained, of all his labors and sacrifices was that the multitude, for whom he worked and suffered, had not yet torn him in pieces. But depression, in masculine natures, stops short at the point where it is sinking into despair, and recoils towards alert and courageous action. Horne was in a mind to shrink from nothing which would enable him to regain his ground in the race for popularity; and he soon had the field clear for a fresh start. Wilkes—who had been dragged into print sorely against his will, and had written only one letter for every two, and hardly one page for every four, of his adversary's—had withdrawn from the controversy with a Parthian fling at Horne's treachery and a flourish about his own sorrows and services.[1] Junius, having signed his redoubted pseudonym for the last time, was making his preparations (a much longer and heavier business then than now) for a journey to the distant shore where he was to fight unmasked and breast to breast with an antagonist of sterner mettle than any

---

[1] "Whether you proceed, sir, to a thirteenth or a thirtieth letter is to me a matter of the most entire indifference. You will no longer have me your correspondent. All the efforts of your malice and rancor cannot give me a moment's disquietude. Formerly, in exile, when I was *urbe patriâque extorris*, I have moistened my bread with tears. The rest of my life I hope to enjoy my morsel at home in peace and cheerfulness, among those I love and honor, far from the malignant eye of the false friend and the invidious hypocrite." The thirteenth letter was duly sent and never answered.

who had gone forth against him either from Brentford or St. James's. As early as June, 1773, his Majesty, little aware of the hidden truth with which his words were weighted, had informed Lord North that, though he knew nothing of the other gentlemen who applied to be appointed on the Council of Bengal, he could vouch for Mr. Francis being a man of talents. With no competitor left to outbid him, and no censor to rebuke him, Horne lay vigilantly in wait for an opportunity of recovering caste in his old party; and while Charles Fox remained in the government there was small probability that he would have to wait in vain.

Mr. William Tooke, of Purley, in Surrey, and a landed proprietor in the East of England, had been a Wilkite up to the time when it became necessary to choose between Horne and Wilkes. Tooke had long been in litigation over a disputed right of enclosure with his country neighbor, Mr. Thomas De Grey, the member for Norfolk. The contention ran its usual course. De Grey, as lord of the manor, erected a fence; and Tooke, who was a commoner, pulled it down. Then came an action for trespass and a challenge to fight from the one side, answered by a citation before the King's Bench from the other; until De Grey, who held that the law's delay was not intended for members of Parliament, got one of his colleagues to introduce into the Commons a private bill which gave him all he wanted. Tooke had nobody to speak for him in the House but Aldermen Sawbridge and Townshend; and such advocates, as he well knew, would do his cause more harm than profit in a contest with the brother of Lord North's ex-attorney-general. He turned for advice to Horne, who at once saw his chance of making himself into a political martyr, and at the same time of serving the interests of as good a friend as ever fell to the lot of one who was seldom anything but his own enemy.

A petition to Parliament was presented from De Grey, and a counter-petition from Tooke; and they were duly dealt with by the Speaker in the expeditious and rather slovenly manner in which nineteen twentieths of the enormous mass of private business that falls upon the House of Commons must necessarily be done, if it is to be done at all. The astonishment of every one who had been present on this very uninteresting occasion was great when in the *Public Advertiser* of the eleventh of February there appeared a letter, columns long, imputing to Sir Fletcher Norton deliberate and corrupt partiality, and charging him in so many words with falsehood, intentional chicane, and premeditated knavery. The members of that Parliament allowed themselves extraordinary liberties with their Speaker;[1] but they had no idea of extending those liberties to the world outside. And yet, when the letter in the *Advertiser* was brought before the notice of the House, some among the milder spirits, weary of the very mention of Privilege, entreated that Sir Fletcher Norton should carry his case to the ordinary courts, which were open to him as much as to any other citizen. But Charles Fox struck in with a clever and well-timed speech which summarily extinguished that pusillanimous suggestion. Was the House of Commons (he asked), with its undoubted and unbounded judicial authority, to implore an inferior tribunal for protection? The King's Bench would never humiliate itself by appealing for redress and defence to the Common Pleas; and what the King's Bench, in majesty and strength, was to the Common Pleas, that, and much more, was the House of Commons to the King's Bench. It was unanimously resolved that Woodfall, the publisher of the *Public Advertiser*, should be ordered to the bar. Woodfall obeyed the summons, and with sorrowful protestations of regret for his share in the transaction, indicated Horne as the writer of the libel. Having got the name of

---

[1] A month after Norton had been chosen Speaker, Sir William Meredith complained that he had been "traduced" from the Chair. Dowdeswell moved a resolution to the effect that Mr. Speaker's words were contrary to precedent and propriety. "Two pillars," said Captain Phipps, "should support that Chair, experience and impartiality. Experience, sir, you tell us that you have not"—and here a hasty call to order provided the gallant officer with the oratorical effect at which he was aiming. Burke, while writing a petition at the bar, quoted "Hamlet" at the Speaker along the whole length of the House; and when he made his celebrated allusion to Junius, the best-turned phrase amidst that inextricable tangle of gorgeous metaphors is the allusion to Sir Fletcher's eyebrows.

the principal, the more reasonable men of both parties were inclined to let the accessory go; but Fox, relieving Thurlow and Wedderburn of their functions as legal advisers of the House of Commons, and North of his responsibility as its leader, and making at least one speech for every fresh character which he assumed, succeeded in committing the government to a proposal that Woodfall should be confined in the gate-house of Westminster. Dowdeswell, however, pointed out that all the precedents were in favor of the House intrusting its prisoner to the charge of its own sergeant-at-arms; not to mention the extreme unlikelihood that a publisher would ever again turn evidence against his authors, if he was to be rewarded for his information by being sent to lie in the common jail. Lord North, who was watching the debate with eyes that he never ventured to close for five minutes together while he had Fox for a colleague, perceived that Dowdeswell had convinced the House, and, with an awkward playfulness which rendered his vexation all the more apparent, entreated the executioner who had bound him to the stake to give him back his liberty of action. But Fox was inexorable; and the prime-minister, driven to vote for a course which he disapproved by a subordinate whom he was beginning cordially to detest, begged his friends to divide against him, and thankfully accepted the humiliation of being beaten on a motion of his own introducing by a majority of more than two to one.

As soon as Woodfall had been disposed of, an order was made out directing the Reverend John Horne to attend on the sixteenth of February. The day came, and the House was crowded, as it always will be crowded when any folly is on foot; but in place of Horne himself, there came a civil letter in which he informed the Commons that he should be very glad to wait upon them if they would be good enough to abstain from addressing him by a title which he no longer recognized. Lord North tried to get the laugh on his own side by observing that Mr. Horne thought, and before they had done with him would have the best of reasons for thinking, an order of the House as infectious as the hand of a bishop; but there was no mistaking that the prevalent feeling even among the ministerialists was rather of shame than of anger. Into what further depths of ignominy (asked William Burke) would a false sense of its honor and an extravagant conception of its privileges debase that which had once been the first deliberative assembly in the world? The latest adversaries (he reminded his hearers) over whom they had triumphed were a milkman and a chimney-sweep; and it was difficult to say at what point of degradation they would stop, so long as they entertained the notion that it enhanced their dignity to have the lowest wretches in God's creation prostrate before them.

On the morrow Horne, only too glad to be captured, was brought up in custody amidst the intense curiosity of a generation among whom a clergyman who had renounced his calling was as rare a spectacle as a monarch who had lost his crown. The appearance and bearing of the culprit disappointed the expectation and conciliated the favor of his judges. Dressed neatly in gray, though without his gown, Horne began by explaining his notion of his own position in respectful and manly words; and the remarks which he interjected in the course of the proceedings were admirably placed, and entirely unanswerable. His main contention was that the law officers had nothing against him except the unsupported testimony of a man who had accused him in order to clear himself. Wedderburn, veiling under a cloud of elegant plausibilities the confession that such was indeed the case, urged the House to adjourn the debate in a speech which Dunning likened to the argument of a prosecutor who should request the bench to allow him a day or two to look about for fresh evidence on the understanding that if time were given, the prisoner should without fail be proved guilty. But the House of Commons, while ready to usurp the authority of the courts of justice, had no intention of binding itself by their rules; and the adjournment was carried in spite of Edmund Burke, who entreated Lord North to remove from sight that "monster of a motion," and to desist from engaging Parliament in a war with individuals, where victory could only be bought with the tears, and defeat would be attended with the scorn, of the whole kingdom.

The affair resulted in the second of the two contingencies which Burke had foreshadowed. When the inquiry was resumed, it appeared that the new witnesses—to secure whom the House of Commons had borrowed a leaf from the code of procedure of the Spanish Inquisition—were compositors from Woodfall's establishment; one of whom had printed the manuscript, but did not know the handwriting, and another had heard his master say that Horne was the author of the letter. Parliament, like the old gentleman in Racine's comedy, had of late years never been happy except when it was sitting as a criminal court; and by this time even the George Onslows had learned enough law to know that a man must not be convicted on hearsay testimony. Fox, balked of his prey, turned angrily upon his brother-huntsmen, and upbraided the ministers for having passed over the publisher, of whom they were sure, in order to get at the writer, who had, after all, contrived to escape their clutches. A mutiny in the ranks of the government seldom fails to produce from the Opposition a copious expression of that sympathy which is more blessed to him that gives than to him that receives. "From the very first," observed Barré, "I augured that this business would end ill, and I felt inconceivable pain for the noble lord. His followers were not to be depended on to fight for him. I know some little about the arrangement of troops; but in my life I never saw a body of regulars cut so wretched a figure." And then, passing from condolence to irony, the orator pointed to the unhappy leader of the House, as he sat between the solicitor-general, who had mismanaged the conduct of the case, and the Commissioner of the Treasury, whose rashness and self-will had been the origin of all the ministerial difficulties. "We have everything," he said, "to hope from the noble lord. He is at present most happily situated. If he wants law, he has but to look to the left; while if he stands in need of common-sense, his spirited friend on the right can abundantly supply him." Amidst a shower of such taunts the curtain was dropped upon the miserable farce, and Horne walked from the bar a free and a made man. The attention which his stroke of judicious audacity had attracted to Mr. De Grey's proceedings in Parliament stayed the progress of the enclosure bill until it had been altered to the satisfaction of all whose interests it affected. Rescued in a hopeless strait, Mr. Tooke repaid his preserver with an affection that was neither short-lived nor barren. Horne, soon or late, received from his grateful friend over eight thousand pounds in money, a second name for himself, and the suggestion of that affected title by which, much better than by its contents, his book is known.[1] But his exertions acquired for him a reputation which extended beyond the garden-walls of Purley, and procured him other benefactors hardly less generous than its large-hearted owner. At every successive crisis in our liberties, when tyranny was so firmly in the ascendant that the hour demanded, not a champion, but a victim, all eyes were turned on the man who had braved the terrors of Privilege; and Horne Tooke always responded to the call, less eagerly and less boisterously as age and wisdom grew on him, but with the same constancy and self - possession as of old. He subsisted till past sixty upon means that were small and precarious; but at length the people, mindful of the hardships which he had undergone in their cause, resolved that so much of his life as was passed outside Newgate and the Tower should be passed comfortably. Liberal subscriptions, followed, as time went on, by substantial legacies, made him richer than he would have become if he had been permitted to wear the one gown or had never thrown off the other.[2] City merchants and Cornish Dissenters could refuse nothing to one whose protest against the coercion of America by fire and sword had landed him in a

---

[1] As a matter of fact, not a line of Horne Tooke's *magnum opus* was written at Purley. The diversions in which he there indulged himself consisted in riding over the Downs by day, and playing piquet with his patron of an evening.

[2] In 1773, when Horne left the Church in order to read for the bar, he had nothing at all. He began the nineteenth century in a large house and grounds at Wimbledon with a clear annuity of eight hundred pounds. His style of living rose, until his friends estimated his yearly expenditure at more than twice that sum; and he died leaving a handsome fortune, a cellar of good wine, and a library which contained a first folio of Shakespeare.

prison from which he did not issue until he had left his health
behind him; and who had been placed in jeopardy of the
gallows by his declared determination that he would not cease
his advocacy of parliamentary reform, as a remedy for domestic misgovernment, because we happened to be fighting with
Jacobins in the Netherlands.

Woodfall was discharged from custody after acknowledging
the enormity of his fault, and imploring the clemency of Parliament in abject terms; but there remained an offender from
whom no apology could be accepted, if, indeed, there had been
the slightest chance that any would be forthcoming. Fox
this time had sinned beyond expiation. There was an impression abroad that, in harassing Lord North, he had acted
under secret orders from the king; and his Majesty had no
right to complain if that impression was strongest in the
minds of those who had known what it was to serve him as
leaders in the House of Commons.   "It is supposed by most
sensible people," wrote Lord Chatham, "that Mr. Charles Fox
did not venture on a line of conduct which almost unavoida-
bly called for the resentment of Lord North without support
from some part of administration, and that *that* part must
have some encouragement from the closet."   But the suppo-
sition was quite unfounded; for the king already disliked
Fox too heartily even to use him as an instrument for plagu-
ing his own prime-minister. His dislike had not its source,
as some aver, in disapprobation of the loose and ill-ordered
life which the young politician had hitherto been leading.
George the Third knew better than to be fastidious about the
private conduct of the peers and commoners who consented
to be the agents of his favorite political system. When Sandwich was appointed secretary of state, the king took special
pains to inform that immaculate statesman of his coming honors in the manner which would be the most flattering and
agreeable to their recipient;[1] and a monarch who went out of

---

[1] "If you have not yet intimated to Lord Sandwich my intentions of
intrusting him with the seals of the Northern Department, I wish you
would not longer defer, as the manner greatly enhances or diminishes
every favor" (George the Third to Lord North, December 14, 1770).

his way to make a Mordecai out of Sandwich was not likely, on moral grounds, to make a Haman of anybody. The king's antipathy to his Junior Lord of the Treasury did not spring from the experience of what was bad in the young man's character, but from the promise of what was good. Whether he abetted the royal policy, or whether he thwarted it, Fox never managed to please his sovereign. The very heat with which the rising orator attacked Wilkes and defended Lowther was ominous and alarming in the eyes of a ruler who cherished every abuse in Church and State, and who felt an uneasy presentiment that, to whatever purpose fire might be put for the moment, its ultimate destination was to burn rubbish. And more distasteful still in the highest quarter was the uncalculating and unflinching chivalry with which Fox espoused any cause, however ostentatiously it might be frowned upon at St. James's, in behalf of which his personal convictions and feelings happened to be enlisted. The spirit and the independence which he exhibited over the Dissenters' Relief Bill and the Royal Marriage Bill were noted down by a master who seldom pardoned and never forgot. The king thenceforward abode in patient assurance that something would ere long occur to justify him in discharging his contumacious servant; and as soon as he had learned the circumstances which brought about the defeat of the government on the question of committing Woodfall to prison, he wrote to the prime-minister as follows: "I am greatly incensed at the presumption of Charles Fox in obliging you to vote with him, and approve much of your making your friends vote in the majority. Indeed, that young man has so thoroughly cast off every principle of common honor and honesty that he must become as contemptible as he is odious; and I hope you will let him know you are not insensible of his conduct towards you."

The delinquent awaited his sentence in joyous equanimity. When he appeared at Almack's on the fifteenth of February, flushed by his successful rebellion of the previous evening, he was asked on all sides whether North had turned him out. "No," he replied. "But if he does, I will write to congratulate him and tell him that if he had always acted with the same spirit, I should not have differed with him yesterday." The prime-minister needed another week's pressure from the palace, and a fresh outbreak of insubordination on the part of Fox, to spur him towards a course of action which was alien both to his good-nature and his indolence. At last he nerved himself to write a letter which was said to run thus: "Sir,— His Majesty has thought proper to order a new Commission of the Treasury to be made out, in which I do not see your name." A similar story is told about a very recent successor of Lord North, and perhaps was invented for one of his predecessors; but whatever the form of the communication may have been, its substance soon became the property of the public. Twenty-four hours after he had been dismissed from office, Fox was again haranguing the House of Commons with an easy magniloquence which provoked a Tory baronet into exclaiming that he talked as if the fate of Cæsar and of Rome depended on his conduct. "The honorable gentleman," remarked the speaker, "is tender in years, but tough in politics, and, if I do not mistake, has already been twice in and twice out of place." And when the sitting was over, and the full-dress sarcasms of debate gave place to the fraternal raillery of the lobby, George Selwyn took the earliest opportunity of setting afloat his view of an incident which, for a month to come, was sure to be in everybody's mouth. "Charles," he said, "for the future I will eat salt fish on the day you was turned out. You shall be my Charles the Martyr now; for I am tired of your great-grandfather, the old one. His head can never be sewed on again; but as yours can be, I will stick to you."

And so Fox was once more out, and out for good; and the first portion of his story had ended in a climax which fitly and harmoniously crowned the preceding narrative. Still of an age before which no English statesman can hope to accomplish great things, he had at any rate given earnest of remarkable qualities. He had shown himself to possess in an unusual degree that recuperative power which is all but indispensable in a career where no one who fights to win can keep himself out of the reach of a knock-down blow. An observant veteran watches with almost pathetic interest the bearing of a young politician who has been flung off the ladder of promotion, or who has brought down upon his head a sudden avalanche of unpopularity; and never did any one pick himself up quicker than Charles Fox, and go to work again with more sublime indifference to jeers and bruises. And while his elasticity of temperament boded well for his own happiness, those who looked to him as a future servant of his country noticed in all that he said and did the unmistakable tokens of an ingrained disinterestedness, which it required only a good cause to turn into heroism. He was not a political adventurer, but a knight-errant roaming about in search of a tilt, or, still better, of a *mêlée;* and not much caring whether his foes were robbers or true men, if only there were enough of them. He was one who, in a venal age, looked to something besides the main chance; who, when he had set his mind or his fancy on an enterprise, never counted the odds that he faced, or the hundreds a year that he forfeited. But with all these generous gifts, his education and his circumstances almost proved too much for him; and it was the instinct of moral self-preservation which drove him to detach himself from his early surroundings, and find safety in uncompromising hostility to that evil system which had come so near to spoiling him.

> "Are wills so weak? Then let not mine wait long.
> Hast thou so rare a poison? Let me be
> Keener to slay thee, lest thou poison me."

Such is the temper in which, fortunately for mankind, rare and noble natures have often revolted against that world whose blighting influence they had begun to feel; and such was the mood of Charles Fox when, sick of a prison-house whose secrets had so early been familiar to him, he dissolved his partnership with Sandwich and Wedderburn, and united himself to Burke and Chatham and Savile in their crusade against the tyranny which was trampling out English liberty in the colonies, and the corruption which was undermining it at home.

INDEX.

ALB

ALBEMARLE, Lord, "Memoirs of Rockingham," 200*n*, 356*n*; portrait of Sir James Lowther, 356*n*.

Almack, 75*n*, 366, 418*n*, 419, 424, 426, 450*f*.

Almon, John, on Charles Fox, 324.

American colonies, some of the grievances of, 96*f*; the Stamp Act, 117; breach with England, 132; coercive measures determined on, 133; Wedderburn's denunciation of the wrongs of, 332.

Anglo-Indians, purchase of boroughs by, in 1768, 125*f*.

Apollonius Rhodius, Charles Fox on, 261*n*.

Articles, Anglican, agitation against subscription to, 373*ff*.

Artois, Comte d', 275.

Askew, Mr., delivers the Middlesex petition to the king, 185*n*.

Augusta, Princess - dowager, 29, 104*f*, 145, 257*n*, 404.

Aylesbury, the representation of, purchased by Wilkes, 141.

BACON, Lord, 99, 100*n*.

Bagot, Sir W., 365, 368.

Barnard, Dr., his influence on Charles Fox, 43*ff*.

Barré, Colonel, 121, 219, 299, 308*f*, 321, 327; deprived of his employments by the king, 111; letter to Lord Chatham, 112*n*; on legal members of the Commons, 329; his denunciation of the Commons, 338, 338*n*; attack on Sir Fletcher Norton, 402; on Horne's letter in the *Public Advertiser*, 447.

Barrington, Lord, moves the expulsion of Wilkes from the House of Commons, 159.

BRI

Bath as a gambling resort, 77*n*.

Bathurst, Lord, letter to Lady Suffolk, 433*f*.

Beckford, Lord Mayor, 169, 224; his remonstrance with the king, 241*f*, 249; Lord Holland's doubts about his prospects in a future life, *ib.*; his denunciation of Lord Holland, 248*f*.

Bedchamber. *See* Household.

Bedford, Duke of, signs preliminaries of peace with France, 24*f*; his followers, 29, 79, 122, 128*f*, 131*f*, 134*f*, 194*ff*, 207*f*, 255, 391, 392*n*; conference with Lord Rockingham, 122*n*, 123; his unpopularity, 187*n*; Junius's slanders on, *ib.*; hunted from West of England, 188; verses on, 188*n*; letter to, from Lord Holland, 253*f*.

Berri, Duc de, 275.

Betting in the last century, 414*ff*. *See* Brooks's; Gambling.

Blackburne, Archdeacon, 374*n*, 377.

Blackstone, Dr., speech on Wilkes, 160; on the Middlesex election petition, 172; his own "Commentaries" cited against him, *ib.*, 173.

Bloomfield, Robert, 210.

Bloomsbury gang. *See* Bedford, Duke of.

Bolingbroke, Lord, 73*n*, 80, 417.

Boswell, J., 152*n*, 332*n*; his work on Corsica, 133*f*, 134*n*; Lord Lonsdale's persecution of, 357*f*; on Charles Fox at the Literary Club, 437*f*.

Bottetort, Lord, 109.

Brentford. *See* Middlesex election.

Bribery, electoral and parliamentary, 90*ff*, 93*ff*, 97*f*, 111*f*, 124*f*, 212*f*, 216*f*, 219*f*, 331, 352. *See* Shoreham, New; Fox, Henry.

Bright, Mr. John, on truth in morals and statesmanship, 115*n*; his speech on the Irish Church Bill, 382.

BRO

Broad Church party, agitation against subscription, 374*ff*.
Brodie, Mr. Peter, 286.
Brooks's, 75, 75*n*, 76, 76*n*; play at, 79*n*, 418*n*, 419; the betting-book, 414*ff*, 425. See Almack.
Bubb Dodington, on Henry Fox, 7; on the fall of Pitt, 23*f*; his dispute with Lord Shelburne, 97*f*.
Bunbury, Sir Charles, on Charles Fox in the House of Commons, 175*n*.
Burgoyne, Colonel, 403.
Burgoyne, Mr., 425.
Burke, Edmund, 106, 110, 151, 161, 165*n*, 166*n*, 171, 175, 194, 220, 279, 307, 343, 345, 347, 366, 406*f*, 413, 432*n*, 433*n*, 446*f*, 452; letter to Lord Rockingham, 70; on George III., 70*n*; on the cause of the discontent under George III., 100*n*, 182; on the reign of George II., 102; on political parties, 107, 120; on the true principle of politics, 115; on Lord Rockingham's acceptance of office, 116*f*; on the persecution of Wilkes, 142*n*; speech in debate on expulsion of Wilkes from House of Commons, 160*n*; on Wilkes, 164*n*; speech on Middlesex election, 170; on Middlesex election petition, 173; on the constitutional questions involved in the persecution of Wilkes, 182*ff*; leads Whig agitation, 184*f*; on Lord Chatham's return to public life, 191; simile on Lord Chatham, 196; on the break-up of personal government, 216; on the unconstitutional proceedings of the House of Commons, 225; his "Discontents" as compared with Johnson's "False Alarm," 228*n*, 229; on political quarrels, 243*n*; reply to Fox on the law of libel, 294*ff*; ejected from the House of Lords, 299*n*; on the "Speaker's eye," 309; his efforts during debates on the press, 309*ff*; reply to Sir Gilbert Elliot, 320*f*; on the trial of Lord Mayor Crosby, 326; and of Alderman Oliver, 338; on the New Shoreham election, 350*f*; attempts to reconcile Fox and Wedderburn, 354; on Sir G. Savile, 364*n*; dislike of arbitrary power, *ib.*; dispute with Charles Fox, 368*f*; on Charles Fox, 369*n*; letter to Fanny Burney, 372*f*; to Lady Huntingdon, 373; on clerical subscription, 381*n*; his reply to Sir W. Meredith, 384; on the re-

CHA

lief of Dissenters, 388*f*; on the Royal Marriage Bill, 400*f*, 402*f*; opposition to Fox's motion for repeal of Lord Hardwicke's Marriage Act, 428; compared with Fox, 428*f*; Dr. Johnson on, 429; on parliamentary oratory, 430; his attacks on the Speaker of the House of Commons, 443*n*.
Burke, William, 300, 338, 343, 446.
Burney, Miss, 109, 372*f*.
Burns, R., 215*n*, 266, 412*n*.
Bute, Lord, 23*ff*, 29, 31*n*, 56*n*, 94, 114, 122*n*, 129, 145, 167, 173, 257, 330, 346, 359, 404.
Byron, Lord, 74*n*; his "Hours of Idleness," 43*n*; his behavior to Lord Carlisle, 54*n*; compliment to Wilkes, 159*n*.

CALCRAFT, Mr., 31*f*, 231*n*.
Cambridge University, contest for the high-stewardship of, 71*ff*; Junius on the high steward and chancellor, 73*f*.
Camden, Lord, 121, 135, 194, 197*f*, 200*f*, 205, 205*n*, 214, 218*n*, 230, 296, 332*n*, 333.
Camden, 2d Lord, 206.
Campbell, Lord, his "Lives of the Chancellors" cited, 173*n*, 205, 330*n*.
Carlisle, Lord, tribute to Charles Fox's schoolboy eloquence, 43, 43*n*; lines on Fox, 43*n*; his attentions to Lady Sarah Lennox, 52*f*; his "necessary banishment," 53*f*; Byron's treatment of, 54*n*; journey across the Alps, 54*f*; with Charles Fox in Italy, 55*f*; his life at Castle Howard, 87; reasons for declining the Bedchamber, 108*n*; his description of 2d Lord Holland, 138*n*, 139*n*; on Stephen Fox, 170*n*; letters to Selwyn on Charles Fox, 393*n*, 423*ff*; on Fox's gambling losses, 423*f*; gives security for Fox's debts, 423; on Selwyn's electoral troubles, 431*f*; other references, 79, 130, 273, 286, 420.
Carlyle, Mr., 9*n*, 19, 141*n*.
Carnarvon, Lord. *See* Herbert, Henry.
Caroline, Queen of Denmark, 399, 399*n*.
Carteret, Lord, on Henry Fox's marriage, 9*n*. See Granville.
Cavendish, Lord John, 115, 120*n*, 161, 318, 354*n*, 376, 433*n*.
Cavendish, Mr. Henry (author of the "Debates"), 170*n*, 175, 182*n*, 295*n*, 351*n*, 367*n*.
Charlemont, Lord, 300*n*.

CHA

Charles II., 2*ff*, 9, 155, 253.
Charlotte, Queen, 48.
Chatham, Lord, on parliamentary corruption, 93; letter from the king, 106*f*; his sympathy with the army and navy, 113*n*; invited to form a government, 119; its composition, 120*ff*; failure of his administration, 121*f*; withdraws from the cabinet, 122; on bribery at the general election of 1768, 125; urgency of the king's letters to, 129*n*; permitted to retire, 135; remonstrates with George III., 189*f*; returns to public life, 190*ff*; Wilkes on, 190*n*; his domestic correspondence, *ib.*; reconciliation with the Whigs, 191; his intended policy, 192; excitement at his return to public life, 193*ff*; Wilkes's pamphlet against, 195*n*; his defence of his assailant, 197; popularity of his orations in public schools, 196*n*; speeches in House of Lords, 196*ff*; influence of, 213*f*; on parliamentary bribery, 220*ff*; speech denouncing official peculation, 296*ff*; reported by Junius, 297; insulted in House of Lords, 299; his treatment by the Peers, 303; on Lord Mayor Crosby's trial in Commons, 327*n*; on Wedderburn's defection from the Whigs, 333; on Lord North's cabinet, 345*f*; advice to his nephew, 376; on Charles Fox's opposition to Lord North, 449; minor references to, 181, 201*f*; 230, 242, 255, 292, 338*n*, 344, 386, 399*n*, 452. *See* Pitt.
Chelsea Hospital, foundation of, 5.
Chesterfield, Lord, 63, 77*n*, 125, 129, 270, 376.
Cholmondeley, Lord, 82, 415.
Christian Club. *See* Shoreham, New.
Church of England, clerical objectors to subscription in, 373*ff*; meeting of objectors, and petition to House of Commons, 375*f*; opposition of the Evangelicals, 377; action of the Commons, 380*ff*; latitudinarian Bishops, 384*f*; secession of Lindsey, *ib. See* Lindsey; Dissenters; Nonconformists.
Churchill, C., lines on Pitt the elder, 24*n*; on Henry Fox, 33*n*, 34*n*; on Lord Sandwich, 69; on Sandwich and Wharton, 148*n*; on his own career as a clergyman, 235*n*; on Wedderburn, 334*n*; his admiration for Wilkes, 148*n*; his death, and character of his

COM

works, 147*ff*; also referred to, 333, 374.
Clarendon, Great Lord, 2*n*, 3, 260.
Clermont, Lord, 417.
Clinton, Lady Lucy, 65*n*.
Clive, Lord, 184*n*, 218*n*, 297; Charles Fox's denunciations of, 436*f*, 436*n*, 437*n*; his great political influence and his death, *ib.*
Clubs, London, one of the objects for which instituted, 414.
Cobbett, W., 374, 440.
Coke, Sir Edward, on men who never prosper, 362*n*.
Colebrooke, Sir George, his bill for increasing the East India Company's army, 306.
Commons, House of, debates on Lord Hardwicke's Marriage Bill, 12*ff*; Pitt the elder's ascendency in, 20*f*; how led by Henry Fox, 27*ff*; approves the peace with France, 28; proscription of the Whigs, 29*f*; its growing hostility to Henry Fox, 30*f*; corrupted by the king, 110*ff*; division on the American question, 117; election of Speaker in 1768, 127*n*; the Wilkes controversy, 139*ff*; debates on Wilkes, 159*ff*; on the Middlesex election, 168*ff*; scenes in and outside the House, *ib.*; conclusion of the debate, 171*f*; Luttrell declared elected, 171, 176; on the petition of the electors, 171*ff*; effect of Chatham's speeches, 199; George Grenville's Bribery Bill, 217*ff*, 353*ff*; abuses at trial of election petitions, 217*n*, 218*n*; proceedings on the remonstrance of the City to the king, 224*ff*; Burke's and Wedderburn's speeches, 225*ff*; annulment of resolution against Wilkes, 242*n*; conditions of success in, 245*f*; discussions on the liberty of the press, 291*ff*; speeches of Fox and Burke, 293*f*, 295*n*; insulted by House of Lords, 299; indignation of, appeased by Charles Fox, 300*ff*; continued ill-feeling towards the Lords, 302*n*; public reports of speeches in, 304*ff*; efforts of the ministerialists to exclude the press from, *ib.*; proceedings against the newspapers, 305; great debate on the press, 307*ff*; the printers reprimanded by, 309*f*; John Wheble's defiance of, 311, 311*n*, 312*n*; Wilkes's practical jokes on, 312*f*; insulted at the Mansion House, 314*f*;

CON

the Speaker's narrative to, 315; coldly received by the House, 316; Welbore Ellis on the situation, 316f; excited debate in, 317ff; inflammatory speech of Sir Gilbert Elliot, 319f; its effect, *ib.*; Burke's reply, 320; Lord North's despondency, 321f; speech of Charles Fox, 322f; defeat of the Opposition, 324; Lord Mayor Crosby before, 325ff, 334ff, 340ff; highhanded proceedings of, 326f; legal and county members of, 327f; Wedderburn, 330ff; canvass of government against the lord mayor, 335n; surrounded by the mob, 336; its members maltreated, *ib.*; speech of Alderman Townshend, *ib.*; helplessness of government, 336f; Alderman Oliver before, 337ff; effect of Charles Fox's speech, 338f; renewed rioting in Palace Yard, 340f; action of the Speaker, 342; speech of Lord North, 343f; the king's friends in, 344; motion of Welbore Ellis, and committal of Crosby, *ib.*; evades its own order, 345; action against Speaker's messenger, *ib.*; dissolution of Parliament, 346; admission of reporters to, 347; effect of New Shoreham election, 350f; quarrel of Fox and Wedderburn, 353f; Sir G. Savile's and Sir W. Meredith's bills, 362ff; speech of Charles Fox, 366, 367, 367n; strange incident of a division in, 368; proceedings on petition against clerical subscription, 379f, 383n; speeches of Burke and Savile, 382f, and of Charles Fox, 383f; petition of the Unitarians, 386; Nonconformists' disabilities, 385ff; petition of Dissenters against Dissenters, 387f; the Church Nullum Tempus Bill, 392ff; proceedings on the Royal Marriage Bill, 401ff; power of Charles Fox in, 408; a German pastor on, 432. *See* London; Lords, House of.

"Concealers," 362n.

Conway, General, 70n, 111n, 120ff, 123n, 157, 209, 401, 403, 408.

Cooke, Mr., 153, 162.

Cornwallis, Lord, 5.

Cornwallis, Marquis of, 213.

Corsica, cession of, to France, 133; struggle for independence, 133f; sympathy for, in England, *ib.*

Courtenay, Mr., 411n.

DIS

Coventry, Lord, 87.

Cowper, W., 85, 91n, 149, 181, 266, 268n, 385n.

Crabbe, G., 266.

Crawford, Mr. (the elder), 252n, 435.

Crawford, Mr., 405, 417, 433.

Crewe, Mr., becomes security for Charles Fox's debts, 423.

Crewe, Mrs., Fox's and Fitzpatrick's verses on, 284.

Cromwell, O., his speech to Long Parliament applied to Lord North's government, 221n.

Crosby, Lord Mayor, 314n, 315f, 325; his popularity, 321f; his progress to House of Commons, 325f; trial of, 326ff; canvass of government against, 335n; drawn in triumph to the Mansion House, 336; again before the Commons, 340ff; stratagem of, 344f; living in state in the Tower, 345f; his liberation, 346.

Cruden, A., anecdote of, 180n.

Cumberland, dispute between the Duke of Portland and Sir James Lowther for possession of Inglewood Forest, 357ff.

Cumberland, Duke of, 15, 18n, 83.

Cumberland, Henry, Duke of, his irregularities, 395, 395n; marries Mrs. Horton, 394.

Cust, Sir John, elected Speaker, 127n.

Custom-house, English, in the last century, 272f.

DALRYMPLE (Lord Bute's poet), 91n.

Dartmouth, Lord, 85, 216.

Dashwood, Sir Francis, 26n, 71n, 141.

Deffand, Mme. du, 271; her acquaintance with Walpole and Fox, 280ff.

De Grey, Attorney-general, 292.

De Grey, Thomas, 303n; his dispute with Mr. Tooke, 442ff, 448f.

D'Éon, Chevalier, his admiration for Wilkes, 179n.

Derby, Lord, 415.

Devonshire, Duchess of, her devotion to Charles Fox, 410, 411n.

Devonshire, Duke of, 28, 41.

Devonshire, Duke of (the friend of Charles Fox), 411, 415f.

Diderot on Wilkes, 234.

Dingley, candidate for Middlesex, 163n.

Dissenters, the king's instructions to Lord North regarding, 114; grievances of, 385. *See* Nonconformists.

DIV

Divorce in England in the last century, 73*n*, 412.
Dodd, Dr., 415.
Dodington. *See* Bubb Dodington.
Domitian. *See* Junius; Francis, Sir Philip.
Dowdeswell, 123*n*, 307, 326, 345, 399*n*, 444*n*, 445.
Draper, Sir William, his defence of Lord Granby, 97; challenges Junius, 372*n*.
Dryden, J., 143*n*; verses of, 267*n*.
Dunning, Solicitor-general, 201, 213, 292, 299*n*, 307, 366.
Dyson, Jeremiah, 109, 118*n*, 215, 307.

EAST INDIA COMPANY, bill for increasing army of, 306.
Eglinton, Lord, 118*n*.
Egremont, Lord, acquires the borough of Midhurst, 126*n*; on Charles Fox's ill-luck at hazard, 418.
Election petitions, curiosities of the trial of in last century, 217*n*.
Eliot, George, her "Daniel Deronda," 58*n*.
Elliot, Sir Gilbert, letter of Hume to, 211*n*; on the jealousy of the English and Scotch, *ib.*; inflammatory speech in House of Commons, 319; otherwise referred to, 344.
Ellis, Welbore, 215, 274, 316, 344, 353.
Emerson on success, 136, 136*n*.
England in the early years of George III., declaration of war with France, 18*f*; fears of invasion, and political crisis in, 19*ff*; triumphs under Pitt, 20*f*; the peace with France, 24; Bute and Fox's administration, 24*ff*; social and moral condition of, 61*ff*; ethics of the higher classes, 75; prevalence of gambling, 77*ff*; drinking and conviviality, 82*ff*; religion among the middle classes, 86*f*; and in the higher, *ib.*; country houses, *ib.*; absence of political principle, 87*f*; the sweets of office under George III. compared with those of the present day, 89*ff*, 100; recipients of State pensions and of the royal bounty, 91*n*, 92*n*, 93*f*; parliamentary corruption, 93*ff*, 124*ff*; her liberties in danger of being bribed away, 95*n*; scramble for political prizes, 97; places, not measures, 98; rapid succession of administrations, 99; general distrust of public men, 99*f*; Burke on the situation, 100*n*; her condition under George II., 102*n*;

FOX

the Rockingham administration, 118*ff*; the general election of 1768, 124; her attitude on the Corsican struggle, 133*f*; indignant at Wilkes's treatment, 150*f*; deadlock of the Lords and Commons, 158*f*; agitation against the Duke of Grafton's government, 186*f*; petitions to the king, 185*n*, 186*f*; joy at Lord Chatham's return to public life, 193*ff*; fall of the Duke of Grafton, 210*ff*; Lord North's administration, 212*ff*; threatened revolution in, 230, 233*ff*; importation of foreign manners into, 271; sympathy for the French émigrés, 277*ff*; English tourists on the Continent, 280; the struggle for the liberty of the press, 306*ff*; agitation in the Church of, 375*ff* (*see* Church of England); effects of French Revolution in, 388; the country and court parties, 390. *See* Commons, House of; Chatham, Lord, etc.
Eton, moral change in, 42*n*; want of discipline at, 42*n*, 43*n*; Dr. Barnard's rule of, 44*ff*; schoolboy effusions, *ib.*
Euripides, Charles Fox's admiration for, 262*f*, 408, 409*n*.
Evelyn, John, on Sir Stephen Fox, 4*f*.

FITZMAURICE, Lord Edmund, his Life of Lord Shelburne, 26*n*.
Fitzpatrick, Lady Mary (married Stephen Fox), 248*n*, 253, 283*f*, 285.
Fitzpatrick, Richard, 56, 76*n*, 281, 411*n*, 415, 434*n*; his friendship with Charles Fox, 283*ff*, 289; his taste for versemaking, 284; part author of the "Rolliad," 285; his devotion to the stage, 285*ff*; his verses on Lord Mulgrave, 291*n*; joins Charles Fox in the defence of New Shoreham, 352*f*.
Fitzroy, Mrs., 78.
Fitzwilliam, Earl, 49, 286, 400.
Fleet marriages, 12*f*; Lord Hardwicke's Bill, 12*f*, 413, 428.
Foley, Lord, 422.
Fontainebleau, preliminaries of peace between France and England signed at, 24; unpopularity of the treaty in England, 25.
Foote, S., 152*n*; his "Nabob," 126*n*, 418*n*; his dramatic performances, 172*n*; his "Cozeners," 352*n*.
"Foundling for Wit," 33*n*, 251*n*.
Fox, Sir Stephen, founder of the Holland family, 1*f*; assists the escape of Prince Charles, 2; Memoirs of, 1*n*;

FOX

enters the service of the prince, 3;
rise of his fortunes, 4; his fidelity to
the Stuarts, *ib.*; embellishes Sarum
Cathedral, 3*n*; his services under
William III., 4; promotes the foundation of Chelsea Hospital, 5; his domestic annals, *ib.*; his death, 6.

Fox, Lady (wife of Sir Stephen), 6; advice to her children, *ib.*

Fox, Stephen (Earl of Ilchester), 7, 9*f*.
See Ilchester, Lord.

Fox, Charles (son of Sir Stephen), 5*n*.

Fox, Henry (son of Sir Stephen), 3*f*, 6*ff*;
his loyalty to Sir Robert Walpole, 7;
story of his marriage, 8*f*; his domestic
relations, 10*f*; opposes Lord Hardwicke's Marriage Bill, 13*f*; his apti-
tude as a debater, 14, 17*f*; his interview with George III., 15; the king's
opinion of him, *ib.*; joins the cabinet,
16; Lord Granville's advice to, 19;
becomes paymaster of the forces, 21;
his financial gains, 22; his will, 22*n*;
on Charles Townshend, 26*n*; his reluctance to enter the cabinet, *ib.*; becomes leader of the House of Commons, 27; how he secured a parliamentary majority, 27*ff*; urged to acts
of spoliation by his colleagues, 29;
general detestation of, 30; hostile mo-
tions in the House of Commons against,
ib.; his quarrel with Lord Shelburne,
31; his retirement from public life,
ib.; obtains a peerage and keeps the
Pay-office, *ib.*; repartee to Lord Bute,
31*n*. *See* Holland, 1st Lord.

Fox, Lady Caroline (wife of Henry Fox),
10, 37*f*, 46, 255*f*, 258. *See* Holland,
Lady.

Fox, Stephen (2d Lord Holland), 38;
Lord Carlisle on, 138*n*, 139. 139*n*;
anecdotes of, 170*n*; high play of, 418*f*;
his bodily appearance, 421*n*; birth of
3d Lord Holland, 425; Mr. Crawford's letter to, 433; other references,
168, 175, 253, 285*f*, 392.

Fox, Charles James (son of Henry
Fox), Memorials of, by Lords Russell
and Holland, 1*n*; birth of, 37; his
boyhood, 37*ff*; idolized by his father,
38*f*; his fondness for the stage, 39*f*;
his precocity, 39; sent to school to
Wandsworth, 40; goes to Eton, *ib.*;
his school-days, 41*f*; goes on the Continent with his father, 42; Dr. Barnard's influence on, 43; his schoolboy
effusions, 44*n*, 45*n*; picture of, by Sir

FOX

Joshua, 45, 46*n*; on verse - making,
46*n*; goes to Oxford, 49; his life and
studies there, 49*ff*; his love for Oxford, 50; letters of Dr. Newcome to,
50, 51*n*; goes to Naples with his father, 51; his companions in Italy,
53*f*; and their proceedings there, 54*f*;
his studies in Italian and French literature, 56*ff*; his talent for taking pains,
57*ff*; makes the acquaintance of Voltaire, 59*n*; returns to England, 59*f*;
what conditions of society he finds
there, 61*ff*; motion for the removal
of Lord Sandwich, 69*n*; his entry
upon public life, 73*ff*; evil influences
surrounding, 74*ff*; Dr. Johnson on,
103*n*; chosen M.P. for Midhurst, 126;
outset of his parliamentary career,
127; his political animosities, 128*f*;
advice to his father, 129*n*; early indication of his qualities, 130; his first
appearance in Parliament, 130*f*; attaches himself to the Duke of Grafton,
135*n*, 136; first years of his parliamentary career, 135*f*; his maiden
speech, 138*f*; sketch of, 139, 428;
canvasses for Colonel Luttrell, 168;
speech in House of Commons, 169;
his opinion of Foote, 172*n*; his reply
to Wedderburn and Burke, 174*f*, 175*n*;
testimonies to his ability, 175, 175*n*;
on Sir G. Savile's censure of the House
of Commons, 200; pays a tribute to
Wilkes's consistency, 243; his rapid
success in the House of Commons,
246; his Parliamentary vagaries, 247,
264; his triumphs over Wedderburn,
247*n*; becomes Junior Lord of the Admiralty, *ib.*; lampooned in the "Foundling for Wit," 251*n*; his father's indulgence to, 252*f*, 254; his studies at
King's Gate, 260*f*; love for the classics, *ib.*; letters to Selwyn and Gilbert
Wakefield, 261*n*; his intended missive
to Bonaparte, *ib.*; his admiration for
Euripides, Homer, and Virgil, 262*f*;
his devotion to literature, 264*f*; his favorite works, 264*n*, 265, 265*n*, 266; at
St. Anne's Hill and King's Gate, 267;
fondness for rustic architecture, 268*n*;
his prodigality, 269*f*; in the society
of great French ladies, 270*f*; his love
for France, 279; his acquaintance
with Mme. du Deffand, 280*f*; at the
Clob à l'Anglaise, 280*n*; Mme. du
Deffand's sketches of, 281*ff*; letter to
Lord Rockingham, 282*n*; his friend-

FOX

ship with Fitzpatrick, 283*f*, 285*f*, 289 ; his talent as a verse-maker, 284*n*, 285*n* ; his fondness for theatricals, and its effect on his oratory, 285*ff* ; Grattan on, 288 ; Selwyn's *bon-mot* on, 289*f* ; speech on the law of libel, 293*f*, 296 ; Burke's reply to, 294*f* ; his resemblance to his father, 305*n* ; on the insult offered by the Peers to the Commons, 300*f* ; on the press inquisition, 305 ; otherwise referred to, 310*f* ; on Welbore Ellis's motion, 318*n* ; on the conflict of the Commons with the City, 322*ff* ; causes of his unpopularity, 323*f* ; John Almon on, 324 ; at the trial of Lord Mayor Crosby, 326*f* ; enunciates a new legal principle, 337 ; at trial of Alderman Oliver, 338*ff* ; popular detestation of, 339*f* ; maltreated by the mob, 341 ; foolish story concerning, 341*n* ; advocates publicity of debate, 347*f* ; his devotion to the king's cause, 348*f* ; his struggle in defence of New Shoreham, 351*ff* ; opposition to G. Grenville's Bribery Bill, 352*f* ; his quarrel with Wedderburn, 353*f* ; speech in defence of Sir J. Lowther, 366*ff*, 367*n* ; its result, 368*f* ; his admiration of Burke, *ib.* ; Junius's attack upon, 370 ; attempts to unmask his antagonist, 371, 372*n* ; seconds Sir W. Meredith's protest against the Criminal Code, 373 ; on religious tests, 331, 376, 382*ff* ; his conduct on the Dissenters' Relief Bill, 388*f* ; later feeling of the Nonconformists towards, 389*n* ; his evil surroundings, 390*f* ; a Quaker's letter to, 391*n* ; popular reprobation of, 391*n*, 392*n* ; quarrels with Lord North, 392*ff* ; leaves office, 393 ; Lord Carlisle on, 393*n* ; his attitude on the Royal Marriage Bill, 404, 406*f* ; reason for leaving office, 405*f* ; effect of his resignation on Royal Marriage Bill, 406*f*, 406*n* ; his victories over the lawyers, 407 ; reasons for his attack on the Marriage Bill, 408 ; his domestic happiness, 408, 409*n* ; fondness for country life, 409*n*, 410*n* ; *vers de société* on, 410, 422 ; his chivalrous respect for women, 410, 412 ; letters to Duchess of Devonshire, 410, 410*n*, 411*n* ; sketched by the Duchess, 411 ; on the death of Pitt the younger, 411*n* ; his legislative efforts in behalf of women, 412 ; his bill for the repeal of Lord Hardwicke's Marriage Act, 413, 428 ;

FRE

eccentricities of his private life, 413 ; records of his bets, 416*ff* ; his ill-luck at hazard, 418 ; verses on his ill-luck at play, 418 ; his fondness for sport, 420*ff* ; his racing adventures, 421 ; his dealings with the Jews, 422*ff* ; his friends go security for his debts, 423 ; his father's liberality to, 425*f* ; his financial catastrophe, *ib.* ; turns his attention towards the bar, 425 ; compared with Burke, 428*f* ; his eloquence, 429 ; on his own and Pitt's oratory, *ib.* ; a Prussian clergyman on, 429*f* ; affection of the Whigs for, 434*n* ; efforts of Lord North to recover his services, 434*f* : fascinates a Tory schoolmaster, 434*n* ; offered a place in the Treasury, 435 ; denunciations of Lord Clive, 436*f* ; his conduct in regard to the press, 437*f* ; at the Literary Club, 438, 438*n* ; on John Horne, 445*ff* ; his opposition to Lord North, 449 ; the king angry with, 450*f* ; Lord North's letter of dismissal to, 451 ; G. Selwyn on, *ib.* ; close of the first part of his career, 451*f*.

Fox, Mrs. Charles, 264, 265*n*, 267*n*, 284*n*, 409*n*.

Fox, Henry Edward (1st Lord Holland's youngest son), 37*n*, 53, 256.

France, declaration of war with England, 18*f* ; *grandes dames* of the old régime, 270*f* ; English visitors to, 272*ff* ; the passage from Calais to Dover, 272*n* ; English visitors shopping in, 273 ; courtesy towards British tourists in, 274*ff* ; French men of letters, 275*ff* ; horror inspired by the Revolution in England, 277*ff* ; and its effects, 388. *See* England ; Walpole, Horace ; Hume, David, Life of.

Francis, Dr., tutor of Charles Fox at Eton, 41*n* ; his connection with the Hollands, *ib.*

Francis, Sir Philip (Junius, Mnemon, etc.), obtains a government clerkship, 41 ; after-dinner abstemiousness of, 82 ; reports speeches in House of Lords, 297 ; Messrs. Parkes and Merivale's Memoir of, 372*n* ; George III. on, 443. *See* Junius.

Frankland, Admiral, on parliamentary privilege, 306*f*.

Franklin, Benjamin, 120*n*, 132 ; on George III. and Wilkes, 156*n* ; on London rioting, 168*n* ; cited, 374.

Frederic the Great on Pitt, 19*f* ; alleged to have been betrayed by Bute, 25; his opinion on Corsica, 134.

Frederic, Prince of Wales, 103*f*; foolish funeral sermon on, 103*n*.

GAMBLING, aristocratic, in the last century, 77*ff*; its deplorable consequences, 80*ff*; Charles Fox's losses, 418, 423*f*. See Brooks's.

Garrick, David, admonished by Wilkes, 180; on private theatricals, 287*n*; his foreign tour, *ib.*; other references to, 240, 399*n*.

Genoa cedes Corsica to France, 133.

George II., policy of, 102; his death, 102*n*; Lord Chatham's estimate of, 118; on spurious and genuine king's speeches, 176.

George III., Henry Fox's interview with, 15*f*; commencement of his reign, 23*f*; gives a place in the cabinet to Henry Fox, 26*f*; countenances the proscription of the Whigs, 28*f*; satisfaction of his court, 30; proposes to Lady Sarah Lennox, 47; the result, 48*ff*; marriage of, 48; letter of, to Lord North, 64; his indulgence to the Duke of Grafton, 75; his theories of government, 70; results of his policy, *ib.*; his temperate and vigorous habits, 83, 84*n*; household of, 85*f*; place-hunting under, 89*ff*; profits and position of crown servants compared with those of the present day, 88*ff*, 100*f*; popular notion of, 103; education of, 104*f*; his preceptors, 105; his intellectual and business qualities, 106*f*; letter to Chatham, 106; political theories of, 106*ff*, 113*ff*; changes of his advisers, 106*f*; attempts to form a party of his own, 107; character and duties of the king's friends, 108*ff*; his private associates, *ib.*; how he manipulated the House of Commons, 111; letter to his minister, *ib.*; his treatment of veterans of the army, 112*f*; his electioneering operations, 113*f*; conduct to Chancellor Legge, 114; invites Lord Rockingham to his councils, 116; plots his fall, 117*ff*; his pledges to Rockingham, 118*n*; popular estimate of him, 119*n*; dismisses Lord Rockingham and invites Chatham to form a government, 119; his theory of party, 120; end of his first Parliament, 123; elections for the new one, 124*ff*; his urgent letters

to Chatham, 129*n*; the quarrel with America, 132; his resentment against Wilkes, 143*ff*; misses his opportunity in reference to Wilkes, 155*ff*; instructions to Lord North, 157, 214*n*, 385; on the Wilkes debate, 162; his speech proroguing Parliament, 176; his unpopularity, 177*f*; his coolness when insulted by the mob, 177, 178*n*; at Drury Lane, 180*n*; receives the Middlesex petition, 185*n*; and petitions from the counties and cities, 186*ff*, 189; action of his ministers against the Whig agitation, 187*ff*; Lord Chatham's remonstrance with, 189*f*; persuades Charles Yorke to accept the great seal, 206*f*; his reluctance to invest the 2d Lord Camden with the Garter, 206; fall of the Duke of Grafton's administration, 210; Lord North as his prime-minister, 212; reign of bribery, *ib.*; the great seal intrusted to commissioners, 214; apparent success of his theories, *ib.*; Junius's strictures upon his rule, 215*f*; character of his agents, 216*f*; expenditure of his Civil List, 219*f*; petitions to, to dissolve Parliament, 221*ff*; his reception of the City remonstrance, 222*f*; joint rebuke of City by Lords and Commons, 226; the Westminster and Middlesex remonstrances, 227*f*; Junius's letter to, and its consequences, 229*f*; deaf to the complaints of his subjects, 231; indignant with his ministers, 232*n*; on Lord George Sackville's duel with Governor Johnston, 302*n*; insists on fighting out the quarrel of press and Parliament, 307; admonishes Lord North to let Wilkes alone, 313; peremptory instructions to his minister, 315; proposes to take the lord mayor to Westminster by water, 324*f*; obstacles to the success of his policy, 355*f*, action of his government in the dispute between the Duke of Portland and Sir James Lowther, 358*ff*; on the Articles of Religion, 379; his hostility to the Nonconformists, 386, 389*f*; his brothers, 394*ff*; his anger at the marriage of the Duke of Cumberland, 394*f*, 397; the Royal Marriage Bill, 397*ff*; high-handed treatment of the Commons, 402*f*; on Sir Philip Francis, 443; his dislike for Charles Fox, 449*f*.

GER

Germaine, Lord George. *See* Sackville.

Gibbon, on Wilkes, 239n; on the reception of English visitors in France, 274; his predilection for French society, 276f; on the French Revolution, 277; on Charles Fox, 405, 434; in the House of Commons, 432.

Gladstone, Mr., on Wilkes, 140.

Gloucester, Bishop of, on the Royal Marriage Bill, 400n. *See* Warburton.

Gloucester, Duke of, marriage of, to Lady Waldegrave, 396f.

Glynn, Sergeant, Wilkes's colleague in the representation of Middlesex, 162, 164, 185, 242, 292f.

Goethe on the English character, 279, 279n.

Goldsmith, Oliver, 164; Charles Fox on the "Traveller," 266n; his "Haunch of Venison," 308n.

Gower, Lord, 123, 209, 215; motion in House of Lords against reporters, 298f.

Grafton, Duke of, 29, 75, 91n, 93, 129, 163n, 165, 193f, 200ff, 207, 209, 212, 303, 395n; his relations with Miss Nancy Parsons, 64n, 65; his administration, 66ff; Horace Walpole on, 69; becomes Chancellor of Cambridge University, 72, 73n; congratulated by Junius, 72, 73; Gray's ode on, 73n; a dinner given by, 94n; as First Lord of the Treasury, 121; seeks alliance with the Bedfords, 122f; becomes prime-minister, 135; Charles Fox's estimate of, 135n; Wilkes's letter to, 150; agitation against his government, 184ff, 189; changes in his administration, 200ff; his resignation and retirement, 209f; Junius's diatribes against, *ib.*; breaking-up of his government, *ib.*; speech of, reported in Woodfall's journal, 297; letter of Junius to, 333; his attack on the Duke of Portland, 356, 358, 361.

Grammont, Count, 6, 427.

Granby, Lord, 97, 135, 157, 194, 200, 213; apology for his part in the Middlesex election, 199.

Grand tour, experiences of the, 55n.

Grantham, Lord, 272.

Granville, Lord, his compliment to Henry Fox, 16n; refuses to accept the Treasury, 19; his advice to Henry Fox, *ib.*

HER

Grattan, Henry, on Charles Fox as an orator, 288; on Burke's Toryism, 364n.

Gray, T., lines on Henry Fox, 34, 34n; ode on the installation of the Duke of Grafton as Chancellor of Cambridge, 73n; on Boswell's book about Corsica, 134n.

Green, Bishop of Lincoln, 389.

Grenville, George, 26, 42n, 91n, 93, 98, 110, 115, 117, 127, 169, 171f, 184n, 186, 191, 213n, 276n, 426n; on the grand tour, 55n; antipathy to king's friends, 110; on motion to expel Wilkes from House of Commons, 159f; on Wilkes's popularity, 182; his Bribery Bill, 217ff, 349, 352n, 353f; proposal for inquiry into the Civil List, 219f; quarrel of Fox and Wedderburn about, 353f; speech of Burke, 354.

Grenville, George (the younger), 55n.

Grenville, James, 214n.

Grenville, Thomas, 42n, 186n.

Grenville papers, 42n, 43n, 65n.

HALIFAX, Lord, 181, 214, 313.

Hamilton, Duchess of, 153.

Hamilton, William Gerard, 95n, 300n.

Harcourt, Lieutenant-colonel, 403.

Hardwicke, Lord, his Marriage Bill, 11ff; its defects, 12f; opposed by Henry Fox, 13f; his philippic against Fox, 15; referred to, 203; Charles Fox's bill for repeal of his Marriage Act, 413, 427, 431.

Hardwicke, Lord (son of the preceding), contests the High-stewardship of Cambridge University with Lord Sandwich, 70f; his apologies for Charles Yorke, 203n; joint author of the "Athenian Letters," *ib.*; his letters cited, 205n; entreats his brother to resign the chancellorship, 207f; grief for his brother's loss, 208.

Harley, Lord Mayor, Lord Holland's memorial of, 255n.

Harris, Mr., 49n.

Hartington, Lord, 218n, 475n.

Hawke, Lord Admiral, 157.

Hayley, W., Charles Fox's appreciation of, 265.

Heine, Heinrich, 215.

Heinel, Mlle., 415.

Herbert, George, 392.

Herbert, Henry, 317.

Hertford College, Oxford, **Charles Fox** at, 49ff, 51n.

HER

Hertford, Lord, 216, 272, 397n, 432.
Hertford, Lady, 78.
Hervey, Augustus, 74n.
Hickey, electioneering agent, 125n.
Hobart, Mr., his frolic at Lady Tankerville's, 66n.
Holbach, Baron d', 147, 238, 274.
Holland, 1st Lord (Henry Fox), defection of his associates, 31f; public
estimate of his character, 32ff;
lampoons and satires on, 33n, 34nn;
his private life, 35f; quarrel with Rigby, 36f; his domestic happiness, 37;
his children, 37n; Holland House,
37n; love for his family, 38f; letters
to Lady Holland, ib.; his dependents,
41n; on his son Charles's studies, 51;
takes him to Naples, 51f; his social
qualities and literary talents, 52; his
verses on Rigby, 52n; his poetical remonstrance to Lady Sarah Lennox,
52n; his stay at Nice with his children, 54; letter from Voltaire to, 59n;
his evil influence on Charles Fox,
74f; his advice to Lord Shelburne,
97; clubs with Lord Ilchester to hire
a borough for their sons, 126ff; his
isolation in English politics, 127; ordered to resign the Pay-office, 127,
255; his advances to the Whigs rejected, 128; considers himself an injured man, ib.; his suit for an earldom refused, 129n; on Corsica and
the Corsicans, 134n; his support
of Colonel Luttrell, 167; delight at
Charles Fox's reply to Burke and
Wedderburn, 175; remarks on Charles
Yorke, 208n; on Charles Fox's parliamentary success, 247f; his reply to
the allegations of Beckford, 249f; his
enormous gains, 250; his communication to Baron Smith, 250n; popular hatred and denunciation of, 251;
character and disposition of, 251ff;
his treatment of his children, 252n,
253; his wealth, ib.; his marine retreat at King's Gate, 254, 258ff; refused a step in the peerage, 256ff; resigned to his lot, 258; careless of his
son's prodigality, 269f; on Burke,
368; antipathy of his family to the
Royal Marriage Bill, 404; his dissatisfaction with Charles Fox, 405; delighted with his son's triumphs over
the lawyers, 407; arranges for payment of Charles Fox's debts, 425;
reason for desiring his son's mar-

ING

riage, 426; his talent as a debater,
428; his satisfaction at seeing Charles
Fox in the Treasury, 435f. See Fox,
Henry.
Holland, Lady Caroline, 270, 321. See
Fox, Lady Caroline.
Holland, 2d Lord. See Fox, Stephen.
Holland, 2d Lady. See Fitzpatrick,
Lady Mary.
Holland, 3d Lord (Henry Richard Fox,
son of the preceding), 1n, 13, 269n,
405, 418; on Charles Fox, 57, 409; on
Lope de Vega, 266n; his birth, 424.
Holland House, 37n.
Holland, Earl of, 37n.
Holt, Lord Chief-justice, 186n.
Homer, Charles Fox's love for, 262n,
408.
Horne, Rev. John, 82n, 152ff; his ac-
tivity during the Middlesex election,
152, 152n; his account of the king's
reception of the City remonstrance,
223n; career of, 439ff; his quarrel
with Wilkes, 441; his letter in the
Public Advertiser, 444f; ordered to
attend at the House of Commons,
445f; letter to the House, 446; his
triumph over the Commons, 447f; his
reputation as a politician, 448n; his
"Diversions of Purley," ib.
Horton, Mrs., 394.
Household of George III., 85f, 108n.
Hume, David, 147f, 270; his sympathy
for George III.'s policy, 210ff; his
dislike of the English people, 211f;
correction of his history, 212; proph-
esies an English revolution, 232; on
cookery and history, 232n; his reception in France, 275f, 276n; on the
different position of literary men in
England and France, 276f; Walpole
on, 276n, 277n.
Hunt, Dr., his conversation with Fox
on clerical subscription, 376.
Huntingdon, Countess of, her crusade
against the latitudinarians, 378ff.
Huntingdon, Lord, and Mr. Lindsey,
378, 378n, 379n.
Hutchinson, John Hely, 300n.

ILCHESTER, Lord, 415; clubs with Lord
Holland to purchase a borough, 126ff.
See Fox, Stephen.
Inglewood Forest, quarrel of Duke
of Portland and Sir James Lowther
about, 358ff; wholesale actions of
ejectment in, 363.

IRE

Ireland the prey of English place-hunters, 95*f*.
Italy, English tourists in, in the last century, 55*n*.

JAMES I., Quieting Act of, 362*f*.
James II., 4, 5*n*.
Jeffreys, Judge, 226*n*.
Jesse, Mr., 269*n*.
Johnson, Dr., 75*n*, 91*n*, 134, 152*n*, 374, 438*f*; on Charles Fox's political power, 152*n*; his anecdote of Lord Shelburne, 132*n*; his suggestion of ducking Wilkes, 145; becomes a political writer, 228*f*; on Garrick, 240*n*; his meeting with Wilkes, *ib.*; Charles Fox's criticisms on his "Lives of the Poets," 263; on lawyers canvassing for briefs, 332*n*; on the Grenville Bribery Act, 352*n*; on Burke's oratory, 429; with Charles Fox at the Literary Club, 437*f*.
Johnston, Governor, his duel with Lord George Sackville, 302*n*.
Junius, on the Duke of Grafton and Miss Nancy Parsons, 64*n*; on Lord Weymouth, 66; causes of his popularity, 69; on the High Steward and Chancellor of Cambridge University, 72*f*; on parliamentary corruption, 93; on George III. and Wilkes, 156*n*; cited, 163*n*; his earlier and later letters, 165*n*; on the Middlesex election riot, 166*n*; his reverence for Wilkes, 178; his libels on the Duke of Bedford, 187*n*, 188*n*; his diatribes on the Duke of Grafton, 209, 210; letter of, to the king, 229*f*, 290; his strictures on Lord Mansfield, 230; his denunciations of Lord North, 231*ff*; his foot-notes, 231; letters to Wilkes, 234*f*; his reports of speeches in the House of Lords, 297*f*; on the tumult in the Lords, 299; referred to, 330*n*, 331; on Wedderburn's treachery, 334; on the maxim "Nullum tempus occurrit regi," 360*n*, 361*n*; replies to, of ministerial writers, 361*f*; attacks Charles Fox, 370; refuses to disclose himself, 371, 372*n*; refuses to fight Sir W. Draper, 372*n*; on marriage of the Duke of Cumberland, 395*n*; letters to the Duke of Grafton and to Wilkes, *ib.*; preparing to go to India, 442*f*; his reply to Horne, 442. *See* Francis, Sir Philip.

LON

KEAN, Edmund, 363.
Kildare, Lord, 54.
King's friends, 108*ff*, 344, 387. *See* George III.; Commons, House of.
King's Gate, Lord Holland's marine retreat, 254*ff*, 255*n*, 258*f*, 268.
Kingston, Duchess of, her revenge on Foote, 172*n*.
Kinnoul, Lord, 250*n*.
Kneller, Sir Godfrey, his picture of Lady Fox, 6.

LARDNER, Dr., on the general election of 1768, 373*f*.
Lauderdale, Lord, 410*n*, 434*n*.
Lawson, Sir Wilfrid, 139.
Lawyers, unpopularity of, 328*f*.
Lee, John, counsel for the Middlesex election petitioners, 171; on Savile's speech on clerical subscription, 382*f*.
Legge, Chancellor of the Exchequer, treatment of by the king, 114.
Lennox, Lady Caroline, 8*ff*. *See* Fox, Lady; Holland, Lady.
Lennox, Lady Sarah, 41*n*, 175*n*, 404; her extraordinary beauty, 46*f*; Horace Walpole on, 46; proposed to by George III., *ib.*; Sir Joshua's picture of, 46*n*; accident to, 47*f*; the king's anxiety about, 47; reappearance at court, and end to her hopes, *ib.*; her own letter on the subject, 48*n*; her children, 48*f*; Lord Carlisle's attentions to, 52; Lord Holland's remonstrance with, 53*n*.
Libel, law of, 289*ff*. *See* Press.
Liberal party, first formation of, 115, 116.
Lincoln, Lord, 9, 10.
Lindsey, Rev. T., his scruples about subscription to the Church of England Articles, 375; his canvass among the clergy, 375*f*; his success with the Whigs, 376; opposed by the Evangelicals, 377; his discussion with Lord Huntingdon, 377, 377*n*, 378*n*; petitions the House of Commons, 378*f*; secedes from the Establishment, 384*f*; Cowper's lines on, 385*n*; also referred to, 392*n*.
Lloyd, Robert, his verses on Wilkes, 180*n*.
London, in the last century, dissatisfaction of, with the government of Bute and Henry Fox, 29; riotous scenes during the Middlesex election, 152*ff*; enthusiasm for Wilkes, 156, 162; collision with the troops, 155; elects

Wilkes alderman, 162; prepares for a conflict with Parliament, *ib.*; inefficiency of the constables, 166, 168*n*; frequency of rioting, 168*n*, 177, 178*n*; excitement caused by the Middlesex election, 168*ff*; deputation of citizens to the king, 177*f*; ballads of the day, 178*n*; remonstrance against the government, 188, 221*f*; reception of the remonstrance, 222*ff*; counter - proceedings in the Commons, 224*f*, 315*ff*; the corporation rebuked by Parliament, 227; elects Wilkes sheriff and lord mayor, 237; makes him chamberlain, 238; conflict with House of Commons, 296*ff*, 314*ff*; action of the City in defence of the press, 310*ff*; scheme of the king against the lord mayor, 325*f*; ovation to the latter in his progress to the House of Commons, 326*f*; his trial, 326*ff*; demonstration of the populace against the Commons, 334*ff*; riot in Palace Yard, 336*f*; cortége of the citizens conducting Crosby to Westminster, 340; renewed rioting, *ib.*; appeased by the Whigs, 342; enthusiastic reception of Crosby and Oliver on their liberation, 346. *See* Commons, House of; Wilkes; Crosby, etc.

Lonsdale, Lord. *See* Lowther, Sir James.

Lope de Vega, 266*n*.

Lords, House of, the debates of 1770, 196*ff*; speeches of Chatham on bribery and the Civil List, 220; on official peculation, 296*f*; speech of the Duke of Grafton, 297; reports of Junius, 297*f*; tumult in, 299*f*; forcible ejection of members of the Commons, 300; rejects bill for relief of the Nonconformists, 387, 389; the Royal Marriage Bill in, 397*ff*.

Loughborough, Lord. *See* Wedderburn, A.

Lowther, Sir James, at Newmarket, 79; instigates the quarrel between Lord George Sackville and Governor Johnston, 301; character of, 357; Lord Albemarle's portrait of, 356*n*; his treatment of Boswell, 357*f*; of the Wordsworths, 357*n*; lines in the "Rolliad" on, 358*n*; claims the estate of Inglewood Forest as against the Duke of Portland, 358*f*; his claim countenanced by government, 360; unseated for Cumberland, 362; whole-

sale litigation by, 363; explanations in the House of Commons, 364; Sir W. Bagot's defence of, 366; defeat of his claims, 370. *See* Portland, Duke of.

Lumm, Mrs., 78.

Luttrell, Colonel Henry, government candidate for Middlesex, 167*n*, 168*ff*; declared the elected member, 170, 176; otherwise referred to, 174, 242*f*, 320, 347, 394.

Lyttelton, 2d Lord, 55*n*, 81, 422.

MACARTNEY, Sir George (afterwards Lord), 41*n*, 128, 266*n*.

Macaulay, Catherine, contemporary opinion of her as an historian, 120*n*.

Macaulay, Lord, 5*n*, 84*n*, 110, 120*n*, 259*n*, 261*n*; on Voltaire's ignorance of England, 85; on Charles Fox's admiration for Apollonius Rhodius, 261*n*; on his favorite passage in the "Alcestis," 409*n*.

Mackintosh, Sir James, on the Royal Marriage Bill, 399*n*.

Malmesbury, 1st Lord, 49*n*.

Manchester, Duke of, 298.

Mann, Horace, Walpole's letters to, 64*n*, 68*n*, 74, 102*n*, 231, 427.

Mansfield, Lord, 75, 98, 134, 142, 146, 154, 155, 165*n*, 198, 201, 240, 299, 391*n*, 398; his charge at the Woodfall trial, 231; dictum on the law of libel, 291; his draft of the Royal Marriage Bill, 400*n*, 406, 441. *See* Murray.

March, Earl of, 79, 143, 158, 273, 274, 415*f*; his correspondence, 74; letter to Selwyn, 80*n*, 81*n*; lord of the bedchamber, 108. *See* Queensberry.

Martindale, Mr., 77*n*.

Masham, Lord, 79.

Mason, W., 33; lines on George III., 84*n*; on Lord Holland, 257*n*; criticism on Fox's and Fitzpatrick's verses, 284.

Massey, Mr., his "History of England" referred to, 401*n*.

Massinger, P., 362.

Medmenham Abbey, 72*n*, 141, 152.

Melcombe, Lord, 23; his dispute with Lord Shelburne, 97. *See* Bubb Dodington.

Meredith, Sir William, speech on parliamentary privilege, 316*f*; on the conflict of the Commons with the City, 335; rescues Lord North from the mob, 341, 343 ; his amendment of Sir G. Savile's Act, 364*ff* ; effect of Charles Fox's speech against, 367*ff* ; move for inquiry into the Criminal Code, 373 ; presents petition of the Broad Church party, 379*f* ; on religious tests, 383 ; complaint against Sir F. Norton, 444*n*.

Merivale, Mr. Herman, 372*n*.

Methodists, the. *See* Wesley, John ; Huntingdon, Countess of.

Middlesex election, strategy of Wilkes's supporters, 152*ff* ; riots, 153*ff*, 165*f* ; enthusiasm in London, 163 ; government candidates, 164*n*, 167 ; inefficiency of the constables, 166 ; candidature of Colonel Luttrell, 166*ff* ; petitions of the electors, 171*f*, 185*n* ; hearing of petition in the Commons, 171*ff* ; Luttrell's election confirmed, 176 ; ballads on, 177*n*, 178*n* ; addresses of the electors to the king, 178*n*, 227 ; re-election of Wilkes, 242*n* ; political results of, 244. *See* Wilkes ; London ; Commons, House of.

Midhurst borough and its voters, 126, 150.

Miller, Mr. (of the *Evening Post*), arrest of, 313 ; proceedings at the Mansion House, 314.

Milton, Lord, 354*n*.

Mnemon (another name of Junius), 360*n*, 361*n*, 372*n*. *See* Junius ; Francis.

Montagu, Viscount, proprietor of the borough of Midhurst, 126, 150.

Montague, Minister of William the Third, 4.

More, Hannah, 385*n*.

Morley, Mr. John, on Wilkism, 151*n*.

Mountford, Lord, 416.

Mulgrave, Lord, Fitzpatrick's verses on, 291*n*.

Mulgrave, Lady, mobbed by Eton boys, 42*n*.

Murray, Attorney-general, 16*f*, 19, 21, 93. *See* Mansfield, Lord.

NABOBS. *See* Anglo-Indians.

Nangis, Comte de, 53*n*.

Napier, Lady Sarah, 6, 48. *See* Lennox, Lady Sarah.

Napier, Sir William, and his brothers, 48*n*.

Napoleon I., 57, 133, 175, 261*n*.

Napoleon III., 216*n*, 278.

Newcastle, Duke of, 9, 16, 19*f*, 21, 24, 29, 107, 218*n*.

Newcome, Dr., Master of Hertford College, 49 ; his letters to Charles Fox, 50, 51*n*.

New Shoreham. *See* Shoreham.

Nice, 53*n*.

Nonconformists, grievances of, 385*f* ; Bill for their relief, 387 ; the king's hostility to, 387*f*, 390 ; Relief Bill rejected by House of Lords, 387 ; petition against abolition of tests, 388 ; Lady Huntingdon's remonstrance, *ib.* ; popularity of Charles Fox among, 389*n*.

North, Lord Chief-justice, 226*n*.

North, Lord, 98, 110, 171, 189, 199, 214, 223, 256, 296, 307*f*, 313, 334, 370, 378*f*, 405, 413, 416, 434*ff*, 443, 445*f*, 449*n* ; becomes Chancellor of Exchequer, 122 ; instructions from the king in reference to Wilkes, 157*f* ; consternation of his cabinet, 158 ; answer to Burke's speech in the Wilkes debate, 160*n*, 161 ; as prime-minister, 212*f* ; wholesale purchase of parliamentary support by, 213 ; Lord Holland on, 212*n* ; further instructions from the king to, 214*n*, 387 ; destination of the seals, 214 ; parries an awkward question, 220 ; on the City remonstrance, 224*f* ; discontent caused by his government, 228 ; his dread of Wilkes, 230 ; Junius on, 231*ff* ; incites opposition to Wilkes, 237*n* ; his squabble with the City, 315 ; orders of the king to, 315, 403 ; difficult position of, 318*f*, 321*f*, 343*f* ; resolves to push the quarrel with the City, 321*f* ; advised by the king how to deal with the lord mayor, 325 ; buys the support of Wedderburn, 332 ; maltreated by the mob, 340*f* ; pathetic speech of, in the Commons, 341*f* ; his civility to the Dissenters, 386*f*, 387*n* ; opposes the Church Nullum Tempus Bill, 392*ff* ; on the Royal Marriage Bill, 401*f* ; his alarm at the desertion of Charles Fox, 405 ; opposes repeal of Lord Hardwicke's Marriage Act, 428 ; efforts to recover Charles Fox's support, 435*f* ; on the Rev. Mr. Horne, 445 ; Charles Fox's opposition to, 449 ; his letter dismissing Fox, 450.

North Briton, No. 45, 143.

Northington, Lord Chancellor, 82*f*, 92, 121, 416 ; his pensions, 93 ; his treachery to Lord Rockingham and advice to the king, 118*f* ; in retirement, 123.

NOR

Northington, 2d Lord, 416, 425.

Norton, Sir Fletcher (Speaker), 246; John Wheble's letter to, 311*n*, 312*n*; requests the sheriffs to quell the riot in Palace Yard, 342; hanged in effigy, 346*n*: Burke's sarcasm on, 402; assailed by Barré, *ib.*; Fox's attack on, 407; accusations against, 444*n*.

Norwich, Bishop of, preceptor of George III., 105.

OLIVER, Alderman, 314*f*, 326; his defiance of the House of Commons, 337; trial of, 337*ff*; committal of, 340, 344; in prison, 345*f*; liberation of, 346.

Onslow, Colonel George, 306, 313, 321; hanged in effigy, 346*n*.

Onslow, Mr. George, 169, 300; on the revival of resolutions against the press, 304*f*; treats with the Presbyterians, 387*n*.

Orford, Lord, Henry Fox's attempt to bribe, 27*f*.

Ossory, Lord, 248*n*, 253, 273, 283, 376, 416, 434; Charles Fox's letter to, 404*f*.

Ossory, Lady, Walpole's letter to, 273.

Oxford, price of the borough of, in 1768, 125.

Oxford, Bishop of, on the Royal Marriage Bill, 400*n*.

PALEY, Dr., 375.

Palmerston, Lord, 415.

Pampellone, Charles Fox's tutor, 40.

Paoli, General, 133, 134*n*.

Paris, English visitors in, 272*ff*; men of letters of, 275*ff*. *See* France.

Parkes, Mr. J., his memoir of Sir Philip Francis, 372*n*.

Parliament in the last century, corruption of, 93*ff*. *See* Commons, House of; Lords, House of; Bribery.

Parr, Dr., 375.

Pay-office, accounts of, 30, 249, 250*n*. *See* Fox, Henry. Holland, 1st Lord.

Payne, Ralph, 169.

Pelham, Henry, 7*ff*, 16*n*, 316.

Pelham, Miss, 9.

Percy, Lord, 1*n*, 3.

Perreaus, the, 415*f*.

Phipps, Captain, 291, 444*n*. *See* Mulgrave, Lord.

Pitt, W. (the elder), 16*f*, 19, 115, 117; political triumphs of, 20; Horace Walpole on, 20*f*; his ascendency in

REY

Parliament, 21; fall of, 23; increase of his popularity in London, 30*f*; as paymaster, 250*n*; fame of his oratory in France, 274. *See* Chatham, Lord.

Pitt, Thomas, Lord Chatham's advice to, 376; brilliant act of self-sacrifice, *ib.*

Pitt, W. (the younger), 123*n*, 409*n*, 411*n*.

Pope, A., 148*n*; the "Dunciad" on the grand tour, 55.

Porson, Prof., on Pitt and Charles Fox, 429.

Portchester, Lord. *See* Herbert, Henry.

Porteus, Bishop of London, 385*n*.

Portland, Duke of, 115, 120, 308*n*, 356; his estate of Inglewood Forest claimed by Sir James Lowther, 359; sensation created by the attempted spoliation of, 360; Sir G. Savile's Act in reference to, 362*f*; Sir W. Meredith's amending bill, 364*f*; chivalrous care for his dependents, 365*f*; Fox's speech against, 366*ff*, 367*n*; result of the quarrel, 370*f*.

Poulett, Lord, 354*n*.

Pratt, Attorney-general, 204.

Pratt, Judge of Common Pleas, 146.

Premier's levees, 93.

Presbyterians in 1768, 374. *See* Nonconformists.

Press, discussions on the, in House of Commons, 291*ff*, 304*ff*, 307*ff*, 437; in the House of Lords, 298*f*; proceedings of the deputy-sergeant against the, 305; reprimand of the printers, 309*f*; action of the City in behalf of the, 310; triumph of the, 347.

Price, U., 53; as an actor, 286.

Priestley, Dr., 270, 374*f*, 375*n*, 378, 386.

Proctor, Sir W., in the hands of the mob, 153; his Irish bullies at the Middlesex election, 164*ff*.

Provence, Comte de, 275.

Pulteney, W. (Earl of Bath), his lamentation over his gambling losses, 77*n*.

Purling, Mr., candidate for New Shoreham, 349.

QUEENSBERRY, Duke of, 75*n*, 278, 415. *See* March, Earl of.

Quieting Acts, the, 361*f*.

RADICALS under George III., 440.

Reynolds, Sir J., his picture of Charles

RIC

Fox, 46 ; of Lady Sarah Lennox, 46*n*; of Lady Waldegrave, 396 ; his candidature for Plympton, 431 ; Selwyn's *bon-mot* on, 431*n*.

Richmond, Duke of (grandfather of Charles Fox), 8*ff*, 75.

Richmond, Duke of, 115, 120*n*, 196, 298*f*, 400, 432*n*.

Richmond, Duchess of, 8*f*.

Rigby, Paymaster and Irish Secretary, 30, 78*f*, 123*n*, 132, 160, 163, 169, 181, 196, 215, 246, 272, 306, 391*n* ; urges Henry Fox to proscribe the Whigs, 30 ; his advice to the city of London, *ib.* ; his defection from Lord Holland, 32*n*, 36*f*; at Holland House, 35*n* ; as Irish Secretary and paymaster of the forces, 65*f*; Garrick's insinuation against, 66 ; his Irish sinecures, 95 ; on the presentation of the Middlesex petition to the king, 185*n* ; his campaign against the Whigs, 187 ; his letter to the Duke of Newcastle, 218*n* ; reason for his opposition to the Grenville Bribery Act, 352*n* ; his appearance in the House of Commons, 500.

Roberts, Hugh, returning officer for New Shoreham, 349, 350*n*.

Robertson, Dr., his "Life of Charles V.," 197*n*, 260.

Robinson, Sir Thomas, 16.

Rockingham, Lord, 29, 98, 115*ff*, 121*f*, 129, 181, 183, 203*n*, 345, 433*n*, 434 ; administration of, 98 ; remonstrates with George III., 110, 118*n* ; invited by the king to assume the government, 116*f*; effects of his administration, 117 ; end of his government, 119 ; retirement of his adherents, 120*n*, 121 ; his conference with the Duke of Bedford's followers, 122*n*, 123 ; his reconciliation with Chatham, 192 ; Lord Hardwicke's letter to, 208*n* ; letter of Charles Fox to, 282*n*.

Rogers, Samuel, 212*n*, 364*n*.

Royal Marriage Bill in the House of Lords, 397*ff*; epigram on, 399*n* ; in the House of Commons, 401*ff*; protest against, *ib.* ; secrecy of the discussions of, 404 ; final vote on, *ib.* ; effect of Charles Fox's resignation on, 405, 406*n*.

Rudd, Mrs., 415, 417*n*.

Rumbold, Mr., candidate for New Shoreham, 349*f*.

Ruskin, Mr., his advice to an Italian

SHE

artist, 58*n*; his criticisms on Homer, 262*n*.

Russell, Lord, his continuation of the "Memorials of Charles Fox," 1*n* ; his "Life of Charles Fox," 42*n*.

SACKVILLE, Lord George, his duel with Governor Johnston, 301, 302*n*.

Sandwich, Lord, as an administrator, 68*f*; scandals of his public and private life, 68*n*; contests the Highstewardship of Cambridge University with Lord Hardwicke, 71*ff*; made postmaster - general, 123 ; lines of Churchill on, 148*n* ; his chaplain, 308*n*; other references to, 91*n*, 92*n*, 132, 141, 143, 158, 195, 198, 201, 215, 240, 449*n*, 450.

Saunders, Admiral, letter of, to Lord Chatham, 112*n*.

Savile, Sir George, 115, 120*n*, 121*n*, 188, 304, 343, 366, 376, 452 ; accuses the House of Commons of corruption, 199*f*; his Nullum Tempus Bill, 362*n*, 363 ; his reply to Burke on clerical tests, 382.

Sawbridge, Alderman, 185*n*, 224, 442.

Scott, Sir Walter, on Holland House, 37*n*.

Selwyn, G., 54, 55*n*, 63, 66*n*, 71*n*, 78, 81, 87, 208*n*, 216*n*, 273, 278, 415, 420 ; Lord Carlisle's letters to, 54*ff*, 423*f*; curiosities of his correspondence, 76*n*, 80*n* ; his daily round of life, 87 ; official sinecures of, 94*f*; price of his borough of Ludgershall, 125 ; his genealogical knowledge, 271*f*; on Fox and Fitzpatrick, 289*f*; in the hands of the mob, 336 ; his election troubles, 431*f*; on Sir Joshua Reynolds's candidature for Plympton, 431*n*; on Charles Fox's second loss of office, 451.

Senior, Nassau, 216*n*.

Seymour, Mr., on the persecution of the printers, 305.

Shebbeare, Dr., 437*f*.

Shelburne, Lord, 29, 31*n*, 121, 134, 201, 224, 292, 332*n*; his quarrel with Henry Fox, 31*f*; on Lord Holland's education of his children, 42*n* ; his political aspirations, 97 ; character of, 131*ff*; his American policy, 133 ; Dr. Johnson's anecdote of, 132*n* ; retirement of, 135 ; letter to Chatham, 399*n*, 400.

Shelley, P. B., 50*n*, 136, 440.

SHE

Sheridan, R. B., records of his wagers, 417n.

Shoreham, New, the election of 1770, 349ff; the Christian Club, 349; effect of election in Parliament, 350f; disfranchisement of the Christian Club, 352.

Smith, Adam, 211, 273.

Smith, Baron, Lord Holland's explanation to, 250n.

Smith, Benjamin, intercepts a letter of Lord North's, 237n.

Smollett, T., 211n.

Society, fashionable, in the early years of George III., gambling and low morality of, 77ff, 80ff; drinking habits and gout, 81ff; absence of religion in, 85; English and French, 271f, 274f, 277f.

Southey, R., 266.

Stanhope, Lord, on Pitt the younger's overtures to the Whigs, 122n, 123n.

Stanhope, Mr., 125.

Stanislaus, Augustus, of Poland, letter of, to Charles Yorke, 205.

St. Anne's Hill, Charles Fox's residence, 58, 267, 409n, 420.

Stavordale, Lord, 80, 126, 424.

St. John, Henry, 273.

Stone, Archbishop, 82.

Strange, Lord, 118, 163.

Strangways, Lady Susan, 45f.

Struensee, John Frederic, 399n.

Suffolk, Lady, 433.

Sunderland, Lady, 6.

Tankerville, Lady, drum - major of, 66n.

Temple, Lord, 55n, 144n, 160n, 162n, 186, 191, 195n, 201, 405, 427.

Tests, clerical, agitation against, 374ff; debates on, in House of Commons, 379ff. See Commons, House of; Lindsey, T.

Thrale, Mrs., on Garrick and Wilkes, 240.

Thurlow, Solicitor - general, 173, 292, 398, 400n, 407, 415.

Tooke, Horne. See Horne, Rev. John.

Tooke, Mr. William, his dispute with Mr. Thomas De Grey, 443ff, 447.

Tories, Henry Fox as leader of the, 27ff; proscription of the Whigs by, 29. See Fox, Henry; North, Lord; Commons, House of, etc.

Townshend, Alderman, 185n, 224, 336, 338, 443.

WAL

Townshend, Charles, 12f, 122n, 123n, 127, 276, 408, 427; Henry Fox on, 26n, 94n; becomes Chancellor of the Exchequer. 121; death of, 122.

Townshend, John, 49n.

Townshend, Lady, her complaint of the royal family, 395f.

Townshend, Lord, 434n.

Townshend, Thomas, 164, 272, 402, 437.

Treasury, epigram on the, 94n.

Trecothick, Alderman, 224.

Turner, Dr., 374n.

Turner, Sir John, 304.

Tyrone, Earl of, 273.

Ulysses, another name of Junius, 370f.

Unitarians in the Church of England, 374ff; grievances of, 386f. See Nonconformists; Dissenters; Priestley, Dr., etc.

Unwin, Mr., letter of Cowper to, 268n.

Victoria, Queen, conditions of office under, compared with those under George III., 89ff, 100f.

Virgil, Charles Fox's admiration for, 263.

Virginia. See American colonies.

Voltaire, visits of Charles Fox to, 59n; on religion in England, 85; on Wilkes, 239n, 240n.

Wakefield, Gilbert, 261n.

Waldegrave, Lord, guardian of George III.'s childhood, 102n, 396, 397n.

Waldegrave, Lady, married to the Duke of Gloucester, 396n.

Walpole, Sir R., 7n, 27, 426, 429; how he provided for his family, 88n, 89; fall of, 218n.

Walpole, Sir Edward, 396.

Walpole, Horace, his account of a fashionable ball, 7f; on Lord Bute's administration, 24n; receives a delicate offer from Henry Fox, 27f; on Holland House, 37n; on Lady Sarah Lennox's beauty, 46f; letters to Mann, 64n, 68n, 74, 102n, 231, 427; on Lord Weymouth, 68; on the Earl of Sandwich, 68f; letters to Conway, 70n; on gambling in the last century, 78, 80; on Lord Cholmondeley's intemperance, 82; his description of Wesley, 86n; his account of his own and his brother's sinecures, 88n, 89; on the death of George II., 102n; on Lord Rockingham's adherents, 120n, 121n; on Stephen and Charles Fox,

WAR

170n, 175, 367; on Wilkes's popularity, 181, 239n, 240n; on the Duke of Bedford, 187n; on Robertson's "Life of Charles V.," 197n; on Charles Fox and Wedderburn, 247n; his migrations to France, 272n; shopping commissions in Paris, 273f; letters to Lord and Lady Ossory, 273; on David Hume and his French admirers, 276n; his acquaintance with Mme. du Deffand, 280; gossip about Lord Mayor Crosby, 314n; on Wedderburn's treachery, 334; on Sir J. Lowther, 358; on the royal family, 395; on the marriage of the Duke of Gloucester, 396, 397n; his account of the gambling at Brooks's, 418n; on things best worth finding, 419; on Charles Fox's debts, 423; on Charles Fox and Wilkes, 426; as chronicler of Charles Fox's follies, 426f; his retirement from Parliament, 426; his objections to political life, 427f; on Charles Fox's motion for repeal of Lord Hardwicke's Marriage Act, 428; on Lord Clive, 436n; other references, 13, 17, 20f, 29, 48, 63, 121, 134n, 176, 178, 416n, 417n.

Warburton, Bishop (of Gloucester), his account of a morning at court, 84n. See Gloucester, Bishop of.

Watson, Bishop, 95n, 379n, 385n, 431n.

Wedderburn, A. (Lord Loughborough), on the Middlesex election, 173f, 247f; Lord Campbell on, 173n; dupes the Opposition, 185f; patriotic speeches of, 225f; his historical precedents, 226n; early career of, 330f; his factitious patriotism, 331f; Chatham's belief in, 332; is made solicitor-general, ib.; causes general astonishment, 333; Churchill, Walpole, and Junius on, 333f; his treatment by the House of Commons, 334; his charges against the Opposition, 342f; his quarrel with Charles Fox, 353f; on the Royal Marriage Bill, 400n; minor references to, 175, 185, 292, 391n, 398, 407, 438f, 447, 452.

Wellington, Lord, 48.

Wesley, John, described by Horace Walpole, 86n; declaration of his followers against Lindsey, 378; his Toryism, ib.; referred to, 440n.

Westminster, address of electors to the king, 227.

Weymouth, Lord, his qualifications for

WIL

the Irish Viceroyalty and as Secretary of State, 66ff; Horace Walpole on, 67f; other references to, 75, 123, 158, 160, 195, 209, 239.

Wharton, Duke of, 148n.

Whately, Mr., his letters in the Grenville papers, 42n, 65.

Wheble, John, his letter to the House of Commons, 311n, 312n; arrest of, 312; proceedings against the Speaker's messenger, 345.

Whigs, proscription of, by Henry Fox, 28ff; roused by the Middlesex election, 183ff; agitation begun by, 185; gathering at the Thatched House Tavern, 184; counter-proceedings of the ministers, 187; call for a dissolution of Parliament, 189; their success in the cities, ib.; Chatham's esteem for, 192; defection of Charles Yorke, 201ff; their demeanor during the quarrel of the city and Commons, 296ff, 337; treachery of Wedderburn, 332ff; their zeal in the cause of order, 342; calumnies against, ib.; visit the lord mayor in the Tower, 345f; on the question of clerical tests, 376; their affection for Charles Fox in later days, 434n. See Commons, House of; Rockingham, Lord.

Whitaker, Sergeant, counsel against the Middlesex petition, 171, 172n.

Whitehead, Paul, 91n.

Wilkes, Mr. Israel, 140n.

Wilkes, John, his description of Sir Francis Dashwood, 26n; on Alpine scenery, 55; on parliamentary bribery, 125; Mr. Gladstone on, 140; his early life and domestic quarrels, 140f; his address to the Berwick freemen, 141n; purchases the borough of Aylesbury, ib.; his profligacy, and cruel treatment of his wife, 141; becomes obnoxious to the government, 142ff; his "Essay on Woman" and North Briton, 143; his duels, 143, 144; correspondence with the secretaries of state, 144n; deserted by his friends, ib.; persecution of, 145ff; goes into exile, 146n; letter from France, 146; outlawed, and remains on the Continent, 147f; becomes literary executor of Churchill, 148f; his failure in the attempt, 149f; narrative of his sufferings, 150; returns to England, and becomes candidate for the city of London, 151; enthusiasm of the citi-

WIL

zens for, 152; his candidature for Middlesex, 152*ff*; proceedings of the judges against, 155; condemned to fine and imprisonment, *ib.*; collision of his partisans with the troops, *ib.*; ingenious application of, to the House of Commons, 158; at the bar of the Commons, 158*f*; Byron's lines on, 159*n*; debate on proposed expulsion of, from the House, 159*ff*; his expulsion voted, 161, elected alderman, 162; re-elected for Middlesex, 163; hostile vote of the House of Commons, 163*f*; again re-elected for Middlesex, 168; great debate on, in the Commons, 169*ff*; his election for Middlesex quashed, 171; petition of his electors, 171*f*; general enthusiasm and testimonials of sympathy for, 178, 179*n*; action against Lord Halifax, 181; causes of his popularity, 182*f*; agitation of his partisans, 183*ff*; his pamphlet against Lord Chatham, 195*n*; Chatham's defence of, 196*ff*; debates in the Lords and Commons on, 197*ff*; flattered by his admirers, 234*n*, 235*n*; Junius's communications to, 235*n*; letter to the lord mayor, 235; limits of his ambition, *ib.*; popular joy at his liberation from prison, 236, 237*n*, 243; elected Sheriff and Lord Mayor of London, 237*f*; opposition of the court, 237*n*, 238; irksomeness of his civic duties, 238; becomes chamberlain, *ib.*; amusements of his leisure, 239; complimented by Lord Mansfield, 240; Walpole, Gibbon, and Voltaire on his social qualities, 239*n*,

YOU

240*n*; his meeting with Johnson, 240; his death, and character of his work, 240*f*; annulment of the resolution of the Commons for his expulsion, 243*n*; on the condition of the press, 291; his leadership of the city in its campaign in behalf of the press, 311; his practical jokes on the House of Commons, 311*n*, 312*n*, 313; testimonial of the Common Council to, 346*f*; his quarrel with John Horne, 441*ff*; minor references to, 69, 70, 91*n*, 121, 314, 325, 345.

Wilkes, Miss, 145, 146, 236, 238, 239.
Wilkes, Mrs. John, 141*ff*.
Williams, Gilly, 79, 432.
Williams, Sir Charles Hanbury, 8, 66*n*.
Wilmot, Sir Eardley, 201*f*.
Wilson, Dr., 185*n*.
Winnington, Mr., 250*n*.
Woodfall, editor of the *Public Advertiser*, trial of, 230; publishes speech of the Duke of Grafton, 297; letter of Charles Fox to, 371; at the bar of the House of Commons, 444*f*; his discharge, 449.
Wordsworth, sonnet of, on Lowther Castle, 357; treatment of his family by Lord Lonsdale, 357*n*.

YORKE, Charles, denounces Henry Fox, 14; vacillation of, 201*f*, 202, 203*n*; career and character of, 203*ff*; joint author of the "Athenian Letters," 203*n*; consents to become chancellor, 206*f*; his remorse and death, 208*ff*.
Yorke, John, 208.
Young, Arthur, 276*n*, 374.

THE END.